Higher
Modern Studies

ALAN BARCLAY, GEORGE CLARKE, ALISON DREW, IRENE MORRISON

Leckie × Leckie

Text © 2007 Alan Barclay, George Clarke, Alison Drew, Irene Morrison

Design and layout © 2007 Leckie & Leckie Ltd

Cover image © Caleb Rutherford / Design Pics Inc. / Alamy

1st edition 2007

ISBN 978-1-84372-377-6

ISBN-10 1-84372-377-8

Published by

Leckie & Leckie Ltd, 3rd Floor, 4 Queen Street, Edinburgh EH2 1JE

tel: 0131 220 6831   fax: 0131 225 9987

enquiries@leckieandleckie.co.uk   www.leckieandleckie.co.uk

Edited by

Tony Wayte, Fiona MacDonald

Special thanks to

Project One Publishing Solutions (content development and editorial), The Partnership Publishing Solutions (project management, design, layout and picture research), Eduardo Iturralde (Illustrations), Andrew Burnet (proofreading), Caleb Rutherford (cover)

Leckie & Leckie is grateful for the following for their permission to reproduce their material:

Dan Chung / Getty (p14); Adam Elder / Andrew Cowan © Scottish Parliament (p16); Adam Elder / Andrew Cowan © Scottish Parliament (p18); Patrick Kovarik / Getty (p36); David Levenson / Getty (p39); Peter Jordan / Getty (p39); Paula Bronstein / Getty (p39); Roy Rainford / Getty (p42); Countryside Alliance (p52); Scott Barbour / Getty (p53); Bruno Vincent / Getty (p66); Michel Gangne / Getty (p71); Scott Barbour / Getty (p77); Christopher Furlong / Getty (p81); Adam Elder / Andrew Cowan © Scottish Parliament (p94); Flying Colours / Getty (p99); George Gutenberg / Beateworks / Corbis (p116); Pixland / Corbis (p118); Image source / Corbis (p118); A. Inden / zefa / Corbis (p123); image100 / Corbis (p136); Keystone / Getty (p167); Pierre Verdy / Getty (p168); Sean Gallup / Getty (p170); William F. Campbell / Getty (p171); Trevor Samson / Getty (p175); Per-Anders Pettersson / Getty (p184); Greg Marinovich / Getty (p185); Per-Anders Pettersson / Getty (p187); Per-Anders Pettersson / Getty (p188); Andrew Wong / Getty (p204); Mike Clarke / Getty (p213); Gregory Costanzo / Getty (p221); Karen Moskowitz / Getty (p221); Erin Patrice O'Brien / Getty (p221); Mandel Ngan / Getty (p225); Phillippe Diederich / Getty (p241); David McNew / Getty (p243); Mike Clarke / Getty (p253); Andreas Rentz / Getty (p253); Jeff J. Mitchell / Getty (p273); Chris Jackson / Getty (p283); Ian Murphy / Getty (p290); Ramzi Haidar / Getty (p294); Jacob Silberberg / Getty (p296); Chris Hondros / Getty (p300); Jung Yeon-Je / Getty (p308); Gerard Malie / Getty (p314); Farzana Wahidy / Getty (p324)

A CIP Catalogue record for this book is available from the British Library.

Leckie & Leckie is a division of Huveaux plc.

CONTENTS

Political Issues in the United Kingdom

STUDY THEME 1A:
Devolved decision making in Scotland

In this study theme you will be expected to have a detailed knowledge and understanding of:

● **DECISION MAKING IN SCOTLAND**

The Scottish Parliament as an arena for conflict, co-operation and decision making; functions; organisation of the procedures for business. The Scottish Executive; the respective roles of the First Minister and the Cabinet. The effects of the electoral system on decision making for Scotland at Holyrood level.

● **REPRESENTATION OF SCOTTISH INTERESTS AT WESTMINSTER**

The distribution of powers between the Scottish Parliament and the UK Parliament; co-operation and conflict between the Scottish Parliament and Scottish Executive and the UK Parliament. The effects of the electoral system on Westminster decision making for Scotland.

● **LOCAL GOVERNMENT IN SCOTLAND**

Role, functions, finance and reform. COSLA, co-operation and conflict with the Scottish Executive. The effects of the electoral system on local authority decision making.

FOUNDING PRINCIPLES OF THE SCOTTISH PARLIAMENT

The Scottish Parliament has four founding principles, which were developed to establish the working methods of the new Parliament that would result in an effective and accountable Parliament, answering the needs of people in Scotland. The founding principles are:

- access and participation
- accountability
- equal opportunity
- sharing power.

Access and participation

The Scottish Parliament is designed to be accessible, open and responsive. Its procedures should promote a participative approach to the development, consideration and scrutiny of policy and legislation. This is achieved in several ways:

- holding Committee **meetings in different places** around Scotland
- **providing information widely** through a professional public information service
- having a modern and transparent Parliament with **simple working practices**:
   —normal business hours
   —proceedings held in public
   —using plain English in proceedings and publications.

Accountability

The Scottish Executive must be accountable to the Scottish Parliament and both must be accountable to the people of Scotland. This is achieved with:

- a **rigorous Code of Conduct** for Members of the Scottish Parliament (MSPs)
- a **strong role for Committees**
- a system of **Parliamentary Questions**, which enables MSPs to question the Executive.

For you to do

- What are the founding principles of the Scottish parliament?
- How do they help to improve democracy in Scotland?

Equal opportunity

The Scottish Parliament must promote equal opportunities for all. This is achieved with:

- an **Equal Opportunities Committee** to ensure that equal opportunities planning, targets and monitoring are established wherever appropriate
- parliamentary operations which are **equally attractive to men and women**
- parliamentary sessions which meet during **normal business hours** on a regular, programmed basis.

Sharing power

Power should be shared between the people of Scotland, the Scottish Parliament and the Scottish Executive. A key element is the Parliamentary Bureau, chaired by the **Presiding Officer**, with representatives from the parties, which organises the

WORD BANK

Presiding Officer: the official who chairs proceedings and organises business in the Chamber of the Scottish Parliament.

programme of business for the Parliament in a transparent way. Further efforts to promote power sharing include:

- the role of the Presiding Officer to **control debate and safeguard MSPs' rights**
- the role of Committees to **initiate legislation, scrutinise and amend** Scottish Executive proposals and have wide-ranging investigative functions
- **encouraging the public to influence legislation** through MSPs and/or through further evidence taking by committees of the Parliament
- **allowing public petitions** to allow the public direct access to influence the work of the Parliament and the law of Scotland.

Internet research

Visit the Scottish Parliament website and find examples of the founding principles in operation to use in essays.

Links to this site and other websites relating to Higher Modern Studies can be found at: **www.leckieandleckie.co.uk** by clicking on the Learning Lab button and navigating to the Higher Modern Studies Course Notes page. LECKIE&LECKIE Learning Lab

THE ELECTORAL SYSTEM FOR THE SCOTTISH PARLIAMENT

The Scottish Parliament uses the **Additional Member System** (AMS) for elections of MSPs. There are 129 elected Members of the Scottish Parliament, of whom 73 are Constituency MSPs and 56 are List or Regional MSPs. The List MSPs are elected from one of the eight regions, with each region returning seven List MSPs.

Constituency MSPs provide the direct link between the constituent and the representative while the List MSPs create the proportionality in the system. (For more information on the workings of AMS and its strengths and weaknesses, see Study Theme 1D, pages 84–107.)

Role of Constituency and List members

Every Scottish Parliament constituent has eight MSPs to represent them – one Constituency MSP and seven List or Regional MSPs. The Scottish Parliament wrote a Code of Conduct for MSPs to control any rivalry between the MSPs. It includes these requirements:

- all MSPs have **equal status**
- all eight MSPs have a duty to **represent the interests of their constituents**
- no MSP should deal with a matter relating to a constituent or issue outwith their constituency or region, unless by prior arrangement.

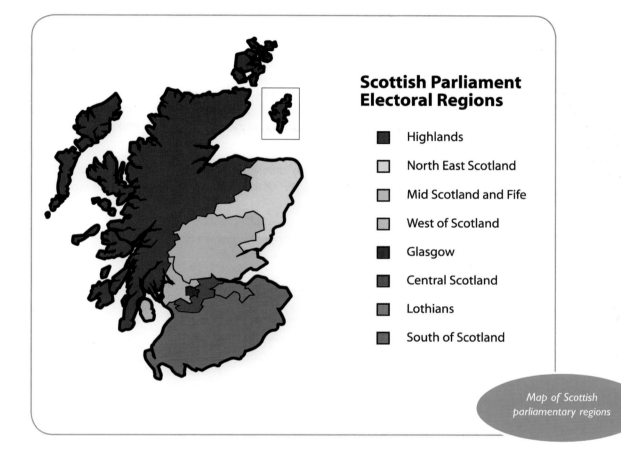

Scottish Parliament Electoral Regions

- ■ Highlands
- □ North East Scotland
- □ Mid Scotland and Fife
- □ West of Scotland
- ■ Glasgow
- ■ Central Scotland
- ■ Lothians
- ■ South of Scotland

Map of Scottish parliamentary regions

A constituent can approach any of their eight MSPs and has the right to expect an MSP to take on their case. In most circumstances, constituents will approach their Constituency MSP first. If a constituent approaches a Regional MSP, he or she must inform the relevant Constituency MSP immediately unless the constituent asks for this not to happen.

MSPs who hold an official position, such as a Minister in the Scottish Executive or Presiding Officer, still act as MSPs on behalf of their constituents.

For you to do

Describe the role of MSPs in Scotland.

Internet research

Visit the Scottish Parliament website to find the name and email address of your Constituency MSP and/or your List MSPs. Email them to ask them for information on how they see their role as individual MSPs, to see if they believe their roles differ, and to ask them how harmonious their relationships are, to use as examples in essays.

Links to these sites and other websites relating to Higher Modern Studies can be found at: LECKIE&LECKIE *Learning Lab*

The impact of AMS

AMS tends to lead to coalition government, with no party having an overall majority. It reflects the will of the electorate and makes each vote relevant. Power is fragmented, with the rise of smaller parties and increased backbench influence. The electorate may become more sophisticated, exercising more choice in their votes.

No overall majorities – coalition government

If First Past the Post (FPTP) had been used to elect the entire Scottish Parliament the outcome would have been significantly different. The table below shows that in the ballot for Constituency MSPs, which is FPTP, the Labour Party was the clear victor and could run Scotland on its own.

SCOTTISH PARLIAMENT ELECTION RESULT 2003								
	Constituency seats (73)			*List seats* (56)			*Total* (129)	
Party	% votes	No seats	% seats	% votes	No seats	% seats	No seats	% seats
Labour	34.9	46	63	32.3	4	7	50	39
SNP	23.8	9	12	20.9	18	32	27	21
Conservative	16.5	3	4	13.3	15	27	18	14
Liberal Democrat	15.1	13	18	9.5	4	7	17	13
SSP	6.2	0	0	7.5	6	11	6	5
Greens	0	0	0	6.7	7	13	7	5
Others	3.5	2	3	9.8	2	4	4	3
Total		73			56		129	

However, the proportionality introduced by the List MSPs meant that the Labour Party was short of a majority by 15 in 2003. This meant the Labour Party had to seek coalition partners to get a majority to run Scotland. They turned to the Liberal Democrats.

They had to negotiate a programme of legislation that was acceptable to both groups. The leaders had to use their negotiation powers to persuade their **backbench** MSPs to accept some compromises. For example, the Labour leadership had to persuade their backbenchers to accept proportional representation (PR) for local authority elections because the Liberal Democrats demanded this in return for their support.

Many Labour MSPs and MPs opposed PR for local government because many owed their position to the work done by local councillors at election time. As the Labour Party will lose control in most local authorities as the result of introducing PR, MSPs felt it would jeopardise their election chances. (For more information on the likely impact of PR on local government elections, see pages 87–89.)

It is likely that AMS will alter the political process in local government in Scotland as it already has in Holyrood. It has created coalition government, given smaller parties more influence and given backbench MSPs greater freedom to influence decisions on behalf of their constituents. AMS has changed the laws that have been passed.

Reflects the will of the electorate

The result of the 2003 election shows the final outcome is close to the will of the electorate. If only the FPTP ballot had been used, the Labour Party would have had 65% of the seats from only 34.9% of the votes. This would have meant that the laws passed in Scotland would have reflected the will of only 34.9% of the voters. However, after the second ballot, the Labour Party got 39% of the seats in the Parliament. Although the party was still over-represented, the number of seats it gained came closer to reflecting the number of votes it received.

Fragmentation of power, the rise of smaller parties and increased backbench influence

In 2003, the electorate realised they could successfully switch their votes from the main parties and elected seven Green Party MSPs, six Scottish Socialist Party MSPs and five independent MSPs.

These small groups present new influences on the politics of Scotland by making political decision making far less predictable. Party managers are faced with shifting coalitions of support which necessitate far more persuasion and negotiation.

Less can be taken for granted and the influence of backbench MSPs is increased. This could make the Scottish Parliament more democratic as issues are discussed and argued fully in the Debating Chamber. But it may also lead to a less effective Parliament as more time has to be spent building up alliances, leaving far less time to discuss the issues. Less may be done because compromise cannot be found on an issue.

In 2004, the five independent MSPs, including Margo MacDonald and Dennis Canavan, formed a loose alliance to get representation on the Parliamentary Bureau which decides what is to be discussed in the Scottish Parliament. This means that the SSP, the Greens and this new group joined the existing four parties with membership of the Parliamentary Bureau, extending the influence of smaller parties over what is to be debated.

For you to do

Do you think the increased influence of smaller parties and independent MSPs enhances or hinders the democratic process in Scotland? Give reasons for your answer.

Internet research

Visit the Scottish Parliament website and find the names of the independent MSPs and the issues on which they fought the 2003 election.
Links to this site and other websites relating to Higher Modern Studies can be found at: LECKIE&LECKIE Learning Lab

A more sophisticated electorate

Scottish voters have become more sophisticated. Many are switching their votes between the first and second ballots, to create checks and balances on the power of the larger parties. Others see a chance to introduce issue politics into the Scottish Parliament. The Scottish electorate have ensured that politicians cannot take their vote for granted.

Why was AMS chosen for the Scottish Parliament?

Since the Scottish Parliament was formed under a Labour administration in Westminster, and it was apparent that Labour would be the losers under the AMS, it's worth asking why it was agreed that AMS would be used for the Scottish Parliament. There are a number of factors:

- new politics
- the desire for proportionality
- the desire to restrict the power of the SNP.

Many people believe it was introduced to create a new kind of politics in Scotland by ensuring that all parties got a fairer representation in the Parliament. It was hoped that AMS would **reduce confrontational politics** and create a **more consensual approach**. Unfortunately the evidence of the first two Parliaments does not indicate that consensus is any greater in the Scottish Parliament than in Westminster.

AMS was chosen as it retained the direct link between constituents and their MSPs but **provided proportionality** in the second ballot. It was also hoped this would encourage greater turnouts.

Some critics suggest the Labour Party chose AMS to ensure the SNP could never achieve a majority of seats in the Scottish Parliament and use it as a springboard for full independence.

Replace AMS with STV?

Following the 2003 elections, many in the Labour Party want to replace AMS with STV (single transferable vote). The threshold to get seats with AMS can be as low as 5% whereas with STV the threshold is higher, at about 25%. This would make it far **more difficult for small parties and individuals to be elected**. The Labour Party is worried about losing its political control in Scotland if more parties are elected. (For more information on STV, see Study Theme 1D, pages 92–93.)

For you to do

Has AMS has made the Scottish Parliament a more democratic institution? Discuss.

Internet research

Visit the Scottish Parliament website and find out the parties of your Constituency and List MSPs. Use recent election results to show the impact that AMS has had on party representation in your region.
Links to this site and other websites relating to Higher Modern Studies can be found at:

Reducing the number of MSPs

The Scotland Act 1998, which set up the Scottish Parliament, set the number of Constituency MSPs as the same as the existing number of constituencies of Westminster MPs in Scotland. In 2005, the number of Scottish MPs in Westminster was reduced from 72 to 59, so the number of MSPs should also have been reduced.

MSPs argued that it would not be practical to run the Scottish Parliament with fewer than 129 MSPs in order to maintain a committee structure that would effectively monitor the work of the Executive. A reduction in the number of Constituency MSPs without a *pro rata* reduction in the number of Regional MSPs would also tilt the balance of power and influence in the Scottish Parliament.

In 2004, the Westminster Parliament, in the face of severe opposition from several Scottish backbench MPs, agreed to keep the number of MSPs at 129 and to amend the Scotland Act.

ROLES AND RESPONSIBILITIES OF THE SCOTTISH EXECUTIVE AND THE SCOTTISH PARLIAMENT

The Scottish Executive and the Scottish Parliament have distinct roles in the government of Scotland.

The **Scottish Executive** is the Government for Scotland for all devolved matters. It has a major influence in deciding the Bills to be introduced into the Parliament and is responsible for making sure that the laws on devolved matters are implemented in Scotland. They operate through a Civil Service.

The **Scottish Parliament** passes laws on devolved matters. The Scottish Parliament elects the First Minister who picks the Scottish Executive. The Scottish Parliament scrutinises the Scottish Executive.

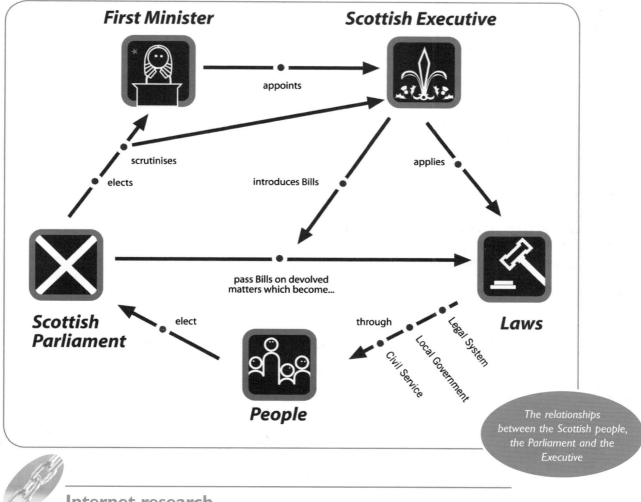

The relationships between the Scottish people, the Parliament and the Executive

Internet research

Visit the website of the BBC News Front Page or newspaper websites to find more information about the negotiations that took place between the Labour Party and the Liberal Democrats to form a coalition in 2003. Find out the names and positions of current Cabinet members.

Links to these sites and other websites relating to Higher Modern Studies can be found at:

APPOINTMENT AND POWERS OF THE SCOTTISH EXECUTIVE

APPOINTMENTS	
Theory	*Reality*
The party, or parties, with the majority of seats in the Parliament form(s) the Scottish Government, known as the Scottish Executive. This is made up of:	The First Minister does not really have a free hand in appointing Ministers to posts.
• the **First Minister** The MSPs elect one of their number who is formally appointed by the Queen. The First Minister appoints ministers, law officers and judges of the Court of Session.	In a coalition government the coalition partners will discuss and agree beforehand who is to be First Minister (usually the leader of the largest party), who is to be Deputy First Minister (usually the leader of the second largest party), and who are to become Ministers from each of the parties.
• the **Scottish Ministers** They are appointed by the First Minister who decides their responsibilities called portfolios.	The First Minister has to appoint people agreed in these negotiations.
• the **Scottish Law Officers** There are two Scottish Law Officers, the Lord Advocate and the Solicitor General for Scotland, who are part of the Scottish Executive. They advise the Executive on legal matters and represent its interests in court. They are appointed by the Queen on the recommendation of the First Minister approved by the Scottish Parliament.	The choices the parties make are also determined by the influence individuals have in the respective parties. People who have strong support from other MSPs have to get important jobs or they might cause problems if left out. So the decision as to who gets which job is not really in the hands of the First Minister.

PROGRAMME	
Theory	*Reality*
The Scottish Executive formulates Government policy on devolved matters. • Once the membership of the Scottish Executive has been formed it decides on its programme. • It introduces Bills into Parliament to be made into Laws to carry out its programme.	In a coalition the programme for the Executive is worked out as a series of compromises by the coalition partners before the Executive is appointed.

Donald Dewar, Scotland's first First Minister

For you to do

Discuss the role and powers of the First Minister for Scotland.

POWERS OF THE SCOTTISH EXECUTIVE

The Scottish Executive has powers to introduce Bills, administer laws on devolved matters and decide the Budget for Scotland.

Introduce Bills

Government Bills are proposals for new laws or amendments to existing laws. They are announced by a Minister from the Scottish Executive in statements during meetings of Parliament. The Executive may also use answers to written questions from MSPs as a way of announcing decisions and publicising documents.

However, it is Parliament that decides which Bills become law and which do not. The Executive must persuade a majority of MSPs to votes for the laws it wants passed.

Administer laws on devolved matters

Through the government departments, the Scottish Executive ensures that laws are carried out on devolved matters.

However, the First Minister and the other Ministers in the Executive are subject to the scrutiny of Parliament. They must respond to written or oral questions at Question Time, defend their positions in debates in the chamber and also in front of committees when they are requested to appear.

Decides the Budget for Scotland

The Scottish Executive decides how to spend the money it is allocated to run services in Scotland.

However, the amount the Executive gets to spend is decided by the UK Cabinet and UK Parliament using the **Barnett Formula**. The Executive can try to persuade the UK Cabinet to change the amount they are given to spend in this *block grant* but ultimately they have no control.

The Scottish Parliament does have **tax varying powers** to raise or lower taxes by 3p in the pound. However, it has not used these powers, and it would be a political gamble to use them, as the Scottish electorate might object to paying higher taxes than people in England, Wales and Northern Ireland. By contrast, if the Scottish Parliament cut the level of taxes, the UK Parliament might use it as an excuse to cut its block grant claiming it was giving Scotland too much.

For you to do

Critically examine the powers of the Scottish Executive and the constraints upon these powers.

WORD BANK

Barnett Formula: part of the mechanism used to decide how much of the total UK tax revenue is allocated to Scotland, named after Joel Barnett, Chief Secretary to the Treasury in the 1974–1979 Labour Government.

Internet research

Visit the Scottish Executive or Scottish Parliament websites to find more information about the powers of the Scottish Executive and the constraints upon these powers. Links to these sites and other websites relating to Higher Modern Studies can be found at:

LECKIE&LECKIE
Learning Lab

WHO IS WHO IN THE SCOTTISH PARLIAMENT?

There are 129 MSPs elected to the Scottish Parliament in elections held every five years. From the elected MSPs, Parliamentary Officers are elected.

Presiding Officer

One MSP is elected by Parliament to serve as the Presiding Officer. There are also two Deputy Presiding Officers. The role of the Presiding Officer is to:

- chair meetings of the Parliament
- convene and chair meetings of the Parliamentary Bureau
- decide on questions raised regarding the rules for parliamentary proceedings
- represent the Parliament in discussions with other parliamentary or governmental bodies, such as:
    - —the United Kingdom Parliament
    - —European institutions
    - —national Parliaments around the world.

The Presiding Officer and the Deputies must act in an impartial manner and on behalf of all MSPs equally

Composition

GENDER COMPOSITION OF THE SCOTTISH PARLIAMENT 2003				
Political party	*Women MSPs*	*Women %*	*Men MSPs*	*Men %*
Conservative	4	17	14	83
Labour	28	56	22	44
Lib Dem	2	12	15	88
SNP	9	33	18	67
SSP	4	67	2	33
Green	2	29	5	71
Independent	2		2	2
Total	**51**	**39**	**78**	**61**

The MSPs do not reflect the composition of the electorate they represent. Women MSPs comprise 39% of the Parliament whereas 51% of the population is female. The Parliament is also mainly middle aged with the majority of members in their 40s and 50s. There are no representatives from any ethnic minority community. Overwhelmingly MSPs are drawn from people who have had an education at university level.

THE WORK OF THE SCOTTISH PARLIAMENT

The main functions of the Scottish Parliament are:

- to **scrutinise** the work of the Scottish Executive
- to **make laws** on devolved matters
- to **debate important issues**
- to **conduct enquiries** and **publish reports**.

The Scottish Parliament also has the power to raise or lower the basic rate of income tax by up to 3p in the pound.

SCRUTINISING THE WORK OF THE SCOTTISH EXECUTIVE

MSPs carefully watch the work of the Scottish Executive, monitoring both what it has done and what it has failed to do. They do this in a variety of ways:

- questions
- motions
- debates
- Decision time
- Members' business.

Much of the important work of scrutinising policy is done by a range of parliamentary committees.

Questions

MSPs table questions to be answered by Ministers about the work of their departments and how it affects the people of Scotland. There are two types of question.

Written questions require written answers and the questions and responses are found in the *Written Answers Report* section of Parliamentary Business on the Scottish Parliament website. These questions are for information. They can be on any subject and may seek very detailed and specific information.

Oral questions require the appropriate Minister to respond during Question Time. Ministers respond to the initial question. The MSP is then entitled to ask a related supplementary question. It is often the supplementary question that is the important question. Ministers and their department civil servants try to anticipate supplementaries and have answers prepared for all eventualities.

Oral questions are used for a variety of purposes. They can be used to get information about the activities of ministers and their departments, but they are also useful to score points by making the minister look ineffectual or incompetent. They can also be used to highlight alternative policies.

Ministers may also have colleagues plant questions so that they can make statements that make themselves and their party look good. Between January and April 2006, there were over 800 answers given to questions raised by MSPs.

Motions

Motions are tabled by MSPs. They are used as the means to **initiate debates** or **propose a course of action**. MSPs can sign up to support motions that have been lodged. Amendments to motions are also lodged by MSPs to allow differing viewpoints to be debated.

The proposer of a motion is given seven minutes to introduce their motion and it is usually replied to by a Government Minister. It is then debated in the chamber. At Decision time MSPs vote on whether to agree or reject the motion. Motions can be on a wide variety of topics such as

- drug treatment and rehabilitation
- local government pensions
- the future funding of Borderline Theatre Company
- congratulations to St Mirren Football Club
- stress experienced by asylum seekers.

Debates

Debates take place in the chamber on a wide variety of subjects. The debate may be about a motion or about legislation. Debates are controlled by the Presiding Officer and his Deputies and the subjects for debate are decided in the Parliamentary Bureau.

During these debates MSPs can raise relevant points and issues on behalf of their constituents and the public in general. They can use the debates to criticise the Executive and force Ministers to defend themselves and their policies, making the Executive accountable for its actions.

Decision time

Decision time takes place at 5 p.m. on Wednesdays and Thursdays, at the end of a day's business. MSPs vote on the passage of Bills, on motions and on debates that have taken place that day. MSPs vote using an electronic voting system.

Members' business

Following Decision time, up to 30 minutes at the end of each meeting of the Parliament may be devoted to Members' business. This means any item of business, other than a Member's Bill, can be introduced by an MSP who is not a member of the Scottish Executive.

Members' business provides a public record of the issue and may generate publicity.

THE PARLIAMENTARY BUREAU

The Parliamentary Bureau consists of representatives of political parties and groupings in the Parliament, chaired by the Presiding Officer. It decides the business programme for Parliament. It sets aside time in Parliament:

- to consider Committee business
- to consider business chosen by political parties not represented in the Scottish Executive
- for the First Minister to make statements to the Parliament about proposed policy objectives or the legislative programme of the Scottish Executive
- for ministerial statements.

THE COMMITTEE SYSTEM IN THE SCOTTISH PARLIAMENT

Committees are far more influential in the work of the Scottish Parliament than committees in the Westminster Parliament. They have been given more powers because the Scottish Parliament has only one Debating Chamber. The powers they have are:

- to scrutinise the Executive
- to examine legislative proposals
- to conduct enquiries and publish reports.

Parliamentary committee meeting

A committee has between seven and 11 MSPs as members. Most have nine. Membership reflects the size of the political parties and groupings in the Parliament. They are chaired by a Convener. A committee can form sub-committees, and can hold joint meetings with other committees. Meetings are normally held in public, and can take place anywhere in Scotland.

There are two types of committee. **Mandatory Committees** must be formed by the Scottish Parliament. **Subject Committees** are formed at the discretion of Parliament and can vary over time in number and subject but they usually shadow the ministerial portfolios of the Scottish Executive.

Mandatory Committees	Subject Committees
Procedures	Education Culture and Sport
Standards	Enterprise and Lifelong Learning
Finance	Health and Community Care
Audit	Justice 1
European	Justice 2
Public Petitions	Local Government
Equal Opportunities	Rural Development
Subordinate Legislation	Social Justice
	Transport and Environment

Scrutiny by committee

A committee can enquire into any issue covered by its remit. It can do this on its own initiative or as required by Parliament. Advisers can be appointed and committees have the power to call Ministers, civil servants, members of organisations and members of the public to give evidence. This means giving evidence or producing documents. They can go on fact-finding visits and meet anywhere in Scotland. MSPs who are not members of a committee can participate in its proceedings but they are not allowed to vote. Committees report their findings to Parliament.

Examining legislative proposals

Committees are involved with Bills as they pass through Parliament – at Stage 1 (the general principles) and at Stage 2 (the detailed examination). Committees have the power to pass, amend or reject Bills.

Committees also have the power to bring forward Bills that have emerged from their discussions and investigations. These are called Committee Bills. In the first session of the Scottish Parliament there were three Committee Bills passed out of 62 in total. For example, the Commissioner for Children and Young People (Scotland) Bill was introduced on behalf of the Education, Culture and Sport Committee.

Conducting enquiries and publishing reports

Committees have the power to call Ministers and parliamentary officials to give evidence in front of them. They can order papers be produced in evidence. They can call expert witnesses, private individuals and representatives of organisations to provide information. They then publish reports to highlight their findings.

For you to do

- What are the procedures of the Scottish Parliament that enable MSPs to scrutinise the work of the Executive?
- Discuss the work of the committees of the Scottish Parliament.

Internet research

Visit the Scottish Parliament website to find examples from Question Times, Debates and/or Motions to illustrate the power of MSPs to scrutinise the work of the Executive.
Visit the website of the 1st Annual Report of the Public Petitions Committee for a case study of its work and successes.
Links to these sites and other websites relating to Higher Modern Studies can be found at:

Petitions

One of the most notable differences between the Scottish Parliament and the UK Parliament is the way in which any individual member of the public can present petitions to the Scottish Parliament. This allows the public to participate directly in the parliamentary process. The Public Petitions Committee (PPC) oversees the management of petitions in Parliament.

A petition can make a request for the Parliament to:

- take a view on a matter of **public interest or concern**
- **amend existing legislation**
- **introduce new legislation**.

However, the PPC cannot interfere with:

- the decisions of local authorities (such as school closures)
- the decisions of Health Boards or NHS Trusts (such as hospital closures)
- cases which are subject to legal or court proceedings or industrial tribunals.

The PPC must consider each admissible petition. The petition should make it clear what action the petitioner wishes the Parliament to take. The PPC may invite the petitioner(s) to appear before it or to provide additional information to assist it in reaching a decision on the action to be taken.

The PPC can decide to take no further action or to send the petition to another committee of the Parliament or to the Presiding Officer or to the Scottish Executive. It can recommend that the petition be debated at a meeting of the Parliament.

Between 1999 and 2003 the PPC considered 620 petitions on topics such as genetically modified crops, fuel poverty, schools, road deaths, allotments, heritage sites and on the issues of the environment and health. Petitions have led to changes in the law, committees of enquiry and changing the views of the Executive.

MAKING LAWS ON DEVOLVED MATTERS

A Bill sets out proposals for legislation. A Bill can be introduced into the Parliament by Ministers and also by Parliamentary committees or by MSPs. There are various types of Bill:

- **Executive Bills** introduced by a member of the Executive
- **Committee Bills** introduced by a member of a committee
- **Members' Bills** introduced by an MSP
- **Private Bills** introduced by an organisation or an individual.

Between 1999 and 2003, 62 Bills were passed by the Parliament. Of these, 50 were Executive Bills (including four Budget Bills), eight were Members' Bills, three were Committee Bills and one was a Private Bill.

The stages of a Bill

The Parliamentary process that a Bill follows varies depending on the type of Bill. The most usual procedure consists of:

Consultation
Stage 1 – General principles
Stage 2 – Details examined in committee
Stage 3 – The final Bill
Royal Assent.

Consultation

The Executive may produce consultation documents to outline its proposals for legislation. These documents are sent out to interested individuals and bodies including the relevant committee. The committee may wish to speak to the Minister at this stage. The committee monitors the consultation and may take its own evidence.

Stage 1 – General principles

At Stage 1, a Bill is sent to the relevant subject committee known as the lead committee, for consideration. The lead committee may take evidence at this stage. Other committees may be involved, such as Equal Opportunities or Finance, which provide the lead committee with information that is included in its report to Parliament.

The Parliament considers the general principles based on the lead committee's report. The Bill can be referred back to the lead committee for a further report, before the Parliament makes its decision. More evidence may be taken.

If the Parliament agrees to the general principles then the Bill goes on to Stage 2. If it does not agree, the Bill falls.

Stage 2 – Details examined in committee

At Stage 2 the Bill receives more detailed line-by-line consideration by:

- the lead committee
- a committee of the whole Parliament
- a different committee
- some combination of the above.

The details are examined and amendments may be made. Any MSP can move an amendment but only the committee members may vote.

Stage 3 – The final Bill

The amended Bill is then considered by the Parliament, which may make further amendments. The Parliament then debates and decides whether the Bill should be passed. At least 25% of all MSPs (33) must vote (whether 'for', 'against' or 'abstain') or the Bill falls.

Once a Bill has been approved, it is then submitted by the Presiding Officer to the sovereign for Royal Assent. If the Bill fails, it is abandoned.

Royal Assent

On receiving Royal Assent a Bill becomes an Act of the Scottish Parliament.

For you to do

- Draw a flowchart showing the passage of a Bill.
- Examine how the work of the Public Petitions Committee relates to the founding principle of access and participation.

Internet research

Visit the Scottish Parliament website to find examples of petitions that have been considered by the Public Petitions Committee and examples of different types of Bill passed by the Scottish Parliament.

Links to this site and other websites relating to Higher Modern Studies can be found at:

HOW EFFECTIVE HAS THE SCOTTISH PARLIAMENT BEEN IN HOLDING THE SCOTTISH EXECUTIVE TO ACCOUNT?

Evidence in favour of the effectiveness of Parliament

The Scottish Parliament holds the Executive to account by asking questions, lodging motions, in debates, in votes and by questioning Ministers in committees. In one parliamentary year MSPs asked 1770 oral questions and 9982 written questions. Therefore the Executive and its officials had to account for their actions or shortcomings over **10,000 times in one year.** The First Minister alone was asked 825 questions, many of which forced him to justify and explain the work of his Government.

In the same year 1334 motions were lodged. Many of these required Executive Ministers to justify and explain the actions of their departments. There were 67 motions discussed during Members' business at the end of the parliamentary day.

There were 458 committee meetings throughout the year. Ministers were called to give oral evidence 103 times and Scottish Executive officials were called 245 times. There were also 403 votes at Decision time.

In the first Parliament (1999–2003), 80% of Bills passed were Executive Bills. However it took an average of 135 days to pass each Bill, so a great deal of time was taken to examine and debate what the Executive was doing.

Presiding Officer versus the Executive

Part of the function of the Presiding Officer is to safeguard the rights of MSPs from being eroded by the Executive. In 2001, the substance of a statement by the Finance Minister was leaked to the press before the statement was made in the chamber. The Presiding Officer refused to allow the statement to be read, which prevented previously planted questions from being heard.

The practice known as *leaking* is common in Westminster, where the Government and ministers regularly inform the press in advance of statements they intend to make. They gain advantage by managing events in this way.

The Presiding Officer said he 'expected to read in the press about what had happened in Parliament, not what was going to happen.' Despite intense pressure from the Executive, the Presiding Officer upheld the rights of Parliament to be treated correctly by the Executive and discouraged the Executive from taking liberties with the rights of MSPs. So the Presiding Officer helped to maintain the effectiveness of Parliament.

Evidence against the effectiveness of Parliament

A **Sewel Motion** allows the Scottish Parliament to let the UK legislate on Scotland's behalf on matters that are devolved. Therefore legislation on devolved matters is enacted without discussion by MSPs.

Sewel Motions are used where it is thought to be more effective to have a nationwide approach (such as powers for the courts to confiscate the assets of serious offenders or where the relationship between devolved and reserved powers is very complex). They can also be used when the UK Parliament is introducing a new law for England and Wales which the Executive believes should also be brought into effect in Scotland, but there is no Parliamentary time available at Holyrood.

Sewel Motions were intended to be used infrequently. However in the first Parliament 41 Sewel Motions were agreed. In the same Parliament 62 Bills were passed. Therefore 40% of devolved legislation was not discussed in the Scottish Parliament. Some critics accuse the Executive of using Sewel Motions to avoid discussion on contentious issues. Between 2003 and 2005, there were a further 26 Sewel Motions.

For you to do

Critically assess the effectiveness of the Scottish Parliament in holding the Scottish Executive to account.

Internet research

Visit the Scottish Parliament and Scottish Executive websites to find examples of Sewel Motions.

Links to these sites and other websites relating to Higher Modern Studies can be found at:

CO-OPERATION AND CONFLICT BETWEEN THE HOLYROOD AND WESTMINSTER PARLIAMENTS

Devolved and reserved powers

Under the terms of the Scotland Act, clear distinctions were drawn between **devolved** matters and **reserved** matters. Devolved matters are those for which the Scottish Parliament has responsibility, and reserved matters are those for which the powers remain with the Westminster Parliament.

Key **devolved** matters include:

- health
- education
- culture and the arts
- local government
- housing
- social work
- police and fire services
- agriculture
- environment
- some aspects of transport, including roads and buses
- renewable energy
- tourism

Key **reserved** matters include:

- the Constitution
- foreign policy
- immigration and nationality
- social security
- defence and national security
- fiscal and economic affairs
- trade and industry
- nuclear energy, oil, coal, gas and electricity
- employment
- some aspects of transport, including national road and rail safety

There is considerable scope for conflict between Holyrood and Westminster in the way legislation is developed for Scotland. Conflict could arise because of **policy differences**, demands for **increased powers**, **finance**, and areas of **overlap** of responsibility.

Policy differences

If the same party is in control in both the Scottish and UK Parliaments, there will usually be agreement on most areas of policy. However, the elections for the UK Parliament traditionally create outright majorities for a single party, Labour or Conservative, while in Scotland the use of PR for elections is likely to create a coalition government made up of two or more parties.

This means it is likely there will be policy differences between the Scottish Executive and the British Cabinet. This situation has already created disagreements over student tuition fees and the funding of personal care for the elderly between the Labour Cabinet in Westminster and the Labour-LibDem coalition in the Scottish Executive.

Conflict would increase if there were a complete separation between the two Governments. For example, if the Labour Party were to win the General Election for the UK Parliament while there was a Liberal Democrat-SNP coalition government in Scotland there would be considerable disagreement.

A Labour-controlled UK Government might reduce the block grant to Scotland.

Reducing finance would damage the SNP and Liberal Democrats as they would have to reduce services (or increase taxes). The coalition might retaliate by targeting the cuts they had to make on Labour-controlled local authorities. The SNP might make political capital if the Scottish voters turned against the Labour Party. The SNP would use their increased popularity and push for independence.

The Conservative Party opposed the Scotland Act, so if they won a UK General Election, they might legislate to restrict the devolved powers or to reduce the Scottish block grant. There are a variety of scenarios that could lead to a constitutional crisis, which could fundamentally alter the existing levels of co-operation between Holyrood and Westminster.

Demand for increased powers

The Scottish Parliament will push for more power. It is in the nature of political institutions to seek to wield as much power as possible. Some politicians consider the Scottish Parliament to be an evolving institution and they actively seek to increase its power. The SNP in particular views the Scottish Parliament as a step on the way to independence. Moves to increase the power of the Scottish Parliament will be resisted by the UK Parliament and will bring the two into conflict.

Finance

The UK Government provides the Scottish Parliament with its income through the Scottish block grant. The Barnett Formula allocated £22 billion in 2003/04.

Many English MPs perceive that Scotland has been treated generously (Scotland receives a higher *per capita* allowance than do the Welsh and Northern Ireland Assemblies) but were willing to accept Scotland's special needs as long as it was wholly represented by the UK Parliament. However, now that Scotland has a Parliament with the power to raise or lower income tax, many English MPs argue that the block grant should be brought into line with the rest of the UK. Any threat to change or scrap the Barnett Formula would be unwelcome in Scotland.

The UK Government is in the process of reducing the extra *per capita* allowance that Scotland gets in the block grant. As this process develops the Scottish Parliament will be blamed for the reduction in the level of services and will be less popular with Scottish voters. To compensate for the reduced block grant, the Scottish Parliament may decide to vary taxes upwards, which again will not be popular with the voters in Scotland. This reduction in the block grant and its consequences could bring the Scottish Parliament into conflict with the UK Parliament.

Areas of overlap

There are areas of overlap between the reserved powers and the devolved powers which could lead to conflict between Holyrood and Westminster. For example, immigration is a reserved matter but the Scottish Executive believes there is a need to encourage some forms of immigration to meet the skills shortage and the falling birth rate in Scotland.

Another example is over the growing energy debate. The development of non-renewable energy such as nuclear is a reserved matter while renewable energy such as wind power is a devolved matter. Currently the UK Government is moving towards the development of more nuclear power to meet the developing energy gap which will involve sites in Scotland, while the Scottish Executive opposes this and seeks to develop renewable energy. There is the potential for serious disagreement where these remits overlap.

Provision of energy is an area for potential conflict between the Scottish and UK Parliaments

SCOTTISH REPRESENTATION AT WESTMINSTER

In 2005 there were 59 MPs representing Scottish constituencies elected to the UK Parliament. Scotland returned 41 Labour MPs, 11 Liberal Democrats, six SNP and one Conservative. Scottish MPs represent the interests of their constituents on reserved matters in the House of Commons.

West Lothian Question

Should Scottish MPs be able to vote on matters that affect only England and Wales when English MPs cannot vote on matters devolved to Scotland? This is the **West Lothian Question** so called because it was originally posed by the West Lothian MP Tam Dalyell.

In 2003, the Labour Government had a majority of just 17 in favour of its plan to set up Foundation Hospitals in England and Wales. They depended on the 46 Labour votes from Scotland. In 2004, the Higher Education Bill, which allowed Universities to charge top-up fees from students, needed the support of its 46 Scottish MPs to secure a majority of only five. Again this policy only affects universities in England and Wales.

This has caused deep resentment from MPs in England and Wales who want the Scottish MPs to be prevented from voting on matters that relate only to England and Wales.

Representation at Cabinet level

Prior to devolution the Secretary of State for Scotland was a high ranking Minister who sat in Cabinet and represented Scotland's interests at the highest level. However, following devolution the post was downgraded and currently it is part of a dual responsibility – Secretary of State for Scotland and Secretary of State for Transport. The Secretary of State represents Scotland on reserved matters within the Cabinet but that influence has diminished.

Scottish Affairs Committee

The Scottish Affairs Committee is appointed by the House of Commons to examine the expenditure, administration and policy of the Scotland Office.

Internet research

Visit the website of the Westminster Parliament and find out the names and parties of the members of the Scottish Affairs Committee. Why are there English MPs on the committee?

Visit the website of the Scottish Parliament and examine the ways in which it has used its devolved powers.

Links to these sites and other websites relating to Higher Modern Studies can be found at:

For you to do

Finance is the single issue most likely to cause conflict between Holyrood and Westminster. Discuss.

THE ROLE OF LOCAL GOVERNMENT IN A DEMOCRACY

Local government has a vital role in the running of the country, in the provision of local services, taking decisions relating to local issues and acting as a watchdog over other governing bodies.

Service provider

Local government is responsible for planning and implementing a wide variety of essential services including education, social work, street lighting, refuse collection and disposal, police, fire, planning and many more. These services have a direct impact on people's lives.

Making decisions on local issues

The principle of **subsidiarity** means that decisions should be made at the lowest possible level. There are decisions best suited to European level, some suited to be taken UK-wide, others for the Scottish Parliament and many can be taken locally. Local government is best placed to take certain decisions because its representatives have detailed knowledge of local needs.

Watchdog

Local government can act as a check on the power of other governing bodies. Local government can alert the electorate to proposed changes from Brussels, Westminster or Holyrood and the impact they will have on local circumstances. Local councils, individually or in collaboration with each other, can question the acts and omissions of other levels of government and try to influence them for the benefit of local people.

POWERS AND RESPONSIBILITIES OF SCOTTISH LOCAL AUTHORITIES

The powers and duties of local authorities are outlined by Acts of Parliament. Local government has four roles and functions:

- provision of services
- strategic planning
- regulation
- community leadership.

Provision of services

Local authorities have responsibility for planning, resourcing and direct provision of a wide range of services. These include education, housing, social work, economic development, public protection, planning, leisure and recreation. Service provision involves providing services directly or working in partnership with other public agencies and commissioning services from the voluntary and private sectors.

Services provided can be divided into three broad categories:

- **mandatory** services which must be provided (such as education for school-age children)
- **permissive** services which may be provided (such as economic development)
- **discretionary** services which allow local government to spend a limited amount of money which will bring direct benefit to the council area.

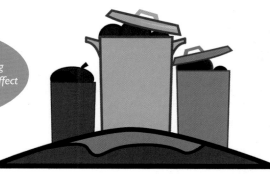

Local authorities are responsible for providing many services which directly affect people's lives

Strategic planning

Local authorities provide a long-term strategic planning framework which sets objectives based on the **needs and priorities** of their constituents. This is used to control and direct the development of services such as road building programmes and the designation of areas for housing, industry and green belts.

Regulation

Local authorities regulate local businesses by the granting of licences to businesses such as taxi drivers, public houses and nursing and residential homes and have **registration and inspection functions** for these licences.

Community leadership

Local authorities take a lead role in issues which cut across the **responsibilities of different agencies** such as social inclusion, community safety and dealing with environmental concerns. Local authorities have to co-ordinate multi-agency responses to these issues.

For you to do

- Draw a mind map of the roles and responsibilities of local government.
- Assess the importance of the role of local government in the democratic process in Scotland.

Internet research

Visit your local authority website to find examples of the powers and responsibilities in your area.
Links to the websites of local authorities and other websites relating to Higher Modern Studies can be found at:

THE CONVENTION OF SCOTTISH LOCAL AUTHORITIES

The Convention of Scottish Local Authorities (COSLA) was formed in 1975 and provides a forum for representatives of Scotland's 32 councils to discuss matters of common concern. When these discussions lead to agreed positions, COSLA discusses them with the Scottish Executive. COSLA is the collective voice for Scotland's local authorities.

COSLA monitors what the Scottish Parliament is planning and keeps individual local authorities aware of proposed changes. COSLA gives evidence to parliamentary committees on behalf of the local authorities. It also gives evidence to and negotiates with the Scottish Executive over local government finance.

LOCAL GOVERNMENT FINANCE

Finance is strictly controlled by the Scottish Parliament. Revenue is raised in four main ways:

- revenue support grant
- national non-domestic rates
- council tax
- fees, charges and sales.

Revenue support grant

The level of revenue support grant (RSG) for local authorities is determined by the Scottish Executive. The final amounts are laid before Parliament each year for approval. Other grants are provided in the same way for specific purposes or services, for example, funding for the police service. The RSG accounts for **60%** of local government spending.

National non-domestic rates

All commercial properties (shops, offices, factories, etc) pay rates based on the rateable value of the properties. These rates are set nationally by the Executive. The local authorities collect the tax but the Executive determines the amount each authority can collect. These rates account for **18%** of local government spending.

Council tax

Council tax is a property tax levied on individual homes. Every residential property is surveyed and placed in one of eight valuation bands (A-H). Each local authority then sets its own council tax level based on its projected expenditure.

If the Executive believes that a local authority is setting council tax too high, it has the power to *cap* the amount the local authority can raise. The Executive has the power to prevent local authorities from raising too much revenue and to force them to cut expenditure. Council tax accounts for **13%** of local government spending.

Fees, charges and sales

Local government raises income from charging for services such as parking, leisure activities and some social work services. These fees and sale account for **9%** of local government spending.

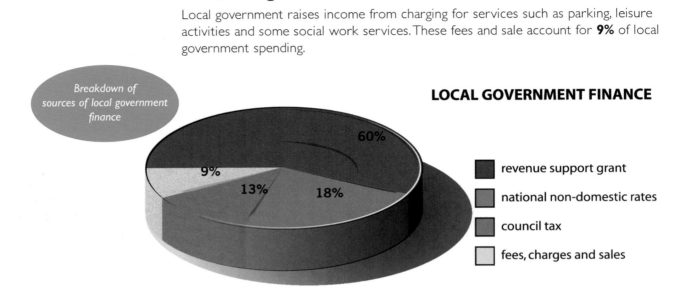

Breakdown of sources of local government finance

LOCAL GOVERNMENT FINANCE

60%

9%

13%   18%

- revenue support grant
- national non-domestic rates
- council tax
- fees, charges and sales

Capital expenditure

Local government can also raise finance for capital expenditure for the development of long-term assets such as the purchase, construction or improvement of land or buildings. Local authorities' capital expenditure is controlled by the Scottish Executive.

Capital expenditure is financed in four ways:

- annually, Scottish Ministers give individual councils permission to borrow specific amounts of money from banks and other financial institutions to undertake particular projects – called **capital consents to borrow**
- receipts from the sale of local authority assets
- grants (such as development grants from the European Union)
- partnership ventures with the private sector – called **private finance initiatives** (PFI).

Scottish Executive controls on local government spending

The Scottish Executive controls local government spending by:

- setting the RSG
- setting the national non-domestic rates
- capping local authority budgets they consider excessive
- undertaking annual audits (via the Accounts Commission for Scotland) of local authority accounts, to ensure the 'economy, efficiency and effectiveness of local government services'
- requiring local authorities to demonstrate they are achieving best value across services by having procedures to audit performance and service provision.

For you to do

Draw a mind map to show sources of local government finance and the controls on it.

Internet research

Visit your local authority website to find examples of how much it gets in grants, how much it raises in council tax and its main items of expenditure.

Links to the websites of local authorities and other websites relating to Higher Modern Studies can be found at: LECKIE&LECKIE Learning Lab

THE IMPACT OF THE ELECTORAL SYSTEM ON THE COMPOSITION OF SCOTTISH COUNCILS

The Local Governance (Scotland) Act 2004 passed by the Scottish Parliament introduced the system of the **single transferable vote** (STV) system for local government elections in Scotland. It is to be used for the first time in 2007.

The switch to STV will make a great difference to the composition of local councils in Scotland. In 2003, the Labour Party controlled 13 of Scotland's 32 local authorities, the SNP and LibDems controlled one each, independents controlled five and in 12 local authorities, no group had a majority.

If STV had been in operation, the election results would have been very different. Approximately five councils would still have been controlled by independents, Labour might have controlled one or two at most, while for the overwhelming majority of councils there would have been no group or party with overall control.

The big losers with the introduction of STV will be the Labour Party whose power base in the central belt of Scotland will be seriously eroded. Many Labour councillors will probably lose their seats. More councils will be opened up as decisions will not be taken in closed group meetings with the full council meeting to rubber stamp them. More decisions will have to be argued out in public.

Coalitions will have to be formed to run councils or groups will be forced to run minority administrations. Councils will have to become more responsive to the popular will of the local electorates. There is the danger that some councils may become locked in

struggles between competing factions which will reduce their effectiveness. If there is a deadlock over setting council tax, however, there is provision for the Scottish Executive to step in and set council tax rates to ensure funding for the authority isn't blocked.

CO-OPERATION AND CONFLICT BETWEEN LOCAL AUTHORITIES AND THE SCOTTISH EXECUTIVE

There are considerable areas of co-operation between the local councils and the Executive, largely because the Labour Party plays such a significant role at both levels. Many of those in the Executive share a common background with those in local government. Many have grown up in the central belt, attended the same universities, joined the Labour Party and served on one of the councils. This helps create common viewpoints. However, there are areas of disagreement, mainly over finance and changes in the electoral system for local government.

In 2003, the COSLA manifesto complained that:

Institutionalised under-funding, unnecessary interference and control from the centre, the over-reliance on management by performance targets, and the inexorable growth of nationally imposed initiatives and partnerships are just some of the issues that need to be tackled if local government is to be allowed to flourish.

Finance

The Scottish Executive controls over 80% of local authority funding. This places constraints on the freedom of action of local authorities. By restricting funding, the Executive can force local councils to restrict the development of local services or to put up council tax by significant amounts, neither of which is palatable to the electorate.

Another area of irritation is that much of the funding is *ring-fenced* so it can only be spent on specific projects decided by the Executive, instead of the local authority.

The Scottish Executive claims that it provides councils with more than sufficient funds, while councils counter that most of the increase in funding is reserved for new initiatives introduced by the Executive.

An example is free personal care for the elderly. Introduced by the Parliament, it was left to local councils to implement. The Executive claims it provides sufficient funds annually to meet the costs. But many local authorities claim it is not enough and are forced to create waiting lists or find loopholes to enable them to set some charges.

Similarly, the Executive claimed it fully funded the McCrone deal in education. However, in order to provide the funds to give primary staff reduced class contact time, some authorities have cut or restricted courses in secondary schools.

Best value procedures also create problems for local authorities. A large amount of time, effort and cost is spent on monitoring services and assessing the efficiency with which they are delivered. This takes scarce funding away from frontline services.

Changes to the electoral system

STV will be used for the first time in Scottish local elections in 2007. Labour councillors tried to use their influence both in the Scottish Parliament and in Westminster to block the change. They objected to the Labour Party giving up its power base in local councils across Scotland. Despite this conflict with the Executive, local authorities had to accept the change.

The change may lead to more conflict in future. Few councils in Scotland will have a single party in control after 2007, and there will be many varieties of coalition, each with separate demands for local government.

These may well create more conflict between local authorities and Holyrood.

COSLA has called for the Parliament and the 32 councils to commit themselves to a joint agreement, called a Covenant, which would set out the basis of their working relationship. COSLA wants a standing Joint Conference where the Executive, MSPs and local government representatives can discuss matters affecting local government.

COSLA has called for adequate, sustainable and flexible funding to deliver agreed national priorities and to allow individual councils to address local priorities. It wants less ring-fenced funding, a recognition by the Scottish Executive of the real costs of core service delivery, and a commitment from the Scottish Executive to fully fund new initiatives that local government is expected to implement.

Internet research

Visit the websites of COSLA, Scottish Executive, your local authority, newspapers and the BBC to find examples of the relationship between local authorities and the Scottish Executive.
Links to these sites and other websites relating to Higher Modern Studies can be found at:

For you to do

To what extent does the Scottish Executive's control of local government spending in Scotland impact on the democratic process at a local level?

STUDY THEME SUMMARY

A range of public bodies is involved in decision making in Scotland, ranging from the UK Government in Westminster, through the Scottish Parliament in Edinburgh, down to local authorities throughout Scotland. The Scottish Parliament is based on the four principles of accessibility, accountability, openness to all, and the sharing of power. The Additional Member System ensures that the number of MSPs elected for each party is a fair representation of how votes are cast. The Parliament is designed to allow the general public to have a more direct input into decision-making activities, through the use of petitions and committee meetings.

The Scottish Parliament has responsibility for specific devolved matters, while the UK Parliament has responsibility for reserved matters which affect the whole of the UK. The Scottish Parliament is supposed to assume a high degree of autonomy over devolved matters, but has been criticised for allowing some decisions to be made for Scotland through Sewel Motions.

Local government in Scotland acts to provide local services such as education, housing, social work and planning, undertake long-term strategic planning and regulation, and provide community leadership. Local government finance is controlled by the Scottish Executive, which can cause conflict between it and local authorities. From 2007, local government elections will use STV, a form of proportional representation, and it is expected that this will have profound implications for the composition of many local councils, requiring more local coalitions between parties and groups.

Exam-style essay questions

Critically examine the effectiveness of the Scottish Parliament in scrutinising the work of the Scottish Executive.

To what extent are there opportunities for conflict between the UK Government and the Scottish Parliament?

Critically examine the relationship between the Scottish Executive and local authorities.

STUDY THEME 1B:
Decision making in central government

In this study theme you will be expected to have a detailed knowledge and understanding of:

- ## THE EXECUTIVE
  The respective roles of the Prime Minister and Cabinet; accountability to Parliament; the role of senior civil servants in the UK political system.

- ## PARLIAMENT (HOUSE OF COMMONS AND HOUSE OF LORDS)
  Parliament (House of Commons and House of Lords) as an arena for conflict, co-operation and decision making; functions; organisation of and procedures for business.

- ## INFLUENCES ON THE DECISION MAKING PROCESS IN THE UK
  The extent of these pressures, their impact and legitimacy.

THE EXECUTIVE

The Executive is the branch of Government concerned with carrying out policy. It is the part of the political system which makes decisions and runs the country. There are several elements of the Executive:

- the Prime Minister
- the Cabinet
- other Government Ministers
- the Civil Service.

House of Commons (elected) House of Lords (mostly appointed)

The Prime Minister Cabinet Ministers Other Government Ministers

The Civil Service Non-political permanent staff (some political appointments)

Parliament

The Executive

The overlapping structure of the Executive and Parliament

In Britain, the party which wins the largest number of seats in a General Election will form the Government. Because of the system of first-past-the-post it is usual for this government to be a **majority government**. In most countries of mainland Europe and in Scotland where proportional representation is used, **coalition governments** tend to be formed. (For more information on types of voting systems, see Study Theme 1D, pages 84–107.)

The Government consists of more than 100 people, comprising about 20 Cabinet Ministers (senior ministers) and junior ministers. These people are chosen by the Prime Minister, usually from his or her own party.

The role of government has grown considerably over the last 60 years. It has taken on the responsibility for many aspects of our lives and we expect the government to deal with problems in the areas of social and economic policy as well as in international matters.

WORD BANK

Coalition government: a government formed with members of more than one political party.

THE PRIME MINISTER

As the role of government has grown, so have the powers of the Prime Minister. This power is based upon the Prime Minister's dual position as head of the Government and as the leader of the majority party in Parliament and election winner.

The Prime Minister now has considerably more power than any other Cabinet colleagues compared with their relative positions in the past. The phrase *first amongst equals* was used to describe the position of the Prime Minister, but this now fails to recognise the additional powers held by the Prime Minister. The role and power of the Prime Minister are not based on formal constitutional powers but are largely based on conventions that have built up over the years and also upon the style and personality of the holder of the position. It has been suggested that the Prime Minister has become more presidential in power, meaning that the Prime Minister has much greater personal authority, and the influence of the Cabinet in making decisions has declined.

For you to do

Give examples of aspects of society where government has a responsibility.

Internet research

Visit the website of the UK Government or 10 Downing Street and find an up-to-date list of the Cabinet members and the positions they hold.
Links to these sites and other websites relating to Higher Modern Studies can be found at:
www.leckieandleckie.co.uk by clicking on the Learning Lab button and navigating to the Higher Modern Studies Course Notes page.

LECKIE&LECKIE
Learning Lab

Powers of the Prime Minister

- The Prime Minster is the **head of the Executive**. The Prime Minister is ultimately responsible for government decisions, and is in overall charge of the Civil Service.
- The Prime Minister **oversees Government policy**, playing the major role in deciding Government priorities while in office and at elections.
- The Prime Minister is the **leader of their party** and the main representative of the party to the public and the electorate.
- The Prime Minister has considerable **powers of appointment**. The Prime Minister chooses the Cabinet Ministers, and will promote or demote members of the Cabinet and other Government ministers in ministerial *reshuffles*. As well as these offices of government the Prime Minister is responsible for other public appointments including the church, senior judges, some university posts, and other public bodies. The Prime Minister also influences the honours system.
- The Prime Minister is the **main figure in Parliament,** where they lead the majority party and speak on behalf of the Government, principally at the weekly Prime Minister's Questions.
- Although not the Head of State, the Prime Minister is the **principal representative** of the country in meetings and negotiations with foreign leaders. Summit meetings with other world leaders give the Prime Minister a major role in foreign affairs.

Prime Minister Tony Blair makes a statement at G8 summit meeting held at Gleneagles in July 2005.

Greater power than other Cabinet members

The historical view of the British Executive was that of collective or Cabinet government and that the Prime Minister was merely the first amongst equals. This is no longer the case and the power of the Prime Minister has increased at the expense of Cabinet colleagues.

- The Prime Minister has the **power to appoint, sack and reshuffle** the Cabinet in order to get the Cabinet that they want. Rivals and enemies can be sidelined or sacked and supporters promoted to influential positions.
- The Prime Minister has a range of **additional powers**, most notably the power to choose the date of the election (with the consent of the monarch).
- Fewer decisions are discussed fully in Cabinet. The increased use of Cabinet committees and decreased use of full Cabinet meetings have reduced the **collective nature of the decision-making process**. The Prime Minister has their own staff and political advisors. This makes the Prime Minister less dependent upon advice from ministers. Ministers tend to be fully occupied with running their own departments, leaving the Prime Minister as the only member of Government with an overall view of Government policy and direction.
- The principle of **collective responsibility**, where all Cabinet members are expected to show public support for Government policies, irrespective of their own personal views, should give the impression of unity behind the Prime Minister.
- The Prime Minister has become the **main focus of the media**. This tends to emphasise the role of the individual as being the main representative of the Government and Government policy. The increased foreign policy role of the Prime Minister has increased this media focus.
- As leader of the winning party in the election the party leader will usually have the goodwill of much of the party. The whips in Parliament aim to ensure the leader has the **support of the backbenchers**, many of whom will owe their election to the success of the party leader.

Whips:
MPs or Peers who have been appointed to act as a business managers and are an essential channel of communication between the leadership and MPs and Lords.

Backbenchers:
ordinary MPs who do not have official positions in Government.

Limits on the power of the Prime Minister

Although the powers of the British Prime Minster have increased over recent years, there are still restrictions on their powers.

- Any Prime Minister needs to retain the **support of their Parliamentary and Cabinet colleagues**. Even three-time election winner, Margaret Thatcher, had to resign after she lost the support of her Cabinet in 1990.
- Ultimately the fate of a Prime Minister will be determined by **voters**. If sufficient voters turn against the Prime Minister and their party in the election then they will lose office. If the party perceive that the Prime Minister has become an electoral liability then they may choose to change the leader before the election in order to increase their chance of success.
- Major **policy disagreements** can weaken a Prime Minister. High profile resignations from the Cabinet over policy issues can seriously weaken the authority of the Prime Minister. Frequent large-scale backbench revolts will also weaken the power of the Prime Minister. Controversial and unpopular policies such as British involvement in the invasion of Iraq caused major difficulties for Tony Blair.

- Although the Prime Minister has the power to pick their Cabinet, they may have to **compromise** over the selections. It may be necessary, in the interests of party unity, to pick rivals. Different wings of the party may have to have representation in order to prevent splits. Some ministers may be appointed because of their ability to run large and complex departments whether or not they are supporters of the Prime Minister. The ability of the Prime Minister to shape the Cabinet can also be affected if a minister refuses to accept a particular post.
- The **media attention** on the Prime Minister can be a double-edged sword. If the attention is positive then the power and status of the Prime Minister will be enhanced. However, if the media image is negative, a daily diet of unflattering photographs and stories which show the Prime Minister in a bad light will weaken their authority.

For you to do

- Explain why the Prime Minister is such a powerful political figure.
- Give reasons why the Prime Minister is more powerful than their Cabinet colleagues.
- What are the limits on the power of the Prime Minister?
- Explain what is meant by saying the media is a double-edged sword with regard to the power of the Prime Minister.

Internet research

Visit the website of the BBC or national newspapers. Find recent examples of high profile events involving the Prime Minister.
Links to these sites and other websites relating to Higher Modern Studies can be found at:

In exam questions you may be asked to 'Discuss' or analyse an issue by saying 'to what extent' something is the case. In these answers you must ensure that you analyse the issue in a balanced way giving evidence and opinions from various sides before you reach a conclusion.

PRIME MINISTERIAL STYLE

Margaret Thatcher

- Most dominant Prime Minister in recent history
- Won three elections with large majorities
- Chose Cabinet members to support her own views
- Reduced importance of collective Cabinet decision making
- Consulted own advisors rather than take departmental advice
- Insisted on pushing through unpopular policies against advice of colleagues
- Seen as autocratic and dogmatic
- Lost support of Cabinet colleagues
- Forced to resign after being challenged in leadership contest

*Margaret Thatcher
(Conservative), 1979–1990*

John Major

- Greater use of Cabinet to discuss policies and make decisions
- Greater mix of opinions represented in Cabinet
- More emphasis on consensus and collegiality
- Won one election in 1992 with relatively small majority
- Faced frequent policy disagreements within party, especially over Europe
- Government perceived as weak, directionless and divided
- Major seen as boring, weak and not in control of party
- Defeated in election in 1997 after splits in policy and allegations of sleaze in the party

*John Major
(Conservative), 1990–1997*

Tony Blair

- Won landslide victory in 1997 after forcing major reforms through Labour Party
- Reduced length and frequency of Cabinet meetings
- Major emphasis on presentation and media image
- Accusations of excessive control over party and spin
- Gave considerable power to Chancellor of the Exchequer, Gordon Brown, in economic policy
- Led party to second major victory in 2001 and again with reduced majority in 2005
- Began to lose support of party members and backbench MPs after decision to support US-led invasion of Iraq and controversial policy decisions on education and health
- Announced in 2005 he would step down before next election

*Tony Blair
(Labour), 1997–present day*

Internet research

Use the internet or textbooks to explain how the different styles of recent Prime Ministers affected their position as PM.

CABINET

The Cabinet consists of around 20–24 members of the Government. Cabinet members are chosen by the Prime Minister. They are required to be accountable for their actions to Parliament, so they must be members of either the House of Commons or House of Lords. Most members of the Cabinet, usually known as **Secretaries of State**, run Government departments such as the Home Office, the Foreign Office or the Department for Education and Skills.

The main roles of the Cabinet are to:

- **propose legislation** to be presented to Parliament
- **supervise the administration** of policy
- **coordinate policies** of different departments
- try and **reach agreement in disputes** between departments.

The Cabinet is chaired by the Prime Minister and meets every week for about an hour. The Prime Minister controls the agenda and following a discussion will sum up the mood of the meeting. Once a decision has been made, Cabinet members must publicly support the decision. This concept is known as **collective responsibility**.

Collective responsibility

Decisions of the Cabinet are binding on all members of the Government. A public display of unity must be maintained by all members of the Cabinet or they must resign from their Cabinet position. Clare Short and Robin Cook resigned from the Cabinet over the Government's policy on Iraq.

Ministerial responsibility

The minister is responsible for all actions and policy decisions within their department. In the past this was interpreted as meaning not only that the minister was accountable to Parliament but that mistakes made by civil servants could lead to the resignation of ministers. Such a course of action is very rare nowadays, although frequent policy or operational failures may lead to hostile press coverage and a loss of confidence in a minister.

Charles Clarke was sacked from his job as Home Secretary in May 2006 following criticism in the media over the release of more than 1,000 foreign prisoners who were not considered for deportation. He was offered other posts in the Cabinet but refused them and was said to have been 'furious' at being dismissed. He has criticised the way he was treated and attacked his successor, John Reid.

With more than 20 members and only meeting for an hour or so a week, the Cabinet cannot effectively discuss and decide all matters of policy. As a result government has made increasing use of a large number of Cabinet committees. It has been said that the greater use of such committees has led to an increase in the power of the Prime Minister since it is they who choose the members of the committees and discussion is increasingly compartmentalised.

The Cabinet Office

The Cabinet Office is the Civil Service department set up to serve the Cabinet. At the top is the Cabinet Secretary, Britain's most senior civil servant who, along with about 40 other senior civil servants, is in regular contact with the Prime Minister's Office in 10 Downing Street. The role of the Cabinet Office, which has some 1,500 civil servants in it, is to timetable meetings, prepare agendas and documents, circulate minutes and service the Cabinet committees.

For you to do

- Explain the meaning of the terms collective responsibility and ministerial responsibility.
- Explain how the power of the Cabinet has been reduced in recent years.

SENIOR CIVIL SERVANTS AND SPECIAL ADVISORS

The Civil Service is the permanent staff of the Government. It is neutral and non-political. Governments may change after elections and ministers may be reshuffled, demoted or sacked, but the civil servants remain in their positions to work with the new ministers.

The role of the Civil Service has three aspects:

- giving **policy advice** to ministers – this has been the role of the most senior civil servants (often known as *mandarins*)
- **day-to-day management of departments** – ministers have overall responsibility for the work of government departments, but officials carry out the administrative functions
- **implementing policy and delivering services**.

The role of policy advisor is a controversial issue. Civil servants are required to be non-party political and provide impartial advice to whichever party leads the Government. Civil servants should be appointed and promoted on the basis of fair appointment procedures and merit, not on the basis of political patronage.

In addition to civil service advisors, the Prime Minister and other ministers can appoint their own *special advisors*. However, the increase in their number and the greater visibility of some of these advisors has led to concerns about the relationship between special advisors appointed by politicians and senior civil servants.

Concerns over the *politicisation* of the Civil Service are not new. Margaret Thatcher took a close interest in the appointment of senior officials, aiming to ensure that people were appointed who would not hamper her own political agenda. Under Labour, the doubling of the number of special advisors in government and the growth of the Prime Minister's own office has increased the concerns.

Special advisors tend to be of two types, concerned either with policy matters or with getting across the government's message to the public and media. These are the so-called *spin doctors*.

Concern has been expressed that career civil servants have been expected to carry out political tasks such as presenting information in a way that would give political support to the governing party. It has been suggested that this occurred in the lead-up to the war in Iraq, although the Government and Civil Service were cleared of this charge by the Butler Report in 2004. A further concern has been over the blurring of the roles of political advisors and senior civil servants, particularly in the cases of Tony Blair's Press Secretary, Alastair Campbell and Chief of Staff, Jonathan Powell. Both were appointed as temporary civil servants into posts traditionally held by career civil servants and were given powers to give orders to civil servants.

For you to do

- Describe the role of the Civil Service in the UK system of Government.
- Explain the traditional view as to how civil servants are recruited.
- Give advantages and disadvantages of the increasing role of special advisors.
- The role of the Prime Minister has become increasingly presidential. Discuss.

Internet research

Use the internet to research some of these issues:

- doubling of special advisors under Labour – still less than 100
- increased number of political appointees affects political neutrality of Civil Service
- special advisors provide advice for ministers which may contradict view of civil servants.

Bicameral:
having two houses
(chambers) of
Parliament.

PARLIAMENT

Parliament is the **legislature** or law-making body at the heart of the British political system. It is a **bicameral system**, made up of two chambers:

● The **House of Commons**

● The **House of Lords**.

Members of the **House of Commons** are called **Members of Parliament** known as *MPs*.
Members of the **House of Lords** are called **Lords of Parliament**, known as *Lords*.

Houses of Parliament in London – site of House of Commons and House of Lords

THE HOUSE OF COMMONS

The House of Commons has several functions within the UK political system.

● **Representation of the people.** All Members of Parliament are elected from a constituency and represent the people of that constituency in Parliament. This provides a direct link between the electorate and Government.

● It **provides the personnel of Government**. In the UK all members of the Government are required to be members of either the House of Lords or the House of Commons. In practice, most members of Government are members of the House of Commons. By convention, the Prime Minister must be a member of the House of Commons. By this means the Executive is accountable to the voters through their elected representatives.

● **Controlling finance.** The House of Commons has sole responsibility for financial matters. Each year the Chancellor of the Exchequer presents the budget to the House of Commons, which must then debate and approve it before the Government can make changes to taxation and spending.

● Provides a **forum of debate between Government and Opposition**. The House of Commons is a debating chamber, and the process of passing laws, holding debates and creating opportunities to question the Government allow the discussion of national issues. This is the embodiment of the democratic principle of free speech. Parliament is televised, allowing the electorate to view proceedings.

● **Legitimises the Government** and its measures. Government policies must go through the correct procedures before they can take effect.

● Seeks to **scrutinise and influence Government**. Parliament is the forum where the Opposition and backbench MPs are able to examine the work of Government and call to account Government ministers.

There are 646 MPs in the House of Commons. MPs are not required to work full-time as an MP and they may have outside interests (although this has recently been reviewed after some MPs were thought to have abused their position and taken payment for asking questions on behalf of commercial interests in Parliament). MPs are expected to register any outside interests and payments and the rules have been tightened since the Nolan Report in 1995. MPs receive a salary of around £60,000 plus accommodation, travel and office expenses.

The work of the House of Commons

Most of the work of the Commons is done through debates with a vote (or **division**) taken after the debate. Proceedings in the House of Commons are conducted by the **Speaker of the House** who is elected by the MPs (currently Michael Martin MP).

The two major functions of the House of Commons are:

- **making laws**
- **control and criticism** of the Government.

Making laws

Laws are made after discussion and debate of **Bills**, which are the documents giving the detail of the proposed new law. When the Bill passes through the required procedures, it becomes an **Act of Parliament** and becomes law. There are no constitutional barriers to the law-making powers of Parliament. However, some people are concerned that UK membership of the European Union has reduced the independence of the British Parliament, since some decisions are limited by obligations resulting from membership of the EU.

The law-making process generally begins outside Parliament with the Government or pressure groups. There are a few limited opportunities for backbench MPs to bring in Private Members' Bills but they are unlikely to succeed unless the Government gives them time and backing.

The Government has the upper hand in the House of Commons.

- They **control the bulk of Parliamentary time**, leaving few opportunities for the Opposition or backbenchers to raise matters of concern.
- They have the **loyalty of most of the MPs** in the house since they are the Government by virtue of their majority following a General Election. Party loyalty and the whips system means that the Government rarely loses a vote in the House of Commons.
- Most Government legislation is introduced in the House of Commons where **the Government's majority should be sufficient to secure its passage**. This process accounts for 55% of the Commons' time each year.

For you to do

- Make up a spider diagram or mind map showing the functions of the House of Commons.
- MPs should be allowed to have paid outside interests. Discuss.
- Why do backbench MPs have little opportunity to introduce laws?

Internet research

Visit the website of the House of Commons and find out the details of your own MP.
Find out the current salary and allowances of MPs. Find their entry in the Register of MPs' interests.
Links to these sites and other websites relating to Higher Modern Studies can be found at:

A Bill becomes an Act in the following stages:

How a Bill becomes an Act

White Paper

A proposed piece of legislation, which contains the general proposals on the Bill. It is circulated for information, comments and consultation.

First Reading

The Bill is introduced into the House, normally by the minister whose department is most concerned with the legislation.

Second Reading

The Bill is circulated to MPs for debate. If a majority do not vote in favour, the Bill will be discarded, so it is not unusual for the Government to introduce a 'Three-line Whip' at this stage.

Committee Stage

The Bill is referred to a standing committee of MPs, made up in the proportion of their party strength in the House, where it is examined in greater detail and where amendments may be made.

Report Stage

The Bill in its amended form is returned to the House where the amendments are debated: there is no division at this stage.

Third Reading

The Bill in its final form is debated for the last time by the whole House and a division is held.

After completing the stages in the House of Commons, Bills other than those concerned with money go to the House of Lords where they go through the same stages. After passing through the House of Lords, the Bill will go to the monarch to receive the Royal Assent. It is a convention that the Queen accepts Bills that have been proposed by an elected Government and have passed through all the stages of Parliamentary procedure. Only after a Bill has been given the approval of each of the component parts of Parliament does it enter the Statute Book and become a law.

For you to do

Make a flow diagram showing the stages in introducing a Bill and passing an Act.

Referendum

In a few cases, voters have been asked directly their opinion on certain matters in a vote on a specific issue called a **referendum**. In recent years these votes have been confined to constitutional matters such as membership of the European Union, devolution for Scotland and Wales, and regional assemblies in England. The Government has announced that any eventual decision on Britain joining the Euro will be put to a referendum.

Control and criticism of the Government

Under the British system, all Government ministers are Members or Lords of Parliament and are responsible to Parliament for their performance as ministers. The function of Parliament is to scrutinise the Government and its ministers and call them to account.

The ultimate power that Parliament has over the Government is a **vote of confidence**. It is rare for such a vote to be called. The last time a Government lost such a vote was in 1979. If a Government loses a vote of confidence in Parliament, the Prime Minister would be obliged to call for Parliament to be dissolved and a General Election held.

The Opposition in Parliament

Her Majesty's Opposition is made up of the MPs of the party with the second largest number of seats following a General Election. The role of the Opposition is to ensure that the policies of the Government are subjected to constant challenge and to make Government accountable for its actions. This is an official role of Parliament and funds are provided to allow the Opposition to do its work. This recognition of the value of the Opposition is seen to embody the principle of free speech.

Functions of the Opposition include:

- ensuring that the Government is **accountable**
- **taking over** the Government when the electorate desires changes in policy
- **co-operating** with the Government in the business of Parliament
- presenting **alternative policy** options.

Criticisms of the role of the Opposition include:

- the pace of Government work is **slowed down**
- challenges to Government may be misconstrued and **operate to the disadvantage of the country**
- the adversarial nature of the British political system tends to **stress difference and encourage conflict** and **rarely seek constructive consensus**.

The main Opposition party will form a Shadow Cabinet, with spokespeople taking on the same areas of responsibility as the Government Cabinet.

The role of the Opposition is often seen as negative, and as opposing for its own sake. To be effective, Opposition should also be seen as constructive, attempting to present itself as an alternative Government with realistic policies.

In periods when the Government has a large majority, the Opposition may become frustrated, believing that Parliamentary opposition is futile due to the Government's in-built majority. In such a situation, opposition to Government policies may come increasingly from sources outside Parliament such as the media, pressure groups and campaigns of civil disobedience.

HINTS & TIPS

> In order to score high marks in essays it is important that you make developed points. Even a long list of unexplained points will score few marks. Remember PEE: make your Point; Explain the point you have made; give relevant Examples to support your point.

Parliamentary scrutiny of Government

There are a number of opportunities for Parliament to criticise the Government:

- Second Reading debates
- Question Time, including Prime Minister's Questions
- Select Committees
- Queen's Speech debates
- Supply Days
- Adjournment debates.

Second Reading debates allow MPs to give their opinions on proposed legislation. The Opposition will make its criticisms and the Government must justify their proposals, after which MPs vote.

Question Time, at the start of Parliamentary business on Tuesdays, Wednesdays and Thursdays, is an allocated time when ministers answer MPs' questions. Parliamentary questions are one way of getting information about the Government's intentions as well as a way for MPs to raise constituency issues with the Government. Recently Prime Minister's Questions was reformed, with one longer session replacing two shorter ones. It was hoped that this would result in more information and considered debate rather than simple point-scoring with *sound bites*, but so far the reform does not seem to have changed the nature of Question Time significantly.

Select Committees were set up to control the Executive by examining and reporting on aspects of policy or administration. Select Committees are constituted on a party basis but may be chaired by an MP of any party. They will shadow the work of a Government department and examine their work, producing reports on the performance of these departments. In their scrutiny of Government policies, the committees question Government Ministers, civil servants and interested bodies and individuals. The members of the committee may build up an expertise and authority in the area they are responsible for. Their reports are often authoritative and, if critical of Government, unlikely to be ignored.

The debate following the **Queen's Speech** at the start of each Parliamentary session provides an opportunity for the main Opposition parties to criticise the Government's proposed programme for the forthcoming Parliamentary session.

Supply days are days which in theory are for the discussion of the Government's expenditure programme but are now given over to the Opposition to choose subjects for debate. There are 20 Supply days in each Parliamentary session.

Adjournment debates are a short period at the end of the Parliamentary day given over to backbench MPs to raise constituency issues or matters of public concern with a Government Minister in attendance.

Internet research

Visit the website of the Opposition.
Find out the current leader of the Opposition and the main shadow spokespersons.
Links to this site and other websites relating to Higher Modern Studies can be found at:

For you to do

- What is a vote of confidence?
- Why is a Government unlikely to lose a vote of confidence?
- Explain the role of the Opposition.
- Why is it important that the criticisms made by the Opposition are constructive?
- What could be the consequences of a weak Opposition?
- Question Time or Select Committees – which is more important in holding the Government to account? Explain your answer.

HOUSE OF LORDS

The House of Lords is the second chamber in the UK's Parliament. It is usually regarded as a valuable safeguard for democracy to have two houses in Parliament in order that the power of one is balanced by the power of the other. In the case of the UK, with a tradition of majority governments and strong party discipline in the House of Commons, the Lords have often been the only effective Parliamentary opposition to the elected Government. The House of Lords now only has the power to delay legislation but this can provide an opportunity for the Government to reflect upon hasty legislation. The House of Lords has more time to debate issues and because of its experienced membership can often bring a high quality of discussion to debates.

Composition of House lords by peer type
April 1999 and June 2000

Legend:
- ■ Life Peers
- ▨ Hereditary Peers
- ▢ Bishops

Before Reform:
- 2%
- 39%
- 59%

After Reform:
- 4%
- 83%
- 13%

(Y-axis: 200, 400, 600, 800, 1000, 1200, 1400)

To many observers, the House of Lords is out of place in a democratic society. Members of the House of Lords are not elected, but gain their place either as **Hereditary peers**, appointed **Life peers**, **Law Lords**, or **Bishops**. The Labour Government elected in 1997 promised to reform the House of Lords and abolished the rights of most Hereditary peers to sit in the Lords. However, further reforms seem to have stalled.

The chart above shows the changed composition of the Lords following the Labour Government's decision in 1999 to abolish the right of most Hereditary peers to sit in the House of Lords.

Functions of the House of Lords

The House of Lords has a number of functions.

- It **makes laws**, along with the House of Commons. Most laws must be passed through the House of Lords. The House of Lords plays an important part in revising legislation and can spend more time in detailed discussions of Bills than the Commons.
- It **holds the Government to account**. The role of the Lords is to scrutinise the work of the Government by considering the legislation they propose, asking ministers questions and sitting on investigative Select Committees.
- It provides **independent expertise**. The range and depth of knowledge and experience in the Lords means that debates can be of a high standard, with those speaking having less concern for party positions than is often found in the Commons.
- It has a **judicial function**. The Law Lords sitting in the House of Lords act as the highest court in the country.

Membership of the House of Lords

There are around 730 members of the Lords at present, and there are four main types.

- **Life peers** are appointed for their own lifetime only. Since 2000 the Appointments Commission has made recommendations for non-political peers (sometimes known as *People's Peers*) and has vetted the suitability of peers nominated by political parties.
- **Law Lords** are senior judges appointed to hear appeals from lower courts. There are currently 12 Law Lords, but this function is due to end in 2009 when a Supreme Court will be set up.
- **Archbishops and Bishops** of the Church of England.
- **Elected Hereditary peers**. Ninety-two of the former Hereditary peers are still allowed to sit in the House of Lords, until the next stage of reform.

As in the House of Commons, many peers are organised along party political lines. They do not represent constituencies and party control is often weaker in the Lords. A significant number of peers are not affiliated to any party and are known as *crossbenchers*. No party has an overall majority in the House of Lords.

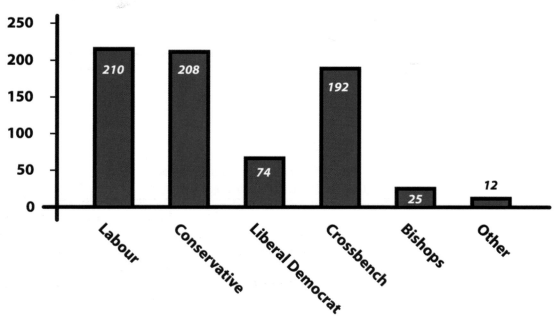

Composition of House of Lords by party and other groups
November 2005

48

Limits on the powers of the House of Lords

As an unelected chamber, it is accepted that the House of Lords will have a lesser role than the House of Commons in passing legislation.

- **Money Bills**, dealing with taxation and public spending, do not have to be passed by the House of Lords.
- Using **Power of Delay**, the House of Lords can delay the passage of a Bill for about a year. However, if the Government reintroduces the Bill in the next session it can be passed without the Lords' approval.
- Under the **Salisbury Convention**, the Lords will not vote against the second or third reading of a Bill if it has been part of the Government's election manifesto promise.

Reform of the House of Lords

The Labour Government elected in 1997 has begun reform of the House of Lords. The first stage has been the removal of the right of most Hereditary peers to sit and vote in the House. All other peers are appointed as Life peers. A commission under Lord Wakeham has produced a report on the future of the House of Lords. It has been very difficult to reach a consensus on the final form of the reformed House of Lords.

Elected	Appointed
Democratic	Not democratic
Could challenge power of Commons	Various sections of society represented
May result in legislative gridlock	Friends of government appointed

It is likely that if reform is agreed it will be some combination of elected and appointed members, with the precise combinations likely to give rise to fierce political debate.

For you to do

- Why is a bicameral system an important safeguard in many democratic societies?
- Make up a table contrasting the House of Commons and the House of Lords.
- Describe the membership of the House of Lords and explain how it is different from the composition in 1999.
- What are the limits on the powers of the House of Lords?
- Explain why it is difficult to reach consensus on the future composition of the House of Lords. You should mention the problems with a wholly elected and a wholly appointed chamber.

Internet research

Visit the website of the House of Lords.
Find out recent items of business in the Lords.
Links to this site and other websites relating to Higher Modern Studies can be found at: **LECKIE&LECKIE** *Learning Lab*

HINTS & TIPS

> **Throughout the year and especially in the months before your exam, read the newspapers, watch television news and use news sites on the internet to give yourself up-to-date examples that you can use in your answers. Has there been a recent campaign run by a pressure group? Has the Government been involved in any major policy initiatives? Has Parliament been discussing and voting on any new laws?**

ROLE OF POLITICAL PARTIES IN PARLIAMENT

Political parties play a crucial role in the political system and are very important to the work of Parliament. It is very difficult to be elected to the House of Commons without being a member and having the support of one of the major parties. (For more information on political parties, see Study Theme 1C, pages 58–83.)

The role of the whips

Each of the main political parties in the Commons appoints a Chief Whip and Assistant Whips. The role of the whips is to maintain party discipline in Parliament. Government whips aim to maintain the Government's majority and get its legislation through Parliament. The role of the Opposition whips is to mount an effective challenge to the Government.

Each week a printed document is issued to MPs by their whips giving guidance on the following week's business. Where an MP's presence and vote is essential a **three-line whip** is called, indicating that the MP must attend. With a **two-line whip**, MPs may be excused if they can arrange a *pair* on the other side who will not vote. A **one-line whip** indicates that the MP's attendance is requested.

The Government's Chief Whip is an important figure in the parliamentary party and has a place in the Cabinet. The whips can also be said to act as the eyes and ears of the Government, providing an important means of communication between ministers and backbenchers.

Whips can apply pressure in a variety of ways:

- **talking to MPs** to try and persuade them of the Government's view
- finding ways of **rewarding loyal MPs** and **withdrawing privileges from rebel MPs**
- temporary **withdrawal of the whip** whereby the MP is denied membership of the Parliamentary party. If the whip remains withdrawn, the MP cannot be chosen as an official candidate of the party, reducing their chance of being elected.

For you to do

- Find out the present party composition of the House of Commons.
- Why do independent candidates have little chance of election in the UK Parliament?
- To what extent is it true to say that Britain is a 'two party' system?
- Parliament has less control over the UK Government than it used to. Discuss.
- Describe ways in which the UK Parliament has undergone recent reform.

Internet research

Visit the websites of the main political parties. Identify the main policies of each of the main parties. Find out how many independent or small parties are represented in Parliament.
Links to these sites and other websites relating to Higher Modern Studies can be found at:

INFLUENCES ON THE DECISION-MAKING PROCESS IN THE UK

Although it is up to MPs to create legislation, there are a number of ways in which members of the public can attempt to influence MPs and Government. One of the most effective ways is through the actions of pressure groups, which can be defined as **organised groups who attempt to influence government in accordance with the views of their membership but who do not seek to govern the country**.

Pressure groups range from small, locally based groups set up to deal with particular issues such as the closure of a local hospital, to sophisticated, world-wide organisations with massive budgets and hundreds of thousands of members and supporters (such as Amnesty International).

Types of pressure groups

- **Cause groups** generally campaign to raise awareness of specific causes. There are two main types of cause group:
  - **sectional pressure** groups attempt to campaign on behalf of people who are unable to campaign for themselves, for example, Shelter, who campaign on behalf of homeless people
  - **attitude groups** attempt to influence public opinion, for example, Greenpeace is an environmental pressure group which attempts to put pressure on governments for the general good
- **Interest groups** operate largely in their own self-interest in order to advance the economic or professional circumstances of their members. Groups such as trade unions, professional associations and employers' organisations are examples of such groups. The British Medical Association represents the interests of doctors and attempts to influence the government to improve health provision.

Lobbyist:
a person who is paid to try to influence the Government on behalf of an organisation.

Pressure group influence

Pressure groups tend to be either *insider* or *outsider* groups. This reflects their relationship with government and will affect the influence they have.

Insider groups have direct access to policy makers such as civil servants or Government ministers. The groups may be helpful and be given an active role in the decision-making process. Insider groups may be consulted by governments at the early stages of the law-making process and be able to influence the eventual law.

This type of group may have influence due to its specialist knowledge or its members may be in an important position with regard to the implementation of the policy and be aware of any potential difficulties in its implementation. Members of the pressure group may also be able to affect the successful introduction of any new law or initiative because of the role they would play in its implementation – the government may wish to ensure that the pressure group supports the policy before it is introduced. A pressure group which opposes the introduction of a policy may be prepared to take action to hinder its successful introduction. As a consequence of their privileged position of access to government, such groups may have to accept certain restrictions upon their actions.

The views of some pressure groups may have a natural affinity with the views of particular political parties. In the past the Labour Party had strong links with the trade union movement and the Conservatives had strong links with the business community. Labour's recent moves to distance itself from some aspects of trade union policies and a wish to appeal to a wide cross-section of the electorate may have weakened the links between itself and the labour movement.

There has been concern over the actions of professional **lobbyists**. Their methods of operation tend to be secretive and out of view of the public. The role of loans, donations and the funding of political parties is also an area of concern since it may be possible for some well resourced pressure groups to appear to buy political influence and prestige. (For more information on funding of political parties, see Study Theme 1C, pages 54–79.)

Outsider groups have no direct access to government. The policy objectives of these groups diverge so much from the views of government that they are largely excluded from the formal process of policy making. A number of groups may wish to retain their independence from government and refuse to accept the compromises and restrictions on their actions which come from accepting insider status.

Outsider groups tend to rely upon high profile public campaigns and the mobilisation of public opinion to influence government decision making. Governments will listen to the concerns of these groups because they are worried about the potential effect on an election if large numbers of voters are seen to be opposed to their policies.

The Countryside Alliance (CA) claims to speak for rural interests. The CA was concerned about the Labour government's attempts to ban fox hunting and found itself moving from having a degree of 'insider' status under Conservative governments to being an 'outsider' under Labour. The tactics adopted by individuals associated with the CA included taking part in demonstrations in major cities and publicity stunts such as the 'invasion' of the House of Commons in September 2004.

Pressure group methods

Pressure groups will employ a wide range of methods to influence those in power.

Countryside Alliance take to the streets in a change of tactics as they become more of an outsider group under a Labour Government

- **Letter writing campaigns** and **petitions** will demonstrate how much support the group has. Delivering petitions to Parliament or Downing Street can provide good media exposure.

- **Large demonstrations** with banners and speeches will often attract the attention of the mass media. This also helps give a boost to the members of the campaign who can see they have large numbers of supporters. Some groups who are unable to mobilise such large numbers of people will often resort to **stunts**, which may involve dangerous or outrageous actions.

- **Lobbying MPs** by sending letters or visiting them at their surgeries or at Parliament. If MPs are aware of a campaign with widespread support, they are more likely to be sympathetic and may even lobby Government Ministers themselves.

- Some pressure groups will employ **professional lobbyists** who are paid to have a more direct route to those in power.

- **Financial contributions** to particular parties, although they have to be declared, may also have an influence on the views of political parties. Some have argued that political parties should be funded by the state in order to remove the possibility of such influence.

- Groups which wish to show how strongly they feel about their cause or feel that legal methods will gain them insufficient attention may resort to **direct action**. Such actions may involve civil disobedience and law breaking. Such tactics run the risk of alienating the public and governments often feel that they cannot be seen to be giving in to the demands of groups using undemocratic tactics.

FATHERS 4 JUSTICE
FIGHTING FOR TRUTH, JUSTICE
& EQUALITY IN FAMILY LAW
www.fathers-4-justice.org

Fathers 4 Justice campaigners dress in superhero outfits and climb onto Buckingham Palace to gain media attention for their cause

For you to do

- What are the main types of pressure groups?
- How do cause groups differ from interest groups?
- What are the main differences between insider and outsider groups?
- How might an insider group become an outsider group?
- Consider each of the methods used by pressure groups. Analyse each one identifying both its advantages and disadvantages as a method to influence government.

Pressure groups and democracy

In a democratic society it is generally accepted that pressure groups have a right to present alternative viewpoints and they often play an important role in allowing greater participation in the political process. Pressure groups give voters a way of influencing the Government and participating in the political process. This is seen to be particularly important at a time when participation in the formal political process is declining, membership of political parties is at an all-time low and turnout in elections is in decline. Disaffection with the political system seems to be widespread but membership of and participation in pressure group activities seems to be high, particularly amongst young people for whom the formal political system seems to hold few attractions.

Some critics argue that pressure groups are not necessarily good for democracy. Pressure groups differ from political parties in that voters have the opportunity to vote for political parties and, if they are in government, to vote them out of office. Pressure groups are self-appointing and not subject to public votes. Even within pressure groups, democratic procedures may not always be upheld. In some cases small unrepresentative minorities may decide policy with little attention being paid to the views of the majority of members. Pressure groups generally put forward minority views and a well organised and powerful group may be able to force minority views, opposed by the majority, upon a government. For pressure groups to be taken seriously by the general public and by government, it is important that they are seen to behave and present themselves in a responsible manner. If they do not, they run the risk of alienating potential supporters and reducing their influence. Some pressure groups have resorted to illegal methods in order to put forward their case and gain publicity for their cause.

HINTS & TIPS

In this topic you are expected to know about Decision Making in Central Government. Make sure any examples you give refer to the powers of Central Government and the UK Parliament and NOT the Scottish Parliament.

Pressure groups are generally thought to be different from political parties:

- they **attempt to influence whichever party is in power**
- they **do not seek to take power** themselves
- they **campaign on single issues** or a narrow range of issues
- they attempt to **enlist public opinion** to influence government
- some pressure groups use elections to **raise the profile** of their own campaigns.

However, pressure groups can evolve to develop parliamentary representation. In Scotland the environmental movement has benefited from the introduction of proportional representation and has been successful in gaining the election of several Green Party Members of the Scottish Parliament.

For you to do

- In what ways are pressure groups different from political parties?
- What advantages does the Scottish Parliament offer pressure groups?
- Pressure groups are an essential part of a democratic society. Discuss.
- Pressure groups are a threat to democracy. Discuss.

Internet research

Visit the websites of these pressure groups:
- Fathers 4 Justice
- Stop the War Coalition
- Make Poverty History
- Greenpeace
- The Countryside Alliance.

Choose at least two contrasting pressure groups, such as cause or interest; insider or outsider, and write a report on the groups you have chosen. Your report should mention the groups' aims, membership, methods, and campaigns. Give an evaluation of how successful the groups you have chosen to investigate have been.

Try to find an example of a case in which a pressure group might be said to have acted irresponsibly.

Links to these sites and other websites relating to Higher Modern Studies can be found at:

THE ROLE OF THE MEDIA

Print and electronic media play an important role in the democratic process.

- Television, newspapers, radio and increasingly the internet provide the information about political issues. Television and radio are obliged to be politically neutral and provide fair and balanced coverage of political issues particularly around elections in their coverage.

- The media not only provide facts but also opinions. Newspapers in particular are free to print opinions and be partial in the presentation of news. Most newspapers present their views in editorial sections and they also employ columnists who give opinions on political matters. Newspapers have become increasingly open about the editorial bias of their political coverage with the selection of stories and photographs giving favourable coverage to the party they explicitly support and giving a negative image of those they oppose.

- The media have taken on the role of investigating and exposing what they see as wrongdoing. In the final years of the Conservative Government under John Major, the popularity of the government was severely weakened by a series of stories in the media exposing political and personal misdeeds which came to be known as *sleaze*. Although generally enjoying favourable press coverage in the early days of its time in office, the Labour Government of Tony Blair has seen increasingly hostile press over allegations of personal wrongdoing, political incompetence, and policy disagreements. Even the *Mirror*, once a stalwart pro-Labour paper, strongly disagreed with the Government over its policy on Iraq. When governments have had large majorities in the House of Commons and as a consequence faced weak opposition in Parliament, the press have often taken on the role of opposition outside Parliament even though they are unelected and not accountable in the way that a Parliamentary opposition is.

- The wide range of newspapers in the UK and the range of opinions they put forward means that governments of whatever viewpoint will be challenged by the print media.

- Influential television and radio programmes such as *Newsnight*, *Question Time* and the *Today* programme give opportunities for journalists to question Ministers and party leaders. Twenty-four hour news programmes and satellite channels mean that stories that ministers would prefer to go away are kept in front of the public's attention.

- Although still relatively new as an influence, the internet is likely to play a bigger role in the future with political blogs often reporting information before the traditional media.

For you to do

- In what ways do the media play a part in the democratic process?
- Compare the coverage of a current political story by two or more different newspapers. What evidence can you find of bias in their articles? Consider images as well as text.

Internet research

Visit the websites of a range of newspapers. What evidence of political bias can you find?
Links to these sites and other websites relating to Higher Modern Studies can be found at:

LECKIE&LECKIE
Learning Lab

HINTS & TIPS

> **Remember that politicians come and go. They may lose elections, Cabinet and other Government posts may be reshuffled, and Opposition leaders may change. Keep up-to-date with senior politicians and the positions they hold.**

IMPACT OF FREEDOM OF INFORMATION LEGISLATION

In January 2005 the Freedom of Information Act (2000) came into force. This legislation gave people in the UK new rights to obtain information held by the Government and other public bodies.

The Act applies to all public authorities in England, Wales and Northern Ireland. (Scotland has its own similar legislation.) The public is entitled to see information from:

- central, regional and local government
- NHS organisations (including GPs, dentists, hospitals and primary care trusts)
- educational institutions (schools, colleges, universities)
- the police and armed forces
- non-departmental public bodies (such as the Charity Commission or the Food Standards Agency)
- publicly owned companies (companies wholly owned by a public authority).

Public bodies covered by this legislation should be proactive in making information freely available and not only provide information when requested. While this greater openness gives greater access to information there are exemptions:

- information about **national security** and related to the security services is absolutely exempt from disclosure
- all other exemptions depend upon whether or not release of the information would be **detrimental to the public interest**. Exemptions may include information that can be shown to prejudice defence, international relations, law enforcement, justice, or commercial interests, if it were made publicly available.

Requests for information may be denied if the cost of providing the information is more than £450 (£600 for central government information).

Although this legislation has only been in force for a short time it does provide a statutory right to obtain information that previously would have remained unavailable. There is a presumption that information will be disclosed both if requested and as a matter of course. In the first month alone after the Act came into force, over 4,000 requests for information were made. Most of the requests came from journalists but political parties also made a number of requests. Delays have occurred in releasing the information, although the Government has targets of replying within 20 days.

For you to do

- In what ways does the Freedom of Information legislation contribute to a democratic society?
- Pressure groups are successful in influencing the democratic decision-making process. Discuss.

Internet research

Visit the Freedom of Information website. Describe the rights of citizens to obtain government information. Links to this site and other websites relating to Higher Modern Studies can be found at:

STUDY THEME SUMMARY

The Executive is the 'doing' part of the political system, responsible for running the country. Traditionally, Britain has been said to have a Cabinet style of Government, but over time, power has shifted. In recent years, the Prime Minister has emerged as the most powerful force in Government. In spite of this dominant position, there are limits on the powers of the Prime Minister.

Parliament's main roles are the passing of laws and the scrutiny of Government. The elected House of Commons is the most powerful part of Parliament. The unelected House of Lords has been reformed to make it more accountable, and will be subject to further reform. The powers of ordinary MPs have been limited when Governments have large majorities, although there have been some notable rebellions in recent years, forcing the Government to amend or change policy.

Both the media and pressure groups can exert pressure on Parliament and Government. As the electorate has become disenchanted with formal political processes, these outside influences have taken a bigger role. The media play an important role in keeping a check on Government and exposing wrongdoing. People who are reluctant to take part in formal political activities may choose to join informal pressure group activities. Most pressure groups use the rights they have in a democratic society to influence politics, but some go beyond their legal rights to pursue their aims.

Exam-style essay questions

To what extent has the changing role of the Cabinet changed in the UK Government?

'The House of Lords should be wholly elected.' Discuss.

To what extent do pressure groups play an important part a democratic society?

STUDY THEME 1C:
Political parties and their policies

In this study theme you will be expected to have a detailed knowledge and understanding of:

- ## POLITICAL PARTIES

  Ideology, membership, organisation and finance; influences on the decisions within parties and on the formulating of party policies; the role of party leaders, MPs, party members, the media and voters.

- ## CONFLICT AND CONSENSUS WITHIN AND BETWEEN PARTIES

  Ideological differences within and between parties; reasons for changes in party ideologies and/or policies.

- ## PARTY POLICIES ON TAXATION, LAW AND ORDER, EDUCATION AND EUROPE

  Trends and differences.

POLITICAL PARTIES IN THE UNITED KINGDOM

Political parties in the UK cover a wide range of political ideologies and range in size from a few hundred members up to a few hundred thousand members for the major parties. The parties to be studied in this theme are the four main parties which have positions of power and influence in the UK and Scottish Parliaments:

- Conservative
- Labour
- Liberal Democrat
- Scottish National Party

These are not the only active parties, or even the only ones with MPs and MSPs, but in terms of the numbers of votes cast in elections, they are the parties with the highest levels of support in Scotland.

HINTS & TIPS

In elections to the Scottish Parliament, the proportional Additional Member System is used for elections. This means that no single party is likely to have enough support to form a government so since 1999, coalitions have been formed.

For you to do

- To help you compare and contrast the four political parties, construct two tables and fill them in as you go through this section, but give yourself plenty of space for adding notes. Your tables should be similar to those below:

	LABOUR	CONSERVATIVE	LIBERAL DEMOCRAT	SNP
Ideology				
Organisation and structure				
Policy making				
Membership				

POLICY	LABOUR	CONSERVATIVE	LIBERAL DEMOCRAT	SNP
Taxation				
Education				
Law and order				
Europe				

- Construct a timeline that you can add to, to show the dates of key events in the history of the four main parties over the last 50 or so years.

THE PARTY SYSTEM IN BRITISH POLITICS

The system of political parties is an essential part of the way Parliament (and hence Government) works in Britain. Using the *First past the post* system (see pages 81–83) the Government is formed from the party which wins most Members of Parliament (MPs) in a General Election. The party with the second biggest number of MPs forms the official Opposition.

Since the end of the Second World War, all British governments have been formed by either the Conservative or Labour parties. In the last three General Elections, there have been some signs that the Liberal Democrats have been gaining ground on the two major parties, but they have not yet been able to convert their share of popularity into a representative number of parliamentary seats. At the time of writing, the Labour Party is the party of government, having won successive UK General Elections in 1997, 2001 and 2005.

The Prime Minister selects senior members of the Government (almost always from his or her own party) to form the Cabinet. Parties always fight General Elections with a **manifesto** of policies, and it is expected that the Cabinet will implement these policies by passing the necessary laws.

Political parties all have the same basic role to play, aiming to:

- generate government policy
- provide choice between alternative policy programmes to persuade voters of the strengths of their particular proposals
- encourage and provide opportunities for political participation
- uphold the national interest.

Internet research

Visit the website of the Electoral Commission and make notes on the numbers of seats won by the parties compared with the numbers of votes. Make comparisons between UK General Elections and Scottish parliamentary elections.

Links to this site and other websites relating to Higher Modern Studies can be found at: **www.leckieandleckie.co.uk** by clicking on the Learning Lab button and navigating to the Higher Modern Studies Course Notes page.

For you to do

- Why do we need political parties?
- What are the aims of political parties?
- What is the relationship between political parties and government?

Party finance and funding

Political parties need large amounts of money to pay for the party organisations and particularly for campaigning activities at elections. Parties receive some funding from individual members, but this is not sufficient to fight successful elections, and the parties rely on large donations from businesses, wealthy individuals and companies. The Labour Party receives considerable support from affiliated trade unions.

Some money is provided to opposition parties to provide funding for their parliamentary activities. This is known as **Short money** (named after Ted Short, Leader of the House of Commons who first proposed the payments in 1974).

In 2000, the Government passed the Political Parties, Elections and Referendums Act 2000 (PPERA). Registered parties have to submit an annual statement of accounts and they have to list all donations over £5,000. There has been concern that the system of donations has allowed rich people or businesses to 'buy' influence over policy. For example, the Formula 1 boss Bernie Ecclestone donated £1million to the Labour Party and some time later, Formula 1 racing appeared to be given favourable treatment over the issue of tobacco sponsorship in sport.

A recent development has been the use of loans to political parties. Until 2006, loans did not have to be declared in the accounts, and both Labour and the Conservatives raised millions of pounds before the 2005 election in loans. These loans have been controversial, with a number of the people making the loans being given peerages. This has raised the question of state funding for political parties.

The case for change

Political parties play a vital role in our representative democracy. They offer alternative policies from which voters choose at elections, organise campaigns to mobilise voters and, perhaps most importantly, they field candidates for public office. In order to carry out these vital functions political parties need adequate funding; without it we risk the health of our democratic system. We have a vital opportunity to stabilise political party membership, to remove the concern that parties are beholden to a few rich backers and special interests, and to create a framework under which parties seek more opportunities to engage with the electorate. And who knows, we may manage to kick-start a renaissance in political party activity. But even if our success is more modest than this, what we do know with absolute certainty is that without reform we can expect only more of the sorry decline we have observed over the last few decades.

What's wrong with the current system of funding political parties?

Under the current system political parties are caught in a vicious circle whereby the perception of sleaze and corruption undermines public trust in politics, politicians and political institutions, thereby depriving them of members and forcing them to rely more heavily on large donations from individuals.

- It creates a dependency between political parties and high value donors
- It creates the perception of sleaze in politics
- Politics becomes increasingly centralised

What do we want from our political system?

It is important that we start defending political parties as public institutions and recognise their importance to our civic as well as political culture. We need to accept that political communication between parties and the public is absolutely essential, and that many traditional methods of organising this are under-resourced and expect too much from too few people. But we should not make the mistake of thinking that political communication and campaigning can be done with anything like the same effect if they are conducted only by central party headquarters and rely upon expensive advertising rather than personal contact. The price of political campaigning – both during and between elections – is the price of democracy. We need to find ways of encouraging and nurturing political activity at local or constituency level. Any new form of public subsidy for political parties should have the aim of encouraging wider political participation, and increasing local political activity.

Source: adapted from an article at http://haydenphillipsreview.org.uk

Internet research

Visit the Electoral Commission website and make a list of the people and companies who have made donations to the major parties.

Go to the Party Funding Review website and read the interim report by Sir Hayden Phillips. Summarise the key points and make notes on how these affect the main parties.

Go to the Guardian website and read the article about the Prime Minister being interviewed by police over the 'cash for peerages' scandal. Comment on the difficulty of ensuring that nominations for peerages or other favours aren't 'bought' by donations and loans.

Links to these sites and other websites relating to Higher Modern Studies can be found at:

For you to do

- Why do people give money to support political parties?
- Using the lists you found in the internet research activity, find any individuals or companies who gave money to more than one party. Why do you think they would do this?
- Describe the main sources of party funding.

Party ideologies

Each political party has an ideology which sets out core beliefs and principles. Party ideologies often have philosophical foundations, but the necessity of winning votes in elections often means that these philosophical foundations are adapted (or even dropped completely) in favour of more popular policies.

Internet research

Visit the politicalcompass website and read about the shifting definitions of left- and right-wing, and how they might be applied to UK political scene. Draw your own 'compass' and progressively label it to show where each party stands on issues such as education, taxation and law and order.

CONSERVATIVE PARTY

The Conservative Party is a centre-right party. It was the dominant party in the second half of the 20th century, holding power for a total of 35 years, most recently from 1979 to 1997 under the leadership of Margaret Thatcher and John Major. Since the landslide election defeat in 1997 and subsequent defeats in 2001 and 2005, it has undergone a number of changes of leadership and undertaken policy reviews to make it more popular with voters. The current leader is David Cameron, MP for Witney, in Oxfordshire.

 Conservatives

Ideology

Over the years, it has been considered to be a pragmatic party and, as a result, its ideology has changed as the political environment has changed. However, there is a core set of beliefs which underpin Conservative party policies:

- the state should not interfere with the rights of the individual
- a free market economy is more effective in delivering economic growth than a state-controlled economy
- Government spending should be kept to a minimum and taxes kept as low as possible
- everyone should have equal opportunities and equal rewards for equal effort.

Membership

The Conservative Party is an affiliation of Conservative associations around the country, and most members of the party join their local association. Like the other major parties, it has had a declining membership since the days of mass party membership in the 1950s.

About 200,000 members voted in the leadership election in 2005. It was reported in January 2006 that the party had gained 16,000 new members since the election of David Cameron as party leader, to give a total party membership of 290,000.

Despite recent efforts by the party to broaden membership, the Conservative Party is still largely a party of the south of England. According to a poll of party members in 2004, a typical member is: 'a 57-year-old woman who lives in a mortgage-free house in the south of England. Only 12% of its members are under the age of 35. More than two-thirds are over 55 and nearly half are retired. These members' children have long ago grown up and left home.'

Internet research

Visit the Guardian website and summarise the main points of the article about the 'typical' member of the Tory party.

Links to this site and other websites relating to Higher Modern Studies can be found at:

For you to do

- Using the internet research, make notes about how important the ideas of the 'typical' member of the Conservative Party are to where you live. Write down some reasons why people where you live might choose to join the Conservative Party.

Funding

The Conservative Party is funded by contributions from constituency organisations, and donations from businesses and wealthy individuals. Like the other parties, its income from constituencies and members has been dropping, and it is increasingly reliant on large donations and loans from a small number of people. In the first few months of 2006, Bob Edmiston, who runs a car-importing company, gave the party £2.1 million.

In 2005, the Conservatives' main sources of funding were:

- donations   £13.5 million
- membership   £0.8 million
- commercial activities £2.4 million
- Short money   £4 million

For you to do

- Why is the Conservative Party having difficulty raising funds?
- Where do the funds come from? Give examples.

Party organisation

There are various strands of organisation within the Conservative Party:

- National party organisation dealing with the membership – much of this party membership organisation is devolved to regional and constituency associations.
- Within the parliamentary party, there are formal structures for the MPs.
- Crossing the boundary between the mass membership and the MPs are a range of policy organisations, or forums, which meet to discuss and develop party policy.

National party organisation

Party members in parliamentary constituencies may have their own constituency association, or they often form larger associations with neighbouring constituencies. The local associations give ordinary members the opportunity to participate in national activities such as the annual conference. Local members campaign locally (for local council elections, for example) and on national issues at General Elections. Constituency members are often involved in fund-raising for the party. Local members have an important role to play in selecting candidates for local and parliamentary elections and in electing the leader of the party.

The headquarters of the Conservative party is the **Conservative Campaign Headquarters** (CCHQ). This looks after all the national administration, and should also act as a link between the national membership and senior party figures.

The **Conservative Party Board** is based in CCHQ and is responsible for the way the party is run, including fund-raising, membership and candidates. It is made up of representatives from different sections of the party representing the local members, MPs and party staff.

The **National Convention** is a national membership body, comprising representatives of the association chairmen and other regional groups. Its most important role is to validate changes to the party rules, such as when the rules for the leadership elections were changed. It is a forum for the views of ordinary party members and acts as a link between the party leader and the members.

The annual **Party Conference** is the major meeting place for MPs and party members. It is an opportunity for senior figures in the party to give speeches, often criticising the Labour Party.

Parliamentary party organisation

The **1922 Committee** is the organisation of backbench Conservative MPs. It is independent of the leader, elects its own officers and holds weekly meetings. Its primary function is to keep the leadership of the party informed of the mood of Conservative backbenchers. It used to be a very important body when the leader of the party was just elected by the MPs, but it has less influence now that the leader is elected by the whole party membership.

There are a number of informal groups of MPs representing different strands of Conservative thinking, such as:

- Tory Reform Group
- Selsdon Group
- Conservative Way Forward
- Bow Group
- Bruges Group.

Policy organisations

The Conservative Party has a number of policy organisations:

- Conservative Party Forum
- Challenge Groups
- Taskforces.

The **Conservative Policy Forum** is one of the oldest policy groups in the Conservative Party. It holds regular meetings and is one of the ways in which members' views are bought to the attention of the leadership.

Following his election as leader in 2005, David Cameron set up a number of **Challenge Groups** and **Taskforces** to develop policy across a wide range of issues. Each group has about 10–12 members (not all are members of the party) chosen for their specialist knowledge. Anyone can contribute to the Challenge Groups through the Conservative party website and through meetings.

Internet research

Visit the Conservative Party website and read about the Challenge Groups and the Taskforces. Make notes about the ways they try to involve the party members in developing policy.

Links to this site and other websites relating to Higher Modern Studies can be found at:

For you to do

- Make notes about the different ways that ordinary members of the Conservative Party can get involved with the running of the party.
- Are the Challenge Groups and Taskforces good ways for a political party to develop new policies? List the advantages and disadvantages of developing policy this way.
- As well as the Challenge Groups and Taskforces, there are other policy groups, and senior MPs also have their own ideas about policy. What difficulties might there be if there are lots of people involved in developing policy?

Electoral success

The Conservatives were the most successful party in the second half of the 20th century. Margaret Thatcher, the Prime Minister from 1979 to 1990, was enormously influential. Her success came at the expense of the Labour Party, and her policies changed the political environment for everyone.

However, even when the Conservatives had a big majority in the Westminster Parliament in the 1980s, they were poorly represented in Scotland, never gaining more than 10 MPs. This low level of representation led to considerable resentment in Scotland against the party.

In the 1990s, support for the party declined. John Major struggled to control different factions of the party which wanted different policies, particularly on Europe. The party was also badly affected by a number of allegations of 'sleaze', which saw a series of scandalous newspaper headlines about Conservative MPs. In the 1997 General Election, the Conservatives suffered a massive defeat. They suffered another heavy defeat at the 2001 General Election. Under the leadership of Michael Howard, the Conservatives lost the 2005 election, but significantly reduced the Labour majority.

In Scotland, the Conservatives have had little electoral success. In 2005/06 they had just one MP in Westminster. Along with the Scottish Nationalists, they are a major opposition party in the Scottish Parliament.

Electing the leader

New rules for the election of the party leader were introduced in 2001. Under these rules, all party members are involved in the election of a new leader (previously, only MPs could vote). A leadership contest takes place either:

- when the current leader resigns, or
- MPs pass a vote of no confidence in the leader.

Leadership candidates put themselves forward to a ballot. If there are only two candidates, there is an immediate election from the whole party membership. If there are more than two candidates, the first ballot will be restricted to MPs to reduce the number of candidates to two. If necessary, there will be successive ballots until there are only two candidates left, with the candidate with the lowest number of votes eliminated at each stage.

David Cameron was elected leader of the Conservative Party in 2005

Once there are only two candidates left, the party membership election takes place, and the winner is simply the candidate who wins the most votes. It has been argued that party members are not very representative of the whole country, so their choice of leader might not be the person most likely to win a General Election.

Michael Howard was elected unopposed in 2003, but resigned after defeat in the 2005 General Election. A new leadership contest was declared. From the initial list of four candidates, David Davis and David Cameron were elected to the party membership ballot, and David Cameron won with 134,446 votes to David Davis's 64,398 votes. This was despite David Cameron having won the support of fewer MPs than David Davis in the first ballot

Party unity and factions

The Conservative Party used to be famous for its internal discipline, with very little public dissent from the official party line. Some divisions have always existed between the right wing of the party and the centre, but these have put to one side at elections. Considerable divisions have existed over the relationship with Europe and these helped cause John Major's defeat in the 1997 election.

The major divisions that David Cameron has to deal with now are between the traditional membership who believe in cutting taxes and reducing public spending, and those who think it is important to make sure the economy is sufficiently stable to support the NHS and education and welfare systems without requiring cuts in spending. Traditional supporters of the party (often former supporters of Margaret Thatcher) are very distrustful of Cameron's emphasis on liberal issues such as the environment.

Internet research

Read the history of the Conservative Party on the party website. Make brief notes on the major events in the party's background over the last 50 years. Add key events to your timeline.
Read David Cameron's article about his first year as party leader on the Guardian website. Make notes about the changes he claims to have made to the party. Links to these sites and other websites relating to Higher Modern Studies can be found at:

CONSERVATIVE PARTY POLICIES

Taxation

Conservatives are traditionally regarded as the party of low taxation. When in Government, they have almost always tried to reduce levels of income tax, so that everyone with a job has less of their income taken in tax. Conservative Governments also try to cut government spending (money spent on the NHS, education, welfare benefits, etc.).

One of the Conservatives' main reasons for having lower taxes is the argument that low taxes promote hard work and enterprise, which contribute to overall economic growth.

In October 2006, the Conservative tax commission came up with these plans:

- total tax cuts worth £21 billion
- cut income tax by 2p
- abolish inheritance tax
- reduce corporation tax from 30% to 25%
- simplify taxes for small businesses.

Internet research

Visit the politics.co.uk website and read about the Conservatives' tax plans.
Visit the Conservative Party website and read what their 2005 election manifesto said about tax. Note any changes in policy between then and now.
Links to these sites and other websites relating to Higher Modern Studies can be found at:

For you to do

- Summarise the main points of the Conservatives' tax plans.
- For each point, give a reason why the Conservatives want to introduce it.
- Why are some people critical of the proposals to cut taxes?

Law and order

Law and order is a devolved matter, so policies in England and Wales are different to those in Scotland. However, the overall approach is the same. Conservative policies include:

- 5,000 extra police a year
- less paperwork and 'political correctness'
- more rehabilitation places for drug addicts
- tougher sentences for career criminals
- prisoners to serve their sentences in full
- more prison places.

Internet research

Visit the Scottish Conservatives' website and read what their manifesto said about law and order.
Links to this site and other websites relating to Higher Modern Studies can be found at: LECKIE&LECKIE *Learning Lab*

For you to do

- Compare and contrast the approaches to law and order in Scotland and England. What are the similarities and what are the differences? Why do you think there might be differences?

Education

Education is another devolved matter and the Scottish education system is different from the English system. Policies in England and Wales include:

- schools to be allowed to set their own priorities and budgets
- headteachers and governors to be given more control over admissions, discipline and expulsions
- grants for pupils who want to study vocational courses
- free after-school clubs available for all pupils
- abolish examinations targets
- abolish university tuition fees.

The Scottish Conservatives have similar policies, described on their website:

- empower headteachers to exclude violent or disruptive pupils
- encourage a greater choice of specialist schools
- give schools greater freedom to set their own priorities
- abolish the graduate tax
- guarantee access to higher education solely on merit.

Europe

The Conservatives' approach to the European Union has been one of the major causes of conflict within the party. Some parts of the party are very keen on membership of the European Union, with all the economic benefits it can bring. However, other parts of the party are very distrustful of the EU and would prefer to withdraw from close involvement with Europe.

The current Conservative policies on Europe were described in the 2005 manifesto:

- Opposition to the EU Constitution; any decisions regarding the EU Constitution would be decided by referendum.
- Britain will not join the Euro.
- Britain will argue for less European regulation.
- The Common Agricultural Policy (CAP) must be reformed.
- Enlargement of the EU should continue with more countries, including Turkey.

For you to do

- Using the information above and what you have found during your internet research, add key points about the Conservatives and their policies to your table.
- Write a few paragraphs describing Conservative policies on the issues mentioned.

LABOUR PARTY

The Labour Party is the main centre-left party in the UK. It formed its first Government in 1929. Since the Second World War, it has had four spells in government.

The Labour Party's greatest achievement was the establishment of the welfare state after the Second World War, which saw the introduction of a comprehensive set of social welfare and health care policies. More recently, the party has moved away from its **socialist** roots and is probably best described now as a centre-left party, with liberal social policies and pro-market economic policies.

Ideology

Labour party ideology has shifted considerably since it was founded over 100 years ago. It was originally a socialist movement, with a strong belief in the role of the state as provider of health care, education, housing and employment, and in public ownership (or nationalisation) of major industries. The party was always seen as the party which represented the working classes. These principles were maintained for most of the 20th century until the 1980s and 1990s.

> **WORD BANK**
>
> **Socialism:** a theory of social organisation based on collective or centralised government ownership, control and distribution of wealth, production of goods and property.

In the 1990s, the leadership of the Labour Party developed the idea of 'New Labour'. New Labour was a description of the way the Labour Party had been forced to change and to adapt to the new politics of the 1990s. The Labour Party is now described as a European-style democratic socialist party.

Some elements of the original ideology are still in place, with a belief in the role of the state as the provider of essential services such as health care and education. However, there is now an acceptance that private-sector, market-based solutions also have a place in the provision of these services. This mixture of the public and private sectors continues to cause conflict within the party. Other elements of current Labour Party ideology include:

- decentralisation of power and open government
- emphasis on personal responsibility – 'tough on crime, tough on the causes of crime'
- recognition and understanding that different people need different solutions to their problems, especially in education.

Membership

Traditionally, Labour Party members were working class men, living in the industrial areas of the country such as the north-east of England and the central belt of Scotland. The modernisation of the party under Tony Blair saw an expansion of the membership into more middle-class areas. The number of members grew to about 400,000 in 1997, but since then have dropped considerably to fewer than 200,000.

A number of trade unions are affiliated to the Labour Party. This means that members of those trade unions give some financial support to the party through their union subscriptions, and they have voting rights in elections within the Labour Party.

For you to do

- What is New Labour? Describe the ideology of New Labour.
- To what extent has New Labour moved away from Labour's traditional roots?
- Why do you think so many people have left the Labour Party since 1997?

Internet research

Visit the Labour Party website and make notes on the different issues you could get involved in. What do these suggest about how the Labour Party views the public's priorities?

Links to this site and other websites relating to Higher Modern Studies can be found at:

Funding

The main sources of funding for the Labour Party are donations and affiliation fees from trade unions. In the period 2001 to 2005, Labour received nearly £66 million, of which over £42 million (64%) came from donations and affiliation fees from trade unions. This funding is declining, as trade union membership has gone down and as a number of trade unions have withdrawn from their links with the Labour Party. In 2001, one of the biggest trade unions, the GMB, announced it was reducing its contribution to the Labour Party by £1 million over four years in protest against proposed reforms of public services.

An increasingly large number of donations come from a small number of wealthy business people. This has attracted considerable criticism, with the accusation that Labour is getting too close to rich businesspeople and is abandoning its working class roots. The Labour Party has also received large loans from wealthy business people.

In 2005, Labour's main sources of funding were:

- donations (including trade union contributions) £13.9 million
- membership £3.7 million
- affiliations £8 million
- commercial activities £3.4 million

Party organisation

The organisation of the Labour Party is similar to that of the Conservative Party, with:

- national party organisation, dealing with regional and constituency branches and links with the parliamentary party
- parliamentary organisation
- policy organisations and forums.

National party organisation

Local parties are based on branches in council wards, making up constituency branches. Members of local parties have a role in selecting candidates for local councils and parliamentary elections. Members elect representatives from the Constituency Labour Party (CLP) to attend the annual conference.

Party conference is the most important national forum. Held annually, the conference used to be the main decision-making body for the party. Resolutions presented at the conference were voted on to become party policy. However, this led to too many resolutions being supported which were unpopular with the whole electorate, so party policy is no longer decided by conference resolutions. Conference is now much more carefully 'managed' so it is less critical of the party leadership.

The **National Executive Committee** (NEC) is the governing body of the party, with representatives of the Government, MPs, MEPs, local councillors, trade unions and constituency parties. It is responsible for the policy-making processes and determines the overall direction of the party. The NEC has a number of sub-committees responsible for internal affairs such as party organisation, and auditing and budgeting party finances.

Parliamentary party organisation

The Parliamentary Labour Party (PLP) is the organisation of backbench Labour MPs. The PLP is responsible for determining tactics within the House of Commons and acts as a link between the MPs and the leadership. PLP meetings can be very important in ensuring that MPs vote to the support the leadership on controversial issues. The Prime Minister attends PLP meetings to answer MPs' questions.

Informal groups within the PLP include the Tribune Group, named from the *Tribune* magazine, and the left-wing Campaign Group.

Policy organisations

The **National Policy Forum** (NPF) is the main body responsible for making policy. It has 184 members, with representatives of constituencies, trade unions, MPs and MEPs, councillors and socialist societies. All the members of the NEC are members of the NPF. The NPF meets two or three times each year.

Work to develop policies is carried out by policy commissions, which meet between full meetings of the NPF. These commissions deal with specific areas of policy, such as Crime, Justice, Citizenship and Equalities, Education and Skills. The commissions have between 16 and 22 members.

Internet research

Visit the Labour Party website and make notes about the different ways members can participate in party activities.
Links to this site and other websites relating to Higher Modern Studies can be found at:

For you to do

● Who provides most of the Labour Party's funding? How does this compare with the Conservative Party?
● Summarise the different organisations within the Labour Party and how they relate to each other.
● Consider the organisation/structure of the Labour Party. Where does the power lie in the Labour Party?
● How easy is it for an ordinary member of the Labour Party to get involved with the making of party policy? How does this compare with the Conservative Party?
● Why might the party leadership not want to follow policy developed by ordinary members?

Electoral success

Labour has had less electoral success than the Conservative party, with four periods in power since the Second World War totalling 26 years to the end of 2006. When Labour won the 2005 General Election, Tony Blair became the first Labour leader to win three successive elections.

When Tony Blair became leader of the party in 1994, the New Labour modernisation programme made considerable changes to the nature of the party. This was a cause of some concern to traditionalists, but the 1997 General Election

Led by Tony Blair, the Labour Party convincingly won the 1997 UK General Election

saw a landslide win for Blair. This was followed by another win of similar proportions in 2001.

In the period 2001 to 2005, some support was lost over a number of issues such as the war in Iraq, the state of the NHS and concerns over pensions. Labour won the 2005 election, but with its majority much reduced.

In Scotland, Labour has been the dominant party for many years. At the 2005 General Election, Labour won 41 of the 59 seats, with the Liberal Democrats second with 11 seats. Most of the Labour seats are in the central belt, particularly in and around Glasgow. In the 2003 elections for the Scottish Executive, Labour won 50 of the 129 seats, and it leads the coalition with the Scottish Liberal Democrats.

HINTS & TIPS

Tony Blair announced that he would stand down as Prime Minister during 2007. Find out about the process of choosing his successor as an example of how Labour changes its leader.

WORD BANK

Electoral college: the name given to the body of voters who are entitled to vote in an election for a particular office.

Electing the leader

The leader of the Labour Party is elected by an **electoral college** of MPs, trade unions and constituency parties. The trade unions and constituencies have to hold ballots for all their members (known as OMOV – One Member One Vote). Each section of the electoral college carries the same weight of votes. Tony Blair was elected leader under this system in 1994.

PERCENTAGES OF VOTES IN THE 1994 LEADERSHIP ELECTION				
Candidate	*Trade unions*	*Constituencies*	*MPs*	*Total*
Tony Blair	52.3%	58.2%	60.5%	57.0%
John Prescott	28.4%	24.4%	19.6%	24.1%
Margaret Beckett	19.3%	17.4%	19.9%	18.9%

Party unity and factions

Unlike the Conservative Party, the Labour Party has been well known for its internal factions and squabbles! For much of the long period in opposition in the 1980s and 1990s, Labour was split and damaged by the differences between the left and right wings of the party. The long period in opposition served to show Labour MPs that indiscipline and in-fighting did not help win elections. Despite the unease that some MPs had about the New Labour modernisation programme, there was relatively little open dissent in the period running up the successful 1997 election.

Paradoxically, the huge majorities after the 1997 and 2001 elections made it easier for MPs to show dissent without actually damaging the Government. An increasing number of issues attracted opposition from 'rebel' Labour MPs, such as:

● university tuition fees
● the role of the private sector in public services
● the war in Iraq (and support for President Bush in general)
● the proposed introduction of ID cards and restrictions on civil liberties
● the 'cash for peerages' scandal.

Despite these difficulties, there are not the same kind of ideologically driven factions within the PLP as there have been in the past.

Internet research

Visit the BBC website and read the article about division and disunity within the Labour Party.

Links to this site and other websites relating to Higher Modern Studies can be found at: LECKIE&LECKIE *Learning Lab*

For you to do

- Compare the ways in which the Labour Party and the Conservative Party choose their leaders.
- What evidence has there been of disagreement within the Labour Party in recent years?
- Add key events in the history of the Labour Party to your timeline.

LABOUR PARTY POLICIES

Taxation

Labour has traditionally spent a higher proportion of gross domestic product (GDP) on public services than the Conservatives, and in order to spend more, it needs to take more tax than the Conservatives. In the 2005 Labour manifesto, the tax policy is described as:

> *Labour believes tax policy should continue to be governed by the health of the public finances, the requirement for public investment and the needs of families, business and the environment.*

Since 1997, Labour has reduced corporation tax to its lowest ever level, reformed other areas of business taxes, and changed the capital gains tax system. They have said they will not increase levels of income tax, and they have introduced tax credits to help families with children.

Labour has been accused by opponents of using **stealth taxes** to raise money in ways that the public might not notice, such as increases in taxes on company cars, increased duties on tobacco, and withdrawing allowances such as mortgage interest tax relief.

Law and order

Traditionally, the Conservatives have been 'hard' on law and order, and Labour have been 'soft'. This has changed over recent years, with Labour taking a hard line on law and order.

Labour has been particularly hard on so-called 'anti-social behaviour'. This is low-level crime and civil disorder, often carried out by teenagers and young adults. One Government response has been the introduction of Anti-Social Behaviour Orders (ASBOs) which place restrictions on individuals such as stopping them from going to certain places (like streets in their neighbourhoods).

The Government has introduced more severe sentences for a number of serious crimes and has built new prisons. Despite this, there are complaints that too many prisoners are being released early and are reoffending on their release.

The Labour Government has had to deal with the issue of Islamic terrorism since the attacks on the World Trade Centre in September 2001. It has introduced a number of measures which are designed to make it easier for the police and security services to detain suspected terrorists. Some of these measures have been criticised as being attacks on civil liberties.

For you to do

- Describe, in detail, the ways in which Labour is dealing with anti-social behaviour and police on the streets.
- Summarise the main points of the Labour manifesto on law and order.

Internet research

Visit the website of the Scottish Labour Party to find out what their manifesto said about law and order. Summarise the main points and compare these with the UK Labour Party.
Links to this site and other websites relating to Higher Modern Studies can be found at:

Education

Labour has spent a lot of money on education since 1997, with more teachers in schools. Tony Blair's conference speech of 1996 is famous for its use of the slogan 'Education, education, education'.

In England and Wales, Labour policy is that all secondary schools should be independent schools concentrating on particular specialist areas, such as music, business, IT and sport. These schools teach the whole range of the National Curriculum but employ specialist staff and develop as centres of excellence in their chosen specialisation. There are currently 2,000 specialist schools in England.

Other policies include:

- greater provision of vocational education
- aim for 50% of young people to go to university
- use of private finance to build and run schools

- parenting orders and fines for parents who allow their children to truant.

In Scotland, policies include:

- reduced class sizes
- an Excellence Standard for top performing schools
- Skills for Work courses
- Educational Maintenance Allowances, providing lower income school students with financial support
- access payments for university students from lower income families.

Europe

Labour is an enthusiastic supporter of the European Union and of expansion of the EU, believing that a strong Europe is good for Britain. So far it has been less enthusiastic about joining the Euro, and Gordon Brown, the Chancellor, has set out five economic tests which must be met before Britain enters the Euro.

Policies given in the 2005 manifesto include:

- support for the idea of a European constitution
- reform of the Common Agricultural Policy
- strengthening EU military cooperation.

Internet research

- Visit the Labour Party website and make notes about their policies on law and order, education, taxation and Europe as presented in their 2005 manifestos. Note any changes between then and now. Add key points about the Labour Party and its policies to your tables.

For you to do

- Write a few paragraphs describing Labour policies on the issues mentioned.
- How true is it to say that the Labour and Conservative parties have moved closer together in their policies?

LIBERAL DEMOCRATS

The Liberal Democrats are the third largest party in the UK parliament. They are a left-centre party, with their roots in the Liberal Party which was one of the main parties in the first 25 years of the 20th century. Since the establishment of the Labour Party as a party of government, the Liberals have not held power. The current Liberal Democrat Party came into being in 1988 with the merger of the Liberal Party and the Social Democratic Party.

At the 2003 Scottish elections, the Liberal Democrats won sufficient seats to enter into a coalition with Labour to form the Scottish Executive, with the party's leader in Scotland taking the position of Deputy First Minister.

Ideology

Whereas the Conservatives have traditional roots in the upper classes and the old notions of a ruling elite, and Labour have traditional roots in the working class movements, the Liberal Democrats do not have the same attachment to any particular class-based political ideology.

Liberal Democrat ideology gives a high priority to civil liberties, with a strong belief in the right of the individual to behave as they wish without interference from the state. Core beliefs include:

- a free, fair and open society, where everyone enjoys the same basic rights
- power should be devolved to the lowest possible level of local government where possible
- a fair voting system where every vote has the same value.

HINTS & TIPS

Although the Liberal Democrats have not held power at the national level since early in the last century, the system of PR used for elections to the Scottish Parliament allowed them to be part of the coalition executive after 1999 and 2003. Use the outcome of the 2007 election to the Scottish Parliament to consider the ways in which parties with different ideologies have to work together to form a coalition.

Internet research

Visit the Liberal Democrats' website and read the preamble to their constitution, which sets out their beliefs. From what you know about the Conservative and Labour Parties, is there very much in the Liberal Democrat beliefs that Conservative and Labour supporters would disagree with?
Make notes on the similarities and differences between the three main parties.
Links to this site and other websites relating to Higher Modern Studies can be found at:

Membership

At the end of 2004, there were just over 70,000 members of the Liberal Democrats, so it is a much smaller party than the Conservatives or Labour.

Funding

The Liberal Democrats do not have the same links to big business or the trade unions as the Conservatives and Labour, and their level of funding reflects this. In 2005, their income was about £8.5 million (about a third of the Conservatives' income and a quarter of Labour income). Almost £4.8 million came from donations, and only £768,000 from membership fees.

The biggest donations came from a company called 5th Avenue Partners Ltd, which gave over £2.4 million (and the legality of this donation was in doubt for some time). The next biggest donation came from the Joseph Rowntree Foundation, which gave £252,000.

The level of funding puts the Liberal Democrats at a serious disadvantage compared with the Conservatives and Labour during election campaigns when huge amounts of money are spent on publicity.

Party organisation

The Liberal Democrats have fewer members than the other main parties so it is not always sensible to try to have small local parties based on council wards. The party has much stronger levels of support in some parts of the country than others, and this is reflected in the way local parties are organised.

National party organisation

The Liberal Democrats have a federal party structure, with power devolved down through a series of national, regional and local parties. The local parties may cover more than one parliamentary constituency, depending on the numbers of members in the area. There are eight regional parties in Scotland.

The headquarters of the federal party is based in London. It looks after UK policy, parliamentary elections and fund raising. The national parties look after the local parties. They also have responsibility for selecting parliamentary candidates, and for specific policies for their country.

There are four main committees responsible for running the business of the party:

- **Federal Executive** – directing, coordinating and implementing the work of the party
- **Federal Policy Committee** – researching, developing and overseeing policy-making processes
- **Federal Conference Committee** – organising and managing the annual conference, which sets party policy
- **Federal Finance and Administration Committee** – planning and administering budgets and finances.

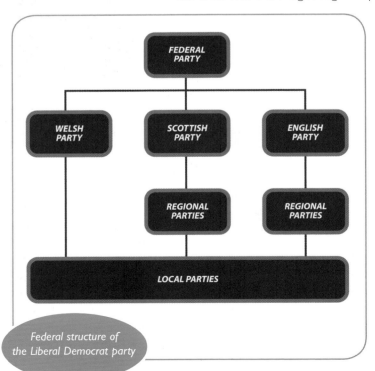

Federal structure of the Liberal Democrat party

Parliamentary party organisation

The Liberal Democrats have far fewer MPs than the other main parties, so most MPs have some official position as spokesperson for something. This makes it much easier for the leadership of the party to exert discipline over MPs, and there are fewer MPs who need to be officially organised. There is no formal organisation for backbench Liberal Democrat MPs.

Policy organisation

Liberal Democrat policy is developed through party conferences held in spring and autumn of each year. Policy development is devolved to the national parties, so there is one set of policy for the federal party which applies of the whole of the UK in specific appropriate policy areas (such as foreign affairs and defence). The national parties in England, Scotland and Wales set their own policies for those countries. Final policy is determined by the Federal Policy Committee, which is responsible for the production of the election manifestos.

As a party with a strong commitment to the grassroots party membership, the Liberal Democrats open their policy debates to every member of the party through policy consultations. A website allows discussion and debate on selected topics.

Internet research

Visit the Liberal Democrats website and look at their policy consultations. Read some of the comments from party members. How will these comments be used to formulate party policy?
Links to this site and other websites relating to Higher Modern Studies can be found at: LECKIE&LECKIE Learning Lab

Electoral success

Electoral success for the Liberal Democrats is a relative term, since they have not held power in UK government for nearly 80 years. The 2005 General Election was their most successful for many years, and they won 62 seats. They are partners in the Scottish Executive coalition with the Scottish Labour Party.

The Liberal Democrats claim that their lack of electoral success is largely a result of the unfairness of the **first past the post voting** system used in UK General Elections (see pages 81–83), so their share of the votes at elections is not reflected in the number of seats they win. If shares of votes corresponded more accurately to numbers of seats, the Liberal Democrats would have enough seats to force their way into coalition partnerships in the UK Government. By contrast, the **additional member** system used in Scottish parliamentary elections (see pages 83–88) means that the Liberal Democrats are able to negotiate the terms of coalition with the other parties.

Electing the leader

Anyone wishing to stand as party leader needs the support of 10% of the MPs and 200 party members from at least 20 different constituencies. If more than one person stands, a postal ballot is held of all the party members, using the Alternative Vote System. This system produces rounds of voting, with the person with the lowest number of votes at each round being eliminated until a winner is declared from the final round of two candidates. In the 2006 leadership election, there were three candidates in the first round. Simon Hughes received the fewest votes, leaving Sir Menzies Campbell and Chris Huhne in the final round. Sir Menzies Campbell won with 57% of the votes.

Sir Menzies Campbell was elected leader of the Liberal Democrats in 2006

Party unity and factions

The Liberal Democrat Party is usually thought to be less divided on ideological grounds than Labour or the Conservatives. Nevertheless, there are different strands of thinking within the party. One group is the Orange Book group, which takes its name from a book written by a number of leading Liberal Democrats, and discusses the role of free-market economics in social issues such as health, pensions and environmental policies. By some standards, this is seen as a right-wing approach which is at odds with the social democrat approach taken by other Liberal Democrats.

For you to do

- Compare the way the Liberal Democrats choose their leader with how the Conservatives and the Labour Party choose their leader.
- Evaluate the claim that the Liberal Democrats' electoral success in the UK is adversely affected by the voting system used.
- Add key events in the history of the Liberal Democrats to your timeline.

LIBERAL DEMOCRAT POLICIES

Taxation

The Liberal Democrats went into the 2005 General Election with a tax policy which proposed an increase in the rate of income tax for high earners and the replacement of the council tax with a local income tax. However, these proposals proved unpopular with voters, and after the election, the Liberal Democrats undertook a review of their tax policies. The main points of their new policies are:

- raise the starting rate for higher rate of tax to £50,000 a year
- abolish the 10p start rate of income tax
- cut the basic rate of income tax
- increase environmental taxes, such as aircraft tax based on carbon emissions, and higher excise duty on high-carbon-emission vehicles.

The main aims of the new tax policies are to make sure the tax system treats everyone fairly and does not put too high a tax burden on anyone. In keeping with their beliefs in local accountability, the Liberal Democrats also want to give more power to local government to raise revenue for local spending.

Law and order

The 2005 election manifesto set out five priorities on law and order:

- 10,000 more police officers
- clamp down on anti-social behaviour with Acceptable Behaviour Contracts
- reduce reoffending by training prisoners so they can get a useful job on release
- make non-violent offenders do hard community work so they are paying back to the community
- increase police resources to improve detection and investigation of crimes.

The Liberal Democrats are strongly opposed to the proposals for Identity Cards.

Education

Liberal Democrat education policies promote the ideas of equal educational opportunities for everyone, so they are in favour of a strong comprehensive system and opposed to charges for university fees. The main features of their policies include:

HINTS & TIPS

> **You may have political views of your own. Do not allow your own views to come through strongly in any essays you write.**

- improve provision for early years education and care
- smaller class sizes for all age groups
- a new curriculum which lets teachers take more control over the way they teach courses
- reduce the amount of testing
- simplify qualification systems to create one system to cover academic and vocational courses together
- abolish tuition fees and reintroduce grants for students from low-income households.

Europe

Traditionally, the Liberal Democrats are the most pro-European of the major British parties. The European Union fits with the Liberal Democrats' ideas of cooperation and federal structures, with power being devolved to the appropriate levels of European, national and local governments. The main thrust of the Liberal Democrats' policies on Europe is to promote greater **decentralisation** within a reformed EU. Other policies include:

- support for the proposed EU constitution, with increased powers for the European and national governments over the EU Commission
- support for the euro
- reform of the Common Agricultural Policy
- improve UK parliamentary scrutiny of European legislation.

WORD BANK

Decentralisation: the process of redistributing and transferring centralised state power to local authorities.

Internet research

- Visit the Liberal Democrats' website and make notes about their policies on law and order, education, taxation and Europe as presented in their 2005 manifestos. Note any changes between then and now. Add key points about the Liberal Democrats and their policies to your tables.

For you to do

- Write a few paragraphs describing Liberal Democrat policies on the issues mentioned.
- To what extent do the Liberal Democrats and the Labour Party have similar policies in two of the following: Education; Law and Order; Taxation; Europe?

THE SCOTTISH NATIONAL PARTY

The Scottish National Party (SNP) is a centre-left political party which campaigns for Scottish independence. It currently has only six MPs in the UK Parliament, but gained nearly 21% of the votes in the 2003 Scottish parliamentary elections, giving it 27 of the 129 seats in the Holyrood parliament.

Membership

In 2006, the SNP had over 12,000 members (compared with about 15,000 members of the Scottish Conservative Party and nearly 19,000 members of the Scottish Labour Party).

Funding

The SNP does not have the same level of financial support from either business or the trade unions as the other main parties. In 2004, its income was £1.3 million, of which £414,163 came from four bequests. Most of the rest of its income came from membership fees and fund-raising activities undertaken by its members, and from commercial income generated by the annual conference. It is often said that Sean Connery is the SNP's biggest donor, but in fact, he stopped giving money to the party in 2001 (although he does still support the party).

Party organisation

The SNP consists of about 250 branches organised at the level of local council wards. These branches are organised into parliamentary constituency associations. The branches are responsible for selecting local council candidates. There are also eight Regional Liaison Committees (covering the Scottish Parliamentary electoral regions) and 32 Council Liaison Committees (covering the local authority areas)

The governing body of the SNP is the **National Council,** which meets at least twice a year. The National Council is made up of representatives from branches, constituency associations, the National Executive Committee (NEC) and members elected by national conference.

The annual **National Conference** is responsible for making policy and electing the party's office bearers and representatives on party committees. Any member of the party can attend the annual conference, but only delegates from branches and associations can vote.

In addition to the annual conference, the SNP holds National Assembly meetings for discussions of policy. Any member of the party can attend and participate in Assembly meetings.

The National Executive Committee is the senior body of the party. It is made up of the party's elected office bearers and 10 elected members (voted for at conference). It meets every month and has overall responsibility for the party's campaign strategy, as well as overseeing the running of the party.

Electoral success

Until Scottish devolution, the SNP had very little influence, having just a few MPs in the Westminster parliament. They were massively outnumbered by Scottish Labour MPs so they were unable to make any inroads on Scottish policy. Their best performance was at the October 1974 General Election, when they won 11 seats, but that is the only time they have reached double figures.

The proportional representation system used for Scottish parliament has given them greater prominence. In the 1999 and 2003 Scottish parliamentary elections they gained 20% and 27% of the seats, respectively, and had a much greater voice in parliamentary debates. However, they still failed to gain sufficient support to be able to win debates on Scottish independence. They will only be able to make progress on this subject when they become the biggest party in the Holyrood parliament.

For you to do

- Why do you think the SNP have had so little influence in the UK Parliament? Has this influence increased or decreased since devolution in 1999?
- Describe the organisation of the SNP. How does it compare with that of the Conservatives or Labour?

Electing the leader

The party leader is elected on a One Member One Vote basis, so all members participate in the election of the leader. The first leader to be elected under these rules was Alex Salmond, MP for Banff and Buchan, in September 2004. He defeated Michael Russell and Roseanna Cunningham, winning over 75% of the votes cast. Salmond had previously been party leader from 1990 to 2000.

Ideology, party unity and factions

The party is generally thought to be a centre-left party with socialist roots, and over the years there have been moves to make it more or less a socialist party. There have also been shifts in the emphasis given to the notion of Scottish independence which have given rise to the terms *gradualists* and *fundamentalists*.

The gradualists favour a step-by-step approach to independence, gained through greater degrees of devolution. Gradualists believe that it is necessary for the Scottish Parliament to prove that it is competent to run the country before there will be widespread support for full independence.

The fundamentalists want to see a more immediate emphasis on Scottish independence, believing that if the SNP do not argue forcefully for independence, then there is little reason for the electorate to support them. Some of the fundamentalists are also sceptical about the devolved parliament since it might seem to place limits on the degree of autonomy that is acceptable.

Internet research

Visit the website of the SNP and make notes about how ordinary members of the SNP can be involved in the running of the party and can contribute to policy making.

Alex Salmond, elected SNP leader in 2004

For you to do

- Critically examine the claim that the SNP will only be able to make progress on the subject of Scottish independence when they become the biggest party in the Holyrood parliament.
- Add key events in the history of the SNP to your timeline.

SNP POLICIES

Taxation

Many of the SNP's tax policies are designed to make Scotland a more attractive and competitive place for international business. SNP policies on taxation include:

- lowering corporation tax to 20%
- reducing business rates to support small businesses
- the use of tax incentives to encourage greater exploration in North Sea oil fields
- 50% tax rate for high earners
- local income tax to replace the council tax.

Law and order

SNP policies on law and order include:

- opposition to the introduction of ID cards
- increased numbers of community police officers
- adjustable fines to reflect the ability to pay, to stop people being imprisoned because they cannot afford to pay fines for minor offences
- new prison options that allow prisoners to work and keep contact with their families, to reduce reoffending rates
- improved rehabilitation programmes for drug addicts.

Education

SNP policies on education include:

- improve provision for early-years education
- reduce class sizes
- early intervention with indiscipline and truancy
- encourage vocational education for S3 and S4 pupils
- improvements to secondary schools which encourage specialisation
- replace student loans with student grants, and write off existing student loan debts.

Europe

The SNP are strong supporters of the European Union. They can see the success of other small independent countries in the EU, and believe that membership of the EU would be good for the Scottish economy. The SNP believe that full independence would enable the Scottish voice to be presented more forcefully in European negotiations, without being diluted by overriding UK concerns.

SNP policies on Europe include:

- opposing efforts to harmonise tax and social security across Europe
- opposing any further European influence over Scottish fisheries
- supporting moves to strengthen cross-border law and order issues while maintaining the Scottish legal system
- support for the euro, but with the decision to join the euro-zone only taken after a national referendum.

Internet research

Visit the SNP website and make notes about their policies on law and order, education, taxation and Europe as presented in their 2005 manifestos. Note any changes between then and now. Add key points about the SNP and their policies to your tables.
Links to this site and other websites relating to Higher Modern Studies can be found at:

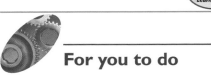

For you to do

- Write a few paragraphs describing SNP policies on the issues mentioned.
- Discuss the policies of the SNP on two of the following: Education; Law and Order; Health; Taxation; Europe.
- Compare the policies of the SNP on devolved issues with those of the other main parties.

Internet research

Visit the BBC website showing the results of the 2005 General Election. Who won in your constituency? Was there a change in your constituency? Were the results in line with national trends? Were there local reasons for any differences?
Using the information on the website and any others, make notes of the success and failures of the main parties in the 2005 General Election.
Look over your tables summarising the key points of the four main parties. Fill any gaps and research further points of interest.
Links to this site and other websites relating to Higher Modern Studies can be found at:

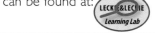

STUDY THEME SUMMARY

In UK parliamentary elections, the three main parties – Conservative, Labour and the Liberal Democrats – win the great majority of votes and seats. However, the share of votes does not match the share of seats, and only Labour and the Conservatives have held power in the UK government since the Second World War. In Scottish parliamentary elections, the proportional representation system means that the share of votes does match the share of seats. The three main UK parties plus the Scottish National Party win the majority of votes, and the Scottish Executive is formed from a coalition of the two parties with the biggest share of the seats.

The four main parties have a range of ideologies which determine their policies on a wide range of issues. Varying degrees of electoral success have been achieved with different policies, and it is common for parties to redefine their policies if they do not achieve success with one set of policies. The Labour Party underwent a major modernisation of policy in the 1990s, and the Conservatives are undergoing a similar exercise in the 2000s.

Devolution in Scotland means that the main parties have separate party manifestos for Scottish elections. Some of the policies will be the same as national manifestos, but devolved issues such as education are completely separate in Scotland.

Exam-style essay questions

To what extent is it true to say that there are few differences between Labour and Conservative Party policies? Discuss with reference to at least two policies.

To what extent has there been of disunity within either the Labour Party or the Conservative Party in recent years?

Choose two of the four main parties in the UK including Scotland. To what extent are there differences in their methods of policy making?

Choose two of the four main parties in the UK including Scotland. To what extent are there differences in their policies on law and order and taxation?

'Political parties should be funded by the state.' Discuss.

STUDY THEME 1D:
Electoral systems, voting and political attitudes

In this study theme you will be expected to have a detailed knowledge and understanding of:

- ## THE UK, SCOTTISH, EUROPEAN PARLIAMENTARY AND SCOTTISH LOCAL GOVERNMENT ELECTORAL SYSTEMS

  Effects on the distribution of power within and among parties, in elected bodies and between the electorate and the elected.

- ## VOTING PATTERNS

  Explanations of voting behaviour.

- ## THE SHAPING OF POLITICAL ATTITUDES THROUGH THE MEDIA

  Opinion polls; referenda; voter participation.

VOTING SYSTEMS

Voters in the UK use a range of different election systems in different elections. Historically, the UK has made most use of the First Past the Post (FPTP) system for elections, and this system is still used for UK General Elections and for many local council elections. More recently, different types of Proportional Representation (PR) systems have been used for Scottish, Northern Irish and European elections, and will be further used in Scottish council elections from 2007. There are a number of different types of PR systems used in different elections.

System	Type of system	Used for	Representative
First Past the Post	Simple Majority	UK Parliament	MPs
Party List System	PR	European Parliament	MEPs
Additional Member System	PR	Scottish Parliament	MSPs
Single Transferable Vote	PR	Northern Ireland European Elections, Northern Ireland Assembly, Scottish Local Government (from 2007)	MEPs, MLAs, Councillors

FIRST PAST THE POST

How the system works

- The UK is divided into 646 areas called **constituencies**.
- Each constituency elects one **Member of Parliament**.
- Voting involves simply **putting an 'X'** next to the name of the candidate you support.
- The candidate with the **most votes wins**.
- The party with the **most seats in Parliament** forms the Government.

The main weakness with the FPTP system is that it does not necessarily produce a result in which the share of seats reflects the share of votes. The table shows the results in the 2005 UK General Election, and it is clear that there is a big difference between the votes cast and the seats won.

UK ELECTION RESULT 2005			
	% votes	seats	% seats
Labour	35.2	356	55.1
Conservative	32.4	198	30.7
Liberal Democrat	22.0	62	9.6
Others	10.3	30	4.6

VOTE FOR ONE CANDIDATE ONLY

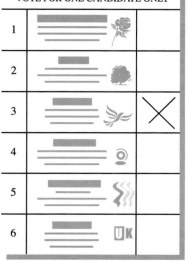

A ballot paper used in a UK General Election

FIRST PAST THE POST SYSTEM	
Strengths	*Weaknesses*
Simple It is simple to understand, voters can clearly see why representatives have been elected; its simplicity may encourage turnout.	**Wasted votes** Only one MP is elected in each constituency, so the voters who did not vote for that MP are not represented. Their votes are wasted – they could have stayed at home and the result would not have been altered. In 2005, in the UK, 19 million voters cast ineffective votes, that is, 70% of those who voted.
Representative The voter can express a view on which party should form the next Government. The system represents the views of the people, as the candidate with the greatest support wins through a fair process.	**Unfair representation** In 2005, Conservative support was spread thinly over most of Scotland. They got 15.8% of the vote in Scotland, and only 1.7% of the seats. The Liberal Democrats got 22.6% of the Scottish vote and a similar share of the seats (18.6%) because they had strong support in a few constituencies and minimal support in most of the others.
Strong Government The system tends to produce single party Governments, which are strong enough to create legislation without relying on the support of any other party.	**Governments elected by the minority** Governments are elected with less than 50% of the vote. In 2005, Labour won 35.2% of the total vote cast, but got 55.1% of the seats in Parliament, giving them power to form the Government. Taking into account the low turnout (61%), only one in five of the registered electorate actually voted for the Government
MP/Constituent link It provides a close and obvious link between the MP and their constituency.	**Lack of choice** There is a lack of choice given to the voters. The candidates are selected by a small number of party members. If the candidate selected for your party has views with which you disagree, you are left with no alternative choice within that party.
No need to change The UK's democracy is one of the strongest in the world. Although it is not perfect, it works, so there is no compelling reason to change.	**Negative/Tactical voting** The system leads to many people casting negative votes, that is, voting against the candidate they dislike most rather than for the candidate they like best.
	Third/Smaller parties disadvantaged The geography of the constituency boundaries means that voters are represented unequally. In 2005, the average number of votes per MP elected was: 26,906 for Labour, 44,373 for Conservative and 96,539 for Liberal Democrats. A two-party system is created by FPTP and smaller parties find it difficult to gain seats.

Internet research

Visit the website of the Electoral Reform Society and make more detailed notes on the advantages and disadvantages of FPTP.

Visit the BBC News website and make notes on seats won, share of the vote, majorities, turnout for the UK and Scotland elections.

Links to these sites and other websites relating to Higher Modern Studies can be found at: www.leckieandleckie.co.uk by clicking on the Learning Lab button and navigating to the Higher Modern Studies Course Notes page.

For you to do

- Use the election results table to make notes on some of the effects of FPTP. Comment on:
  —strong single-party Government – what is the Labour Government's majority?
  —two-party politics – what is the combined number of seats and percentage votes for Labour and Conservative?
  —third parties unfairly represented – compare the percentage of votes and percentage of seats for Labour and for the Liberal Democrats.
  —unrepresentative Government – compare the percentage of votes for Labour with the percentage against.
- Discuss whether the First Past the Post system of election is bad for democracy.

PROPORTIONAL REPRESENTATION SYSTEMS

All Proportional Representation (PR) systems work on the principle that the number of seats won by a party should be roughly in proportion to the number of votes gained. However, there are different systems which work in different ways and are used in different elections:

- **Party List** system, used in European Parliament elections
- **Additional Member** system, used in Scottish Parliament elections
- **Single Transferable Vote** system, used in European and Assembly elections in Northern Ireland, and in Scottish Local Government elections from 2007.

PARTY LIST SYSTEM: EUROPEAN PARLIAMENT

How it works

- Each party draws up a **list of candidates** ranked according to the party's preference.
- Electors vote for a **party**, not for a person.
- If a party gets 30% of the vote then the top 30% of candidates from their list is elected.
- There can be a **national** list when the entire country is one constituency, or a **regional** list where the country is divided into large multi-member regions. A **quota** may be used to calculate the number of votes required to win in a region.

Quotas

In the European Parliament elections, a method called the **d'Hondt formula** is used to allocate seats. Seats are allocated in successive rounds. In each round, votes cast for each party are divided by the number of seats the party has already been allocated in the region plus 1. The party with the highest remaining total in the round wins the seat.

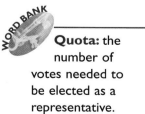

WORD BANK

Quota: the number of votes needed to be elected as a representative.

The system is demonstrated by a three-party, five-seat example below.

	Party A	Party B	Party C	
Votes	700	400	300	
Round 1	**700**	400	300	Party A **wins** with 700/1 = **700**
Round 2	350	**400**	300	Party B **wins** with 400/1 = **400** (Party A has 700/(1+1) = 700/2 = 350)
Round 3	**350**	200	300	Party A **wins** with 700/(1+1) = **350** (Party B has 400/(1+1) = 200)
Round 4	233	200	**300**	Party C **wins** with 300/1 = **300** (Party A has 700/(2+1) = 233; Party B has 400/(1+1) = 200)
Round 5	**233**	200	150	Party A **wins** with 700/(2+1) = **233** (Party B has 400/(1+1) = 200; Party C has 300/(1+1) = 150)
Total seats	3	1	1	

D'HONDT SEAT ALLOCATION

PROPORTIONAL REPRESENTATION: PARTY LIST SYSTEM

Strengths	Weaknesses
Proportional List systems guarantee a high degree of party proportionality. If a party receives 32% of the vote, then it will get 32% of the seats in Parliament. Every vote has the same value. No votes are wasted.	**MP/Constituent link is lost** Voters have no choice over candidates. They only vote for a party. This means the MPs elected are no longer directly accountable to their constituents. The MP/Constituent link is lost.
Simple The system is also very simple for voters, who have only to make one choice for a party.	**Power with the parties** Parties can stifle independent and minority opinion within their ranks. Party leaders select who is on the List. MPs become accountable to their party instead of to their constituents.
Fairer representation It is fairer to smaller parties who are more likely to gain seats under this system.	**Under-representation** Party lists do not help to ensure fair representation for traditionally under-represented groups in society, such as ethnic minorities, women or the working class. Party leaders are most likely to choose people from a similar background to represent the party.
Coalition Government Coalition Governments are very likely to result using this system. Coalitions represent a broader range of opinion. Parties are forced to compromise and more extreme policies are avoided.	**Coalition Government** Many people believe that coalitions are weak and that the policies of such governments will be weak and unrepresentative of the views of the people. Sometimes it is difficult to negotiate and achieve compromise, making it difficult to get things done. No-one voted for the coalition or their compromise policies.
	Unsupported policies Some coalitions may need the support of small parties that got little support in the election. In return for their support the small parties may expect several of their policies enacted – policies which most voters rejected.

Coalition: In a situation where no single party can get a majority of its representatives elected, the only way an effective government can be formed is by an alliance of more than one party.

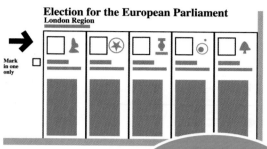

Election for the European Parliament
London Region

A ballot paper used in a European Parliament election

The Party List System was used in the 2004 European elections. The results are shown in the table below. (There were also three MEPs elected in Northern Ireland using a different election system, Single Transferable Vote.)

2004 EUROPEAN ELECTIONS			
Party	% votes	seats	% seats
Conservative	26.7	27	36.0
Labour	22.6	19	25.3
UK Independence Party	16.1	12	16.0
Liberal Democrat	14.9	12	16.0
Green	6.3	2	2.7
SNP	1.4	2	2.7
Plaid Cymru	1.0	1	1.3
Others	1.1	0	0

Contrast the results of the European elections with the 2005 UK General Election results, which used the FPTP system.

2005 UK GENERAL ELECTION				
	% votes	Actual no. seats (using FPTP)	Estimated no. seats (using PR)	Difference (had PR been voting system)
Conservative	32.4	198	209	+11
Labour	35.2	356	228	-128
Liberal Democrat	22.0	62	142	+80
Other	10.3	30	67	+37

For you to do

- Use the election results tables to make notes on how the Party List system could improve representation in the UK.
- To what extent does the Party List system improve representation in elections?

Internet research

Visit the website of the Electoral Reform Society to find out more about how the Party List System is used in the European Parliament.

Links to these sites and other websites relating to Higher Modern Studies can be found at:

LECKIE&LECKIE
Learning Lab

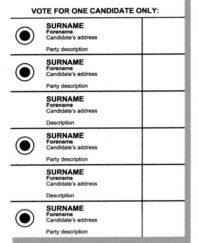

ADDITIONAL MEMBER SYSTEM: SCOTTISH PARLIAMENT

The Additional Member System (AMS) is a combination of FPTP and the Party List system. The purpose is to keep the best features of FPTP but at the same time introduce proportionality between parties through Party List voting.

How it works

- Each voter has **two votes**, one vote for a **Constituency MSP** using **FPTP**, and one vote for a **Regional** (or **List**) **MSP** using **AMS**.
- Seventy-three seats are allocated to the **single-member constituencies** and 56 to the **regional party list**, with eight regions having seven members each.
- The percentage of votes obtained by the parties in the Party List vote determines their **overall number of representatives for each region**; the Party Lists are used to top up the FPTP seats gained by the party to the required number.

PROPORTIONAL REPRESENTATION: ADDITIONAL MEMBER SYSTEM	
Strengths	*Weaknesses*
MSP/Constituent link There is a directly accountable MSP for each constituency.	**MSP conflict** It creates two types of MSP, one with a constituency role and duties and one without such a base. MSPs are often from different parties.
Proportionality The results are broadly proportional.	**Lack of accountability** Regional List MSPs are not directly accountable to any voters, just to their party leadership, and have no direct constituency.
Strong Government In Scotland the Labour/Liberal Democrat coalition Government has introduced policies that demonstrate independence from Westminster (such as free personal care for the elderly).	**Unrepresentative Government** A coalition is likely to result, such as the Labour/Liberal Democrat coalition. In return for their support, smaller parties like the Liberal Democrats may expect several of their policies enacted – policies which most voters rejected.
No wasted votes Each elector has at least one effective vote. Even if they see no chance of their candidate winning in the single member constituency, people can use their second vote for a party they support and still have a limited say through an additional member. Conversely, because the first vote does not determine a party's total representation, a voter can use it to express personal support for a candidate without necessarily using the second vote to help that candidate's party.	**Low turnout** It is argued that voters may be confused by the new voting system and be discouraged from voting. This might be supported by the fact that at the 2003 Scottish Parliament election the turnout was only 49.4%, compared with 59% in 1999.
Wider representation The Regional List vote allows many smaller parties to gain representation. Small parties and independents gained 17 MSPs in the Scottish Parliament in 2003: seven for the Scottish Green Party; six for the Scottish Socialist Party; one from the Scottish Senior Citizens Unity Party, and three independents. Of these 17 MSPs, 15 are 'additional members' elected on the regional lists.	**Power with the parties** As in the Party List system the parties have complete control over choosing their Additional Members.

SCOTTISH PARLIAMENT ELECTION RESULT 2003					
Party	% Vote Constituency	% Vote Regional	Seats Constituency	Seats Regional	Seats Total
Labour	35	30	46	4	50
SNP	24	21	9	18	27
Liberal Democrat	15	12	13	4	17
Conservative	17	16	3	15	18
Green	0	7	0	7	7
Scottish Socialist	6	7	0	6	6
Save Stobhill Hospital	1	0.5	1	0	1
Scottish Senior Citizens	1	2	0	1	1
Others	1	4.5	1	1	2

For you to do

- Use the 2003 election results table to make notes on the effect of AMS on representation.
- What are the advantages and disadvantages of the system used to elect the Scottish Parliament?
- Critically examine the view that AMS provides better representation than FPTP.

In the Glasgow Regional Vote, Labour gained the highest percentage of votes, but they did not gain any additional List seats. The use of the AMS system ensured that the other five parties all gained representation even though they had been unsuccessful in the constituency vote.

Internet research

Visit the website of the Electoral Reform Society to find out more about how AMS is used in the Scottish Parliament and also in the Welsh Assembly and London Mayoral elections.

Visit the Scottish Parliament website and make detailed notes on the 2003 election results.

Visit the Scottish Parliament website to find out how the result was calculated for your region. Look at Glasgow for an example of how AMS improved small party representation.

Links to these sites and other websites relating to Higher Modern Studies can be found at:

Why was AMS chosen as the voting system for the Scottish Parliament?

The White Paper that preceded the Scotland Bill in 1997 justified AMS as the electoral system for the Scottish Parliament on the grounds that its greater proportionality would build stability into the overall settlement, because it was felt that FPTP would have given Labour an automatic outright majority, and PR was likely to produce coalition governments in Scotland. Given the strength of the Labour Party in Scotland, it's worth asking why Labour would vote for a system that would reduce their control of power in Scotland.

Although the Labour Party would currently benefit from the outright majorities brought about by FPTP, there was no guarantee that such a situation would continue. In many constituencies the SNP was the second party. Should the SNP make a breakthrough and become the majority party in the Scottish Parliament, they would use it as a mandate to move for an independent Scotland. This would create a constitutional crisis which Labour would prefer to avoid.

It was argued that the greater degree of proportionality would help overcome the increasingly poor turnout at elections. One reason put forward for the poor turnouts was that many elections were foregone conclusions so people did not bother to vote. Others suggested that there were so many wasted votes under FPTP that many voters simply gave up on elections. PR would encourage more participation and underwrite the importance and success of the new Scottish Parliament.

Therefore it is argued that the Labour Party supported the introduction of AMS to prevent the SNP from achieving single party-government in Scotland and using this as a mandate for independence.

SINGLE TRANSFERABLE VOTE: NORTHERN IRELAND ASSEMBLY AND SCOTTISH LOCAL GOVERNMENT

How it works

- The country is divided into **large multi-member constituencies**. For Scottish local government this will involve three or four councillors per ward. Larger wards have correspondingly more councillors.
- Voters **rank the candidates**, putting a '1' for their favourite, a '2' for the next, and so on. They do not have to rank all candidates or vote only for one party.

You may vote for multiple candidates
Place a '1' by your first choice candidate, '2' by your second choice, '3' by your third choice etc.

Lennox, James (Liberal Democrats)	1
Barr, Michael (British National Party)	
Kay, Angela (Green Party)	2
Singh, Nikita (Labour)	3
Brown, Patricia (Conservatives)	

An STV ballot paper

PROPORTIONAL REPRESENTATION: SINGLE TRANSFERABLE VOTE	
Strengths	*Weaknesses*
Voter/MP link Most voters can identify a representative that they personally helped to elect. This personal link also increases accountability.	**MP/Constituency link** It can be argued that it breaks the link between an individual MP and his or her constituency.
Strong Government Only a party or coalition of parties which could attract more than 50% of the vote could form a government.	**Not as proportional as other PR systems** The system does not produce such accuracy in proportional representation of parties as the Party List system or AMS.
Simplicity It is simple for voters to use.	**Complexity** The counting of results is complex. Voters may not understand how their representatives are elected and so may be deterred from voting.
No wasted votes There is no need for tactical voting. Voters can cast a positive vote and know that their vote will not be wasted whatever their choice is.	**Disliked by politicians** Many MPs with safe seats would lose the security they feel now.
Voter choice Voters can choose between candidates within parties, demonstrating support for different wings of the party or for individual candidates.	

- The number 1 choice (**first preference vote**) is most important. But if the candidate already has more than enough votes to be elected, or too few to stand a chance, the vote will be used to help the next choice of that voter (the vote, or the unused part of the vote, is **transferred**).
- Candidates who poll a **certain proportion of the vote** or **quota** (25% in three-member wards, 20% in four-member wards), are elected. This means that the main parties will be represented roughly in proportion to the votes they have polled.

Internet research

Visit the website of the Electoral Reform Society to find out more about the STV System and how it is used in the Northern Ireland Assembly.
Look at the Electoral Reform Society website briefing on the arguments for local government election reform. Analyse the local government election results after 2007. Links to these sites and other websites relating to Higher Modern Studies can be found at:

For you to do

- Design a grid or diagram to summarise the strengths and weaknesses of each election system.
- With reference to at least two systems, assess the effectiveness of PR in improving representation for minorities.

You are all useless numpties

vote here

VOTING SYSTEMS AND THE DISTRIBUTION OF POWER

Voting systems are not neutral. This means that the way Governments are elected can vary according to the type of voting system used. The example of the UK General Election in 2005 showed how different systems, FPTP and PR, would have produced quite different results. Voting systems affect:

- the relationship between the constituent and their representative
- the relationship between the elected representative and the political party they belong to
- the relationship between parties and the nature of political parties
- the voting behaviour of the electorate.

The relationship between the constituent and representative

There is direct accountability with FPTP. For each constituency there is one representative who is directly responsible to each constituent. If any constituent does not feel their representative is working on their behalf they can vote against them at the next election.

With PR, accountability is not so direct, since with some systems of PR there may be several representatives. For example, with STV there may be as many as five representatives for one constituency. Which one is responsible for dealing with a constituent's complaints? With a List System the representative is allocated a constituency after the election so there is no direct relationship between the representative and the constituents. With AMS in the Scottish Parliament elections each voter has eight MSPs to represent them – one Constituency MSP and seven Regional MSPs. Each voter has a clearly accountable Constituency MSP but the role of the Regional MSP is not as clearly defined. Therefore the type of electoral system used alters the relationship between representative and constituent.

HINTS & TIPS

> **The period before elections is a particularly good time to compare the policies of the parties on different issues.**

The relationship between the elected representative and their political party

FPTP has created an **adversarial** system. The success of the elected representative is dependent on the success of their party. Usually FPTP gives power to party leaders who are successful because many representatives will owe their seats to the popularity of the party and its leadership. So they will support the party on all issues in order to maintain the party's appearance of being united and worthy of winning votes. Members of the other parties will support their parties, thereby creating an adversarial situation.

PR tends to leads to more **consensual** politics and often leads to a coalition government. There is a necessity to compromise in coalition government because there is no one party able to govern on its own. Party leaders may have less power or influence over their party because in a coalition individual representatives do not depend on the leadership for their electoral success to the same extent as in FPTP. However, in some PR systems such as the Party List system and the Regional Lists in elections for the Scottish Parliament it gives the party leaders much more power over their backbenches. Individuals can be placed near the top or the bottom of the lists as a result of pressure from the leadership and this will determine whether or not they are to be elected next time round. Consequently MSPs may be careful not to antagonise their leaders.

Full chamber of the Scottish Parliament

The relationship between parties and the nature of political parties

First Past the Post leads to a **confrontational two-party system**. Two main parties often compete with each other to score points irrespective of the case either is presenting. Other parties sit on the margins as they have limited representation in the Parliament and limited influence.

PR tends to produce a **consensual multiparty system** because two or more parties must combine and compromise to achieve Government.

The nature of the electoral system employed will have an impact on the nature of political parties. The winner-take-all nature of FPTP means that successful political parties must be large, so they accept a broad membership with wide-ranging ideas on many subjects. The party then seeks an acceptable compromise it hopes will win the votes of the public. In the UK Parliament the Labour and Conservative Parties dominate. Within the Conservatives there are many who are in favour of membership of the European Union and others who are Euro-sceptics. Within Labour there are those who support a programme of nuclear power stations and others who oppose it. Both parties have to accommodate a wide range of views if they wish to gain power.

With PR parties will be smaller and more focused on a range of issues. Smaller, more extreme parties are more likely to pick up seats with PR than with FPTP. For example, it would be easier for parties like the National Front to get a small number of representatives elected. Issue parties like the Green Party also have a better chance of getting representation. So with PR there will be many more smaller parties representing a wide variation in political views.

The voting behaviour of the electorate

FPTP can encourage voters to vote for a party other than the one they really want. This is called **negative voting**. If voters feel that their preferred candidate has little chance of being elected they may use their vote as a protest or vote tactically to keep their least preferred candidate out or may not vote at all. It also reduces the vote for smaller parties who may be seen as unlikely to gain any electoral success.

PR, however, can encourage positive voting and discourage tactical voting as smaller parties have more chance of electoral success. However, the Regional Lists in the Scottish Parliament elections can also encourage some protest votes. Voters may vote for a preferred candidate but express displeasure with a party in their second vote. In the 2003 Scottish Parliament election, the second vote allowed voters to express support for the Scottish Socialist Party, the Green Party and also for a number of Independent candidates. All of them gained representation.

For you to do

- Compare the effect of different voting systems on the interrelationships between constituents, elected representatives and political parties.

INFLUENCES ON VOTING PATTERNS

Between 1945 and 1970 there was stability in voting patterns. Most voters in the UK remained loyal to the two main parties – the Conservative Party and the Labour Party. Most changes in Government were the result of small swings from one major party to the other. Third parties had less than 10% of the vote.

In the 1970s there was a drift in voter loyalty away from the Conservatives and Labour towards the Liberal Democrats who doubled their vote share with around 15–20%. In Scotland and Wales the SNP and Plaid Cymru benefited from an upsurge in support which created a four-party system.

Since 1970, the UK electorate has become increasingly less loyal to one party and voting patterns became more volatile and less predictable. The period 1979–1997 was a time of fragmentation in class voting, increased voter volatility and partisan **dealignment**. The gap between the Conservative and Labour parties grew to over 10% in the four elections in these years. In 1997, the swing in votes from the Conservative Party to Labour was over 10%. Voters were demonstrating they were willing to desert the main parties and switch between them in increasing numbers.

WORD BANK

Dealignment: the trend of voters abandoning traditionally strong loyalty to a political party based on their social class.

95

Voting patterns can be investigated across a range of criteria:

- Social class
- Age
- Gender
- Party affiliation
- Ethnicity
- Issues
- Image and personality
- Location.

Social class

Class used to be a strong indicator of voting intentions. (For more information on social class, see Study Theme 2, pages 111–113).

In the 1966 election, there was a clear class basis for voting. Voters in the A, B and C1 class groups voted solidly for the Conservative Party while C2, D and E, who make up the manual working class, voted solidly for the Labour Party. Loyalty was so strong for the respective political parties that a political scientist, P. J. Pulzer, was able to write in 1967 'Class is the basis of British party politics; all else is embellishment and detail.'

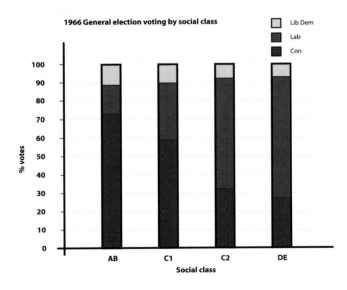

Class dealignment by the 1980s changed voting patterns.

- In the 1980s the UK became increasingly middle class as working class occupations were disappearing.
- The Labour Party lost traditional working class support.

- Conservatives and Liberal Democrats attracted an increasing amount of the shrinking working class vote.

In the 1990s, the voters became increasingly volatile.

	VOTING PATTERNS AND SOCIAL CLASS (%)						
	1992 General Election			1997 General Election			
Class	Con	Lab	Lib Dem	Con	Lab	Lib Dem	% swing Con to Lab
AB	56	20	22	42	31	21	12.5
C1	52	25	15	26	47	18	24.0
C2	38	41	17	25	54	13	13.0
DE	41	50	15	21	61	13	15.5

The Labour Party began to drop the policies that it thought appealed to the working class such as nationalisation and support for the trade unions and began to adopt policies designed to attract middle class voters such as low taxation. This was called *New Labour*.

In 1997, Labour won a clear majority of the C1 votes for the first time. The swing between 1992 and 1997 for C1 voters was 24% from Conservative to Labour. Between 1997 and 2001 the effect of class continued to decline, and dealignment became even more pronounced.

- Labour continued to lose support among the C2s and the DEs while the Conservatives made gains.
- Conservatives lost votes among the ABs and C1s whilst Labour made gains.
- There was little difference between the parties in their policies. With no clear class-oriented messages class-based voting will not take place.
- In 1987, 47% of Labour voters said that the Labour Party was looking after the interests of the working class, but by 2001, only 9% said the Labour Party was looking after working class interests.

Social class used to be considered an important influence on voting behaviour. There is still some residual class loyalty when voting but social class on its own is no longer a reliable predictor of voting intentions.

Internet research

Visit the website of the **Guardian** newspaper to read in more depth about differing views on the influence of class on voting.
Links to this site and other websites relating to Higher Modern Studies can be found at:

For you to do

● Using the election results of 1997 to 2005, to what extent do you think social class remains a predictor of voting intentions?

Age

Age does influence voting behaviour. The Conservatives gain votes among the over-50s, while younger and first-time voters are more likely to vote Labour. This behaviour has remained true over the last four elections.

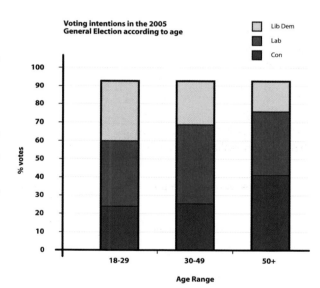

The reasons for this pattern are not clear but there are possible explanations.

● Different age groups have had different experiences of life. Older voters may be more 'conservative' by nature whereas those in the 30–49 age group with families may be concerned with issues like health and education. These are issues in which Labour has held the lead in opinion polls.

● Older voters may be more likely to stick to 'traditional' voting patterns and less likely to change voting allegiances. A large number of the 50+ age group would have been voting Conservative in 1979 when they were aged 23+ and the Conservatives were in power, and there is still a strong Conservative vote in that age group.

● How parties handle different issues may influence the age groups differently. The issues which concern the young most differ from the general voting public.

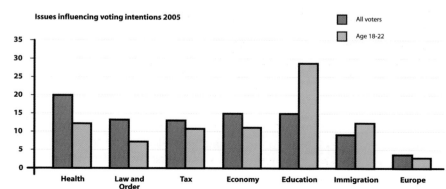

Young voters are less likely to vote and are less engaged with formal politics (see page 106 for information on turnout). This trend may become important for political parties as engaging young voters could be the key to future electoral victory.

	Certain to vote (%)	Certain not to vote (%)
18–22 year olds	26	18
All voters	62	10

Source: ICM 2005

Gender

In the 1950s and 1960s more men voted Labour and more women voted Conservative. This could be explained by Labour's strong links with the male dominated trade unions. In the 1997 and 2001 elections there was no significant difference between the way the genders voted. In the 2005 election, however, a slight difference in voting patterns between the genders did re-emerge as women became more likely to vote Labour than men. Gender does not have a significant effect on voting behaviour but that may be changing.

VOTING PATTERNS FOR MEN AND WOMEN (%)									
	Labour			Conservative			Liberal Democrat		
	1997	2001	2005	1997	2001	2005	1997	2001	2005
Men	44	42	34	31	33	34	17	18	23
Women	44	42	38	32	33	32	17	20	22

Source: Observer Politics

Party affiliation

A significant number of voters used to have a strong long-term commitment or affiliation to one party, often linked to social class, but dealignment has changed this. The polls of 2005 showed that 36% of voters were willing to change their mind. Even among those with a stated voting intention, some 16% said they would consider voting differently from their original intentions.

Internet research

Visit the MORI website to analyse the polls of voting intentions just before the May 2005 election. Look at the factors that voters identify with, the different parties and leaders. Also look at the strength of identification with each party. Summarise some key facts and figures. Links to this site and other websites relating to Higher Modern Studies can be found at:

Floating (undecided) voters are increasingly important. In pre-election polls in 2005, 13% of those who definitely intended to vote were undecided as to who they would vote for. It would have taken a 10% swing to the Conservatives to change the outcome of the 2005 election. A 13% swing would have given the Conservatives a majority of 88. Undecided or floating voters can have a significant impact on elections.

Personalities and policies are increasingly important. Party affiliation is now less important than the influence of policies and leaders, which could explain the willingness of voters to change their mind as parties change leaders or adopt new policies. Voters are increasingly likely to change their party affiliation. Other factors are more important in determining voter behaviour.

Ethnicity

Black and minority ethnic (BME) voters are less likely to vote than white voters. In 2001 the BME turnout was 48%, compared with 59.4% of all registered voters.

Compounding the low turnouts, only three in four of those entitled to vote in the BME community are actually registered and turnout is lowest in the poorer communities. The low levels of participation may be due to the feelings of alienation caused by deprivation and religious intolerance amongst many BME communities.

David Lammy MP (Lab) at the 2005 General Election

According to the 2001 Census, 7.9% of the UK population is from a minority ethnic group and yet in 2005 there were only 15 BME MPs out of 646 (2.3%). There were 113 BME mainstream candidates in the election. The BME vote could have a significant impact on elections. It has been calculated that in 70 seats the margin of votes between the MP and their nearest challenger was less than the number of black votes in the constituency. If a party wins all these black votes then the results in 70 constituencies would be changed. This could make the black vote the 'swing' vote.

The BME vote goes largely to Labour. In 2005 BME voters, in particular those of African or Caribbean descent, were more likely to vote Labour than the general population. Asian communities also gave a lot of support to Labour, but that support was not as strong as in the past, with the lowest level of support registered by voters of Bangladeshis origin. In previous elections, the Conservative Party had gained significant support from Asian communities but in 2005 the Liberal Democrats benefited.

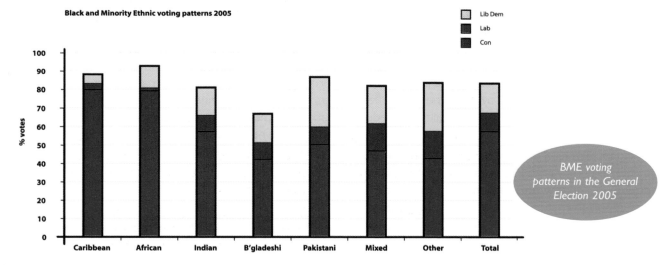

BME voting patterns in the General Election 2005

The BME voting behaviour can be related to social class, age and issue voting. There are higher numbers of social class AB among the Asian communities and the AB group are less likely to vote Labour than Conservative. Age is also a factor influencing the BME voting pattern, as the Liberal Democrats gained support among the younger BME voters. This could be explained by the strong feelings about the Iraq war among the young and the deliberate targeting of the young by the Liberal Democrats. It may also be that Government policy on issues such as immigration generated a lot of opposition among ethnic minorities and this opposition is expressed more by the young whereas older voters retain residual loyalty to Labour.

Issues may have influenced voter behaviour: BME voters identified asylum (7%) and immigration (6%) as the most important election issues. Pre-election polls in 2005 found a lack of confidence in Labour's handling of these areas. However, BME groups were not significantly different from the general public in this and so it may just reflect a general loss of support for Labour.

The BME vote could make a significant difference to results in key areas. The BME vote is strong for Labour but some not among all groups. This could be explained by other factors such as social class or issue voting.

Issues

Issue voting has become an important influence on election results. A MORI poll conducted on 15 April 2005 showed that party policy on national and local issues is very important in influencing voters, with 54% stating that policy on national issues is very important to them and 45% that policy on local issues is very important. This was more important than the parties' leaders or the quality of the local candidate.

What parties stand for and how well they are perceived to be handling the issues important to voters can influence an election result. In 1997 Labour had a landslide victory. Polls showed they were regarded as best able to handle the issues that are most important to voters. They maintained a lead in the polls in 2001 although it was reduced and by 2005 the Labour lead was significantly reduced. Labour's majority was reduced in 2001 and again in 2005.

The issues identified by voters as being most important to them in deciding how to vote in 2005 were **health**, **education**, and **law and order**. These have been the most important issues over the last three elections. How parties are perceived as handling issues that are important to voters can influence elections.

MOST IMPORTANT ELECTION ISSUE	
Health	73%
Education	62%
Law and order	50%

Source: MORI May 2005

LABOUR PARTY LEAD ON KEY ISSUES (%)			
Issue	*1997*	*2001*	*2005*
Health	+49	+28	+13
Education	+39	+27	+9
Law and order		+22	+4

Source: ICM & MORI

Internet research

Visit the BBC news website to read about how specific issues such as the war in Iraq can affect voters. See pages 104–105 for information on opinion polls. Links to these sites and other websites relating to Higher Modern Studies can be found at: **LECKIE&LECKIE Learning Lab**

Image and personality

The images of the main party leaders are important in influencing voters. Trust in the party leaders and their perceived ability to become Prime Minister influences voter behaviour.

In 2005 Tony Blair was perceived as being the most capable leader, with the best understanding of world problems and the best able to handle a crisis. In contrast, Charles Kennedy (at the time, leader of the Liberal Democrats) was rated highest for honesty and trustworthiness. It would seem that an image of strong leadership matters most and, despite doubts over his honesty and a view that he was out of touch, Tony Blair was rated as the best option for Prime Minister.

	Would describe as trustworthy	*Would not describe as trustworthy*	*Don't know*
	%	%	%
Tony Blair	32	61	7
Michael Howard	36	52	12
Charles Kennedy	61	25	14
Gordon Brown	52	36	12

Source: MORI, 29 April 2005

	Mr Blair	Mr Howard	Mr Kennedy
	%	%	%
A capable leader	34	18	18
Good in a crisis	19	5	2
Understands world problems	24	12	11
Tends to talk down to people	27	22	2
Rather narrow minded	15	22	6
Too inflexible	20	12	4
Has sound judgement	9	9	10
More honest than most politicians	10	9	31
Down-to-earth	15	7	31
Understands the problems facing Britain	25	21	21
Patriotic	16	22	12
Has got a lot of personality	25	6	13
Rather inexperienced	3	10	35
Out of touch with ordinary people	36	30	7
No opinion	11	21	23

Source: MORI, 27 April 2005

Location

There are strong regional variations in voting patterns. The Conservatives dominate in the South-East of England and Labour are stronger in the Midlands, the North of England and in Scotland. This is a voting pattern that has continued over several elections, although the line dividing the North and South has shifted. Since Labour came to power in 1997 the dividing line has moved south as the Midlands and London became Labour territory. Conservatives still remain the strongest party in the South of England outside London.

There are regional differences in voting behaviour. In Scotland there is a four-party contest although the Conservatives are poorly represented at present. In the cities and the central belt, Labour dominate although the Liberal Democrats have gained a foothold in Edinburgh. In the Highlands and Islands the Liberal Democrats dominate. In the North-East it is SNP, Liberal Democrats and Labour. In the Borders it is a three-way split between Liberal Democrats, Conservative and Labour.

Wales is dominated by Liberal Democrats in the centre but in the North and South it is a contest between Labour, Plaid Cymru and to a lesser extent Conservative.

Regional variations in voting patterns at the 2005 General Election

London

The South-West of England is a three-party race with Conservatives the strongest, followed closely by Liberal Democrats and the Labour Party in third place.

The South-East of England is dominated by the Conservatives but London is dominated by Labour, while the Midlands is largely a contest between Labour and Conservatives.

Geographical differences in voting may be explained by residual class loyalty, despite recent dealignment. The Labour vote is strongest in areas where there is a significant working class such as inner city London and central belt Scotland. The Conservatives dominate in the relatively affluent South-East.

For you to do

● Try to develop an acronym to remember all the factors that may influence voting behaviour: Class, Age, Gender (could be Sex), Party affiliation, Ethnicity (could be Race), Issues, Personality (could be Image), Location (could be Place or Geography).
● Rank the various factors that affect voting behaviour in order of importance. Give reasons to justify your decision for each one.
● Discuss whether image and issues have become the most important influences on voting behaviour.

THE MEDIA AND VOTING

People's political opinions are also shaped by the political information that they receive from a whole range of sources. An important source of political information in today's society is the mass media, comprising television, newspapers, radio and the internet.

Television

Television is the most widely used form of media. Surveys have shown that the average person in the UK watches 25.2 hours of television per week and 96% of the population watch television at least once per week.

Television is the main source of political information; 51% of adults consider television to be their main source of political information, with news broadcasts being the most used source followed by current affairs programmes such as *Newsnight* or *Question Time*. During elections, TV is even more heavily used as a source of information.

The public have a high level of trust in television reporting of politics. Television is regulated and all channels are required to ensure their political coverage is impartial.

Television may actually influence only a relatively small number of people. For the undecided voter who does not make up their mind until the last few days of a campaign, television may have a strong influence, and it is this small number of voters who can swing an election.

Politicians and parties use television to promote a positive image. The appearance, dress, speech and manner of political leaders is carefully managed. **Soundbites** for television are carefully planned. Speeches are reduced to concise statements that can be given extensive TV news coverage and convey an important message. However, by reducing issues to 'catchy' phrases, soundbites may trivialise issues and viewers are not fully informed.

Television has huge potential to shape political attitudes as it is the favoured and trusted source of information for the majority of the population. Political parties invest a great deal in trying to take advantage of the potential of television to influence the electorate, despite the fact that over half of voters have already made up their minds about how they will vote and nearly a half of voters pay little attention to political news coverage. However, it only needs a small percentage swing to change an election outcome.

Newspapers

Newspapers are an important source of political information. British people buy more newspapers per head of population than most of their European counterparts.

Newspapers are not neutral. The press is independent of government control and is in a powerful position to influence public opinion. Newspapers can decide which news stories are covered and how they are covered, which then influences the way a story will be interpreted by readers. Most newspapers are open in their support for particular political parties. *The Sun*, with the highest weekday tabloid circulation, supports Labour whereas the *Daily Express* is Conservative. These strong political affiliations may influence readers but newspapers may also simply reflect their readers' views. Also, newspapers change affiliation. In 1992 *The Sun* supported the Conservatives but by 1997 they had shifted to support Labour who were the predicted election winners. Newspapers have claimed to swing election results.

Political parties recognise the influence of newspapers. The importance of the press's influence on voters is clearly recognised by party leaders who actively court newspaper owners like Rupert Murdoch. Newspapers have campaigned for legislative change and parties have taken notice. The long-running campaign by *The News of the World* for changes in the laws on sex offenders is an example.

Newspapers can form opinion. People who read newspapers have stronger political opinions than those who do not. It may be that newspapers can influence political opinions or it may be that people with strong political opinions are more likely to buy newspapers.

Yet newspapers are also limited in their impact on voting behaviour. Only 10% of people believe newspapers have any influence on the way they actually vote. Only 41% of *Sun* readers voted Labour in 2005 as did 23% of *Financial Times* readers although both newspapers support Labour. Open support for a party does not automatically translate into votes.

Readers do not trust newspapers to be accurate and impartial in their reporting of political information as much as they trust television reporting.

Internet research

Visit the websites of some of the national newspapers and compare the way they report the same stories. Consider use of images as well as text. Look for the difference between straight news reporting and opinion columns.

Visit the politics.co.uk website to find articles about the ways newspapers can influence readers.

Visit the BBC website and find stories about the Government's reaction to the *News of the World* sex-offender campaign.

Links to these sites and other websites relating to Higher Modern Studies can be found at:

The internet

There is a huge growth in the use of the internet as a source of information and communication. Political parties all have websites, political news is available on-line and there are many political organisations, blogs and discussion forums which can be accessed on-line.

Information and Communications Technology (ICT) is being promoted by government as a channel to engage voters. In 2002 a parliamentary select committee identified ICT as the way forward to increase accessibility and participation among the public, but only 1% of people regard the internet as their main source of political information and only 1% regard the internet as the most accurate and impartial source of information.

For you to do

- Make up a table or a mind map to summarise the impact of the media on voting. Include the extent of use, the extent of influence, and trust.
- Critically examine the influence of the media on voting behaviour.

HOW DO POLITICAL PARTIES USE DIFFERENT MEDIA?

Party election broadcasts

Party election broadcasts (PEBs) are an important media tool, particularly during election campaigns. More than half of voters (58%) claimed to pay attention to PEBs during the 2005 election campaign, and more than a half of voters also felt that PEBs had influenced their decision either a little (39%) or a lot (16%).

Labour PEBs engaged more voters. About 50% of voters watched a Labour PEB, while 44% watched a Conservative PEB, and 40% watched a Liberal Democrat PEB. The other parties had fewer PEBs and were only watched by about 5–10%.

The net effect of PEBs seems to be to confirm party preferences: 63% of Labour voters watched at least one of their party's PEBs (63%), slightly fewer Conservative voters watched a Conservative PEB (60%), and 55% of Liberal Democrat voters watched one of their party's PEBs. Labour again proved better at engaging their own voters.

PEBs are popular. The Labour Party makes best use of PEBs as they engage more voters. PEBs can influence voting decisions but it may only be to confirm existing preferences.

Spin

Spin doctors or special advisors are increasingly used by political parties to manage the media. In 2005 the Labour Government had 72 special advisors at a cost to the public of £5.5m. During the 2005 election campaign Labour paid £530,000 to a former advisor to Bill Clinton and a further £47,000 to the former Government advisor Alastair Campbell. The Conservatives spent £441,146 on hiring the Australian election advisor Lynton Crosby.

The use of special advisors has attracted much criticism. They are consulted as part of government policy making, and so have a great deal of political influence. Yet they are unelected and therefore unaccountable to the voting public.

Opinion polls

There a number of opinion poll companies that regularly monitor voting intentions and public opinion on key political issues for political parties and for the media. Companies include MORI, ICM, YouGov, Populus, NOP and Communicate.

Opinion polls reflect the effect media reporting of events and issues can have on voters. For example, following 'Triple Whammy Wednesday', April 26 2006 (the day when Charles Clarke was forced to resign as Home Secretary, Patricia Hewitt the Health Secretary was booed and John Prescott the Deputy Prime Minister admitted an affair), the polls showed Labour at an all time low. Both ICM and MORI found support for Labour at 32–34% and 68% of people dissatisfied with the Government.

Opinion polls can influence political decision making. Political parties commission polls and react to the results when forming policy. However, opinion polls are often inaccurate in predicting election outcomes. They have a sampling error of +/- 3%. They sample nationwide support for a party but cannot predict the outcome for individual seats. They are only a snapshot of opinion and that opinion can vary from day to day. Opinion polls famously got it wrong in the 1992 General Election when a Labour win was widely predicted but did not materialise.

Internet research

Visit the BBC website and study its polltracker to see how party support moves in relation to events.
Read the article on the BBC website about the accuracy of opinion polls. Note the examples of when they were and were not accurate.
Links to these sites and other websites relating to Higher Modern Studies can be found at:

For you to do

● Make up spider diagrams for each of PEBs, opinion polls and spin to summarise key points on the influence of the media on voting behaviour.
● Assess the importance of PEBs, opinion polls and spin in the political decision-making process.

Referenda

Referenda are not used often in the UK. There have been a total of nine referenda but only one, on membership of the EEC in 1973, has been UK-wide. There have been two each on the constitutional futures of Scotland, Wales and Northern Ireland, and one for London. Referenda are used to gauge public opinion on constitutional issues, but governments are not bound by the results.

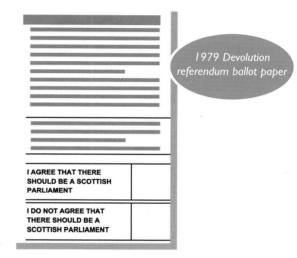

1979 Devolution referendum ballot paper

| I AGREE THAT THERE SHOULD BE A SCOTTISH PARLIAMENT | |
| I DO NOT AGREE THAT THERE SHOULD BE A SCOTTISH PARLIAMENT | |

Generally the outcome is what the government already expects, because the government can structure the referendum to create a desired result. This happened in 1979 in the referendum on Scottish devolution. The Government was pressured into having a referendum, but they did not want a **Yes** vote. To ensure a negative result, they created a condition that 40% of the **electorate** would have to vote in support of devolution for Scotland. Even though the majority voted **yes** for devolution, a low turnout meant that fewer than 40% of the electorate voted for devolution, giving the Government the result they wanted.

Internet research

Visit the Electoral Commission website and find out more about the referenda in the UK, the questions asked, the results and turnout.
Links to this site and other websites relating to Higher Modern Studies can be found at: LECKIE&LECKIE Learning Lab

Turnout

Voter turnout at elections is low and generally declining. Only 61% of the electorate voted in 2005 and of them 35% voted Labour. This means the Government was elected by just 21% of the electorate. This raises the question of whether the Government has the mandate of the people.

Parliament	1997	1999	2001	2003	2004	2005
UK Parliament	71%		59%			61%
Scottish Parliament		58%		49%		
Scottish local elections		60%		50%		
European Parliament		24%			39%	

Voter turnout is particularly low among the young. More 18–34 year olds voted during the 2004 live final of **Big Brother** than voted in the 2005 General Election.

Low turnout is blamed on lack of trust in politicians. A survey of non-voters after the 2005 election found nearly a half would be more encouraged to vote if they felt politicians' promises could be trusted. Only 15% of non-voters blamed apathy for their lack of turnout.

The Government wants to re-engage voters and different voting methods are being made available to improve turnout.

- Postal voting is now available to all voters. (However, postal voting was the subject of several fraud inquiries in 2005.)
- Voting by text, computer or at supermarkets was trialled in English local elections in 2002.

To broaden the range and appeal of candidates, other changes have been proposed.

- The Electoral Administration Act, introduced from 2006, has lowered the minimum age of candidates to 18.
- Reducing the threshold for candidates to lose their deposit to 2%. (However, this was rejected by MPs in the House of Commons.)

PR will be used in Scottish local elections from 2007. PR has not improved election turnout in the Scottish Parliament, but European Parliament election turnout improved between 1999 and 2003 when the List System was introduced.

Internet research

Visit the UK Politics page on the BBC website to find out more about the arguments for and against electoral changes such as postal votes and text voting.
Links to this site and other websites relating to Higher Modern Studies can be found at:

For you to do

- Examine the proposals for electoral changes to re-engage voters. How successful do you think each one will be? Give a reason for each of your decisions.
- Critically examine the issue of low turnout in elections in the UK.

STUDY THEME SUMMARY

Voters in the UK use a number of different voting systems for different elections. The First Past the Post system is used in UK General Elections and is a simple system, but can lead to very unfair election results where the numbers of seats won is not in proportion to the number of votes cast. This type of voting system makes it very hard for smaller parties and independents to win seats. Different types of Proportional Representation systems are used in other elections and produce results which give a better representation of minority parties.

Until recently, voting patterns were quite easy to predict, based on factors such as social class, age, gender and ethnicity. These factors are losing importance, and more prominence is being attached to issues and party leaders' personalities. There are also considerable regional differences in voting patterns.

People's voting intentions are influenced by the way the media present politics. TV is the most widely used and trusted form of media, and the use of election broadcasts during election campaigns can have significant impact on undecided voters. Most newspapers have a particular political stance, but this does not always dictate the way readers vote. Voter turnout is generally low in all UK elections, and various efforts are being made to improve this situation.

Exam-style essay questions

Critically examine the claim that Proportional Representation is a more democratic voting system than First Past the Post because it gives voters more choice and results in a more representative Parliament.

Assess the importance of different factors on voting behaviour.

To what extent does the media influence political attitudes and voting behaviour?

Social Issues in the United Kingdom

STUDY THEME 2:
Wealth and health inequalities in the UK

In this study theme you will be expected to have a detailed knowledge and understanding of:

- Evidence of inequalities in wealth and health; causes of inequalities in wealth and health; consequences of inequalities in wealth and health.

- ## WITH REFERENCE TO ETHNICITY AND GENDER

  The extent of social and economic inequalities; the nature and effect of government responses to deal with these inequalities.

- ## THE PRINCIPLES OF THE WELFARE STATE

  The debate over the provision of funding of health care and welfare; individual and collective responsibility.

SOCIAL CLASS

There are a number of formal and informal ways used to measure social class. The old simple distinctions of upper, middle and lower class are now not considered acceptable, and methods to measure class status include considerations of occupation, income, education and a number of other factors.

The Government has used several models to measure social class, including:

- the Registrar-General's Model of Social Class
- the National Statistics Socio-Economic Classification.

There are also sociologists' models, including:

- the Hope-Goldthorpe Scale
- Hutton's 30:30:40 model.

There are also informal ways of measuring social class which classify people according to buying habits and overall lifestyle, as used by:

- the Institute of Practitioners in Advertising
- the National Readership Survey.

The Registrar-General's Model of Social Class

The Registrar-General's Model of Social Class (RGSC) divides the population by occupation. It was used for most of the 20th century and many statistics are still presented this way. This model is very simple to use but because it is occupation-based, it misses out large sections of the population such as the unemployed, the elderly and spouses.

SOCIAL CLASS	EXAMPLE OCCUPATIONS	
A Professional occupations	Accountant, doctor, clergyman, university teacher	Middle class
B Intermediate occupations	Pilot, farmer, manager, police officer, teacher	
C1 Non-manual skilled occupations	Clerical, sales representative, shop assistant, secretary	
C2 Manual skilled occupations	Butcher, bus driver, electrician, miner	Lower class
D Partly skilled occupations	Bus conductor, bar person, postal worker	
E Unskilled occupations	Labourer, office cleaner, window cleaner	

The National Statistics Socio-Economic Classification

The National Statistics Socio-Economic Classification (NS SEC) was introduced in 2001, and covers most of the population. However, it is still based on occupation and misses out social and cultural influences as well as differences in income across the same status.

SOCIAL CLASS	EXAMPLE OCCUPATIONS
1.1 Large employers and higher managerial occupations	Company director, senior civil servant
1.2 Higher professional occupations	Doctor, lawyer, teacher
2 Lower managerial and professional occupations	Nurse, journalist, police
3 Intermediate occupations	Clerk, secretary
4 Small employers and own account workers	Publican, farmer, painter and decorator
5 Lower supervisory and technical occupations	Plumber, TV engineer, butcher
6 Semi-routine occupations	Shop worker, hairdresser, bus driver
7 Routine occupations	Labourer, waiter, refuse collector
8 Never worked and long-term unemployed	Non-working spouse, unemployed for various reasons

The Hope-Goldthorpe Scale

The Hope-Goldthorpe scale uses occupation to measure class, but also tries to reflect supervisory/management responsibility, so, for example, a supervisor of butchers would have higher status than a butcher.

SOCIAL CLASS	EXAMPLE OCCUPATIONS	
1 Higher grade professional	Company director, senior manager	Service class
2 Lower grade professional/administrator	Manager in small business, higher level supervisor	
3 Routine non-manual	Clerical, sales	Intermediate class
4 Small proprietor/self-employed	Small farmer, electrician, plumber	
5 Lower grade technician/supervisor	Lower level supervisor of manual workers	
6 Skilled manual	Electrician, butcher	Lower class
7 Semi-unskilled manual	Farm labourer	

Hutton's 30:30:40 Model

The Hutton model moves away from simply using occupation to measure class and brings in ideas such as gender but it is limited in value because it is too simple and the group categories are too broad.

SOCIAL CLASS	GROUP CHARACTERISTICS	
1 Advantaged	● Full-time or self-employed (held their job for 2 years) ● Part-time workers who have held their job for 5 years ● Strong and effective unions or professional associations ● Range of work-related benefits ● Mainly male workers	Top 40%
2 Newly Insecure	● Part-time and casual workers ● Declining employment protection and few benefits ● Large numbers of female workers ● Self-employed (especially manual workers) ● Fixed-term contract workers	Intermediate 30%
3 Disadvantaged	● Unemployed (especially long-term) ● Families caught in poverty trap (e.g. single parents) ● People on government employment schemes ● Casual part-time workers	Bottom 30%

Informal ways of measuring social class

There are a number of ways of measuring social class used by organisations other than government departments and sociologists. These have been designed specifically to meet the needs of particular organisations. One example is the **Institute of Practitioners in Advertising** (IPA) grouping. Unhelpfully, this uses the same classification labels as the RGSC, but the classifications themselves are different:

A Higher managerial, professional and administrative

B Middle management, professional and administrative

C1 Supervisory, clerical and junior management

C2 Skilled manual workers

D Semi and unskilled manual workers

E Pensioners, casual workers, unemployed.

Another informal method, the National Readership Survey (NRS) classifies certain groups according to lifestyle:

A Affluent achievers

B Thriving greys

C Settled suburbans

D Nest builders

E Urban ventures

F Country life

G Senior citizens

H Producers

I Hard-pressed families

J Have-nots

K Unclassifiable

Internet research

Visit the National Statistics website and read about the NS SEC classes. Think about where your parents and other adults you know would fit in the scale. Do you think the scale gives an accurate reflection of class? Links to this site and other websites relating to Higher Modern Studies can be found at:

www.leckieandleckie.co.uk by clicking on the Learning Lab button and navigating to the Higher Modern Studies Course Notes page.

MEASURING WEALTH

In order to make any meaningful comparisons, it's necessary to have agreed definitions of wealth, and to differentiate between an individual's wealth and a country's wealth.

Individual wealth

Wealth is a monetary measure of the assets a person owns and is accumulated over a person's lifetime. Most individual wealth in the UK is held in three forms:

- property
- savings
- pension rights.

In the UK, there is considerable inequality in individual wealth. In 2004, the richest 1% of the population owned 23% of the national wealth, and the richest 10% owned 54% of national wealth, while the poorest 50% owned just 5% of the national wealth.

A country's wealth

A country's wealth is measured in **gross national product** (GNP) or **gross domestic product** (GDP). GNP is a measure of a country's total economic activity over a period of time (usually a quarter or a year). It includes wealth brought into the country from overseas investments minus the profits from investments removed from the country by foreigners. GDP is a measure of the total economic activity within a country over a given period.

To make comparisons between the relative wealth or poverty of people who live in different countries, GNP and GDP are divided by the total population of the country to give GDP per head or GNP per head.

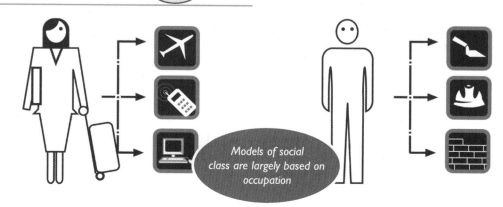

Models of social class are largely based on occupation

POVERTY

Poverty can be defined in different ways, and it is usual to distinguish between **absolute** poverty and **relative** poverty.

Absolute poverty

Absolute poverty was defined in 1995 by the UN as *'a condition characterised by severe deprivation of basic human needs, including food, safe drinking water, sanitation facilities, health, shelter, education and information. It depends not only on income but also on access to services.'*

Relative poverty

Relative poverty is measured by comparing the living standards of individual people against what is expected by society at a point in time.

Ways of measuring poverty

There are a number of ways of measuring poverty in the UK:

- Households Below Average Income
- Income Support levels
- the Poverty and Social Exclusion Survey.

Interestingly, the different methods say different things about poverty levels in the UK.

Households Below Average Income

This definition of poverty used by the UK Government is the income level which is **60% of the median income level**. Each year the Department of Social Security publishes statistics for poverty in the *Households Below Average Income* (HBAI) report.

The HBAI report calculates the median income for different families depending on the number in the household. The median income is the middle income which has half the households above and the other half below.

HBAI POVERTY LEVELS, 2003–04		
Family size	*Median weekly income*	*60% Median weekly income (poverty level)*
Couple, no children	£336	£201
Single, no children	£205	£123
Couple, 2 children aged 5 and 11	£490	£294
Single, 2 children aged 5 and 11	£359	£216

Income Support levels

Income Support is paid to people who are aged between 16 and 59 and who are not working because they are lone parents, registered sick or disabled, or care for someone who is sick or elderly. Each person's entitlement is calculated by measuring their circumstances against criteria laid down by statute. Income Support levels are determined by political decisions.

AVERAGE WEEKLY PAYMENTS MADE TO INCOME SUPPORT CLAIMANTS BY FAMILY TYPE (FEBRUARY 2005)				
All claimants	Single without dependants	Single with dependants	Couple without dependants	Couple with dependants
£86.66	£61.57	£105.50	£79.90	£137.62

Source: Department of Work and Pensions, 2005, Table IS 1.7

Poverty and Social Exclusion Survey

The Poverty and Social Exclusion (PSE) Survey was undertaken by teams from four universities and the Office of National Statistics. A representative sample of the population were asked to identify items from a prepared list that a British household should not be without. People were then asked to identify which items they had and those they did not have because they could not afford them.

More than half the population considered 35 items as essential. Over 90% of the population perceive 'beds and bedding for everyone', 'heating to warm living areas of the home', a 'damp-free home', 'visiting friends or family in hospital' and 'medicines prescribed by doctor' as items which British adults should have access to. Among the items that a significant number of people could not afford were replacing broken electrical equipment, home redecoration, savings of £10 per month, spending money on themselves, holidays and replacing worn out furniture.

A separate list was compiled for children. The top necessities were fresh fruit or vegetables, three meals a day, new properly fitted shoes, warm waterproof coat, celebrations on special occasions and books of their own.

The PSE identified four groups:

- poor
- those vulnerable to poverty
- those who have recently risen out of poverty
- those who are not poor.

People who lacked two or more of these essential items were classed as poor.

POVERTY LEVELS, 1999		
	Poor	*Not poor*
Equivalent weekly income (PSE scale)	£183	£382
Equivalent weekly income (HBAI scale)	£205	£409

The PSE Survey is different from other measures of poverty. Instead of using a statistical calculation to provide a value for the poverty line, it analyses and measures **social perceptions** of what poverty and social exclusion mean and then measures the extent to which society suffers from these things. Similar surveys were carried out in 1983 and 1990 (under the name *Breadline Britain*) and comparison between these surveys enables trends in poverty to be identified.

Internet research

Visit the Joseph Rowntree Foundation website for more information on the PSE Survey.
Visit the websites of the Department for Work and Pensions (DWP) and Income Support to get up-to-date figures on poverty levels to use in essays.
Links to these sites and other websites relating to Higher Modern Studies can be found at:

For you to do

- Draw up a table that compares the different measures of poverty.

CHANGES IN CLASS STRUCTURE

OCCUPATIONAL CLASS IN GREAT BRITAIN 1911–1991 (% OF EMPLOYMENT)		
	1911	*1991*
Managers and administrators	3.4	15.1
Higher professions	1.0	5.3
Lower professions	3.1	13.9
Employers and proprietors	6.7	3.3
Clerical workers	4.5	15.4
Foremen, supervisors	1.3	3.8
Sales	5.4	5.6
Manual workers	74.6	37.7

Source: Skill Change and the Labour Market: Gender, class and unemployment by Duncan Gallie, 2000

The class structure in Great Britain changed enormously in the 20th century. Between 1911 and 1991 the number of **manual workers** fell from three quarters of all workers to just over one third. Over the same period there was a large increase in the numbers involved in **middle class occupations** (managerial, professional and clerical). This trend has continued since 1991.

Another structural change has been in the number of women participating in the workforce. In 1911, fewer than 30% of women were in employment and so women were placed in the same social class as their husbands. Today nearly half of all workers are women. Most of these women work in service industries and professional occupations. The modern class structure based on occupation is more relevant because it includes more of the population.

POVERTY IN THE UK

Compared with a life of poverty in a developing country, poverty in the UK might seem like an overstatement, but for the people affected, the impact on their lives can be very severe. A life in poverty means that standards of health, education, and employment are all impaired, and it is very hard to move out of poverty.

Reasons for changing levels of poverty

Levels of poverty in the UK have changed considerably over time, for a range of reasons. Actual levels of income and spending capacity are affected by economic change, which is related to Government policy. Government policies also have an impact on levels of support for poor people. Membership of the European Union has also had an effect through its social and economic policies.

Changing social expectations

The PSE Survey shows that society has changed its expected living standards. Items such as refrigerators, deep freezes, washing machines and TVs were once seen as luxuries, but are now seen as necessities.

Essential items in a modern kitchen were considered luxuries 50 years ago

Consequently **relative poverty is rising** as society expects more. The PSE Survey found that the proportion of households living in poverty increased from 14% in 1983 to 21% in 1990 to over 24% in 1999, partly due to increasing social expectations.

Economic change

As the structure of the economy changes the levels of poverty are affected. As technology develops, products appear and disappear, and **international competition** affects our economy. People find themselves unemployed or in new jobs, either gaining new skills or becoming deskilled, or in higher paid or lower paid employment. All of these changes have an impact on the levels of poverty in a country.

Changes in the **global economy** also have far-reaching consequences on poverty. The increased use of oil pushes up prices for oil and gas for UK consumers and increases the price of manufacturing. Competition from Eastern Europe, the Far East, China and India for cheap labour has led to job losses in the UK.

Economic changes in the UK and internationally affect unemployment levels

Government policy

Government collects tax and decides which groups receive **welfare benefits** and how much they get. It decides whether or not to have a **National Minimum Wage** and what level it is to be set at. It decides the level of state pensions and at what age they can be accessed.

The Government influences the economy in its policies towards industries through **taxation**, **support** and **procurement**. The Government has huge **spending power** in areas such as Defence, Health and Education, and can seriously influence the economy of the UK as a whole or regions within the country by how much and where it places its orders.

EU Membership

Membership of the European Union has had a significant effect on poverty in the UK. Through its social and economic policies, it has **provided benefits** but also **created problems** for the UK economy and its citizens. Scottish fishermen have lost jobs as a result of fishing quotas, while regions such as the Highlands have benefited from funding to improve the infrastructure which has brought employment and wealth to the region.

For you to do

- Draw a diagram to summarise the main reasons for poverty.
- Make a list of items you consider to be essential in your household. How many of these are included in the PSE Survey? Consider whether you think the PSE Survey gives good coverage of essential items. Are there items which you think should be added to or taken off the PSE list of essential items?

Extent of poverty in the UK

The extent of poverty in the UK depends on the measure used. However, both the HBAI definition of poverty and the PSE Survey indicate that around a quarter of the UK population are poor.

POVERTY LEVELS IN THE UK POPULATION, 1999	
Poverty level	*%*
Poor	25.6
Vulnerable to poverty	10.3
Recently risen out of poverty	1.8
Not poor	62.2

Source: PSE Survey

FACT

People also faced varying degrees of poverty:

- 9.5 million people could not afford to keep their homes adequately heated, damp free or reasonably decorated
- 8 million could not afford essential household items such as fridges, telephones and carpets or to replace worn out or broken furniture
- 7.5 million people cannot afford to participate in social activities such as visiting friends and family, attending weddings and funerals, or having celebrations on special occasions
- one third of British children go without at least one of the things they need, like three meals a day, toys, out-of-school activities or adequate clothing; 18% go without two or more of these items
- 6.5 million adults go without essential clothing and about 4 million cannot afford a diet which has fresh fruit and vegetables and two meals a day
- over 10.5 million people cannot afford to save, insure their house contents or spend even small amounts of money on themselves.

Poverty rates are higher amongst:

- women
- children
- adults living in one-person households, including single pensioners
- large families
- families with a child under 11
- young people
- those who left school at age 16 or under
- households with no paid workers
- separated/divorced households
- lone parent households
- local authority and housing association tenants
- households dependent on Income Support.

Different groups of people are more vulnerable to poverty than others

The groups vulnerable to poverty are changing. Since 1997, the Government has targeted pensioners and families with dependent children, and as a result of such policies, there are now 700,000 fewer children and 500,000 fewer pensioners living in poverty. However, the number of working-age adults without dependent children living in poverty has increased by 300,000.

For you to do

- Poverty affects few in the UK and is mainly caused by unemployment. Discuss.

CAUSES OF INEQUALITIES IN WEALTH

There are a range of factors which lead to inequalities in wealth across the population. Government policies can have significant impact on levels of employment and social inclusion. Other factors such as gender, race, age, and location will all have an impact on wealth.

Government policy

Government can use a number of policy initiatives to address wealth inequalities. There will be different initiatives for those who are employed, and those who are not employed (or are in low-paid employment). For people in employment, the main policy areas of concern are **taxation**, **employment law** and general **economic policy**, while for those not in work, or in low-paid work, **benefit policy** will be of prime concern.

Taxation policy

The level of taxation affects people's income. If the tax burden is high then people will either have less income (due to high levels of income tax and/or national insurance) or be able to buy less because the price of goods has been increased (through VAT and excise duties). The **burden of taxation** can be shifted between groups in society such as between the rich and the poor.

Direct taxation in the UK is much lower than in our European neighbours, as is the level of Corporation Tax that companies have to pay. However, the overall burden of tax is higher in the UK because we pay far more in **indirect taxation** through VAT and excise duties. This reduces the tax burden on the rich who would pay more in income tax and puts more of the burden on to the poor who have to pay a higher percentage of their income in indirect taxes such as VAT.

The introduction of **Working Tax Credit** has helped reduce the effect of income tax on those workers in the poorest paid jobs in the UK.

Benefit policy

Governments decide benefit levels and on which groups to target benefits. In recent years benefit levels have been allowed to fall behind the increases in earnings in the UK making those dependent on benefits relatively poorer. Some sections of the population such as **pensioners** and **children** have seen some of their **benefits increased** or new ones introduced that have helped lift some of them out of poverty.

Economic policies

Government can take actions to stimulate the economy in order to reduce unemployment and reduce poverty or they can make decisions that will create higher unemployment. These economic policies will also lead to changes in interest rates (set by the Bank of England) and this will make lending from banks and building societies more expensive or less expensive which will then increase or reduce poverty.

Employment laws

Over the past 20 years governments have altered the laws regarding employment and trade union activity which has made it easier for employers to dismiss workers and more difficult for trade unions to protect workers' rights and win higher wages. More recently, the EU has forced the Government to take actions to protect workers. The Labour Government has introduced **Minimum Wage legislation** which has helped **raise income levels**. Women and ethnic minorities have been helped by **equal rights and discrimination legislation**.

Unemployment

In April 2006, 5.3% of the UK population or 1.6 million people were unemployed and the trend was increasing. Unemployment is caused by a variety of factors. There are **large-scale economic and political factors** that affect the nation or regions and there are **personal reasons** which affect individuals.

Economic and political factors include:

● structural and technological changes
● Government policies (already mentioned)
● competition and world trade
● European Union policies.

Factors that affect individuals include:

● education
● lifestyle choices.

Structural and technological changes

The economy is constantly changing. Over the course of the 20th century the economy has seen the decline of heavy industry such as coal mining and ship building and the rise of light industry such as motor car manufacturing. Primary industry and secondary industries have declined in importance while the tertiary or service sector of the economy has become the most important contributor to GDP. This is **structural change**.

SECTORS OF THE ECONOMY	WHAT THEY DO	EXAMPLES
Primary	Extract raw materials	agriculture, forestry, fishing, mining
Secondary (or manufacturing)	Process raw materials into useful products	shipbuilding, computer assembly
Tertiary (or service)	Provide services to improve living standards	banks, shops, call centres

Structural change often occurs as a consequence of **technological change**. As new products and processes are developed, jobs are created in new areas and lost in others. Heavy manufacturing has declined and has been replaced by the electronic manufacturing and the service sector. Robots have replaced assembly-line workers in many factories. Digital cameras have caused photo developing factories to close and hence created employment in one area and reduced it elsewhere.

Competition and world trade

The UK is part of a **global economy** and UK unemployment is affected by events and activities in other areas of the world. When UK companies set up call centres in India where labour costs are much lower, it creates unemployment in the UK. When foreign produced goods such as footwear, clothing and electronic goods are produced far more cheaply in China, it creates unemployment in the UK. **Foreign competition** has had a significant impact on many British industries such as textiles and coal mining, resulting in unemployment.

The global economy goes through cycles of boom and recession. These changes may be caused by events such as wars. For example, the uncertainty brought about by the war in Iraq forced up the world price of oil which had an impact on manufacturing costs that could create unemployment. In the late 1990s problems in the Japanese economy led to a recession in the world economy which then led to unemployment in the UK.

Problems with global warming and other natural disasters can create nervousness in international stock exchanges. World trade is built on confidence and if international stock exchanges show signs of nervousness, it can start a fall in stock and commodity prices that will lead to recession. UK employment levels are affected by the **world trade cycle** and **natural and man-made international events**.

European Union policies

European Union policies can have a major impact on British industries. For example, the **Common Fisheries Policy,** which introduced landing quotas and restricted fishing days has led to a serious **decline in employment** in the fishing industry in North-East Scotland. By contrast, other policies such as the European **Regional Development Fund** and the **Social Fund** have helped to reduce unemployment in various parts of the UK by **developing the infrastructure** and assisting with retraining schemes to help rebuild industrial blackspots.

Internet research

Visit the website of BBC News to find up-to-date examples of Government changes, global events or EU policies that have created employment or unemployment.
Visit the Direct Government website to find more detailed information on Government and taxation. Links to these sites and other websites relating to Higher Modern Studies can be found at:

For you to do

- Design a diagram or table to summarise how government policies and international events can influence inequalities in wealth.

Education

Education has a significant impact on rates of employment in the UK. The higher the level of education the more likely a person is to be in employment.

EMPLOYMENT RATE BY HIGHEST QUALIFICATION, 2005	
Qualification	**%**
Degree or equivalent	88
Higher education	85
GCE A level or equivalent	77
Trade apprenticeship	81
GCSE grades A* to C or equivalent	75
Qualifications at NVQ level 1 and below	69
No qualifications	48

Source: *Social Trends 36*

Lifestyle choices

Lifestyle choices can make a person unemployable. Alcohol abuse or drugs misuse can lead to serious underperformance and make a person a liability in dangerous or hazardous working environments. Ill health brought on by obesity can mean a person is unable to continue working. Coronary heart disease or osteoarthritis resulting from obesity can prevent a person from being able to work.

For you to do

- Describe the main causes of unemployment in the UK.

Low pay

Low pay is concentrated in specific sectors of the population. Despite equal opportunities legislation, **women** are still often paid less than men for equivalent jobs. **Certain sectors of the economy**, such as catering and cleaning, are poorly paid. Some **regions** of the country have little well-paid employment. The **low pay–no pay** cycle amongst unskilled workers is a recurring issue for many.

People who live in households where at least one person is employed account for 40% of those living in poverty. Low wage poverty has increased in the UK over the past decade. In Scotland in 2004, the median gross weekly income for full-time employees was £392.70, but for those in the bottom 10%, it was less than £220.90 per week (while at top end of the scale, the top 10% earned more than £742.40 per week).

Women are more likely to be employed in low paid jobs than men. This is partly due to their role as carers for the young, sick or elderly which prevents them developing careers and requires them to find part-time employment or low paid work that has suitable hours. This forces many women into low paid sectors of the economy such as sales, catering, cleaning, etc.

The median income for women was about £75 per week less than for men. The lowest paid sector of the economy is 'sales occupations' in which people earn £245 per week. Other areas of low pay are personal services such as health care and child care, hotel and restaurant sectors. Women comprise **80% of low paid workers in the public sector**.

Another factor affecting pay rates is **geography**. Some regions of the UK, such as the North-East of England, have more low paid employment than others. The median income for London is £556 and the South-East of England is £450 whereas in the North-East of England it is £386. In Scotland, rural areas such as the Borders and Moray have the highest levels of low paid workers whereas in the cities such as Aberdeen and Edinburgh the proportions of low paid workers are lower.

One reason for low pay in rural areas is the nature and availability of employment. Work is often seasonal in nature (in agriculture and tourism) and in sectors that are traditionally low paid. There are also fewer jobs available so the employers do not have to increase wages to compete for workers.

Finally the **no pay–low pay** cycle affects people in low paid jobs, who face much greater job insecurity than those in better paid work. Many unemployed people have no skills, are much less likely to receive training and therefore can only get a foothold on the employment ladder in very insecure employment. About **40% of those in low paid employment** are not in the same job six months later. Job insecurity leads to low self-esteem, stress and ill health which adds to the problems finding and holding down a job.

For you to do

- Thinking about the social classes defined earlier in this theme, do you think unemployment affects all groups equally?
- What geographical factors in your area affect local employment?

Social exclusion

Social exclusion describes the general conditions that surround poverty. It is the result of economic and social changes that have occurred in UK society in the last 50 years. Conditions contributing to social exclusion include **long-term unemployment**, the increase in **separation**, **divorce** and **lone parenthood**, and the increase in **anonymity** and **social isolation** in urban areas as neighbourhood and social networks decline.

Social exclusion includes:

- exclusion from a **decent standard of living**
- exclusion from the **labour market**
- exclusion from **services**
- exclusion from **social relations**.

Exclusion from a decent standard of living

People who live in poverty cannot afford a decent **standard of living**. Many do not have a good diet with fresh food and a suitable balance of meat, fish, fruit and vegetables. They cannot afford appropriate clothing and they often live in substandard housing. They cannot afford to furnish or decorate it or provide the heat to give their children a separate room to study in. (See pages 114–115 to remind yourself about the nature of poverty in the UK.)

Single parent and child

Exclusion from the labour market

People who are excluded from the labour market due to lifestyle choice, ill health or disability, lack of skills, having to care for others or old age have a high risk of living on a low income. While many low income employees face social exclusion and many who are not in work have sufficient income to have a comfortable life, labour market exclusion remains an important risk factor for exclusion from other aspects of life.

Exclusion from services

Poverty leads people to be at risk of being excluded from services. Some people may not be able to **attend hospital** or **access a doctor's surgery** if they cannot afford the transport or if there is no provision in their area. Some families may not be able to **access education** because they cannot afford the necessary equipment or lack adequate accommodation for study and rest.

As many as one person in 14 are excluded from essential public or private services. The **non-availability** of services is a much larger problem than **affordability**. Over 5% of the population have been disconnected from water, gas, electricity or telephone and more than 10% use less than they need because they cannot afford it.

Exclusion from social relations

One fifth (20%) of the population is excluded from three or more social activities such as visiting friends and relations or celebrating special occasions such as birthdays because of affordability. One person in eight has no friend or relation outwith their household that they meet on a daily basis.

lone parent families spend less on themselves than almost any other group of people in the UK.

Longevity

Women **live longer** than men but they earn less during their working lives and as a consequence have **fewer savings** or make **fewer contributions** to provide for a pension in their retirement. Women's poverty extends into their old age. A considerable proportion have no pensions in their own right because they have spent their lives as carers rather than as earners or their careers have been curtailed by family or they were divorced. They are forced to depend on means-tested benefits in their old age. Female poverty is deeper and longer than male poverty.

Internet research

Visit the Equal Opportunities Commission website to find up-to-date information on the relationship between gender and poverty.
Links to this site and other websites relating to Higher Modern Studies can be found at:

For you to do

- Using information from the Equal Opportunities Commission website, make notes on the differences between men and women which are related to poverty. Remember to look for factors other than just income and employment.

Race

Race, or ethnic origin, contributes to wealth inequalities in the UK. Some ethnic groups are at **higher risk of poverty** than others, while issues of **culture** and **education** have an impact on employment undertaken, and hence on income. Despite legislation, ethnic workers still suffer from **discrimination**. Poorly educated members of ethnic groups are at a particular **economic disadvantage** when the national economy is in decline.

RISK OF BEING ON LOW INCOME* BASED ON ETHNIC CHARACTERISTICS, 2004/05	
Ethnic group	%
White	18
Indian	30
Pakistani/Bangladeshi	52
Black Caribbean	25
Black non-Caribbean	45
Chinese	36
* Defined as 60% below median income after housing costs.	

Source: DWP – HBAI

Risk of poverty

Members of different ethnic minority communities are all at a **higher risk of poverty** than the majority white community. Overall the greatest level of poverty is to be found in the Pakistani and Bangladeshi communities who have poverty rates nearly three times that of the white community. The lowest rate of poverty among ethnic minority groups is in the black Caribbean community, but this rate of poverty is still 40% higher than the rate for white people.

Culture

There are a range of cultural issues which affect ethnic groups in different ways. Pakistanis and Bangladeshis are mainly Muslim and have a strong belief in a family structure in which the **woman looks after the home and children and the man is the breadwinner**. Generally they want to have larger than average families. As a consequence, a large number of children and only one person working, very often in low paid employment, means that a high proportion of households have incomes below the HBAI median income level.

Within the Caribbean community the prevailing culture is moving away from marriage as the basis of people's relationships often leaving women with the **sole responsibility for bringing up children**. About 34% of the poor in the Caribbean population are in single parent households compared with 24% in the general UK population. However, a higher proportion of Caribbean women work full-time than white women and they have higher levels of income.

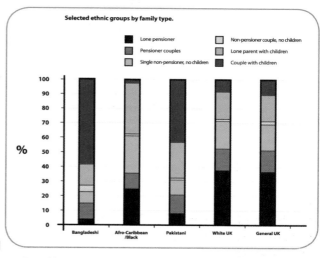

Selected ethnic groups by family type.

Legend: Lone pensioner, Pensioner couples, Single non-pensioner, no children, Non-pensioner couple, no children, Lone parent with children, Couple with children

Source: Race, Place and Poverty: Ethnic groups and low income distribution by Michael Noble and Lucinda Platt, Joseph Rowntree Foundation

Education

Income and employment often depend on educational attainment. Pakistani and Bangladeshi men and women have significantly **lower qualifications** than other groups, and 40% of Bangladeshi males and 49% of Bangladeshi women have no qualifications. Therefore they are at a disadvantage in the labour market and have to depend on low income employment or benefits. Pakistani and Bangladeshi households receive a large proportion of their incomes from **mean-tested benefits**.

However, the educational attainment in the Indian and Chinese communities is significantly higher than for whites. Culturally these communities **value**

HIGHEST QUALIFICATION HELD: BY SEX AND ETHNIC GROUP, 2004 GREAT BRITAIN (%)						
	Qualification					
	Degree or equivalent	Higher education	GCE A level or equivalent	GCSE grades A* to C or equivalent	Other qualification	No qualification
Males						
White British	18	8	30	19	10	14
Indian	30	6	17	11	22	15
Pakistani	15	4	15	16	22	29
Bangladeshi	11	2	10	12	25	40
Black Caribbean	11	6	26	24	15	18
Black African	24	9	18	14	25	12
Chinese	33	4	13	10	21	19
Females						
White British	16	10	19	29	10	16
Indian	21	6	16	16	24	18
Pakistani	10	4	14	20	18	35
Bangladeshi	5	2	12	17	15	49
Black Caribbean	15	13	16	33	14	10
Black African	17	9	15	15	26	18
Chinese	29	6	10	8	26	21

Source: Annual Population Survey, Office for National Statistics

education highly and therefore they are increasingly employed in higher skilled employment. The Indian community have high levels of employment, and their earnings are close to those of white workers. Although overall their rates of poverty are higher than for white households, these groups are prospering.

Discrimination

Individuals from ethnic minority communities continue to have to overcome the barrier of **discrimination**. Recently, researchers have shown that ethnic minority applicants who had similar CVs, applying for the same jobs, were asked to attend interviews less often than a white applicant. Employment tribunals continue to make judgements against employers for race discrimination in the workplace. Public Attitude Surveys such as the Home Office Citizenship Survey report that ethnic minorities and the public generally feel race discrimination is still a problem in employment. Fluency in the language, particularly in first generation immigrants, is often a problem and may lead to greater discrimination.

REASONS FOR BEING REFUSED A JOB, BY ETHNIC GROUP, 2005				
Reasons	*White*	*Asian*	*Black*	*Mixed race*
Race	2	20	27	24
Religion	1	10	2	–
Colour	1	13	25	8
Respondents who had been refused a job in last 5 years	717	338	334	77

Source: 2005 Home Office Citizenship Survey

Internet research

Visit the website of the Commission for Racial Equality to find case studies of discrimination.
Links to this site and other websites relating to Higher Modern Studies can be found at: **LECKIE&LECKIE Learning Lab**

Economic disadvantage

Without qualifications, Pakistanis and Bangladeshis are particularly vulnerable to **changes in the economy**. Unskilled workers are always the first to be fired in an economic downturn and the last to be hired when the economy improves. Many are stuck in the no pay–low pay cycle. Businesses are often situated at some distance from housing and without private transport many find it difficult to commute to and from work as the journey times on public transport, if it is available, would be too long.

Pakistani and Bangladeshi communities are concentrated in regions that have experienced some of the worst economic declines in the UK in recent years, so many have experienced long-term unemployment. They also report 50% more health problems than the rest of the community so are more likely to be off work and lose income (and possibly employment).

Age

Both the **young** and the **old** are vulnerable to poverty. Government policies since 1997 have been successful in reducing the numbers of children and old people who live in poverty. Despite these targeted policies, significant proportions of both groups still face poverty in their daily lives.

Children

The HBAI Report indicated there were 3.5 million children living in households with below 60% of median household income. This represents a fall of 700,000 since 1997. These figures represent **27% of all children**. However, children in different categories face different levels of risk.

Children who were at particular risk were in **lone-parent families**, children of couples where the **parents are unemployed** or work only part-time, those in **families with three or more children**, or where either **a parent or a child is disabled**.

The impact of low income on children is far reaching. **Diet** and **health** can suffer. They are less likely to enjoy a balanced diet with sufficient fruit and vegetables and this will have an impact on their health. Living in **substandard housing** will also have a serious impact on health. Poor children living in damp houses have a higher than average risk of suffering from asthma and report twice the rate of long-standing illnesses. They are lighter at birth and grow shorter in height.

Poor children do less well at school. They cannot afford to participate in all activities, take more time off through ill health and do not achieve the same level of **qualifications** as children from more affluent homes.

For you to do

● Draw a mind-map to show the different factors which contribute to poverty amongst ethnic minorities in the UK.

FAMILY TYPE	PERCENTAGE OF CHILDREN IN POVERTY
Lone parent	48
Working part-time	13
Working full-time	27
Not working	72
Couple with children	20
Both working full time	2
One full-time one part-time	6
One full-time one not working	21
Neither working	72
Number of children	23
One	23
Two	30
Three	50
No disabled adults	25
One or more disabled adults	40
No disabled children	27
One or more disabled child	30
White	25
Mixed	39
Asian	47
Indian	33
Pakistani / Bangladeshi	57
Black	43
Chinese	44
All children	27

Source: DWP – HBAI

This disadvantage continues into adult life where, through lack of qualifications, they are at greater risk of **ill health,** are part of the **no pay–low pay** cycle and become involved in **alcohol** or **substance abuse**. They are more likely to become involved in **crime** and **the penal system** and end up in **abusive relationships**.

Poor children have a higher than average chance of ending up as poor adults and find it increasingly difficult to escape this cycle of deprivation, so pass the constraints on to the next generation.

Pensioners

In 2003/04, there were 2.0 million pensioners living in households with less than 60% of median household income. The risk of pensioners living in poverty is increased if they are **female**, as they get **older** and if they **do not claim benefits**.

RISK OF PENSIONER POVERTY	
Characteristic	*Pensioners in poverty (%)*
Pensioner couples	61
Single pensioners	39
Male	8
70 and under	2
71 to 75	2
75 and over	4
Female	31
70 and under	10
71 to 75	5
75 and over	16
Gender	
Male	35
Female	65
Benefits received	
Disability Living allowance	5
Attendance Allowance	4
Pension Credit	22
Housing Benefit	17
No Benefit	63

Source: DWP – HBAI

Pensioner poverty has fallen since 1997 because the Government has targeted help on this group. It has fallen from 2.7 million in 1997 to 2.0 million in 2005. In 2006, the state pension was £84.25 per week for a single person and £134.75 for a couple. However, the Family Budget Unit suggests that a single pensioner needs around £125 per week to pay for the basics of a healthy diet and adequate heating. The state pension is the single most important source of income for pensioners, so an inadequate pension causes pensioners to suffer from poverty.

Until 1980, increases in the state pension were linked to increases in **average earnings**, so pensioners kept pace with the increases in living standards. After this link was abolished, the falling value of the state pension meant increasing numbers of the elderly were allowed to drift into poverty in retirement.

Pensioners with company pension schemes or private pensions have some protection from poverty but this is subject to some uncertainty. The cost of final salary schemes has been a problem for many companies and for many employees the value of their final pension is not guaranteed. Women are less likely to have access to such pensions; 50% of men have access to a non-state pension but only 25% of women have alternative pension provisions. Women who have not worked would also have made insufficient National Insurance contributions to entitle them to a full pension (or indeed any pension at all).

Most pensioners who have lived in poverty through their lives, have had no option but to depend on the state pension in retirement. The jobs they had did not provide a pension and they were not able to afford a private pension. They are forced to rely on what little savings they have or apply for means-tested benefits to raise their living standards.

In order to avoid poverty in retirement, many women are reliant on means-tested benefits, but these entitlements are often not claimed in full because of the complexity of the system and because of personal pride.

Internet research

Visit the websites of Help the Aged, Age Concern and the Family Budget Unit to find up-to-date information, statistics and case studies on the impact of poverty on the elderly and families with children.

Links to these sites and other websites relating to Higher Modern Studies can be found at:

For you to do

- Draw a flow-chart showing the factors which affect children born in low income households. Think about the ways in which child poverty can lead to a cycle of poverty.
- What are the factors which make female pensioners more likely to experience poverty than male pensioners?

Geography

Poverty levels are not the same in all regions of the UK. Poverty is greater in the North of England, Scotland and Wales than it is in the London and the South-East of England. Differing levels of unemployment are significant, with the unemployment rate in Scotland being 5.2% at the end of 2004, compared with 4.9% for the whole of the UK. The North–South divide is highlighted by other indicators, such as income levels and house prices, which are higher in London and the South-East of England, while levels of ill health are worse in the North of England and Scotland.

Many would argue that there is no North–South divide. They point to the fact that poverty exists side by side in all areas of the UK. London has six of the poorest boroughs in the UK despite being the wealthiest city. In Scotland there is a wide gulf between the richest constituency in Edinburgh and the poorest in Glasgow.

The average income in the poorest constituency in Glasgow is approximately half that of the richest in Edinburgh while the poorest has four times as many Income Support claimants. There are more than double the number of home owners in the richest constituency and twice as many car owners. The poverty is underlined in the figures for life expectancy. Life expectancy for men is 13 years more in the richest constituency while only just over half of 15 year olds in the poor constituency can expect to reach their 65th birthday.

The Scottish Index of Multiple Deprivation shows that pockets of wealth and poverty exist side by side throughout Scotland. Areas of West Central Scotland including Glasgow City, West Dumbartonshire and Inverclyde suffer the greatest concentrations of multiple deprivation with parts of Shettleston experiencing some of the worst deprivation in the UK.

The areas that are most deprived coincide with areas of low income work and unemployment. Many of the poorest areas in the UK are economic blackspots where large proportions of the population have poor skills or qualifications. Health is poor and there is a high incidence of anti-social behaviour and alcohol and drug abuse. Individuals become enmeshed in a cycle of deprivation and a way of life from which it is difficult to break out. It is this combination of economic conditions and social problems that develop over time to create inequalities in various areas throughout the UK.

Internet research

Visit the websites of the Scottish Index of Multiple Deprivation and the National Policy Institute to get more up-to-date information on regional variations in poverty throughout the UK.
Links to these sites and other websites relating to Higher Modern Studies can be found at:

For you to do

- Draw a mind-map of all the factors contributing to inequalities in wealth throughout the UK. Show the interrelationships between the different factors.
- What are the main causes of social exclusion in the UK?
- The gap between the rich and poor in the UK will only get bigger. Discuss.
- Describe the economic and social causes of unemployment/poverty in the UK.

CAUSES OF INEQUALITIES IN HEALTH

There are major inequalities in health across the population. Factors which affect health inequalities include physical factors such as age, ethnicity and gender, and cultural and social issues such as lifestyle, employment and income, social exclusion and location.

Age

There is a gradient of reported ill health as people grow older. The most healthy people, both male and female, are those in the 16–45 age range. The **least healthy people are those over 65**. As people age they begin to experience increasing ill health either through long-term illness or disability. Only 3% of children under five have chronic conditions whereas the figure for those over 90 is 75%.

As people age the body begins to wear out and becomes increasingly slow and unable to repair itself. People take or are able to take **less physical activity** than they once did.

The effects of a lifetime of work, physical activity and consumption begin to take their toll as people age. Working in **physically demanding conditions** may lead to problems with worn joints and stress problems in areas such as the spine. If the atmosphere people breathed was polluted then they may have problems with breathing or cancer.

PROPORTION OF POPULATION REPORTING 'GOOD' STATE OF GENERAL HEALTH: BY SEX AND AGE, 2001/02						
	Males			Females		
	16–44	45–64	65 or over	16–44	45–64	65 or over
England	73	56	38	69	54	37
Wales	66	53	32	72	53	25
Scotland	68	53	36	66	59	39
Northern Ireland	72	48	31	66	47	26

Source: General Household Survey, Office for National Statistics; Continuous Household Survey, Northern Ireland Statistics and Research Agency

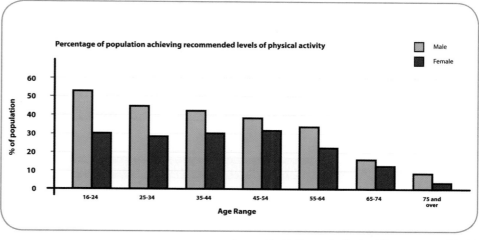

Source: Health Survey for England, Department of Health

Sports injuries may lead to increasingly painful conditions. Those who smoked may suffer a variety of problems with breathing, heart or cancer. Overconsumption of alcohol may create problems with the liver as well as loss of brain cells affecting mental processes.

As people grow old, it is more likely they will develop **mobility problems** due to arthritis, and will develop problems with their **eyesight**. **Dementia** is a major problem, with over 700,000 dementia sufferers in the UK, of whom 98% are over the age of 65.

For you to do

• Think about the old people you know, like your grandparents, and consider whether they have age-related health problems. Are their problems only related to their age, or are they also related to other issues like work, diet, smoking, exercise, etc?

As a result, we place greater demands on NHS services as we get older. Those aged 75 and over have demand levels that are twice the average: 25% of the over-75s attend hospital compared with just 14% of the general population. The elderly also need to have personal services provided for them such as help with washing, eating and taking medicine.

In the UK more elderly people die from hypothermia than in many neighbouring countries such as Finland and Germany which have considerably harsher winter climates. Even in the city of Yakutsk in Siberia, where temperatures plummet to -40°C, there are fewer deaths than Britain in winter. Elderly people are particularly susceptible to the cold especially if they keep their heating turned down because they are poor. It is estimated that 30,000 people die each year from hypothermia and Age Concern estimates that every time the temperature drops 1°C below average, 8,000 more elderly people will die.

Race

Race, or ethnicity, has a role to play in health inequalities. Some races are more susceptible to certain diseases than others. Levels of infant mortality are affected by ethnicity. Cultural differences such as smoking and alcohol consumption have an impact, and social issues such as poverty, harassment and discrimination also generate differences in standards of health.

PERCENTAGE OF PEOPLE WITH A LONG-TERM ILLNESS: BY AGE AND ETHNIC GROUP, ENGLAND AND WALES CENSUS, 2001					
Age	White (%)	Asian/Asian British (%)	Black/Black British (%)	Mixed (%)	Chinese/Other ethnic group (%)
0-15	4	4	5	5	3
16-49	10	10	10	11	5
50-64	26	40	34	32	22
All people aged 65 and over	51	60	54	49	48

Source: Commission for Racial Equality

PEOPLE REPORTING 'NOT GOOD HEALTH': BY ETHNIC GROUP AND AGE IN ENGLAND AND WALES, 2001				
	50-64		16-64	
	Male (%)	Female (%)	Male (%)	Female (%)
White	15.3	14.2	8.0	8.2
Indian	18.3	25.2	6.9	9.4
Pakistani	28.9	36.1	9.6	12.2
Bangladeshi	34.0	32.9	9.2	10.8
Black Caribbean	21.4	24.0	8.7	10.9
African	12.0	16.6	4.5	5.8
Chinese	10.3	10.3	3.2	4.1

Source: Review of the occupational health and safety of Britain's ethnic minorities

Asians report greater levels of ill health than other groups in the population. Black Caribbeans are also more likely to report 'not good health'. Africans and Chinese are less likely than the general population to report poor health. However, it is only in the 50+ age group that there is any significant difference in long-term limiting illness between minorities and the majority population.

Diseases

Racial groups differ in their risk of suffering from certain diseases. **Diabetes** is a particular problem for Pakistanis and Bangladeshis who are over five times more likely to suffer from it than the general population. Indians of both genders are three times more at risk.

Pakistani and Bangladeshi men and women face a higher risk of **heart disease** than average whereas the Chinese face a lower than average risk. Black Caribbean women also face a higher risk. Diet has a significant part to play in these variations.

Infant mortality rates

Infant mortality rates are higher for **ethnic minority mothers born outwith the UK**. The infant mortality rate for mothers born in the UK was 7.8 in 2002, whereas it was 14.5 for mothers born in Pakistan and 15.4 for mothers born in the Caribbean.

Smoking

Bangladeshi men are more likely to smoke than any other group followed by black Caribbean men. However, Indian, Pakistani and in particular Chinese men are less likely to smoke compared to the general population.

Irish women are more likely to smoke than the general population, while Chinese, Indian, Pakistani and Bangladeshi women are less likely to smoke compared to the general population. Smoking has a significant impact on health, particularly in the rates for cancer and respiratory problems.

Alcohol consumption

The 1999 Health Survey for England found that members of all ethnic minority groups were less likely to drink alcohol than the general population, while those who did drink consumed smaller amounts. Only 7% of men in the general population were non-drinkers,

whereas 13% of black Caribbean men, 30% of Chinese men, 33% of Indian men, 91% of Pakistani men and 96% of Bangladeshi men did not consume alcohol.

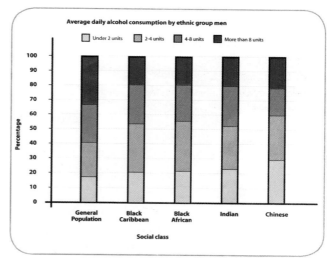

For women the figures were even higher: 12% of women in the general population did not consume alcohol whereas 18% of black Caribbean women, 41% of Chinese women, 64% of Indian women, 97% of Pakistani women and 99% of Bangladeshi women did not drink alcohol.

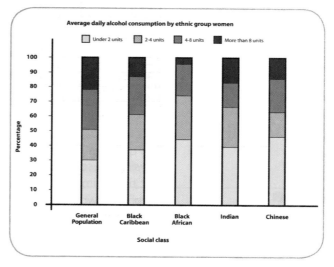

Poverty

Just as in the general population, poverty in ethnic groups has an important impact on health. Those groups that have incomes closest to the general population average, such as Indians, Africans, Asians and Chinese, record health levels close to the general levels. Those

Mortality rates differ

Men have higher mortality rates for a variety of common illnesses, such as lung cancer, heart disease, injuries and suicide. Men tend to develop heart disease 10 years earlier than women. Women are less likely to develop tuberculosis but are at greater risk of developing diabetes because of differences in their immune systems. Women are more likely to report illness at an earlier stage and are therefore more likely to make use of their doctor and be admitted to hospital.

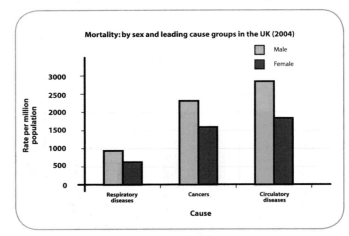

In the UK, the most common causes of death in both men and women are cancer and circulatory diseases. However, women are more likely than men to die from strokes when they are much older, while men get heart attacks at an earlier age. Women have higher death rates for conditions that are related to increasing age.

Health-related behaviour

Women tend to smoke less and consume less alcohol than men which is good for their general health, but they take less exercise than men which does not help.

In 2003 in England and Wales, twice as many men per 100,000 died from alcohol-related causes compared with women. In the previous year in Great Britain, the rate of lung cancer was 90% higher for men than for women.

Internet research

Visit the websites of the Department of Health and the Office for National Statistics and find the relative levels of smoking and alcohol consumption for men and women. Compare this with the incidence of lung cancer and alcohol-related diseases. Links to these sites and other websites relating to Higher Modern Studies can be found at:

Diet and obesity

Men tend to have a poorer approach to their diet than women. Across the income scale they consume less fruit and vegetables and their salt intake is significantly higher, resulting in health problems. About 64% of Scottish adult men and 57% of Scottish adult women are either overweight or obese. The higher percentage of obese men means that greater numbers of men are at risk from the effects of illnesses associated with being overweight.

Different living and working conditions

Men tend to be employed in more dangerous occupations than women so are more likely to die early from diseases or injuries connected with their work. Pressures on men from social expectations mean that they are more likely to suffer from health problems and death related to smoking, alcohol and fast driving.

Women are more likely than men to suffer from injuries sustained at home. In addition, women's traditional domestic responsibilities lead them to suffer from higher levels of anxiety and depression compared to males, particularly if they are poor and are lone parents.

Internet research

Visit the website of the Scottish Health Survey 2003 and see how your health compares with the averages for Scottish males and females.

Links to this site and other websites relating to Higher Modern Studies can be found at: **LECKIE&LECKIE** *Learning Lab*

For you to do

● Examine the differences in health problems people are more likely to suffer now or in older age because of gender?

Lifestyle and social class

Some factors in health inequalities are straightforward physical factors, such as gender, ethnicity and age, over which the individual has no choice. There are other factors which do result from individual choice, such as **lifestyle choices**, **diet and smoking** and personal circumstances, such as **unemployment** and **wealth**.

A person's lifestyle relates to their **social class**, whether or not they are **unemployed** and whether or not they suffer from **social exclusion**. The way of examining mortality is to calculate the Standard Mortality Ratio (SMR). If the figure is above 100, then the death rate

is higher than average, if it is lower than 100 then the death rate is lower than average. The chart shows that there are considerable differences in the SMR for men and women of different social classes, and those in lower social classes (D and E) are more at risk of disease and have a higher mortality ration than average.

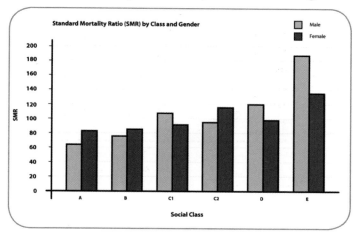

The higher mortality rate is due to a range of factors, including:

● poorer diets
● poor housing leading to illnesses as asthma and hypothermia
● increased rates of smoking.

The disadvantages start young. Mothers who do not have a good diet when they are pregnant or who smoke or abuse alcohol or drugs or who do not get sufficient medical attention during pregnancy are at greater risk of still births. When new-born infants are taken home they are at greater risk of hypothermia if they are going into a cold damp house or if they are looked after by inadequate parents. The mortality rate is double for infants whose parents are in social class E (unemployed, low income and socially excluded).

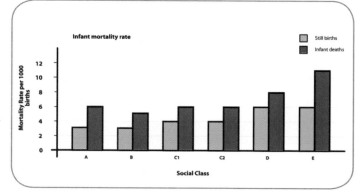

AIDS

Men and women who have unprotected sex with partners of either gender whose previous sexual experiences are unknown run the greatest risk of getting AIDS. Drug users who choose to share needles are also at risk. The lifestyle choices a person makes is a major factor affecting the quality of their health.

AIDS BY PROBABLE ROUTE OF INFECTION 2002							
	Sex between men	*Injecting drug use*	*Sex between men and women*	*Blood/blood products*	*Mother to infant*	*Other/not known*	*Total*
United Kingdom	14,522	1,285	13,005	495	1,038	1,516	31,861
Scotland	546	391	504	40	51	40	1,572

Sources: *adapted from Health Protection Agency Communicable Disease Surveillance Centre; Institute of Child Health (London); Scottish Centre for Infection and Environmental Health*

Lifestyle choices

People's health is affected by the myriad of lifestyle choices that are there to be made. Smoking, alcohol, exercise, diet, dangerous recreational activities, foreign travel and many other factors have a major impact on the health of an individual. AIDS is a good example of how lifestyle choices can put a person at risk of ill health.

Diet

People from lower social class groups do not eat as healthily as those from higher groups. They tend to eat more fried foods, and eat less wholemeal bread, fruit and vegetables. This will lead to those in lower social classes having more health problems related to diet.

Smoking

The biggest single cause of inequalities in the death rate between different classes is smoking. Death rates from smoking are two to three times greater for people in disadvantaged social groups than for those who are better off.

Long-term or persistent smokers are at the greatest risk. Those in the disadvantaged groups who smoke start to smoke at an earlier age. Nearly half of men (47%) and 41% of women in routine and manual occupations were regular smokers by the age of 16 compared to 32% of men and 25% of women in managerial and professional occupations.

People in the upper social classes are more likely to stop smoking. Nearly 70% of those in the professional class who smoked at one time had given up whereas less than 40% from the unskilled class have quit. Peer group pressure and greater willingness to react to the health messages coming from the medical profession have encouraged those in the higher classes to stop whereas the peer group pressure and pressures of an impoverished lifestyle force the unskilled in the other direction.

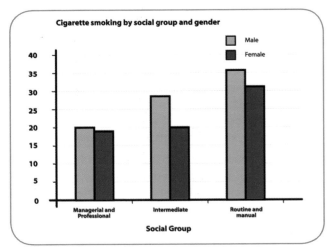

Unemployment and health

The Health Development Agency published a report in 2005 entitled 'Worklessness and Health – what do we know about the causal relationship?'. This report concluded there was a direct relationship between *'mortality and unemployment for all age groups, with suicide increasing within a year of job loss, and cardiovascular mortality accelerating after two or three years and continuing for the next 10-15 years.'* It went on to say that *'studies illustrate that during the anticipation and termination phase of factory closure, illness and health service use increase, the rate of hospital admissions doubles and conditions such as heart disease and higher blood pressure increase.'*

Young people who are unemployed have lower levels of general good health and more health problems than those who are employed. They suffer from more anxiety and depression, higher rates of smoking and higher suicide rates. Those with health problems are less successful in finding employment than those with good health so the problem becomes self-perpetuating and deeper. Financial stress and the resulting material deprivation are partly responsible for poor health among the unemployed.

There is an extremely complex series of relationships between ill health and unemployment. Poor health is both a cause and a result of unemployment.

Increased wealth

As people become wealthier their **social habits** change. In Scotland there has been an increase in drug taking and alcohol-related disease and hospitalisation figures have exploded over the past ten years. Alcohol has become relatively cheaper and more available.

Increased wealth can also mean more **processed foodstuffs** forming part of the regular diet and an increase in **alcohol consumption**. At the same time social and technological changes have made work less **physically demanding**. Instead of walking or using public transport we drive from door to door and take the lift rather than the stairs. We no longer have rise from our seats to change the TV channel and more children play computer games in their bedrooms than go out to play games.

The combination of increased food intake and reduced physical activity means that increasing numbers are obese and suffer from the resulting heart attacks, strokes blood vessel damage and kidney failure.

Obesity in Scotland

- Scotland now has the second highest rate of obesity in the world behind USA
- Over the past 40 years the incidence of type 2 diabetes has increased from 1% of the population to 10%
- Today 20% of schoolchildren are overweight and some children as young as five have fatty streaks on their arteries
- Many 50-year-olds face an increased risk of angina and are able to live longer only due to medication

Obesity levels in Scotland are increasing

Internet research

Visit the Advanced Higher Modern Studies website in Learning and Teaching Scotland to find a PowerPoint presentation which illustrates impact of lifestyle on health.

Links to this site and other websites relating to Higher Modern Studies can be found at: LECKIE&LECKIE *Learning Lab*

For you to do

● Explain how lifestyle choices affect a person's health.
● Explain how increasing wealth has both positive and negative impacts on health.

Geography

Geographic location has an impact on health largely as a result of economic factors such as **employment** and **health service provision**. Location will also have a bearing on lifestyle choices.

Two Scotlands – rich and poor?

WORD BANK

Morbidity:
the incidence and severity of sicknesses and accidents in a defined group of people.

Mortality:
a measure of the rate of death from a disease or illness within a defined population.

Economic activity

People's health varies in different parts of the UK as a consequence of the economic wellbeing of the area and the availability of health services. The general health of a region will be affected by the levels of unemployment and the type of work available in that area. If it is an area of high unemployment then **morbidity** and **mortality** rates will be higher than if there are high levels of well-paid employment.

If the main employment is in low income sectors of the economy, then the risk of poor health will be higher. Similarly, if the work available is in a high risk industry such as mining or deep-sea fishing, poor health will be more widespread. Other factors may be culturally specific to the region such as the diet or levels of smoking or alcohol use.

Health service provision

The provision of health services will affect health. If people are served by GPs and clinics close to where they live, they will be more likely to seek help at an earlier stage and so catch problems before they get too serious. If the local hospital is close at hand and specialises in care that the patient needs then their chances of survival from such things as heart attacks and road traffic accidents is improved.

The phrase *postcode lottery* in health has developed to describe geographic inequalities in health in the UK. Inequalities in service provision such as doctor, dentist and hospital provision vary throughout the UK. Decisions made by health trusts about which operations, treatments and drugs to fund mean that people with the same health problems in neighbouring areas may receive differing levels of treatment. Health is better in London and the South of England compared to other parts of the UK because this area has the highest incomes and the lowest unemployment and it is well served by the NHS. For most cases, mortality rates are lower in London and the South-East of England.

Lifestyle choices

People who live in London and the South-East of England **drink considerably less** than their counterparts in other areas of the UK, and they **smoke a little less**. They are also likely to take **more exercise** and have a **healthier diet**. These differences stem from the fact that there is greater wealth in London and the South-East and there is more employment in the higher class occupations.

Internet research

Visit the Office for National Statistics website and find the General Household Survey pages (chapter 7). Find information on regional variations in health issues such as overall states of health, mortality rates, and figures for cigarette smoking and alcohol consumption.

Links to this site and other websites relating to Higher Modern Studies can be found at:

In Scotland the health divide is also related to wealth and poverty. Inequalities in health are clustering in pockets that exist beside each other. The richest constituency in Edinburgh has far better health statistics than the poorest constituency which is in Glasgow.

Health and wealth inequalities in two constituencies in Scotland

CATEGORY		RICH CONSTITUENCY	POOR CONSTITUENCY
Wealth and income	Average gross income	£31,478	£17,170
Life expectancy	male	76.5 y	63.9 y
	female	81.6 y	75.9 y
Proportion of 15-year-olds reaching 65	male	83.6%	54.7%
	female	78.7%	73.4%
Death rates/100,000 of the population	heart	92	182
	stroke	43	68
	lung cancer	33	74
	drug related	42	153
	smoking	351	987
General health	Long-term limiting illness	16%	32%
	Self-assessed – health not good	7%	21%
	Adults unable to work due to disability	7%	28%
Smoking	Smokers	30%	50%
	Smoked during pregnancy	23%	36%
Obesity	male	63%	56%
	female	51%	53%
	pre-school children	24%	21%
Alcohol (excess of recommended intake)	male	32%	38%
	female	19%	13%
Exercise	male	40%	34%
	female	30%	24%
Daily fruit consumption	male	48%	38%
	female	62%	52%
Teenage pregnancies		4.7%	7.2%
Lone parent households		15%	35%

Note: most figures have been rounded   *Source: Public Health Institute of Scotland*

Internet research

Visit the website of the Scottish Public Health Observatory (ScotPHO) to find up-to-date and comprehensive statistics on geographic differences in health throughout Scotland.
Links to this site and other websites relating to Higher Modern Studies can be found at:

For you to do

- Using the Scottish Public Health Observatory website, find the constituency or community profile for the area you live in. Make notes on the data for the categories shown in the table above and think about the reasons for the relative health statistics in your area compared with the overall Scottish average.
- Describe the main causes of inequalities in health in the UK.
- Examine how wealth affects health.

THE DEBATE ABOUT HEALTH CARE AND WELFARE PROVISION

The political debate about the provision of welfare and health care polarised around the arguments between the **individualists** and the **collectivists**. Individualist argue for **greater self-sufficiency on the part of the individual** while the collectivists argue it is the **state's responsibility** to provide the necessary help. In UK political party terms, the individualists were largely found in the Conservative Party while the collectivists were in the Labour Party.

The Labour Government introduced the National Health Service (NHS) in 1948 based on a collectivist model. Provision would be **free at the point of need** and paid for by general taxation. They believed that the health of the nation would improve as people benefited from free medical care and that costs would then fall. However, the cost of health care has risen every year as medical knowledge develops and people live longer, making greater demands on the NHS.

From 1945 to 1979, there was a general agreement in terms of the collectivist approach with the argument centring on the level of government support. After 1979, Thatcherite Conservatives put the individualist approach into action. They argued it was the individual's responsibility to find employment and look after their family. The state would provide minimal help. Welfare levels should be low enough to encourage recipients to find work.

They saw society divided into the **deserving poor** such as the elderly and the disabled and the **undeserving poor** such as unmarried mothers and young people who should be looking for work rather than living off benefits. In its final years the 1979–1997 Conservative Government trimmed its individualist philosophy.

The Labour Party came into power in 1997 with a more collectivist approach but they diluted their collectivism with the philosophy of **personal responsibility**. The state would provide support for people who were in need but it would also provide the means and the incentive for individuals to find their way back into useful employment. With their **welfare-to-work** philosophy there would be no right to remain on welfare indefinitely.

Paying for health care

In the area of health provision, individualists argue that individuals should provide for their own health care through private insurance and the private sector. They argue the state should give financial incentives to people who take out private insurance. The collectivists want public health provision paid for by taxation.

Health care is a political problem for all political parties. People want the best and fullest health care but do not want pay the high tax levels needed to pay for it. People in the UK pay just over 7% of GDP towards health care. This is a low level of spending compared with our nearest neighbours. In the USA, health care spending is approximately double the amount compared to the UK (although a much higher proportion of this spending comes from private health care schemes).

After 1979, the Conservatives gave greater support for private health care and promoted tax incentives for private health insurance. They tried to bring more private enterprise into the NHS by privatising non-medical services. They also tried to create a market in the NHS so that competition between GPs and hospitals would lead to improved funding efficiencies.

They introduced managers to streamline and make hospitals more efficient. A perception developed that this approach resulted in deteriorating services and longer waiting lists.

Elected in 1997, the Labour Government set about removing the many of the *marketplace structures* in the NHS and replacing them with a *mixed economy structure*. While they wanted a collectivist approach to provide public services they were also willing to embrace private practice to reduce the growing waiting lists. They encouraged private hospital beds (which in the past they would have taken all steps to eliminate). The use of **Public Private Partnerships** (PPPs) was extended for building new hospitals.

Public Private Partnership: a collaboration between public bodies like local authorities and local health boards and private companies. PPPs usually use private funding to help build expensive building projects like hospitals and schools.

The current Conservative philosophy has changed too – both parties have moved to very similar positions on the collectivist–individualist spectrum. Currently both parties hold the position that the public want a publicly funded health service to provide their health care but both see advantages in using the private sector to meet their targets for improvements in provision.

The key issue facing any government is the funding of health care and welfare provision. The cost of the NHS continues to grow. Part of the problem of funding new hospitals has been deferred, to be paid by later generations through the mechanisms of the PPP system. The most pressing welfare issue facing successive governments is what to do about pension provision in the UK. As the number of elderly people increases and the working population gets proportionally smaller, the ability to service the costs of pensions will be strained.

STRATEGIES THAT TARGET WEALTH INEQUALITIES

Since 1997, the Labour Government has promoted **social inclusion** as a central feature of its social welfare programme. The aim has been to help those who were excluded from work to gain employment and remove them from benefits by using incentives and creating pathways into employment. For those who were unreasonably reluctant, benefits would be reduced or stopped altogether.

The **income differential** between work and benefits has been increased to make work more attractive. A time limit has been placed on Job Seeker's Allowance, which is the main benefit for the unemployed, so moving from welfare into work is made more attractive. The Labour Government targeted two particular groups – households with children and pensioners – as groups they wanted to assist out of poverty.

Strategies to encourage more people into employment

A wide range of Government strategies have been designed to encourage people into employment. Different strategies have been developed to address the needs of different groups of society, such as young people and school-leavers, single parents, disabled people, and the long-term unemployed. Emphasis has been placed on the notion that it is better to be in employment and have the necessary skills for employment than to be reliant on benefits. The different strategies include:

- Jobcentre Plus
- The New Deal
  — for young people
  — the long-term unemployed
  — lone parents
  — disabled people
- National Minimum Wage
- Working Tax Credit
- Child Tax Credit
- Skillseekers
- Modern Apprenticeships.

Jobcentre Plus

Jobcentre Plus is a network consisting of job centres and social security offices in all large towns and cities. Jobcentre Plus helps a person find suitable employment and claim the correct benefits when unemployed. Clients have a personal advisor to help them negotiate their path back into employment.

Jobseeker Direct is a phone service which provides information about vacancies in the local area and beyond. **Jobpoints** are touch-screen kiosks which allow people to search all available jobs in all offices throughout the UK.

The Jobcentre Plus website provides online job searches through a nationwide list of vacancies. It also provides application forms, assistance with creating CVs, advice on writing letters of application and other aspects of finding employment.

The New Deal

The New Deal is the Government's central strategy for helping the unemployed back into employment. There are several New Deals for different categories of unemployed people. **Compulsory** schemes are:

- New Deal for Young People, for those aged 18–24
- New Deal 25 Plus, for those aged 25–49
- New Deal for Musicians is part of New Deal for

Young People and New Deal 25 Plus; it is a scheme to help aspiring musicians into a new career in the music business.

There are also a number of **voluntary** programmes:

- New Deal 50 Plus, for the unemployed who are 50 or over and who want to work
- New Deal for Lone Parents, for single parents who are not working or working 16 hours or less and whose youngest child is under 16
- New Deal for Disabled People
- New Deal for Partners, for the partners of people who are in receipt of a range of benefits.

When a person joins a New Deal programme they are allocated a personal advisor who remains with the individual throughout their time in the programme. They assess the individual's needs and create a personalised pathway into employment. There are various types of help available, including:

- work experience with an employer or voluntary organisation
- training for a specific job
- developing the type of skills that employers might want
- help with job applications (such as writing CVs and job application letters)
- developing interview techniques.

Internet research

Visit the website of Jobcentre Plus to find up-to-date information and more details of the New Deal. Links to this site and other websites relating to Higher Modern Studies can be found at:

Tax Credits and the Minimum Wage

Jobcentre Plus and the New Deal are designed to **help people gain employment**. A second set of strategies are designed to **help those in employment but with low incomes**. These strategies involved the introduction of tax credits and a change in the level of benefits to increase the differential between those dependent on benefits and those who are working. A National Minimum Wage was introduced in 1999 to further increase the differential.

Working Tax Credit

Working Tax Credit (WTC) allows working people on low incomes to pay less tax on their wages and so retain more of their income. It was introduced to avoid the benefit trap which caused people to lose income when returning to work. Many found they were worse off in low-paid employment compared with benefits when the costs of going to work, such as travelling and childcare, were deducted from a low wage.

Families on WTC are also eligible for childcare tax credit. For a lone parent, or a working couple who work for at least 16 hours a week, childcare tax credit is worth up to 70% of childcare costs of to a maximum of £300 a week for two or more children or £175 a week for a single-child family.

Child Tax Credit

Child Tax Credit is paid to all families with children and a combined income less than £58,000 per annum (2005 levels). It is paid directly to the carer. It is means-tested and those on higher incomes will get progressively less. In 2005/06, households were paid a 'family element' of £545 per year or £1,690 if the child was in its first year. Families with less than £50,000 a year get at least £545 a year from the 'family element'.

Households that have incomes up to £13,910 a year qualify for the 'child element' of £1,690 a year for each child. Child Tax Credit is targeted on households with children to reduce the levels of child poverty in the UK.

The National Minimum Wage

The Labour Government introduced a National Minimum Wage (NMW) to give workers a reasonable hourly rate. In 2006 the NMW for an adult (22 and over) was £5.35 per hour. (This gives a weekly wage of £214 before tax for a 40-hour week.) The Government intends to encourage more low-paid workers to move back into work because of the increased wage levels.

The combination of Tax Credits and the National Minimum Wage has created a significant differential between the income from benefits and the income from being in low paid employment, and has largely eliminated the benefit trap.

Internet research

Visit the is4profit website to find up-to-date information about the National Minimum Wage.
Links to this site and other websites relating to Higher Modern Studies can be found at: LECKIE&LECKIE *Learning Lab*

For you to do

- What are the National Minimum Wage rates for 16–17 years olds and 18–21 year olds?
- Are there any types of business which do not have to pay the National Minimum Wage?

Skillseekers

Local Enterprise Companies (LECs) run programmes for young people aged 16–24 by encouraging employers to train them in a recognised workplace qualification. **All 16–18 year olds** are eligible for Skillseekers training. The LECs provide financial support by assisting with the cost of training. Most young Skillseekers are trained by an employer but LECs provide some training places for those who have had difficulty finding employment.

Skillseekers work towards Scottish or National Vocational Qualifications. Each Vocational Qualification is comprised of units covering different aspects of a particular job. Skillseekers are able to work through them at their own pace. The training is flexible to match an individual's ability, the needs of the employer and the level of qualification the Skillseeker hopes to achieve.

Internet research

Visit the Careers Scotland website to find more details and case studies for Skillseekers.
Links to this site and other websites relating to Higher Modern Studies can be found at:

Modern Apprenticeships

Modern Apprenticeships are targeted at the 16–24 age group, although they can be undertaken by people of any age. They offer work-based training leading to Scottish Vocational Qualifications (SVQ) Level 3 or above. Apprentices work with an employer who offers a range of training identified in a framework, developed by the National Training Organisations. The most popular frameworks in Scotland are Construction, Customer Services, Business Administration, Motor Vehicles, Engineering, Electrotechnical and Hospitality. Students also undertake day release work in a Further Education college.

Modern Apprenticeships include a Core Skills element which covers communication, numeracy, problem solving, working with others, and information technology

In 2005/06, there were just over 34,000 Modern Apprentices currently in training in Scotland. Businesses have found several benefits to becoming involved in the Modern Apprenticeship scheme. It has helped develop the quality of their workforce and has helped retain staff.

Benefit payments

In addition to the strategies described to help people find work, there are a number of benefit payments which help those who are temporarily or permanently out of work. These include payments to pensioners and people who cannot work. These benefits include:

- Jobseeker's Allowance
- Income Support changes targeted at children
- Pension Credit
- Winter Fuel Payment
- other benefits for those on low incomes paid by national government
- benefits paid through local authorities.

Internet research

Visit the Scottish Enterprise website to find case studies and more detailed statistics about Modern Apprenticeships.
Links to this site and other websites relating to Higher Modern Studies can be found at:

For you to do

- List the various strategies the Government has developed to address poverty. Is the Government doing enough? Can you think of other ways to help people in poverty?

Jobseeker's Allowance

Jobseeker's Allowance is paid to people who are able to work, are available to work and are actively seeking work. It is a benefit paid to those taking part in a New Deal scheme. Anyone unwilling or unable to take part in the New Deal has their Jobseeker's Allowance withdrawn.

Jobseeker's Allowance lasts for a maximum of six months by which time the claimant will be expected to have found a job or have moved into full-time training or education.

Internet Research

Visit the Job Centre Plus website to find more details about the Jobseeker's Allowance. Links to this site and other websites relating to Higher Modern Studies can be found at:

Income Support

Income Support is for people between 16 and 60 who cannot work because they are **incapable** (because of illness or disability) or because they **care for a sick or disabled person** or they are a **lone parent** responsible for a child under 16.

Income Support is a means-tested benefit and depends on age, family size, disabilities, and other personal circumstances. Income Support cannot be claimed by people working more than 16 hours per week or who have a partner who works more than 24 hours per week. People studying full-time and those with capital or savings over a certain level are not entitled to claim.

The rules governing Income Support are very complex so it is difficult to work out the entitlements that claimants have. As a result many people do not claim the full levels of Income Support they are actually entitled to claim. The level for Income Support payments are set by Parliament.

Income Support claimants are entitled to claim other benefits such as Housing Benefit and Council Tax Benefit, free prescriptions, free NHS dental treatment, vouchers for glasses, and help with fares to hospital for hospital appointments. They can also get grants and loans from the Social Fund and free school meals.

The complexity of the system means that many people do not claim their Income Support entitlements

Pension Credit

Pension Credit provides a minimum income for pensioners. In 2006, a single pensioner with an income under £114.05 and a couple with income under £174.05 will receive a pension credit to make up the difference. (For example, a couple whose combined state pensions and occupational pension is £150 will receive pension credit of £24.05.) Pensioners with extra needs such as caring needs or particular housing needs may be able to claim more. Pension Credit is means tested although everyone aged over 75 gets a free TV licence.

Winter Fuel Payment

The Winter Fuel Payment is a **one-off annual payment** to pensioners to help with the cost of keeping warm through the winter. It is paid on a sliding scale depending on age and circumstances. Those aged 60–79 get either £100 or £200. Those aged 80 or over are entitled an extra £50 or £100, so could get up to £300. It does not depend on the level of savings.

Internet research

Visit the Pension Service website to find up-to-date information about Pension Credit and the Winter Fuel Payment.

Links to this site and other websites relating to Higher Modern Studies can be found at: LECKIE&LECKIE Learning Lab

Other benefits

There are a range of other benefits for those on low incomes paid by national Government:

- free prescription charges
- free eye tests and spectacles
- free dental treatment.

In addition, there are other benefits for those on low incomes paid through local authorities

- Housing Benefit
- Council Tax Benefit
- free school meals
- clothing vouchers.

Internet research

Visit the website of the Department of Health or the Department of Work and Pensions for more information on these benefits.

Links to these sites and other websites relating to Higher Modern Studies can be found at: LECKIE&LECKIE Learning Lab

Sure Start

Sure Start is a Government programme designed to help children and their carers overcome the problems of social exclusion. It integrates child care, early education, health and family support services for families with children under five years old to promote the physical, intellectual and social development of babies and young children.

There are over 500 local Sure Start programmes helping 400,000 children from disadvantaged backgrounds. In Scotland all local authorities provide Sure Start services. Sure Start is focused support, dealing with small pockets of disadvantage both in urban and rural areas.

Sure Start Children's Centres in the most disadvantaged areas provide high quality early learning with qualified teachers and day-care provision for children throughout the year. They also provide child and family health services including ante-natal services. The centres also provide family support and outreach services actively making contact with disadvantaged families in their homes to encourage them to make use of the Centres. They also have links with Jobcentre Plus to support parents and carers who wish to get training or employment.

In less disadvantaged areas, Sure Start provides a basic level of services with a more selective level of support and outreach services that targets particular individuals.

Internet research

Visit the Sure Start website for a comprehensive review of the scheme.
Links to this site and other websites relating to Higher Modern Studies can be found at:

For you to do

- Government measures to help meet the financial needs of the poor are focused on particular groups. Discuss.

EFFECTIVENESS OF GOVERNMENT POLICIES IN TACKLING WEALTH INEQUALITIES

The Government devotes a great deal of effort and money to social policies aimed at helping those with low incomes. However, it is important that the policies are assessed on a regular basis to ensure that the spending is providing effective support. Regular monitoring allows changes to be made to the various services in order to improve the outcomes. In developing these policies, the Labour Government set a range of targets which address unemployment, low pay, child poverty and pensioner poverty.

Unemployment

The combination of the New Deal, Working Tax Credit and the National Minimum Wage has increased the differential between benefit levels and low paid work. It has helped to increase the employment rate by an average of 2.5% in the past four years and brought unemployment down from 7% to 5%.

The New Deal has helped many people back into work with over three-quarters of people on New Deal schemes going into sustained employment.

Low pay

The National Minimum Wage has helped to increase the income of over one million workers, 75% of whom were women.

Child poverty

The policies introduced by the Labour Government since 1997 have reduced the number of children living in poverty by 1.3 million. Tax credits have enabled 40% of lone mothers to escape poverty, leaving only 8% of lone working mothers living in poverty.

However, the high cost of child care is often a barrier preventing parents from working, and can make people worse off in work than on benefits. Affordable, accessible, high-quality child care is essential for paid work to be a more secure ladder out of poverty for lone parents.

In 1999, the Government set itself the goal of halving child poverty by 2010. It is currently on track but continuing reductions are getting progressively harder. If economic conditions do not continue to improve then the goal might not be achieved.

Despite some successful Government strategies, many children in the UK still experience poverty

Pensioner poverty

Pension Credits and Winter Fuel Allowances have helped reduce pensioner poverty in the UK. In 1997, 27% of pensioners had an income of less than 60% of median income. By 2003, this had fallen to 21%.

However, large numbers of pensioners still suffer the effects of poverty. Despite the Winter Fuel Allowance, it is estimated that between 20,000 and 50,000 people aged 65 and over die during a British winter. Many of these deaths could have been avoided if the elderly had better standards of housing. Countries in Europe with harsher winters have lower winter death rates.

One reason for the continuing pensioner poverty is the complexity of the **benefit system** for pensioners and the fact that it is heavily **means tested**. Pensioners may be eligible for up to 23 state benefits and entitlements. One pensioner in three does not claim Income Support. Of those pensioners who are entitled to claim, 33% do not claim Council Tax Benefit, and 10% do not claim Housing Benefit.

This problem could be overcome by increasing the state pension to a level that supports pensioners adequately without forcing them into the labyrinth of means-tested benefits. However, governments are concerned about the country's ability to fund pensions in the future. With an ageing population the tax burden on the working population could be too much for it to bear by the middle of the century.

The Government commissioned Lord Turner, the head of the Pensions Commission, to conduct an inquiry and report on the future of pensions in the UK. The **Turner Report** proposed raising the age of retirement to 68 by 2050 and in return increasing the basic state pension in line with earnings, not inflation. It should become a flat rate payment for all pensioners. It was also proposed that all employees should be part of a National Pension Savings Scheme (NPSS) so they could save extra to make up their income in their retirement.

The Government did not accept the Turner Report in its entirety but it did agree to restore the link between pensions and earnings by 2012 in return for raising the retirement age for both men and women to 68 by 2050.

As the elderly form an increasing proportion of the population, the funding of pensions becomes a more significant issue for individuals and government

For you to do

- Critically assess the range of Government policies to reduce poverty and unemployment.

STRATEGIES TO DEAL WITH HEALTH INEQUALITIES

The NHS was introduced in 1948 by the Labour Government as a collectivist answer to health provision in the UK. It was part of the sweeping welfare reform originally proposed in the *Beveridge Report on Social Insurance and Allied Services*. This proposed a system of state welfare that would provide support 'from the cradle to the grave'. It was to fight the five social evils of **want**, **disease**, **squalor**, **ignorance**, and **idleness**. A universal welfare state would provide a comprehensive health service, public housing, free and universal secondary education, and full employment, as well as welfare benefits to assist those in need.

William Beveridge trained as a lawyer before the First World War, but served as an economist to advise Government on National Insurance and Old Age Pensions. He became director of the London School of Economics in 1919 and in 1941, he was asked by Ernest Bevin, a Government Minister, to conduct a review of the ways Britain should be rebuilt after the Second World War. His report, published in 1942, proposed a scheme of National Insurance, which gathered contributions from all working people and a system of health care provision and benefits to ensure a minimum standard of living for all. The proposals were adopted by the Attlee Government following the War. The NHS was established in 1948 and a system of social security provided security 'from cradle to the grave'.

The principles of the NHS were that the state was to take collective responsibility for a **universal and comprehensive range of health services** with equality of access for all.

The state took the responsibility to fund a centrally directed NHS from general taxation. It would remove inequalities in access and in the quality of health provision. The whole population would be entitled to the full range of health services free at the point of need. It would be responsible for improving the nation's health through education and prevention as well as for diagnosis and treatment. Health provision would be equal in every area and access would be equal irrespective of wealth.

The Acheson Report

The Acheson Report which was published in 1998 provided an analysis of the health of the UK. The proposals it made for addressing the problems it had highlighted became the basis of the Labour Government's policies towards health care. Its conclusions pointed to the strong relationship between social class and ill-health and its solutions centred on actions that would be targeted at the less well off in order to reduce the impact of poverty on health.

all policies likely to have a direct or indirect effect on health should be evaluated in terms of their impact on health inequalities, and should be formulated in such a way that by favouring the less well off they will, wherever possible, reduce such inequalities.

(Acheson Report 1998)

The report called for:

- an increase in benefit levels for women of childbearing age, expectant mothers, young children and older people.
- more funding for schools in deprived areas, better nutrition at schools and an emphasis on 'health promoting schools'.
- restrictions on smoking in public places, a ban on tobacco advertising and promotion, increases in the price of tobacco and provide nicotine replacement therapy on the NHS.

Recent government strategies for tackling health inequalities have tried to put the emphasis on structures and programmes aimed at prevention.

STRUCTURE OF THE NHS

Health care in the UK is divided into two parts, primary care and secondary care. Primary care is concerned with the health services such as general practices, dentists and opticians which cater for general and routine health care. Secondary care is more specialist care, usually delivered in hospitals.

Although the National Health Service operates equally in England, Scotland, Wales and Northern Ireland, it is organised in slightly different ways in the different countries, with differing structures and lines of responsibility.

Primary care

Primary care consists of a range of services such as general practitioners (GPs), nurses, dentists, pharmacists and opticians. It is normally the **first point of contact** for the public seeking medical help and advice. It caters for general health problems and routine medical care as well as preventative care. In recent years it has been given responsibility for more specialist treatments such as minor operations in order to bring medical care closer to the point of public contact.

Primary care is provided through:

- **local GP practices:** teams which include GPs, nurses, health visitors and midwives, physiotherapists and occupational therapists who provide diagnosis and treatment for medical problems as well as preventative treatments and health education; this primary care is free at the point of need
- **dental practices:** provide check-ups and treatments such as fillings and extractions as well as dental education; some practices take only private patients, others take only NHS patients while others take a combination of both
- **pharmacists or chemists:** dispense prescription medicines and health care advice
- **opticians:** test eye-sight and prescribe and fit spectacles
- **NHS Walk-in Centres:** there are 66 Walk-in Centres in England which provide 'no-appointment' advice and treatments for minor conditions; they are run by NHS nurses and provide treatment for minor illnesses and injuries and give medical advice
- **NHS Direct:** is a 24-hour phone service giving health advice usually staffed by nurses.

Secondary care

Secondary care also referred to as **acute care**. It is normally accessed by a referral from a GP, an optician or other health professional. It may also be accessed via Accident and Emergency (A&E) services in hospitals when patients can present themselves if they suddenly feel very ill or have had an injury. They will also be taken to A&E in an ambulance as the result of an accident. In A&E they may be discharged after treatment or advice or they can be admitted to a hospital ward for further care.

Following referral from a primary care practitioner, a patient may attend a specialist clinic for an outpatient's consultation or may be admitted to a hospital ward as an inpatient or a day care patient for observation or specialist treatment such as surgery.

Secondary care is provided through:

- **hospitals:** provide planned treatment following referral from GPs and the health professionals as well as emergency treatment
- **NHS Foundation Trusts:** these are hospitals that are run by local managers and staff. A hospital with a good performance record can apply to become an NHS Foundation Trust. Such hospitals are still part of the NHS, but the hospital has more freedom in the way it is run and how it provides services, so staff have more power to make decisions.
- **Ambulance Trusts:** run the paramedic and ambulance services. These are the local organisations responsible for responding to 999 calls and transporting patients. They responding to life-threatening and urgent conditions such as heart attacks and road accidents. Depending on the nature of the emergency a rapid response vehicle, crewed by a paramedic and equipped to provide treatment, may be dispatched. Ambulance staff assess patients at the scene and decide whether they need to go to hospital.

Structure of health provision in England

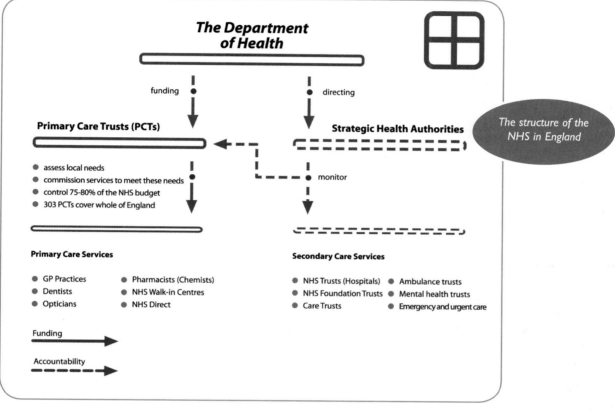

The Department
of Health

funding directing

Primary Care Trusts (PCTs) Strategic Health Authorities

The structure of the
NHS in England

● assess local needs
● commission services to meet these needs monitor
● control 75-80% of the NHS budget
● 303 PCTs cover whole of England

Primary Care Services **Secondary Care Services**

● GP Practices   ● Pharmacists (Chemists) ● NHS Trusts (Hospitals) ● Ambulance trusts
● Dentists   ● NHS Walk-in Centres   ● NHS Foundation Trusts ● Mental health trusts
● Opticians   ● NHS Direct   ● Care Trusts   ● Emergency and urgent care

Funding

Accountability

Source: Learning and Teaching Scotland
(Social Issues: Health and Wealth Inequalities in the UK)

The Department of Health

The Department of Health is the Government department in charge of administering the NHS. It lays out standards and working practices for the NHS and social service departments in England. It sets the priorities for the NHS and provides the funds for service delivery.

Strategic Health Authorities

Strategic Health Authorities (SHAs) have the responsibility for local strategic planning in England's 28 authority areas. They oversee the Primary Care Trusts and NHS Trusts (hospitals) and monitor their performance. They ensure that national priorities laid down by the Department of Health are fully implemented in their areas.

Primary Care Trusts

Primary Care Trusts (PCTs) control 75–80% of the NHS budget and it is their responsibility to provide appropriate medical services in their area. They have to ensure there is the correct balance of medical services such as GP practices, hospitals and dentists to meet the community's medical needs.

PCTs must make sure that their services can be accessed by everyone who needs them and they must listen to patients' views on services and act on them. They are responsible for carrying out annual assessments of GP practices in their area.

PCTs report directly to their local SHA. As well as buying and monitoring services, they also help local GP practices, NHS Trusts and other parts of the NHS consider how to deliver better care to the communities they serve.

Structure of NHS provision in Scotland

There are 14 Unified Health Boards responsible to the Scottish Executive for providing health services in their area.

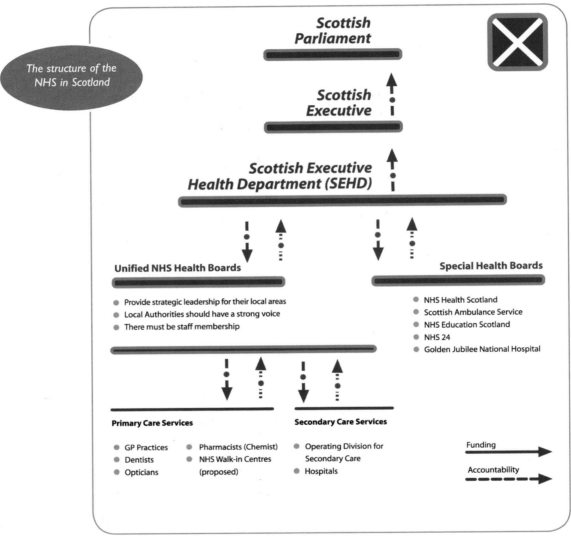

Source: Learning and Teaching Scotland (Social Issues: Health and Wealth Inequalities in the UK)

For you to do

- In what ways does the structure of the health service in Scotland differ from that in England and Wales?

The Scottish Executive Health Department (SEHD)

The Scottish Executive Health Department (SEHD) lays down strategic objectives and national priorities for the NHS in Scotland and monitors the performance of each NHS health board.

Unified NHS Health Boards

Health Boards have the responsibility for local planning and service provision.

Community health partnerships (CHPs)

CHPs have the responsibility to provide health services in the areas they serve. They are run by representatives of the primary care professionals and local authorities.

Hospitals

A hospital is run by what is called an Operating Division for Secondary Care which is responsible to the NHS Board.

THE ROLE OF THE PRIVATE SECTOR IN HEALTH CARE

Most health care in the UK is delivered through the publicly funded National Health Service. There is also a significant role for private sector health care, through private medical insurance and private hospitals. The private sector is also playing a part in the NHS through Public Private Partnerships (PPPs) and through the requirement for compulsory competitive tendering for the provision of certain services.

Private Medical Insurance

Private Medical Insurance (PMI) is available from a number of insurance companies for those who can afford it. Premiums can be quite high, averaging over £1,000 per person per year. Premiums vary depending on the level of cover required and a person's age and general health. A healthy middle-aged person might be charged £750 for basic private insurance, while premiums rise significantly as a person grows older and has more need for expensive health care services (for example, a coronary artery bypass can cost £17,500). Premiums exclude pre-existing medical conditions, chronic conditions and cosmetic surgery.

Private medical insurance allows people to get fast treatment from a medical professional and at a time and place of their choice. In the past, people taking out PMI have been offered tax incentives but the current Government ended tax relief. The Conservative Party would encourage the expansion of PMI.

There are nearly 7 million people in the UK covered by PMI with 2 million buying personal cover and the rest in company schemes. The total value of PMI is around £3 billion.

Private hospitals

In England there are around 230 private hospitals and 3,000 pay beds in NHS hospitals, providing around £15 billion in medical care annually. Around 20% of non-urgent surgery is done in private hospitals. PMI pays for 75% of treatment, with 20% privately funded and 5% paid for by the NHS.

In Scotland there are nine private hospitals with 900 beds. The Scottish Executive has block-booked beds for around 500 knee and hip replacement operations in an attempt to cut waiting lists.

Two major influences in the uptake of private medical insurance are waiting lists and waiting times for hospital appointments and operations. In 2004, over 86,000 people in Scotland were waiting for hospital treatment. PMI sales increased by 60% in the three years to 2005. Waiting times are longer in Scotland than in England.

The Labour Party has traditionally been opposed to private health care and has in the past actively sought to eliminate it. However, in 2000, the Labour Government signed an agreement with the private sector to provide services to ease the pressures on the NHS at certain times (such as during winters, when the bed demand is at its highest).

There has been a 400% increase in NHS-funded operations in the private sector since the agreement was signed. There have been concerns in the Labour Party about this agreement because the expansion of the private sector will take staff from the NHS and cause more shortages.

Most nursing homes and other residential provision for the long-term care of the elderly and the majority of mental health hospitals are provided privately.

Private Finance Initiative

The Private Finance Initiative (PFI) is the method of funding used to finance Public Private Partnerships (PPPs), and is the Government's favoured way of financing the building of new hospitals. The Labour Government has approved 15 major PFI hospital schemes in England and three in Scotland.

PFI operates with a group of companies including a financial backer, a construction company and a management contractor. The group agree a contract to build and maintain a hospital over a period of time. The NHS agrees to pay a fixed annual fee to use the hospital. If the NHS decides it no longer needs the hospital it must continue to pay the fee agreed until the contract expires.

In a PPP hospital the NHS will employ the medical staff but the catering, porters, security and maintenance staff will be employed by a private contractor. Such hospitals usually have extensive private provision. Medical provision will remain free but people will be able to pay for better food or a private room.

The benefit of PFI for the Government is that it can have new hospitals built now without the high costs being met out of current taxation or cuts in services elsewhere. The drawback is that it will cost far more for taxpayers in the future. The companies building the hospitals have to borrow at higher rates than the Government can and will make a profit. Both these things will be reflected in higher fees. They may also cut costs to create higher profits, and this may result in inferior provision

The Government refuses to divulge what these PFI contracts cost, citing 'commercial confidentiality'. However, the profits made by private consortiums in other PFI contracts show that 200% plus is not unusual.

One concern with PFI contracts is that medical staff may find that the developments in these hospitals may be determined by commercial considerations and not medical need, so profitable activities may take precedence over less profitable activities, regardless of the actual needs of the local community. Non-medical staff may find their pay and conditions squeezed in the interests of increased profit and this will affect morale and efficiency.

Compulsory Competitive Tendering

Compulsory Competitive Tendering (CCT) was introduced into hospitals as a means of introducing business efficiency into non-medical services. The NHS has to put contracts for all domestic, catering and laundry services out to tender and accept the lowest bid. To reduce costs and ensure profits, private contractors have cut wages and conditions and reduced the number of staff. This can have an impact on standards of health care.

In 1986 the NHS employed nearly 70,000 full-time domestic cleaning staff. By 2005, this number had been reduced by nearly half. Over this period, medical staff and patients have complained of a deterioration in the service provided, particularly in hospital cleanliness. There has been a huge rise in MRSA in hospitals in recent years; MRSA is estimated to kill over 5,000 people each year and costs the NHS over £1 billion every year in treatment. It is thought that CCT cost-cutting practices may have resulted in lower standards of cleanliness in hospitals, contributing to the spread of MRSA.

Internet research

Visit the websites of BBC News or the *Guardian*. Find more information on the private sector in the NHS to use in essays. Find out about targets being set by governments (such as reducing waiting times for cancer treatments or hip operations), and see if these targets are being met.

Visit the websites of the Health Education Board for Scotland and the Department of Health to find out more about health-related policies being promoted by Government. Find information on changes in Government funding and the numbers of health professionals to use in essays evaluating the effectiveness of Government strategies in addressing health issues.

Visit the website of the Scottish Executive Education Department to find out about its Healthy Living policy. Then look at the website of your local authority to find out what is being done in your area to promote healthy school meals.

Links to these sites and other websites relating to Higher Modern Studies can be found at:

For you to do

- Consider the role of the private sector in the UK. Draw up a table giving the positive and negative impacts on overall medical care in the UK.
- Evaluate the effectiveness of Government policies in addressing health inequalities in the UK.
- The NHS is no longer free or universal. Discuss.

STUDY THEME SUMMARY

A range of different measures are used to classify social class in the UK. Such classifications are important in order to assess what policies are needed to address health and wealth inequalities, and to measure the success of these policies. Poverty can be defined as either absolute or relative. Although few, if any, people in Britain suffer from absolute poverty, there is still significant relative poverty, affecting about a quarter of the population. Risk of poverty is affected by national economic and political factors, and by personal circumstances such as education and lifestyle. Poverty affects different groups in society to varying degrees, according to age, gender, ethnicity and regional location.

Health inequalities affect people in similar ways to poverty. Different groups in society are vulnerable to ill health in different ways, according to age, gender, ethnicity and regional location. Ill health can result from lifestyle choices such as diet, smoking, over-consumption of alcohol and lack of exercise.

The Government has a wide range of targeted policies to address poverty in the UK. The main strategies are to encourage people to seek and take employment instead of relying on benefits by increasing the differential between being on benefits and being in work, and to provide financial support for those unable to work due to ill health or as a result of their role as carers. A major challenge for the future will be the adequate funding of pensions.

The National Health Service has been the major provider of health care in the UK since 1948. The founding aim of the NHS was to provide free cradle-to-grave support for everyone, funded from general taxation. Ever-increasing costs and expectations make it hard for the NHS to meet all the health needs of the whole population.

Exam-style essay questions

Critically examine the claim that the UK has become a more equal society.

Assess the importance of the factors that cause inequalities in health and wealth and the interrelationships between them.

To what extent have government policies aimed at moving people from dependence on welfare to paid employment been effective?

International Issues

STUDY THEME 3A:
Republic of South Africa

In this study theme you will be expected to have a detailed knowledge and understanding of:

- ## THE SOUTH AFRICAN POLITICAL SYSTEM

  The role and powers of the South African Government at national, provincial and local levels.

- ## POLITICAL ISSUES

  Participation and representation. Political parties and support from different groups. Political trends.

- ## SOCIAL AND ECONOMIC ISSUES

  The nature and extent of social and economic inequalities; demands for change; the effectiveness of Government responses and the consequences among and within different racial groups.

BACKGROUND TO SOUTH AFRICA'S LAND AND PEOPLE

South Africa is located on the southernmost tip of the continent of Africa. It has an area over 1.2 million square kilometres (nearly 15 times the size of Scotland). The land varies from fertile green valleys, supporting a rich agricultural industry, to large semi-desert areas.

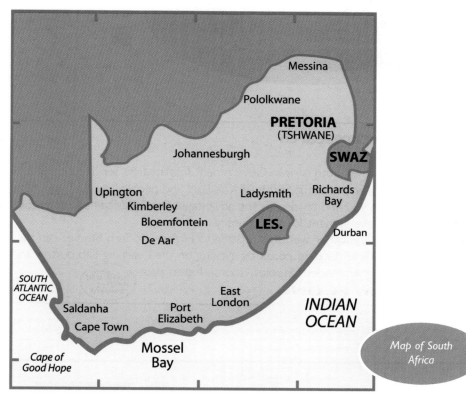

Map of South Africa

South Africa is the world's leading producer of gold, diamonds and many other minerals. It is the wealthiest country in Africa, having strong financial and manufacturing sectors. However, it is also one of the most economically and socially unequal societies in the world.

South Africa has a uniquely varied racial mix. Over 45 million people live in South Africa. Almost 77% are black (or African), 11% white and 9% coloured (the South African description for people of mixed African, Asian and white descent). About 2% are Indian/Asian.

The white population is made up of two distinct groups: Afrikaners, of Dutch descent, and the remainder, mainly of British descent. The Afrikaners were early settlers, arriving in Africa in the 17th century and establishing a country free of the religious persecution they had experienced in Europe. They became the dominant force in South African politics and developed the Apartheid system to preserve South Africa as their homeland.

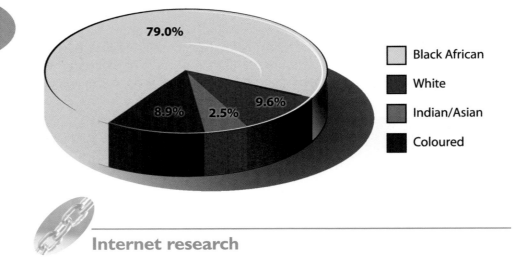

Population distribution by race

79.0%

8.9%   2.5%   9.6%

- [ ] Black African
- [ ] White
- [ ] Indian/Asian
- [ ] Coloured

Internet research

Visit the website of the South African Government Information Service or the CIA Factbook to find out more about South Africa's land and people.

Use the information you find to identify the advantages South Africa has which could lead to successful development for the country.

Links to these sites and other websites relating to Higher Modern Studies can be found at: **www.leckieandleckie.co.uk** by clicking on the Learning Lab button and navigating to the Higher Modern Studies Course Notes page.

LECKIE&LECKIE
Learning Lab

FACT

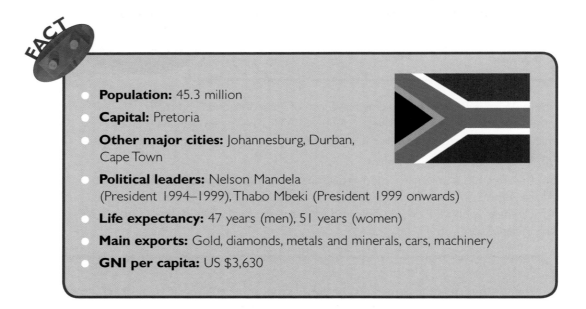

- **Population:** 45.3 million
- **Capital:** Pretoria
- **Other major cities:** Johannesburg, Durban, Cape Town
- **Political leaders:** Nelson Mandela (President 1994–1999), Thabo Mbeki (President 1999 onwards)
- **Life expectancy:** 47 years (men), 51 years (women)
- **Main exports:** Gold, diamonds, metals and minerals, cars, machinery
- **GNI per capita:** US $3,630

APARTHEID

From 1948 to 1994, South African politics were based on Apartheid, a policy of separation of the races. Under Apartheid, only white people had the right to vote, and the white minority Government enforced a strict system of political, social and economic discrimination.

Apartheid involved the forced re-settlement of hundreds of thousands of people to create racially segregated areas. People of different races were forbidden to marry or live in the same area. The best jobs were reserved for whites. Non-whites had to carry **Pass-books** if they were in white areas. Different races went to different schools and even had to stand in different queues in the post office.

Apartheid came under pressure within South Africa and from the international community. In the late 1980s, the white minority Government began negotiations which led to the eventual end of Apartheid. The first democratic elections open to all South Africans were held in 1994. More than 10 years after the end of Apartheid, South Africa is now a democratic society with one of the most liberal and tolerant constitutions in the world.

Apartheid era sign showing segregation on beaches

You will not be asked specifically about the Apartheid years in an exam. However, years of economic, social and political inequality have left a legacy that South Africa is still dealing with today. It is important to have a broad understanding of Apartheid in order to appreciate how much life has changed since 1994 and the legacy that still needs to be overcome by the Government and people. South Africa also acts as a model to other countries around the world on how to achieve peaceful reconciliation between different groups.

For you to do

- Find out who coined the phrase 'rainbow nation' to describe South Africa. Why is it a suitable name for the country?
- Explain how generations of social, economic and political inequality under Apartheid can still have an effect today.

Politics under Apartheid

Under Apartheid, white South Africans had a monopoly of political power. Only whites could vote in elections and be elected to Parliament. Parties opposed to Apartheid such as the African National Congress (ANC), Pan Africanist Congress (PAC) and the Communist Party (CP) were banned and it was an offence to be a member. The leaders of these parties were either in jail (Nelson Mandela, Walter Sisulu, etc.) or in exile (Thabo Mbeke, Oliver Tambo).

In the latter years of Apartheid, coloureds and Asians were given the vote for segregated Parliaments, but blacks were still not allowed to vote. Eventually in 1990, the ANC and other anti-Apartheid parties were legalised and Mandela and other political prisoners were released.

The first truly democratic elections in South Africa took place in 1994. The ANC won the election decisively with 63% of the vote and Nelson Mandela became the country's President.

Nelson Mandela, imprisoned for 27 years for his opposition to Apartheid and elected in 1994 as South Africa's first Black President

GOVERNMENT IN SOUTH AFRICA

South Africa is a constitutional democracy with a three-tier system of government and an independent judiciary. The national, provincial and local tiers of government have their own legislative and executive authority.

The Constitution

The Constitution of the Republic of South Africa was approved in 1996 and is the supreme law of the land. No other law or Government action can supersede the provisions of the Constitution, but the Constitution can be changed by a vote with a two-thirds majority in Parliament.

Internet research

Visit the website of the South African Government Information Service to gain further information on the South African Constitution.
Links to this site and other websites relating to Higher Modern Studies can be found at:

For you to do

- What evidence is there that the South African Constitution aims to achieve social justice?
- What evidence is there that the South African Constitution is one of the most liberal and tolerant in the world?

Structure of South African Government

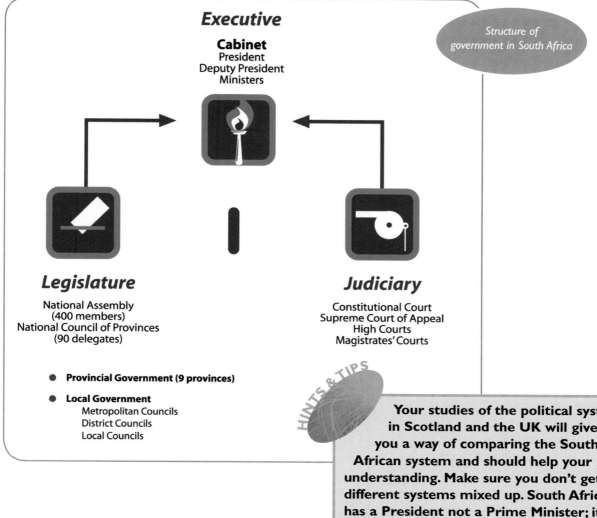

Structure of government in South Africa

Executive

Cabinet
President
Deputy President
Ministers

Legislature

National Assembly
(400 members)
National Council of Provinces
(90 delegates)

- Provincial Government (9 provinces)
- Local Government
   Metropolitan Councils
   District Councils
   Local Councils

Judiciary

Constitutional Court
Supreme Court of Appeal
High Courts
Magistrates' Courts

HINTS & TIPS

Your studies of the political system in Scotland and the UK will give you a way of comparing the South African system and should help your understanding. Make sure you don't get the different systems mixed up. South Africa has a President not a Prime Minister; it has a National Assembly not a House of Commons.

Parliament

Parliament is responsible for making the laws in South Africa. Parliament consists of the National Assembly and the National Council of Provinces.

The National Assembly:

- has no more than 400 members
- is elected for a five-year term
- consists of seats awarded to each political party using a system of proportional representation involving a mixture of national and regional lists.

The National Council of Provinces:

- consists of 54 permanent members and 36 special delegates, and elects its own chairperson (10 representatives from each of the nine provinces)
- represents the interests of the provinces.

The Executive

The President is elected by the National Assembly.

- He is the Head of State and leads the Cabinet.
- The President may not serve more than two five-year terms in office.

The Cabinet consists of the President, the Deputy President and 25 Ministers. The President appoints the Deputy President and Ministers, allocates their powers and functions, and may dismiss them.

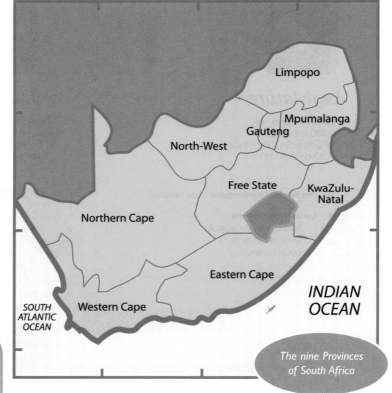

Thabo Mbeki has been President since 1999 and will be required to stand down at the next election in 2009

Provincial government

Each of South Africa's nine provinces has its own provincial government.

- Provincial laws are passed by a provincial legislature and executive power is in the hands of the provincial Premier and Executive Council.
- Provincial legislatures vary in size between 30 and 80 members and are elected at the same time as the National Assembly, every five years.
- Provinces share responsibility with the national Government over areas such as agriculture, education, health, housing and welfare.
- Provinces have complete responsibility for services such as planning, recreation and roads and traffic.

HINTS & TIPS

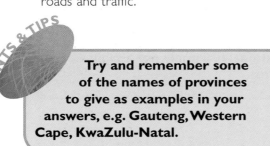

Try and remember some of the names of provinces to give as examples in your answers, e.g. Gauteng, Western Cape, KwaZulu-Natal.

The nine Provinces of South Africa

Local government

- Members of municipal councils are elected every four years.
- South Africa has 284 municipalities, responsible for a limited range of services in cities and district and local councils.
- Municipal councils are mainly responsible for the delivery of services such as water, sanitation, electricity and refuse collection.
- Since 2000, national Government has transferred more resources to local councils.

The judiciary

The Constitutional Court is the highest court in the country.

- It consists of 11 judges (eight men and three women at the moment).
- Judges are independent and are required to be impartial; they cannot be members of Parliament, the Government or political parties.
- They may serve for a non-renewable term of between 12 and 15 years but must retire at the age of 70.
- The President appoints judges, after consultation with the leaders of political parties represented in the National Assembly, from a list of names submitted by the Judicial Service Commission.
- Decisions of the court are binding on all parts of the Government.

For you to do

- Describe the political structure in South Africa today.
- Draw a simple diagram showing the institutions of government in South Africa under the headings Legislature; Executive; Judiciary.
- What is the evidence that South Africa is a democratic society?

Internet research

Visit the website of the South African Government Information Service to gain further information on South Africa's system of Government.
Use the BBC or other similar websites to find out about cases on which the South African Supreme Court has ruled recently.
Links to these sites and other websites relating to Higher Modern Studies can be found at: LECKIE&LECKIE *Learning Lab*

THE FIRST DECADE OF FREEDOM

The elections in 1994 were held under an interim Constitution. The election was greeted with great enthusiasm with voters queuing for many hours to vote. For the majority of voters, including most members of the new Government, it was the first time they had enjoyed the right to vote in their own country.

Thousands of voters wait patiently to cast their votes in South Africa's first multi-racial elections

The interim Constitution divided South Africa into nine new provinces, and required a Government of National Unity (GNU) to be formed after the election by all parties with at least 20 seats in the National Assembly.

The African National Congress (ANC) won the election with 63% of the vote. The main opposition came from the National Party (NP), which gained 20% of the vote nationally, and a majority in the Western Cape (almost wholly from white voters). The Inkatha Freedom Party (IFP) received 10% of the vote, mainly in its KwaZulu-Natal base. The NP and the IFP joined with the ANC to form the Government of National Unity until 1996, when the NP withdrew. The ANC-led Government embarked on a programme to promote the reconstruction and development of the country and its institutions and agree upon a new Constitution for the country.

For you to do

- What was the result of the election in 1994?

POLITICAL PARTIES IN SOUTH AFRICA

South Africa has an active multi-party political system, with over a dozen parties represented in Parliament. The ANC is the majority party in the National Assembly and dominates the country's nine provinces. But opposition parties play an important role. The main parties in South Africa today are the ANC, the Democratic Alliance (DA) and the IFP.

African National Congress *(293 seats in the National Assembly)*

- Formed in 1912 to defend the rights of Africans and fight for freedom.
- Banned by the Apartheid Nationalist Government. From 1961 it was an underground and exiled organisation.
- In February 1990, the Government lifted the ban and released Nelson Mandela and other political prisoners.
- In the 1994 elections the ANC won 63% of the vote. Nelson Mandela became South Africa's first democratically elected President.
- In the 1999 elections the party increased its majority to just short of two-thirds of the total vote.
- In 1999 Thabo Mbeki succeeded Mandela as leader of the ANC and President of the country. The ANC enjoys strong support from most of the black majority population in South Africa as a result of its historical role in fighting against Apartheid. It has strong support in all provinces of South Africa gaining support also from some whites, coloureds and Asians. Social and economic policies aimed at the black majority also mean it has widespread support among the most disadvantaged sections of society.

HINTS & TIPS

In a new democracy, political parties and alliances frequently change. Monitor the media for any changes. According to the Constitution of South Africa, Thabo Mbeki must stand down at the next election. Pay attention as to who becomes the leader of the ANC since they are almost certain to become the next President of South Africa.

Democratic Alliance *(47 seats in the National Assembly)*

- The Democratic Alliance, formerly known as the Democratic Party (DP), is the main opposition party in the National Assembly.
- Tony Leon became DP leader in 1996, introducing a more aggressive approach to opposition politics. The DP's campaign slogan for the 1999 elections – 'Fight Back' – gained it a substantial number of white voters who were disillusioned with the New National Party.
- It increased its vote from 1.7% in 1994 to about 10% in 1999 and over 12% in 2004, making it the official opposition.
- In 2000 the DP joined forces with the New National Party to form the Democratic Alliance (DA) (but in late 2001 the NNP withdrew from the Alliance).
- The Democratic Alliance receives most of its support from the white community. It also receives votes from coloureds in the Western Cape. It is the only opposition party to have won seats in all the provinces.

Inkatha Freedom Party
(23 seats in the National Assembly)

- The IFP, led by Mangosuthu Buthelezi, draws support largely from Zulu-speaking rural areas of KwaZulu-Natal.

- Inkatha was transformed into a political party in July 1990, championing **federalism**, the right of different areas to have a significant degree of autonomy in determining their own affairs.

- Since the 1994 elections, members of the IFP have occupied Cabinet positions at national level. In KwaZulu-Natal, it shares executive positions with the ANC in the provincial legislature.

- The IFP has failed to extend its base beyond its traditional supporters in KwaZulu-Natal and even here is under pressure from the ANC. It has some support from migrant workers in Gauteng.

Federalism: a system of government in which power is shared between the national and regional (state or provincial) governments.

There are a number of smaller political parties active in national and local politics:

- United Democratic Movement
- Independent Democrats
- African Christian Democratic Party
- Freedom Front Plus
- National Democratic Convention (Nadeco)
- Pan Africanist Congress
- United Christian Democratic Party
- Minority Front
- Azanian People's Organisation
- South African Communist Party

Political change

The ANC have dominated politics since 1994, but other parties are still developing and changing, more than 10 years after the first democratic elections. Some redistribution of the political scene took place in September 2005. Five new parties were formed,

none of which have actually contested any election. Of these, Nadeco is the largest, with four seats in the National Assembly, followed by the United Independent Front, with two seats, and three parties each with one member of the National Assembly.

The New National Party (formerly the National Party which ruled South Africa for over 40 years during the Apartheid era) has now disbanded. Support for the NNP had declined from 20% in the 1994 election, and despite alliances with other parties, it was disbanded in 2004. Most of its former representatives now belong to the ANC.

Within the ANC, tensions exist between different wings of the party. Some members believe the pace of progress is too slow and there are rivalries over the replacement for Thabo Mbeki when his term of office ends in 2009.

Internet research

Visit the website of the South African Government Information Service to gain further information on the current state of the parties in South Africa.

Visit the websites of the main political parties in South Africa.

Find out from whom each of the parties receives most of their electoral support.

Links to these sites and other websites relating to Higher Modern Studies can be found at:

For you to do

- Give evidence to support the view that South Africa is a multi-party democracy.
- Compare and contrast the three main political parties in South Africa.
- Explain why the ANC has the largest support of any party in South Africa.
- What is the evidence that South Africa is a society still in the process of political change?

TO WHAT EXTENT IS SOUTH AFRICA A DEMOCRATIC SOCIETY?

South Africa is widely viewed as having made enormous progress in establishing a multi-party, multi-racial democratic society since the end of Apartheid. However, there are still questions raised about the extent to which South Africa is a stable democratic society.

South Africa has a written Constitution which guarantees political rights and freedoms. The powers of the various parts of the political system are stated in the Constitution and the Constitution can only be changed by a two-thirds majority vote in Parliament. However, following the 2004 election, the ANC gained control of more than two-thirds of the seats in the National Assembly, giving them the power to change the Constitution. In practice the ANC have not attempted to use this dominance to make changes to the Constitution, but some opposition parties are concerned that they may try in the future.

Although South Africa has a three-tier political system, the national level is most powerful. The white minority, coloureds and Asians as well as minority African groups such as Zulus feel that they have little autonomy. Prior to the 1994 elections, groups such as the Afrikaners and black groups such as the Zulus were pressing for more power to be given to provincial Governments while the ANC were in favour of more power being held by central Government. There are some moves for more powers to be exercised at provincial and local levels, but the most important powers are still held centrally.

South Africa has had three general elections since the end of Apartheid in 1994, as well as elections for lower level institutions and local councils. There has been a smooth transfer of Presidential power from Nelson Mandela to Thabo Mbeki. Elections are conducted under a system of proportional representation ensuring the election of a wide range of political parties at all levels but particularly in the National Assembly where almost a dozen parties have members. Worries have been expressed, however, about the gradual increase in the power of the ANC, who now control over two-thirds of the National Assembly and dominate all nine of the Provincial Assemblies. Turnout in elections has also been declining since the euphoria of the first and second elections. However, at over 75% in the 2004 election, turnout is still high by international standards.

The ANC faces opposition from the large number of parties that are represented in the National Assembly. The Democratic Alliance has been effective in challenging the ANC on its policies and over allegations of incompetence and corruption. However, the opposition parties are small and divided amongst themselves. They have been plagued by instability, resignations, reformations and changing allegiances. Within the ANC itself, the leadership often faces opposition from factions who are concerned about the slow rate of progress in making social and economic progress.

South Africa has an independent judiciary and an independent media. The Constitution provides for freedom of the press. The media have often been critical and prepared to challenge the ANC. Leading members of the ANC have been accused and convicted of serious crimes. Deputy President Jacob Zuma was sacked following his alleged involvement in a bribery scandal and he has also faced trial on charges of rape. He was acquitted of the charge of rape and was reinstated to his position within the party as deputy leader; subsequently the corruption case against him collapsed but his credibility may have been seriously weakened. Although South Africa enjoys freedom of speech there have been concerns that the ANC and Thabo Mbeki are intolerant of opposition. A row erupted between the President and Archbishop Desmond Tutu, in 2004, when the Archbishop criticised the ANC and the Government over their policy of black economic empowerment (for more information on black economic empowerment see page 180).

The role of the media

The South African Constitution guarantees freedom of expression including freedom of the press and media. South Africa has a lively and robust media with a large number of competing newspapers. Reporters Without Borders (the journalistic equivalent of Médecins sans Frontières) ranks South Africa's press as the 26th freest in the world, just ahead of the United Kingdom. Ownership of most newspapers, however, is in the hands of four major corporations. The press has played a significant role in scrutinising the Government which, given the ANC's dominant position in Parliament, is an important democratic safeguard. The press has often embarrassed the Government with allegations of corruption and misgovernment.

South Africa has a varied and relatively free press and broadcast media

Television came late to South Africa although there is now a range of channels from both state and private broadcasters. The main broadcaster is the state-owned South African Broadcasting Corporation which has been criticised for pro-Government bias.

Role of pressure groups

South Africa is a relative newcomer to a democracy where all citizens have the right and opportunity to vote, and pressure group activity is still at a fairly early stage of development. The ANC have often been suspicious of independent and critical pressure groups operating outside the ranks of the ANC itself, seeing them as showing disloyalty. This suspicion has given greater weight to those who accuse the ANC of undemocratic tendencies.

The trade union movement organised under the banner of COSATU is a major force and its members have occasionally flexed their industrial muscle to protest about the slow pace of social and economic improvement for the poorest sections of South African society. However, COSATU and the Communist Party form a triple alliance with the ANC, and most of the pressure applied by COSATU takes place within the alliance rather than from outside.

Case study: Treatment Action Campaign

The AIDS crisis in South Africa has led to the establishment of an effective pressure group. The South African Government's slow response to the HIV/AIDS crisis led to the formation of the Treatment Action Campaign (TAC), led by Zackie Achmat. TAC was started in 1998 with the aim of putting pressure on the Government to increase public access to antiretroviral drugs (ARVs). Achmat, himself HIV-positive, publicised the situation by refusing to take ARVs until they were available to all South Africans. In March 2003, TAC laid culpable homicide charges against the Health Minister and her Trade and Industry colleague, claiming that the pair were responsible for the deaths of 600 HIV-positive people a day in South Africa who had no access to ARV drugs.

The Government eventually approved plans to provide public access to the drugs in November 2003. The Government's change in attitude towards ARVs was partly a result of a court battle in which GlaxoSmithKline and other pharmaceutical companies agreed to allow low-cost generic versions of their drugs to be produced in South Africa. This made South Africa one of the first African countries to produce its own AIDS drugs.

Internet research

Visit the websites of TAC and the media in South Africa.
- What are their aims?
- What tactics have they used to try and achieve these aims?
- How successful have they been?

Links to these sites and other websites relating to Higher Modern Studies can be found at:

For you to do

- What is the evidence that South Africa has a healthy and free media?

ELECTION RESULTS: FACTS AND FIGURES

NATIONAL ASSEMBLY ELECTION RESULTS						
Party	**1994**		**1999**		**2004**	
	Votes (%)	Seats	Votes (%)	Seats	Votes (%)	Seats
African National Congress (ANC)	63.1%	252	66.3%	266	69.7%	279
Democratic Alliance (DA)	1.8%	7	9.5%	38	12.3%	50
New National Party (NNP)	20.5%	82	6.9%	28	1.7%	7
Inkatha Freedom Party (IFP)	10.6%	43	6.6%	34	6.9%	28
United Democratic Movement (UDM)	–	–	3.4%	14	2.3%	9
African Christian Democratic Party (ACDP)	0.4%	2	1.4%	6	1.6%	6
Freedom Front (FF)	2.2%	9	0.8%	3	0.9%	4
Pan Africanist Congress (PAC)	1.2%	5	0.7%	3	0.7%	3
Others	0.2%	0	4.4%	8	4.0%	14
Total	100%	400	100%	400	100%	400

Source: IEC www.elections.org.za

SEATS WON IN PROVINCIAL ASSEMBLIES, 2004									
Region	**Party**								
	ANC	DA	NNP	IFP	UDM	ACDP	FF	PAC	Others
Eastern Cape	51	5	0	0	6	0	0	1	0
Free State	25	3	0	0	0	1	1	0	0
Gauteng	51	15	0	2	1	1	1	1	1
KwaZulu-Natal	38	7	0	30	1	2	0	0	2
Mpumalanga	27	2	0	0	0	0	1	0	0
Northern Cape	21	3	2	0	0	1	1	0	2
Limpopo	45	2	0	0	1	1	0	0	0
North West	27	2	0	0	0	0	1	0	3
Western Cape	19	12	5	0	1	2	0	0	3

TURNOUT IN ELECTIONS			
	1994	1999	2004
Number who voted	19,533,498	15,977,142	15,612,667
Turnout (%)	n/a	87.1	75.5

For you to do

- Study the information in the three sources above.
  – Describe the trends in support for political parties in the results of the national elections between 1994 and 2004.
  – How does the state of the parties differ across the nine Provincial Assemblies?
  – To what extent is South Africa, in reality, a one-party state?
- What conclusions can you draw about the extent of democracy in South Africa? Consider: the political institutions, the party system, and election results in South Africa.

SOCIAL AND ECONOMIC ISSUES AND INEQUALITIES

Under Apartheid, South Africa was one of the most racially unequal societies in the world. Following the 1994 elections, millions of non-Whites in South Africa who had suffered under Apartheid were eager to see a real change in their circumstances. However, the huge scale of the inequality in almost every aspect of peoples' lives and the growing population meant that the task would be enormous in scope and cost. The Government also had to be careful in its economic strategy since so much of the ownership and control of the economy was still in the hands of the white minority, and most of the skilled and professional workers were white. The international community were also concerned that drastic policies which could destabilise the economic situation in South Africa should not be enacted.

South Africa is still suffering from the inequalities of health, education, employment, housing and land ownership imposed during the Apartheid era. The ANC Government would argue that they are making a bold start of tackling these problems.

Land distribution and reform

The aim of Apartheid was the separation of the races. Most land was allocated to the white population. Blacks made up over 80% of the population but were only allowed 13% of the land. This was generally the poorest, least fertile land which lacked the rich mineral resources of much of South Africa. Many thousands of black families were cleared from land which had been allocated to whites.

Land reform has become one of the main aims of the South African Government and is being tackled in two main ways: by **restitution** of land to those who were forced from their land, and by **redistribution**, involving the transfer of Government-owned land to disadvantaged communities.

The strategy for restitution was to be based upon a voluntary principle with payments to landowners being made at market values. This approach is known as the 'willing buyer/willing seller' approach and aimed to transfer 30% of white-owned farmland over five years.

Progress in land distribution has been slower than many blacks hoped for.

- More than 90% of commercial farmland remains in the hands of 50,000 white farmers.
- Many land claims have been caught up in bureaucracy and it is difficult for claimants to prove their case.
- Many white farmers have also resisted attempts to take their land.

The Government has increased the grants available for the purchase of land. It has also adopted powers to take farms from their owners without going to court, although the Government has said this power would only be used in the last resort and confiscation would only be allowed where black South Africans could prove the land had been theirs and had been unfairly seized. Full compensation would still be paid to the white owners.

The Government is under pressure from a growing Landless People's Movement (LPM), which claims to have 100,000 members and has threatened farm invasions. As yet, land seizures of the kind seen in Zimbabwe have not happened in South Africa. LPM is pressing for the Government to **expropriate** (deprive) private landowners of land which is not being productively used and wishes to end the requirement to pay market prices for land acquired.

For you to do

- Briefly describe the land issue the Government has to deal with.
- What has the Government done to deal with this issue?
- How successful has the Government been in dealing with land inequality and reform?

Factfile: Land

- 3.5m hectares of land have been redistributed since 1994
- 0.75m hectares of state land have been redistributed
- 1.7m hectares of state land are still available for redistribution
- More than 1,500 South African farmers have been killed in land-related violence since 1991
- Between 1995 and March 1999 only 41 land claims were settled
- The Land Claims Commission has now settled 45,000 of the 79,000 claims submitted

The economy and employment

South Africa is richer and the economy is more stable than ever before.

- Growth is nearly 6%, consumer confidence is increasing, and the country's credit rating has been upgraded allowing it to borrow at better rates.
- A budget deficit of just 0.5% of GDP is the lowest for 25 years.
- Sales of vehicles and property are breaking records thanks to a growing black middle class.

Despite some good economic progress, the poorest members of South African society are still disadvantaged.

- Although jobs have been created, it has not been enough to keep up with the huge numbers entering the labour force for the first time.
- Much of the discontent about the slow rate of progress for the poorest comes from within the ANC and from its core supporters.
- There have been protests about the lack of basic services and there is concern about the solidity of the ANC vote in the future.
- Hundreds of thousands of vacancies remain unfulfilled due to a shortage of suitably skilled workers (partly caused by an inadequate education system).

The Government is trying to balance economic policies which:

- do not threaten the business community *and*
- encourage foreign investment *but also*
- meet the aspirations of those in South Africa who suffered most under Apartheid *and*
- are impatient to see an improvement in their standard of living.

Black economic empowerment

The Black Economic Empowerment Act of 2004 requires companies to go beyond the previous measures involving the transfer of a proportion of shares into black ownership. In order to be compliant with the Black Economic Empowerment (BEE) legislation, firms must now:

- have a proportion of blacks in upper and middle management positions
- undertake appropriate training programmes
- buy a proportion of materials from other companies which are BEE compliant.

There are concerns that the costs of achieving compliance will increase the overall costs of doing business. There are also worries that the legislation will only increase the demand for the relatively small number of suitably qualified black candidates for senior management positions and will do little to improve the position of the black majority.

The black middle class is growing, probably doubling since 2000. Estimates put it at 22–40% of the black population. The rise in luxury car ownership and house purchase among middle class blacks is evidence of larger numbers of affluent black South Africans. However, it has been suggested that much of the growth in middle class jobs for blacks has been in the public sector with private sector firms contributing relatively less, leading to the strengthening of the BEE legislation.

The ANC is facing growing unrest from its traditional supporters. People are fed up waiting for jobs and basic services such as electricity, clean water and sanitation. 'We used to like the ANC because it brought freedom. But freedom is not enough,' said Solly Nyathi, an unemployed 18-year-old. As well as jobs and decent schools, he said, his community wanted tin shacks replaced with decent houses. 'Until we get that it will be dangerous for the ANC.' Unemployment is not evenly spread amongst the different racial groups. In 2005, the unemployment rate among black Africans was 31.5%, 22.4% among coloured people and only 5.1% among white people.

For you to do

- Briefly describe the issues of the economy and employment the Government has to deal with.
- What has the Government done to deal with these issues?
- How successful has the Government been in dealing with these issues?

Factfile: Poverty

- 12m people (a quarter of the population) live in tin shacks, a 50% rise over the past 10 years
- 1% of people live below the international poverty line of $1 a day
- 658,000 jobs were created in the past 12 months
- The official unemployment rate is about 26% but trade unions claim the real rate is nearer 40%
- 80% of homes are connected to the National Grid and 68% of poor people receive a free water ration.

The position of Afrikaners in South Africa today

Afrikaners dominated South Africa during the Apartheid years and have seen great changes in their fortunes since 1994. They have virtually no political power within the National Assembly with the Freedom Front holding only a handful of seats and the former Afrikaner bastion, the NNP, now defunct. The Afrikaners have always seen themselves as African and so, unlike other disillusioned whites, have no other 'homeland' to re-settle to. Attempts to set up their own white homeland (or *volkstaat*) within South Africa came to nothing. Significant numbers of Afrikaners, who previously enjoyed a comfortable lifestyle, are now finding themselves in poverty and living in shanty towns, a position only blacks would previously have found themselves in.

The policy of Africanisation is threatening their culture and language with many *Afrikaans* place names being replaced by African language names. Afrikaans is being taught less frequently and many Afrikaners fear it will die out completely.

Since many Afrikaners are farmers and live in relatively isolated rural areas they feel particularly vulnerable to rural crime and the frequent attacks on isolated farms and the loss of life that often results. They look with alarm at the violence and farm takeovers in neighbouring Zimbabwe and fear that this could become their fate.

Although the frustration of the Afrikaners has led to acts of terrorism by a few extremists, the authorities have dealt swiftly with such activities.

HINTS & TIPS

Although blacks in South Africa are the most likely to be living in poverty and most whites are still wealthy, do not oversimplify by stating that all whites are rich and all blacks are poor. The end of Apartheid has seen the development of a significant, very affluent black middle class while some whites have fallen on hard times and are living in poverty.

Health

Considerable inequalities continue in health care provision in South Africa. For the majority in South Africa, health care is limited to quite basic primary health care provided free by the state, while for the wealthy, high quality private health care is available.

The health system in South Africa consists of both a public sector and a private sector.

- The public sector is under-resourced and over-used: 40% of all health expenditure is spent by the state but this sector is expected to deliver health care to 80% of the population.
- In 2000, only 24% of the total expenditure on drugs was accounted for by the state.
- The bulk of health spending in the country is by the private sector which sees to the health needs of only 20% of the population.
- The majority of health professionals, with the exception of nurses, work in the private sector.

Public health expenditure makes up 11% of the Government's total budget with most of this money being allocated to and spent by the nine provinces.

There is a variation in the standard of health care across the different provinces with poorer provinces struggling to meet the health care needs of their populations.

With the end of Apartheid, the Government began to take steps to expand health care to reach all citizens.

- White-only hospitals were opened to all.
- Since 1994, about 3,000 clinics have been built or upgraded, and 125 new mobile clinics introduced.
- There are now more than 3,500 clinics in the public sector.
- Free health care for children under six, and for pregnant or breastfeeding mothers, is available.
- Programmes were established to tackle basic health issues in the black community.
- Hundreds of foreign doctors were employed, mainly in rural areas where the shortages of trained staff were most serious.
- Newly qualified South African doctors must now complete a year of community service in understaffed hospitals and clinics.

Before these changes could have a significant impact on health, the extent of the HIV/AIDS problem became apparent and placed an almost overwhelming burden on the struggling health care system.

For you to do

- Explain the difference between health resources available for the rich and poor in South Africa.
- What steps have the South African Government taken to improve health in recent years?

Internet research

Visit the website of the South African Information Service and find up-to-date information on health care in South Africa.

Links to this site and other websites relating to Higher Modern Studies can be found at:

Impact of HIV/AIDS

HIV/AIDS in South Africa

- Approximately 5.6 million South Africans were living with HIV in 2003.
- South Africa has the fifth highest prevalence of HIV in the world.
- The UNAIDS Global Report estimated the number of AIDS-related deaths in South Africa in 2003 ranged from 270,000 to 520,000.
- Given the numbers of people infected and dying, South Africa is regarded as having the most severe HIV epidemic in the world. This epidemic is still several years away from reaching its peak.
- New infections are still increasing and show no sign of reaching a natural limit.

The HIV/AIDS epidemic has forced the Government to divert medical resources to this condition, away from other major health problems such as tuberculosis and malaria.

The impact of HIV/AIDS is obviously heaviest on those who become ill, but there are also further consequences.

- When a breadwinner becomes ill **income is lost** and scarce household resources are used to provide care.
- **Burden of caring**, particularly **children** caring for terminally ill parents, and the trauma of bereavement and orphanhood. In 2004, it was estimated that there were 2.2 million orphaned children in the country, nearly half of those due to AIDS-related illnesses.
- The **burden of care and support** has fallen heavily on the shoulders of already poverty ridden rural communities, where sick family members return when they can no longer work or care for themselves.
- There is a **huge stigma** attached to HIV/AIDS.
- **Economic growth is reduced** through the impact of HIV/AIDS. Productivity is reduced through illness and firms are faced with the cost of death benefits and spouse's pensions as well as the need to train new workers.
- The **medical insurance industry** also faces high levels of payouts to AIDS victims.

Reasons for South Africa's HIV/AIDS problems

South Africa has more people living with HIV/AIDS than any other country in the world. The factors which have led to this situation are complex and varied.

- **Poverty**
  - —The highest levels of HIV/AIDS infections are amongst blacks, with lower rates for coloureds and Asians and by far the lowest rate amongst whites, which corresponds with the distribution of wealth in South Africa.
  - —Poverty leads to poor nutrition which lowers resistance to infection.
  - —Good health care is inaccessible to those with low incomes.
  - —Poverty limits availability of expensive drugs and medical treatment.

- **Breakdown of traditional patterns of behaviour** has led to a high level of mobility and weakening of family ties.
- The **migrant labour system** leads to the separation of family members and a high level of prostitution.
- High levels of **sexual violence** have increased the rate of transmission of HIV/AIDS.
- High levels of **sexually transmitted diseases** reduce resistance and increase the level of infection.
- **Unequal role of women** means that young women have the highest level of infection.
- Low use of **condoms**.
- The **stigma** attached to issue of HIV/AIDS has meant that many of those infected are reluctant to submit to testing and therefore continue to pass on the infection to others.
- Limited availability of drugs and medical treatment due to the **reluctance of the health ministry** to sanction the use of proven treatments.

Government attitude

The Government was slow to appreciate the seriousness of the HIV/AIDS problem. This can be partly blamed on the focus on other priorities immediately after 1994 as well as a degree of personal embarrassment on the part of Nelson Mandela. However the attitude of President Mbeki has contributed to the seriousness of the problem. He questioned the link between HIV and AIDS, and also questioned statistics on HIV infection and AIDS-related mortality. It took court action to compel the Minister of Health to implement a mother-to-child transmission prevention programme. In April 2002 the Cabinet agreed that antiretroviral drugs (ARVs) should be made available to all rape victims, and that Government should consider introducing ARVs into public health. In 2003, Cabinet announced the rollout of a comprehensive AIDS treatment plan that would offer free ARVs. However, Health Minister Tshabalala-Msimang continued to advocate a traditional diet of beetroot, olive oil, African potato and garlic for people with HIV.

Despite all these setbacks, proper treatment is becoming more widely available as health facilities develop the capacity to manage patients on ARVs. The Government has increased the budget allocation to enable the targets for the treatment plan and other HIV/AIDS initiatives to be met. The Government continues to invest in prevention efforts as the core of its HIV/AIDS strategy and promotes good nutrition as well as traditional medicine. At the same time, there are a range of social benefits available to people living with HIV/AIDS and impoverished households.

Efforts to stem the tide of new infections have only had limited success, as behaviour change and social change are long-term processes, and factors such as poverty, illiteracy, and gender inequalities cannot be addressed in the short term.

Internet research

Visit the websites of the South African Information Service and groups dealing with AIDS in South Africa. Find up-to-date statistics on levels of HIV/AIDS in South Africa and the effects on the population.
Links to these sites and other websites relating to Higher Modern Studies can be found at:

LECKIE&LECKIE
Learning Lab

For you to do

● Describe the extent of the HIV/AIDS problem in South Africa.
● How does this problem impact on South Africa?
● How has the attitude of the Government hampered progress in dealing with HIV/AIDS?
● What progress, if any, has been made in dealing with AIDS in South Africa?

Education

Under Apartheid, education was separate and unequal between the races. This inequality was one of the main ways in which the white minority maintained their position of dominance. For a whole generation of young blacks, boycotting education was seen as part of the struggle against Apartheid. Others saw no point in education as a means to make progress for themselves. This left the education gap between black and white even wider.

Education accounts for over 20% of public spending, but the Government admits that it is not enough, with the biggest problems being in the poorer, rural areas.

Although formerly whites-only schools have been opened up to black students, huge inequalities still remain. The gap in educational attainment is shown in the table below.

Many black students still have inadequate education facilities

HIGHEST LEVEL OF EDUCATION ATTAINED THOSE AGED 20+ IN SOUTH AFRICA, 2003					
Race	*No schooling*	*Some/ completed primary*	*Some secondary*	*Completed secondary ('matric')*	*Higher education*
Black	22.3%	25.4%	30.4%	16.8%	5.2%
Coloured	8.3%	28.2%	40.1%	18.5%	4.9%
Asian	5.3%	11.9%	33.0%	34.9%	14.9%
White	1.4%	2.0%	25.9%	40.9%	29.8%

Source: *Statistics South Africa*

The education system is a mixture of state provision and private. Government provides a minimum level of funding in state schools but parents are expected to contribute to top up this provision. Affluent parents are able to contribute most and their children receive the best education. A small proportion of pupils and students attend private schools and universities. The inequality in education reflects the wider inequalities in living standards in the society and remains one of the main factors in the overall economic inequalities in South Africa.

There is an enormous shortage of suitably qualified teachers in state schools. The proportion of unqualified teachers in the system is higher than it was 30 years ago. Examination pass rates show a huge variation with the pass rates in the state-funded public schools attended by the majority of blacks being the worst. Increasing numbers of black parents are making sacrifices to get their children into independent or private schools although the fees remain prohibitively high for most. Inadequate school qualifications and high fees prevent most black students progressing from school to university.

For you to do

- Describe the differing levels of success in education by different racial groups.
- Explain the inequalities in education in South Africa.
- What progress has been made in tackling educational disadvantage in South Africa?
- Explain why education is seen as a key programme for tackling disadvantage in South Africa.

Internet research

Visit the website of the South African Information Service and find up-to-date information on education in South Africa.

Links to this site and other websites relating to Higher Modern Studies can be found at:

Crime

South Africa has high levels of crime and violence. Crime is a huge problem and preoccupies many whites. White South Africans who can afford to do so will take many measures to try and protect themselves and their families.

- High fences topped by razor wire surround their homes.
- CCTV cameras, guard dogs and private security patrols are amongst the security measures taken by whites.
- Gun ownership is common and even from a young age, many white South Africans take lessons in the use of firearms.

South Africa continues to have one of the highest crime rates in the world

HINTS & TIPS

HIV/AIDS and crime are major problems in South Africa, but there is no need to exaggerate their significance. Do not rely on anecdotes in your answer at the expense of reasoned examples.

Although many whites are concerned about levels of crime and violence, it is blacks living in the townships who are most likely to be the victims of crime, with violent crime being a particular problem. The level of sexual violence including rape is particularly high and is a contributing factor in the high incidence of HIV/AIDS. It has been estimated that a woman is raped every 26 seconds, that only one in nine rapes is ever reported, and only 7% of reported cases lead to conviction.

The reality and perception of crime as a major problem is of concern to the Government. Potential foreign investors may be deterred if the safety of their employees cannot be guaranteed, and potential tourists may be deterred from visiting. Both impacts have a negative effect on the economy.

Lack of success in reducing crime levels provides an opportunity for opposition parties to attack the Government. Although the Government is spending more on law and order, failure to deal with crime is bad for the image of the Government. Law enforcement forces are ineffective and South Africa has seen a rise in vigilante groups as well as private security firms.

Reasons for the high level of crime in South Africa

- Apartheid was an **inherently violent** system, kept in place by the white controlled state, including the police forces.
- The police and security forces are still **not trusted** by the black population.
- There are huge number of **weapons** in circulation in South Africa.
- Police officers are **poorly paid** for a very dangerous job, and new recruits lack training.
- The court system is often **unable to convict** suspects.
- Greater **freedom of movement** causes greater fear among some whites.
- **Alcohol abuse** is a major cause of crime.
- The huge **gap in the economic and social positions** between the richest and poorest is still one of the worst in the world.
- The rapid **urbanisation** of the population and the influx of immigrants from other African countries mean that here are many people who cannot find a legal way of making a living.

Urbanisation: the movement of large numbers of rural people into urban areas, usually in search of better jobs and living conditions.

Government response to crime

The Government has massively increased the police budget, which has gone up five-fold in 10 years. They have introduced new laws to tackle crime and shortcomings in the criminal justice system, introducing minimum sentences and tighter bail conditions.

The Government claims that the official statistics show a fall in crime, in particular, the number of murders. They say this is the most reliable measure of success since virtually all murders are reported to the police. Critics, however, point out that the fall in murders can largely be attributed to the fall in politically motivated violence and that although this is to be welcomed it does not indicate any real fall in the level of criminally associated murders.

For you to do

- Why are the black and white people so concerned about the level of crime?
- What are the reasons for high levels of crime in South Africa?
- What problems do high crime levels cause the Government?
- What policies have the Government of South Africa introduced to tackle the problem of crime?
- How successful have the Government been in tackling crime in South Africa?

Internet research

Visit the website of the South African Information Service and find up-to-date information on crime in South Africa.

Links to this site and other websites relating to Higher Modern Studies can be found at:

Housing

A shortage of decent housing was one of the most pressing challenges facing the new Government in 1994. At the time it was estimated that there was a need to build over 2 million new houses to deal with the shortage. The 1996 Constitution states that everyone 'has the right to have access to adequate housing' and that the state 'must take reasonable legislative and other measures, within its available resources, to achieve the progressive realisation of this right.' Provincial and local governments share responsibility with the national government for delivery of adequate housing.

Housing conditions in many rural areas have improved little over the last 10 years

High levels of unemployment and low wage levels contribute to a major affordability problem in South Africa, and the ability to pay for housing is severely limited among most families in the country. The Government has adopted a strategy to provide subsidy assistance to households that are unable to satisfy their housing needs independently.

The housing subsidy scheme is aimed at the poorest of the poor, yet the income level has not been changed from R 3,500 per month or less, meaning one has to be poorer in real terms today than a decade ago to qualify for a subsidy. HIV/AIDS has compounded the problem as people spend their income on health care rather than housing.

The process of urbanisation means that the housing situation in urban areas is even more difficult. The building of 1.5 million new houses means that a larger percentage of the population now lives in formal houses.

The Government has not achieved its goal of 350,000 houses per year and the number of people living in inadequate housing has increased. Population growth and urbanisation combine to increase the need for housing at a rate as fast as or faster than it is being built.

Some progress has been made in providing services. Free basic water is now widely available and free basic electricity is now becoming available. But it will be at least a decade before these services are available to all.

Factfile: Housing

- In 1994 there was only one formal brick house for every 43 Africans compared to one for every 3.5 whites.
- The urban backlog alone was estimated as at least 1.3 million units in 1994.
- Between 7.5 and 10 million people lived in informal housing such as shacks in squatter camps and back yards of black township houses.

Achievements

- 1.6 million new houses built for the poor
- 70% households have access to electricity
- 9 million more people have access to water

Challenges

- 2–3 million new homes are still needed
- 7.5 million people are still in need of adequate housing
- Many cannot afford basic services

The provision of clean water supplies to all South Africans remains a major priority for the Government

Internet research

Visit the website of the South African Information Service and find up-to-date information on housing in South Africa. Links to this site and other websites relating to Higher Modern Studies can be found at:

LECKIE&LECKIE
Learning Lab

For you to do

- Make up a table for housing and basic services. On one side put down progress made so far, on the other side put down things still to be done.
- Draw a mind map showing the interrelationships between social and economic inequalities facing South African people. Annotate the mind map further to show what the Government has done to address specific issues and where more needs to be done.
- What evidence is there of social and economic inequality in South Africa?
- Discuss the claim that despite the end of Apartheid, blacks and whites still live largely separate and unequal lives.
- South Africa has been an example of a success in making social and economic progress for all its citizens. Discuss.

STUDY THEME SUMMARY

From 1948 to 1994, South Africa was governed by the racist policy of Apartheid. In 1994, the country's first democratic elections were held and there has been a largely peaceful transition from the Apartheid regime to a multi-racial society which accepts the legitimacy of the new Government. Nelson Mandela was elected in 1994 as the country's first black President, and in 1999 he was replaced by Thabo Mbeki. South Africa is a constitutional democracy, with three levels of government – national, provincial and local – and an independent judiciary. Power is largely centralised in the national government and there are some concerns that the dominant ANC may use its two-thirds majority in the Parliament to effect constitutional change.

The first decade of democratic freedom has been a time of flux in the political scene – alliances forming and changing, parties dissolving, new parties being created. There are more than a dozen parties represented in the National Assembly, but the three main parties are the ANC, the DA and the IFP. The ANC also dominates at the level of provincial government. Its dominance increases the importance of scrutiny and criticism by organisations outside the government scene, such as pressure groups and the media.

The years of Apartheid have left a legacy of massive social and economic inequality. The ANC Government has been given praise by the international community for its handling of the economy. Much has been achieved, but there are still massive challenges for the Government, such as addressing an unemployment rate of about 26%, helping the 5.3 million people with HIV/AIDS, improving educational and housing provision for the disadvantaged, the massive wealth inequality, crime rates (actual and perceived). There is now a significant black middle class, but the Government must also handle the growing impatience of the poorest section of the black population over the slow pace of progress, whilst being mindful that some whites are concerned about favouritism being shown towards blacks, and that some whites are leaving the country and taking valuable skills and experience with them.

Exam-style essay questions

Describe the main features of the political system in South Africa.

Critically examine the claim that there is no effective opposition to the African National Congress.

Examine the effectiveness of the South African Government in dealing with two of the following issues: health, housing, employment.

STUDY THEME 3B:
The People's Republic of China

In this study theme you will be expected to have a detailed knowledge and understanding of:

- ## THE CHINESE POLITICAL SYSTEM

  The role and powers of the Chinese Government at national, provincial and local levels.

- ## POLITICAL ISSUES

  Participation and representation. The role of the Chinese Communist Party and the extent of political opposition. Political trends.

- ## SOCIAL AND ECONOMIC ISSUES

  The nature and extent of social and economic inequalities; demands for change; the effectiveness of Government responses and the consequences for different groups.

BACKGROUND TO CHINA'S LAND AND PEOPLE

China occupies a large portion of south-east and central Asia. It has an area of over 9.5 million square kilometres, making it the fourth largest country (in terms of area) in the world after Russia, Canada and USA (and about 120 times bigger than Scotland). It is the most populous country in the world, with a population of more than 1.3 billion people. The land varies enormously, from deserts in the west, tropical forests in the south and high mountains in the south-east.

China has huge reserves of many natural resources, including coal, petroleum and natural gas, and minerals such as iron ore mercury, tin, tungsten, antimony and manganese. It also has significant reserves of uranium and huge potential for hydro-electric power. About half the land area is under agricultural use, although there are major problems with soil erosion and desertification.

There are many ethnic groups in China, but the majority of the population are Han Chinese, comprising over 90% of the population.

China is a Communist state, although the type of Communism being practised now is very different to the Communism of Chairman Mao in the 1950s and 1960s. The country is in a state of transformation, as it moves from a *centrally controlled economy* in which government plans and controls all elements of the economy to a *market economy* which is becoming increasingly important in the global economy. Despite these changes to the way in which the government controls the economy, China remains a *one-party state* without the democratic structures which are common in other market economies.

China has the world's fourth largest economy, and with its rapid growth, is predicted to become the largest economy by 2020. It is the third largest importer and exporter in the world, and the rapid expansion of the economy is driving a major construction boom, making it the major consumer of steel and concrete. It is a permanent member of the UN Security Council, and is considered by some to be an emerging superpower to rival the USA.

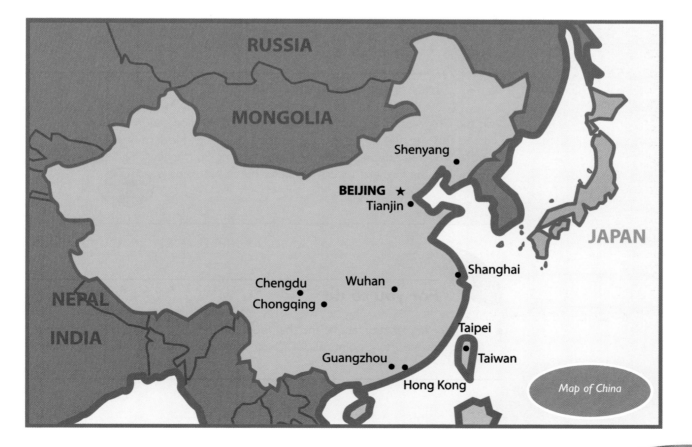

Map of China

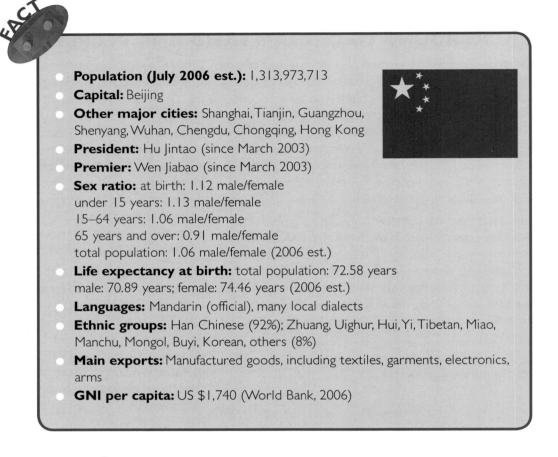

- **Population (July 2006 est.):** 1,313,973,713
- **Capital:** Beijing
- **Other major cities:** Shanghai, Tianjin, Guangzhou, Shenyang, Wuhan, Chengdu, Chongqing, Hong Kong
- **President:** Hu Jintao (since March 2003)
- **Premier:** Wen Jiabao (since March 2003)
- **Sex ratio:** at birth: 1.12 male/female
  under 15 years: 1.13 male/female
  15–64 years: 1.06 male/female
  65 years and over: 0.91 male/female
  total population: 1.06 male/female (2006 est.)
- **Life expectancy at birth:** total population: 72.58 years
  male: 70.89 years; female: 74.46 years (2006 est.)
- **Languages:** Mandarin (official), many local dialects
- **Ethnic groups:** Han Chinese (92%); Zhuang, Uighur, Hui, Yi, Tibetan, Miao, Manchu, Mongol, Buyi, Korean, others (8%)
- **Main exports:** Manufactured goods, including textiles, garments, electronics, arms
- **GNI per capita:** US $1,740 (World Bank, 2006)

Internet research

Visit the CIA World Fact book website and read the information about China. Links to this site and other websites relating to Higher Modern Studies can be found at: **www.leckieandleckie.co.uk** by clicking on the Learning Lab button and navigating to the Higher Modern Studies Course Notes page.

For you to do

- Using the information above and that found on the CIA website, make brief notes about five important points about China. Think particularly about the population.

THE STRUCTURE OF THE CHINESE GOVERNMENT

The Constitution establishes China as a **one-party state**, with the Communist Party being the only party allowed to hold power. Despite this, the structure of the Chinese Government is quite complicated because of the overlapping relationship between the Communist Party and the Government.

The Communist Party of China (CPC) dominates all aspects of Chinese politics and controls all the workings of government. The current Chinese Head of State, President Hu Jintao, is also the General Secretary of the CPC.

The structure of China's government is determined by the Constitution, with a number of tiers of central, provincial and local government. At each level of government, there are party and non-party members on all relevant bodies, but party members tend to be more influential.

The political system of China depends on a series of elections to Peoples' Congresses at different levels, from village up through the provincial structures to national level. Only the lowest level of elections for village committees are genuinely open elections subject to direct popular vote. This makes it possible for independent members to be elected to village committees, but they cannot hold positions of power, and they are not able to organise in such a way as to be able to elect members for the next highest level of People's Congress.

One-party state: a state in which only one party is allowed to form the Government and no opposition parties are allowed.

Internet research

Visit the Chinatoday website, and find the pages for the Government and the Communist Party of China. Read and take brief notes about the committee structures in the Party and the Government. How many members of the CPC also hold senior positions in the Government?
Links to these sites and other websites relating to Higher Modern Studies can be found at:

For you to do

- Describe the structure of the CPC, the structure of the Government, and how they overlap. How much independence do you think the Government has from the Party?

GOVERNMENT	COMMUNIST PARTY OF CHINA
President/Head of State (*Hu Jintao*) Formally elected by the **National People's Congress** (in a single-candidate election), but in practice, the President is selected after negotiations within the CPC.	**General Secretary** (*Hu Jintao*) Heads the **Secretariat of the Communist Party of China** (CPC) and is most senior figure of the **Politburo Standing Committee**.
Premier/Head of Government/Prime Minister (*Wen Jinbao*) Chosen in the same way as the President. Member of the **Standing Committee of the Politburo of the CPC**, and chairs the **State Council of the Government**.	
National People's Congress (NPC) Highest legislative body in government. Heavily influenced by the CPC, but becoming less dependent. **Chairman of NPC** is also member of **CPC Politburo**. 3,000 delegates, who meet annually for about two weeks at about the same time as the **Chinese People's Political Consultative Committee**.	**Politburo** Most senior committee of the CPC, consisting of 19–25 members, meeting every month. Role of Politburo is to oversee the CPC. Members are nominally appointed by the **Central Committee of the CPC**. Members of the Politburo also hold positions in the Government. The **Standing Committee of the Politburo** comprises the senior leadership of the CPC and its members are the most influential people in the country. Membership includes the **Party General Secretary**, the **Premier** and the **Chairman of the NPC**.
Standing Committee of the NPC A committee of the NPC with 150 members, convened between annual NPC meetings. Has the power to modify legislation (within limits).	**Party Congress** Theoretically the highest body in the CPC, but it only meets every five years and most decisions are agreed before the meetings.
Chinese People's Political Consultative Committee (CPPCC) Political advisory body, consisting of CPC members and non-CPC members. Discussions tend to be dominated by debates about the principles of Chinese Communism.	**Central Committee** The highest body in the CPC between Party Congress meetings. Has about 300 members, but has no formal authority. However, its members include leading figures in the Government, army and party.
State Council of the Central People's Government The chief administrative body of Government, chaired by the Premier, which includes the heads of all government departments. Most members of the State Council are also senior members of the CPC.	

REGIONAL AND LOCAL GOVERNMENT

Regional and local government structures are similar to the national structure in the way the powers are largely determined by the CPC. Provincial and local leaders are all appointed by the CPC.

At a regional level, China is governed as 22 provinces (although Taiwan is claimed by China as a 23rd province), five autonomous regions and four municipalities.

The **four municipalities** – Beijing, Shanghai, Tianjin and Chongqing – are the major cities in China and are considered so important that they are under central government control.

The **five autonomous regions** – Guangxi, Inner Mongolia, Ningxia, Tibet and Xinjiang – have large ethnic minority populations and have a degree of autonomy from the national government.

There are also **two Special Administrative Regions** – Hong Kong and Macau – which have a much greater degree of autonomy than the autonomous regions and operate under very different political and economic structures.

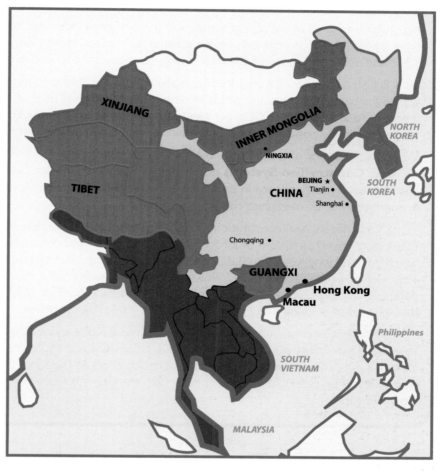

Provincial government

Within the 22 provinces of mainland China, there are further subdivisions of local government: the prefecture, county, township and village. Each level of government has a People's Congress, elected on a regular basis every three or five years (depending on the level). Although there are elections to the People's Congresses, local government leaders are appointed by the CPC, so the CPC retains considerable control over local government.

It has been estimated there are 700,000 villages in China, each with its own village committee. Village elections were introduced in 1988, and are held every three years. They were introduced by the government to help maintain social and political order at a time of much change and potential conflict. Village committees oversee the administration of the village, including land and property management, health and utilities. (Chinese villages can have populations up to 10,000 people, although the average is between 1,000 and 2,000.)

Hong Kong

Hong Kong consists of a group of islands and some mainland territory on the south-east coast of China. The total area is just 1,104 square kilometres. The British leased Hong Kong from the Chinese government in 1842, and under the terms of the lease, Hong Kong reverted to Chinese sovereignty in 1997.

As a British colony, Hong Kong developed an enormously strong economy, becoming a major international centre for banking, finance and global trading. It has the highest level of GDP per head of population in the whole of Asia, and a higher GDP per head of population than the UK, France, Italy and Germany. It is one of the most densely populated areas of the world, with 6,300 people per square kilometre.

When the territory of Hong Kong reverted to Chinese control in 1997, it was given special status under the **One Country Two Systems** policy developed by the Chinese Government. This gave Hong Kong a high degree of independence in the way it is governed and allowed Hong Kong to carry on as a capitalist economy within a Communist country.

Hong Kong has its own constitution called the **Basic Law**. This spells out the basic civil rights (such as freedom of speech, freedom of association, religious belief and conscience), and the democratic structures which govern Hong Kong. The Basic Law states that the capitalist system which existed in Hong Kong before 1997 will be maintained until 2047. However, there is already conflict between civil rights as guaranteed in the Basic Law and laws passed by the Chinese Government. A number of large pro-democracy demonstrations have been held in Hong Kong to try to influence government policies.

There is a difficult balancing act for politicians in Hong Kong and in China. The Chinese Government wants to exert greater control over Hong Kong, but it does not want to damage the economy, so it needs to be careful about how it tries to influence the administration. At the same time, the Hong Kong administration also needs to be careful about how it deals with the Chinese Government so that it does not appear to be challenging it.

The People's Liberation Army

The People's Liberation Army (PLA) is the third pillar of authority in China along with the Government and the CPC. With over 2 million troops, it is the largest army in the world.

The PLA is controlled by the Central Military Commission (CMC). There are actually two Central Military Commissions, one belonging to the state and one to the CPC, but their members are usually the same people. The Chairman and Vice-Chairman of the CMC are usually civilian leaders of Government, but the other members are active officers of the PLA. Because of the way members are appointed to the state and party CMCs, the CPC effectively controls the PLA.

For you to do

- Describe the problems for the Chinese Government posed by Hong Kong.
- Draw a diagram showing the different levels within the Chinese Government – from the very top to the bottom.

POLITICAL PARTIES IN CHINA

Politics in China is dominated by the Communist Party, which has been in control of the country since the revolution in 1949. There are a number of small parties which are recognised by the Government and are allowed to participate in Chinese politics. There are also a number of illegal parties and parties in exile, which are not allowed to participate in Chinese politics.

Communist Party of China

The Communist Party of China (CPC) was founded in 1921, and with over 70 million members, it is the largest political party in the world. The CPC can be considered to be one of the three bodies of power in China, the others being the Government and the People's Liberation Army, and there are strong links between these three bodies. Under the terms of the Chinese Constitution the CPC is the only party allowed to hold power at the national level.

The CPC has recently attempted to modernise China, making significant changes to the type of communist ideology it promotes. Whilst maintaining an authoritarian one-party state, it has moved away from a controlled centrally planned economy to a market economy. The result has been rapid economic growth and improved living standards for many Chinese.

Corruption

'We see the fight against corruption as a top priority, a pressing task that has great influence on the overall development of the country.' — President Hu Jintao, at anti-corruption conference October 2006

4 Chinese Judges Charged With Bribery

Four Chinese judges have been charged with taking bribes to fix cases, a news report said Friday, following a warning by President Hu Jintao that corruption is threatening China's well-being.

The cases in the eastern province of Anhui come amid a widening, high-profile corruption scandal in Shanghai, but there was no indication the cases are related.

Zhang Zimin, former president of the Intermediate People's Court in Fuyang, a city in Anhui, stood trial Wednesday on charges that he took more than $162,000, the official Xinhua News Agency said.

Zhang was accused of taking bribes to arrange jobs and intervene in trials, Xinhua said. It said no verdict had been reached.

A Communist Party official and former judge in Fuyang, Shang Jun, is charged with taking $114,000 in bribes, Xinhua said. It said two other former judges, Liu Jiayi and Wang Jianmin, face similar charges.

The government has punished thousands of officials in a multiyear effort to stop widespread corruption that threatens to erode public acceptance of communist rule.

A senior prosecutor said this week that more than 17,500 officials have been punished this year for corruption.

Source: from Associated Press, 27 October 2006

Membership of the CPC has grown in recent years, largely because membership is seen to be advantageous either financially or politically. In some places it has become common for branches to pay members to attend regular meetings.

Internet research

Read the rest of the article about corruption at the AP News website.
Links to this site can be found at: LECKIE&LECKIE *Learning Lab*

For you to do

- Why is corruption rife in China? Give evidence to show the extent of corruption.
- Why is the Government trying to clamp down on corruption?

Other legal parties in China

There are eight legal political parties apart from the CPC, including the Revolutionary Committee of the Kuomintang, the China Democratic League, the Chinese Peasants' and Workers' Democratic Party and the Taiwan Democratic Self-Government League. Unlike most multi-party democracies, these parties do not to act as an Opposition to the Government, but they are allowed to participate in Government discussions.

Although these parties are allowed to make their voice heard, they are not allowed any formal organisational status, so they have no legal way of raising party funds or political campaigning.

Banned parties in China

Opposition parties are not formally banned in China, but a wide range of laws prevent such parties being formed. These laws generally include crimes such as subversion (attempting to overthrow the state), sedition (inciting hostility against the state), and the leaking of state secrets. Because of this, any opposition parties exist in exile and their supporters in China are liable to be arrested if their activities become known to the authorities.

Parties in exile include:

- the **China Democracy Party** – based in the USA and founded in 1998 by activists who had been involved in the 1989 Tiananmen Square protests
- the **Inner Mongolian People's Party** – also based in the USA, this group campaigns for the independence of Inner Mongolia
- the **National Democratic Party of Tibet** – campaigns for Tibetan independence.

Separatist and nationalist movements in China

A number of regions of China have strong separatist movements, which campaign for independence from China. Both Tibet and Inner Mongolia were invaded by China and the citizens have been placed under Chinese rule against their will.

The Chinese Government and the Tibetan government-in-exile even disagree over the area that can be called Tibet. At its simplest, it can be said that there was once an independent Tibetan nation which is no longer independent from Chinese rule. There is a strong Tibetan nationalist movement, with an established government-in-exile, based in India under the leadership of the Dalai Lama. The current position of the government-in-exile is not to seek full independence but to accept Tibet as an autonomous region of China.

Inner Mongolia was taken over by the Chinese at the end of the Second World War and various neighbouring territories were added on to it. Over the course of history, Inner Mongolia has not had a single national identity and this may explain why the nationalist movement does not have the same level of support as the equivalent movements in Tibet and Taiwan.

Taiwan is a large island off the south coast of China. It was formerly a part of China, but after the Chinese Civil War in 1949, a separate government was established in Taiwan. This government called itself the Republic of China and claimed sovereignty over mainland China. Similarly, the government in mainland China, called the People's Republic of China, claimed sovereignty over Taiwan. The precise status of Taiwan is still confused and the dispute between the governments continues to cause difficulties. Over recent decades, Taiwan has established itself as a powerful industrial democracy.

Dissidents in China

The recent economic liberalisation has not been matched by similar liberalisation of the political system. Dissent against the Government is strongly discouraged. The Ministry of State Security was established in 1983 to monitor the activities of political dissidents and to collect domestic and foreign intelligence. The extent to which the Chinese Government will act to suppress dissent was shown dramatically in 1989 when democracy campaigners gathered in **Tiananmen Square** in Beijing and hundreds of protesters were allegedly killed by the Chinese army. Many of those involved in the Tiananmen Square protests are still held in prison.

The Chinese Government accepts certain religious and spiritual groups, but a number of illegal religious groups exist despite the dangers of belonging to them. The Falun Gong movement is the most widespread of these illegal religious groups, and members are regularly arrested, ill-treated, and in the worst cases, tortured and executed. (See also pages 212–216 for more information on the Chinese Government's approach to human rights issues.)

Internet research

Choose one of the illegal/exiled parties. Find its website and make up a spider diagram to show the following: name of party; when it was formed; why it was formed; its position now in China; what its aims are; example/s of protest. Write a short paragraph using this information.
Research examples of political activity – the dissident Zhao Changqing using the Wikipedia website and the separatist Uighurs using the WorldWide Religious News website. Make notes on the Government's reaction to such activities.
Links to these sites and other websites relating to Higher Modern Studies can be found at:

The role of the middle and business classes in politics

Surprisingly, the growth of the middle and business classes – the result of successful economic reforms – has not led to growing pressures for greater democracy in China. Since 1989, the Government has taken actions to try to prevent middle class activism:

- clamping down very hard on political organisations which attempt to promote democratic reforms
- winning over the middle classes by making their lives easier if they conform to the requirements of the CPC and the Government.

Many members of the middle classes have been allowed to join the CPC and have gained positions as Government officials, with good, well paid jobs and preferential treatment in housing, education and health care.

It is not possible to say whether this situation will last. As people become richer, they will travel more and gain more experience of the rest of the world. If they begin to feel their standards of living are not as good as elsewhere, they may begin to show more dissent in opposition to the Government.

Opportunities for political participation

For the ordinary citizen, there are few opportunities for political participation. With the exception of local government elections, there are no opportunities for citizens to vote for the leadership of the country, and membership of the CPC is only permitted after a formal application process, which involves extensive screening and approval.

However, there are a considerable number of organisations which do allow some degree of political action. The most prominent of these are the Federation of Trade Unions and the All-China Women's Federation. These organisations are related to the CPC but do have their own aims to promote. For example, the Federation of Trade Unions calls for reform of trade unions. In 2004, trade union membership in China was 137 million, although it should be recognised that employees of government agencies or state-owned businesses are given automatic membership of a trade union. Independent trade unions are not allowed.

Political activity is dominated by men, with few opportunities for women to participate. At the lowest levels of government, this is generally explained by women's lack of confidence resulting in their reluctance to stand as candidates, and the continuing attitude that sees women as being incapable of leadership. The All-China Women's Federation is attempting to address these problems by targeting sexist attitudes and promoting equality, and by actively working to improve women's skills and abilities.

For you to do

- If China is a single-party state, why are other political parties allowed?
- To what extent is China a democracy?
- Assess demands for political reform in China.

THE MEDIA IN CHINA

In the past, all the media – television, radio and newspapers – were controlled by the Government and acted as the propaganda arm of the Government. Many of the large media organisations are still agencies of the Government, and so it is not surprising that there are restrictions on what is allowed in the media. However, there are also independent privately owned newspapers and magazines which have more freedom than the state-controlled media. It is harder for the Government to control new technologies such as the internet.

Foreign media companies can operate in China, but they need a Government permit which is not always given. Similarly, foreign companies can invest in Chinese media companies. Three foreign TV companies (Viacom, CNN and BBC World) are allowed to broadcast in China, although in restricted areas. The Chinese Government banned foreign satellite TV stations in 2005 in order to apply greater control over what could be broadcast.

The main newspaper in China is the *People's Daily*, which is the official newspaper of the CPC. There are a wide range of other newspapers, covering most elements of society, with newspapers for peasants, workers, and the middle-classes, and covering subjects ranging from the economy and technology to diverse cultural issues.

It is estimated that there are now about 700 terrestrial TV channels, 3,000 cable channels, and about 1,000 radio stations. The national broadcaster, Chinese Central Television (CCTV) is overseen by the Government, with the propaganda department having responsibility for content. The head of CCTV is a Government minister, and all senior staff are appointed by the Government.

Radio is a growing medium, with a number of privately owned organisations having extensive radio networks alongside the two state-owned national radio networks. A notable development is the growth of talk radio stations, with discussions of a wide range of topics, including levels of political debate which could not have been tolerated a few years ago.

Magazines and journals cover a wide range of social and political issues. There is considerable freedom for political discussion and magazines will often publish articles critical of the Government. Only in extreme cases will the Government take action against journalists. Economic liberalisation also means that the media are less reliant on the Government for funding and are free to generate their own revenue through advertising.

The internet is a growing source of information in China. It is estimated that one billion people in China (about 75% of the population) will have internet access by 2010. The internet allows users to read unregulated news which they would not get from the normal media in China. The Government has tried to block access to certain websites through the use of firewall and routing filters. The search engine company Google was involved in controversy when it agreed to Chinese Government demands to launch a censored Chinese version of its search engine in 2006. (See also pages 212–213 for more information on freedom of speech.)

Internet research

Visit the Google website to find the official explanation for their decision to launch a censored version of their search engine. Comment on and evaluate the arguments given.

Visit the BBC website and read the article about the Chinese authorities allowing access to Wikipedia. Make notes and compare the Wikipedia decision with the Google decision.

Links to these sites and other websites relating to Higher Modern Studies can be found at:

For you to do

- Give examples of how the Government controls different parts of the media.
- Why is the use of the internet expanding in China?
- Why does the Government see this as a potential problem?

PROGRESS TOWARDS A MARKET ECONOMY

China has been reforming its economy since the late 1970s, but only recently has it become a major power in the world economy. After the Second World War, the economy was dominated by the state. The Government controlled every aspect of business and industry. The Government developed Five Year Plans, which laid out the ways in which all commodities were to be made. The emphasis was heavily on agriculture, to meet the needs of the growing population, and on steel production.

However, these Five Year Plans and the centrally controlled economy proved ineffective in meeting the needs of the population, and large numbers of the Chinese population were living in poverty. In 1981, it is estimated, over half the population was living in poverty.

The economy was reformed progressively:

- from the late1970s, farmers were allowed to sell surplus produce on the open market (instead of selling through Government agencies at fixed prices)
- restrictions on what farmers were allowed to produce were removed
- rules about industrial production were relaxed, allowing factories to produce things for which there was a demand instead of having to fill government quotas (even when there was no demand for a particular item)
- there has been further easing of restrictions on private ownership of businesses – about 70% of the gross domestic product of China now comes from the private sector. The whole package of reforms has been remarkably successful, and the Chinese economy has grown at an annual rate of 9.4% over the period 1980 to 2005. Poverty levels have dropped dramatically from 53% in 1981 to 8% in 2001.

The decline of state ownership

State ownership in the economy is now largely restricted to heavy industry and utilities. Most of the state-owned enterprises are inefficient and fail to make a profit. Reforms of these organisations are likely to lead to massive unemployment, but the Government is determined to press ahead with plans for reform and to sell, merge, or close most state-owned enterprises.

A major factor in the economic reforms of state-owned enterprises is the need for **private and foreign investment** in expensive industries. Heavy industry and utilities such as electricity generation and telecommunications need huge amounts of money. To compete internationally, Chinese industries need to be able to invest in expensive new technologies and new expertise. The Government cannot afford the levels of investment needed, so the reforms have to allow for private and foreign investment.

The decline in state-owned enterprises has widespread implications. Previously, state-owned enterprises provided a great deal of **social support** to employees, former employees and their families. Health care, education, housing and pensions were provided by the employers, so almost every aspect of a worker's life was looked after by the state. As the state withdraws from these enterprises, people are fearful of losing many of these additional benefits as well as their jobs.

The Iron Rice Bowl

In the 1950s, the Communist Government provided comprehensive employment and social welfare programmes for the urban population. Virtually everyone was guaranteed a job for life, and along with that job went guaranteed access to food, education, healthcare and housing. This system was known as the **iron rice bowl**. All elements of the iron rice bowl were controlled by the state, right down to allocating rice rations.

The economic reforms launched in the 1980s took away the protection of the iron rice bowl. Workers no longer had guaranteed jobs for life, and many were made unemployed and so lost access to the social benefits they once took for granted. Smashing the iron rice bowl has been one of the most significant social developments in China in the last 25 years.

Employment and unemployment

The economic reforms have led to the closure of a great many unprofitable and inefficient state-owned enterprises. Those that are still operating have had to improve their efficiency in order to compete in the new market economy. Consequently, unemployment levels have risen – from 1997 to 2000, the number of jobs in state-owned industries declined by 43 million, while the number of jobs in the private sector increased by only 16.5 million.

Many of the old industries (such as textiles) were either relatively unskilled, or used skills which are no use in high-tech manufacturing industries. Workers from these industries either have to undergo retraining, or take poorly paid unskilled work, but many of them have failed to find new jobs. In some areas, it is estimated that 20% of the working population are unemployed. Agricultural workers face similar difficulties. As farms try to improve their efficiency, many farm workers are forced to leave their homes and migrate to the cities to try to find work, where they often face discrimination.

One way the Government is tackling these problems of unemployment is by giving financial benefits such as tax breaks and loans to new industries if they agree to take on workers who have lost their jobs in the old industries. Many workers, particularly women, are taking early retirement.

Foreign investment in China

A major part of the economic reforms has been the way in which foreign companies have been allowed to invest in Chinese companies. At first, foreign companies had to form **joint ventures** with Chinese companies, but this restriction has been eased and although licences are still needed, foreign companies are now encouraged to invest and develop businesses in certain industrial sectors and in particular geographical regions.

In 2004, total foreign investment in China was $153 billion. The main business sectors are banking, high technology industries, electronic manufacture, entertainment, and retailing. The countries with the highest levels of investment are Hong Kong, the British Virgin Islands, Japan, South Korea and the USA. Many foreign businesses are taking advantage of the low cost of wages in China, which helps them reduce production costs. In 2005, Chinese exports were worth $762 million, having grown by 28% from 2004.

Internet research

Visit the Business Week website and read the article on joint ventures. Describe the changing nature of joint venture operations in China – what are the implications of these changes?
Links to this site can be found at: **LECKIE&LECKIE** *Learning Lab*

Environmental impacts

The rapid growth of the Chinese economy, based on manufacturing industries, is having major impacts on the physical environment. There are virtually **no pollution controls** on factories and their emissions. Air pollution is a major cause of illness, particularly in the cities. One study has shown that children in some of the big cities are being exposed to such high levels of lead pollution that their mental development is in danger of being impaired.

Much of the pollution in cities is caused by the increasing numbers of cars, trucks and lorries. Many Chinese cars are much more polluting than vehicles in more developed countries. Future improvements arising from better engine technology may be overwhelmed by the growth in the number of cars as the population grows richer.

Many parts of the country suffer from **water shortages** and **water pollution**. Water shortages affect the economic development of cities in some regions, and water pollution has made the shortages even more challenging. Only 30% of city waste water is treated, so huge quantities of untreated polluted water are discharged into urban water systems.

One of the major environmental impacts is through the increased demands for energy and electricity. China has massive reserves of coal which is cheap to mine, so much of the industrial growth is fuelled by coal. Coal-fired power stations release huge

China is a major source of international pollution:

- One estimate suggests that a quarter of the pollution over Los Angeles has drifted across the Pacific Ocean from China.
- To meet energy demands, a new coal-fired power station is opened every week of the year.
- China emits more greenhouse gases than any other country, apart from the USA.
- 116 million people in Chinese cities breathe air considered very dangerous to health.
- Seven of the world's 10 most polluted cities are in China.

amounts of pollution into the atmosphere, including greenhouse gases such as carbon dioxide (contributing to global warming), and sulphur dioxide, which causes acid rain. In the south and south-west of China, acid rain is damaging agricultural land.

The increased demand for electricity has caused other environmental damage. New hydro-electric schemes are being built, with massive dams creating reservoirs and drowning large areas of land. The biggest hydro-electric scheme is the **Three Gorges Dam**. Work began in 1994 to build the world's biggest dam across the Yangtse River and create a reservoir 600km long. Nearly 2 million people have been forced out of their homes to make way for the reservoir. The ecosystems surrounding the river will be destroyed and many animal habitats will be lost.

The Chinese Government has been slow to take action against industrial pollution, but is it starting to implement new environmental laws, as well as introducing laws aimed at conserving energy and promoting energy efficiency. It is currently trying to introduce water quality standards and pollution controls to prevent factories from discharging untreated waste products into rivers. Thousands of inefficient old buses and taxis are being replaced, and civil servants have to cycle or take public transport, to reduce the numbers of cars on the roads. Factories are being moved out of city centres to improve air quality.

Internet research

Visit the New Internationalist and CNN websites to research some of China's big developments – the Funan Rivers project and the Three Gorges Dam project. Make notes summarising key aspects of these projects. Links to these sites and other websites relating to Higher Modern Studies can be found at:

For you to do

● Summarise the difficult tasks facing the Chinese Government – balancing the need to reform the economy and raise of living standards with the need to protect the people and the environment.

Agricultural reform

About half of China's working population is involved in agriculture, and the country is the world's biggest agricultural producer. The most important feature of the agricultural reforms was the **household responsibility system**, introduced in the late 1970s and early 1980s. Under this scheme, land which had previously been held collectively by local government and communes was transferred to individual households. Other reforms which helped the farming sector were the reduction of government controls and the lowering of taxes.

As a result of these reforms, the profitability of Chinese agriculture has improved and incomes of the rural population have grown. This has allowed farmers to invest in new technologies and in fertilisers, which has helped improve production levels even further.

However, increased agricultural production has come at an environmental cost. **Fertiliser runoff** is a major cause of water pollution, and land affected by **soil erosion** has increased by about 32% to 1.53 million square kilometres over a 40 year period. This soil erosion and the resulting runoff into rivers affects the availability of irrigation water, the output of hydroelectric power schemes and causes problems with river flood control.

Internet research

Visit the NPR website and read the stories about the price of industry and agricultural reform being paid by some Chinese villages and farmers. Make notes about the different ways the reforms affect different people. Links to this site can be found at:

CHINA'S ROLE IN THE WORLD ECONOMY

Increasing trade with the rest of the world is a key element of the Chinese economic reforms. China joined the **World Trade Organisation** (WTO) in 2001. This sets rules for the levels of subsidies that China can give its farmers and industries, and on the degrees of tariffs applied to imports. The rules mean that there is now much more open competition in China. With such a huge population and a growing economy, China is a very important market for major Japanese, Asian, European and American businesses.

China's role in the world economy has changed dramatically over the past 25 years, but most notably since it joined the WTO. The graph below shows the growth in China's trade with the rest of the world, with exports from China growing from $249.2 bn in 2000 to $762 bn in 2005 – a threefold increase in just six years.

China's gross domestic product (GDP) has grown 10-fold since the economic reforms began, and it now has the second-highest GDP in the world, after the USA (although GDP per head is still relatively low).

China is a major producer and exporter across a wide range of industrial sectors. In the early stages of its economic growth, most of its exports were relatively low-value items such as clothing and cheap consumer items. More recently, foreign investment has helped China play a leading role in the manufacture and supply of high technology equipment and industrial equipment.

China is also making a major transition from providing a cheap labour force simply assembling products for foreign companies. In 2006, it was announced that China would spend 2.5% of its GDP on research and development, so that it will be less reliant on imported technology and can produce more of its own high technology equipment. It is also increasing the numbers of students studying science and engineering at Chinese universities, and is using tax incentives to try to attract back to China the large number of students who have migrated elsewhere.

China's biggest imports are industrial commodities such as minerals, metals and fuel. It also imports large quantities of electronic components like computer micro-chips and lasers which are used in the assembly of high-tech equipment.

The speed and the size of the growth of the Chinese economy is important for the global economy in a number of ways:

- international manufacturers now have access to a huge number of potential Chinese customers
- international manufacturers now have access to a much cheaper workforce
- Chinese consumption affects **world prices** of many materials.

The size of China's role in the world economy is big enough to affect inflation rates and interest rates around the world. This means that decisions taken in China can have an impact everywhere.

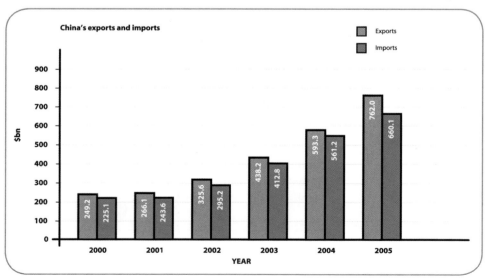

China's exports and imports

Internet research

Visit the China Embassy and BBC News websites and read the articles about China's dispute with the EU and the USA over textiles imports in 2005 and the docking of the 'Christmas goods ship'. Make brief notes about the importance for China of trade with other countries. Links to these sites and other websites relating to Higher Modern Studies can be found at:

LECKIE&LECHIE
Learning Lab

For you to do

- Summarise the key points about the role of China in the world's economy, including reference to advantages of WTO membership.
- To what extent has China become a market economy?

SOCIAL AND ECONOMIC ISSUES

Despite the growth in the Chinese economy, there is still much inequality in Chinese society. Although the overall number of people living in poverty has declined, there are very big gaps between the richest and poorest parts of Chinese society.

Economic inequality

According to a report by an American consulting group, the top 0.4% of Chinese families (about 1.5 million) own over 70% of the nation's wealth. Much of this accumulation of wealth has come about as a result of corruption amongst members of the CPC. At the end of 2000, the top 3.5% of the population earned more than ¥20,000 annually, while 50% of the population earned less than ¥2,000. This makes Chinese wealth inequality the most extreme in the world.

There is a big gap between incomes in urban and rural areas. In 2004, it was estimated that on average, urban incomes were 3.2 times higher than rural incomes.

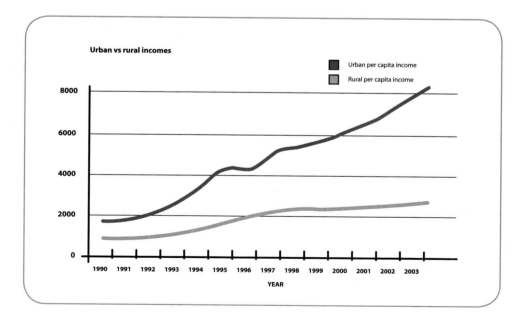

Internet research

Visit the website to read about the Great Western Development plan, the five-year project designed to attract foreign investment and build infrastructure in the poor, western regions of China. Make notes on the aims of the plan and its effectiveness in lifting people out of poverty.

Links to this site can be found at:

Social inequalities

There are also considerable inequalities across a range of social issues such as health care, education and housing. These differences are most apparent across different geographical regions and between urban and rural areas.

Education inequalities

All children are required to have nine years of education, which is usually made up of six years of elementary, or primary, education and three years of junior education. This nine-year compulsory education is mostly delivered, but there are regions where some children will drop out early. Education may be compulsory, but it is not free. The fact that parents have to pay for their children's education is one factor behind drop-out rates.

In 1995, the illiteracy rate in rural areas was 78% higher than in urban areas. Across the whole country, the illiteracy rate among girls is more than double that for boys. This gender gap appears to have got worse in the 1990s. Although the Government is attempting to correct this difference (renovating rural schools, promoting compulsory education in rural areas and distributing free schoolbooks to poor families), illiteracy rates are still much worse for girls than boys. The gender gap continues at higher levels of education, with only 25% of undergraduates at university being women.

Rural areas also have fewer teachers per head of population than urban areas.

Standards of education vary across regions. In Tibet, fewer than 1.5% of children receive any kind of secondary education and only half the population can read and write. In contrast, in cities such as Beijing and Shanghai, about 60% of the children receive secondary education, and nearly 98% of the population are literate.

Internet research

Visit the **People's Daily** and UNESCO websites to take notes about the reforms to rural education and some of the pressures in the education system.

Links to these sites and other websites relating to Higher Modern Studies can be found at:

For you to do

- Why is education important to the Chinese Government?
- What are the problems in education in China, and how is the Government tackling them?

Health care inequalities

Although China is a Communist country, health care is not free for all Chinese, and individuals often have to rely on private medical insurance to get decent health care. In 2004, 15% of rural residents had medical insurance compared with 50% of the urban population, again highlighting the difference between the urban and the rural situation.

Health care facilities are much better in cities than in rural areas. There are many more beds and health care professionals per 1,000 people in urban areas than in rural areas, and the gap appears to be getting wider. Life expectancy varies considerably across the country – 65 for a farmer in a rural province compared with 74 in a rich urban province.

Infant mortality rates are a standard way of assessing health care, and there are significant differences for different groups:

- rural rates are more than double those of urban areas
- girls experience higher infant mortality rates than boys.

Housing and urban overcrowding

The economic reforms were accompanied by a population shift from rural areas to urban areas, and China now has 660 cities, of which 48 have populations over 1 million. The **urban population has increased** from 190 million people in 1980 to 560 million people in 2005, with 43% of the population living in urban areas. This rapid growth in the urban population has put great pressure on all aspects of living in these cities, such as transport, housing, energy supplies, and water and sanitation.

The economic reforms have changed the patterns of land ownership, and there is now an **active housing market** in the cities. Although the supply of housing has struggled to meet the demand, it is generally considered that housing standards for most people have improved. In a survey in the mid-1980s, it was found that about a quarter of residents of China's cities were living in a space of less than 43 square feet. Housing was controlled by CPC officials and party membership and status were important factors in the allocation of housing.

In 1999, the state and state-owned enterprises gave up their control of housing and all existing properties were sold to tenants. Private developers were encouraged to build new housing projects. In 2003, it was estimated that there were over 37,000 property development companies in China, and many hundreds of thousands of new homes have been built. This new building has seen cities expanding over very wide areas, and the resulting **urban sprawl** is having a major impact on the environment.

For you to do

- Summarise the ways in which inequalities can be seen when comparing the circumstances of rural and urban Chinese. Add to this summary as other issues arise.

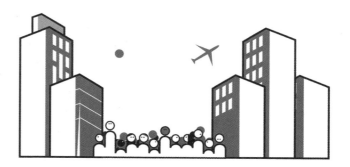

Urban sprawl: uncontrolled and unrestricted expansion of urban areas into neighbouring rural areas.

Internet research

Visit the NASA website and find the satellite images of the expansion of the city of Shenzhen. Describe what the pictures show.

Visit the Chinese Embassy and China.org websites and read and make notes about the rapid expansion of China's cities and the Government's responses to it.

Links to these sites and other websites relating to Higher Modern Studies can be found at:

For you to do

- What are the problems caused by the growing urban populations?
- Assess the Government's responses to these problems.
- Make notes about the implications of urban sprawl in China. Think about the resources needed to build and maintain the huge new cities and think about the planning needed to minimise the damage done to the environment.
  (*Hint:* Imagine if planning authorities wanted to double the size of Glasgow. What issues and factors would they need to take into account?)

Crime

It is difficult to discuss crime in China because the Chinese Government is reluctant to publish figures of the numbers of crime committed. It is often said that crime is relatively rare in China, because the police responses to criminal activity are very harsh.

Chinese law has two categories of crime – serious crimes are classified as **criminal** offences, while less serious crimes are classified as **minor** offences. In cases such as theft, the scale of the theft will determine whether it is called a criminal or minor offence. Possible penalties for criminal offences include the death penalty.

Chinese police claim high levels of success in responding to crimes. For example, in the first three months of 2006, they claim to have solved nearly one-third of criminal cases, and over 80% of minor offences. However, critics argue that these success rates are achieved only because suspects are not given fair trials.

Most crime is related to property, theft and money. Recent police campaigns have seen levels of violent crime reduced.

Drug-related crime has risen over recent years, with many of the same drug problems as those in Europe and the USA, and related crimes such as **theft** and **prostitution** are increasing. The Government is very concerned about the spread of drug use because of the damage it is thought to do to society, particularly among young people.

Drugs and AIDS

Drug use, and in particular, heroin addiction, in China is a growing social and health problem. At the end of 2004, there were 791,000 registered drug addicts (although the real figure is thought to be much higher).

Intravenous (injected) drug use is officially described as the major cause of HIV/AIDS in China. It is estimated there are 120 million migrant workers, who are mainly single young men, living in dormitories in the big cities. They have easy access to drugs and are regular users of prostitutes, so their activities are affecting themselves, the prostitutes they use, and other men who use prostitutes. The United Nations estimates there are 127,000 prostitutes in China with HIV/AIDs, or about 20% of the total number people infected with HIV/AIDS.

In response to these problems, China has developed **Four Frees and One Care** programme, which offers free HIV testing, free antiviral drugs to people with AIDS, free drugs to pregnant women, free education for AIDS orphans, and economic help for people with HIV/AIDS. Regional governments are undertaking programmes such as drug rehabilitation clinics, HIV testing and the distribution of free condoms to reduce the spread of the disease.

Organised crime

China has particular problems with **organised gang crime**, or as one Chinese report describes it 'crime perpetrated by highly organised local evil forces'. Criminal gangs are involved in the whole range of criminal activity, but the greatest concern is the gangs involved in drug trafficking, prostitution and people trafficking, gambling, and smuggling.

Smuggling is a massive activity in China. It is estimated that there are 350 million smokers in China, and high import tariffs make cigarette smuggling very lucrative. It is estimated that in the years from 1999 to 2004, goods worth about $24 billion were smuggled into China.

People trafficking involves smuggling people illegally either from one part of China to another, or out of China completely. Many Chinese people pay large amounts of money to trafficking gangs who arrange for them to be transported to foreign countries to work. The smuggled workers are often forced to live in very poor overcrowded conditions for very low levels of pay. Girls and young women are often tricked into believing that they will be given a good job, only to be sold as a wife or to brothels where they are forced to work as prostitutes. The Chinese Government does not like to admit the scale of the trafficking problem, and efforts to crack down on it are not very effective.

The Chinese take fraud very seriously. In September 2004, four people were executed for fraud worth $15 million. Two of the people executed worked for two of the big state-owned banks. These executions were part of a drive against white-collar crime as China was preparing to sell shares in the state-owned banks.

In 2002, six people were executed in Guangdong province for their role in an export tax fraud involving almost $4bn.

For you to do

- What are the problems related to drugs in China? Draw a mind map to show the connections between different factors.
- What solutions are being tried?
- Summarise the main problems in inequality in China, and what the Government is doing to address these problems. Highlight the interrelationships between the factors of health, education, employment and housing.
- To what extent has the move to a market economy made China a more unequal society?

Internet research

Visit the Utopia-Asia and the China.org websites and read the articles abut the links between drug use and HIV/AIDS. Summarise the key points and how the Government is tackling these problems.

Visit the Amnesty International website and read about the 'strike hard' anti-crime campaign.

Links to these sites and other websites relating to Higher Modern Studies can be found at:

HUMAN RIGHTS IN CHINA

The Chinese Constitution and freedom of speech

In 2004, the Chinese Constitution was amended to include the statement:

The State respects and preserves human rights.

Article 35 of the Constitution states:

Citizens of the People's Republic of China enjoy freedom of speech, of the press, of assembly, of association, of procession and of demonstration.

Article 36 of the Constitution states:

Citizens of the People's Republic of China enjoy freedom of religious belief. No state organ, public organisation or individual may compel citizens to believe in, or not to believe in, any religion; nor may they discriminate against citizens who believe in, or do not believe in, any religion. The state protects normal religious activities.

The constitutional amendment seems to establish sound principles of human rights. However, human rights organisations such as Amnesty International and Human Rights Watch regularly express their concerns about human rights violations in China. These violations are often built into systems of government.

Freedom of speech

Despite the constitutional right to free speech, there is considerable censorship in China.

- major media organisations are controlled by the Government
- foreign-owned media have to be **licensed by the Government** in order to publish or broadcast in China
- favourable references to democracy and pro-democracy movements, to independence movements, or to certain religious groups are effectively banned
- the Central Propaganda Department (CPD) is a Government organisation that monitors the media to make sure that their output conforms to the requirements of the Communist Party
- the CPD also controls the official news agency Xinhua
- the arrest of journalists and closure of media outlets is usually a last resort for the authorities; even so, in 2004, 338 publications were closed and in 2005, 32 journalists were imprisoned.

The rise of the internet has presented the Chinese Government with particular problems. Used in certain ways, the internet will help Chinese companies develop new products and grow their business. Used in other ways, it could help the Chinese population to learn more about their country than their Government wants them to know. To regulate access to information, the Government blocks access to websites which it does not approve of. It has been estimated that the Government has between 30,000 and 50,000 people monitoring internet traffic.

Internet research

Visit the *New York Times* to read about the prosecution of a journalist who wrote about high-level activity in the CPC.
Visit the *Financial Times* and Council on Foreign Relations websites to read about the Chinese Government's approach to the internet.

For you to do

- Think about the way you use the internet. How would it be different if you were living in China? What sorts of things would you not be able to do? Do you think that restrictions on using the internet are good for the Chinese people?
- The Chinese Constitution guarantees its citizens freedom of speech. Give examples that show how the Government supports or inhibits this freedom.

Freedom of religious belief

Although the Constitution gives Chinese citizens freedom of religious belief, they are restricted to religious organisations which are registered with the Government. Approved religious bodies must not have any loyalties outside China – according to the Government, this is to prevent political interference or influence.

There are five **Government-recognised religions** which are monitored through religious associations:

- Chinese Buddhist Association
- Chinese Catholic Patriotic Association
- Protestant Three-Self Patriotic Movement
- Chinese Islamic Association
- Chinese Daoist Association.

For example, Catholics in China have to choose between the Chinese Catholic Patriotic Association, which is the official state-registered church, and the Roman Catholic Church headed by the Pope in Rome. There are about 13 million Catholics in China. Of these, about 5 million follow the state-registered Church, and 8 million are loyal to the Roman Catholic Church. The Chinese Government rejects the Pope's leadership of the Catholic Church in China. State restrictions included the refusal to allow Pope John Paul II to visit Hong Kong in 1999.

More serious restrictions on freedom of religious beliefs are made against a group called the **Falun Gong**. Falun Gong is a relatively recent religious belief system which became popular in the 1990s. The Chinese Government declared it illegal in 1999, describing it as a cult involved in illegal acts against the state. Since the group was banned, many practitioners have been arrested, some of whom claim to have been tortured while in police custody. The Chinese Government rejects claims that nearly 3,000 Falun Gong practitioners have died while under arrest.

Because of concern over by the links between Islam and separatist movements in Xinjiang, in south-west China, there are Government restrictions on the use of religious materials and only the Government publisher, the Xinjiang People's Publication House, is allowed to publish books dealing with Islam. Many mosques and Koranic schools in this region have been closed down, and unauthorised teachers and imams arrested.

More tolerance is shown towards unauthorised religious groups which do not have any obvious political or nationalist tendencies. In some areas, Government officials work with church groups (Buddhist, Catholic, and Protestant) in building schools and healthcare facilities in poor communities. In these cases, European and American groups have been encouraged to provide social services as long as their religious activities are not given a high profile.

Internet research

Visit the Phayul website and read about religion in Tibet and the extent to which it is tolerated. Visit the US Department of State website for a more general discussion about religious toleration in China. Make brief notes on the extent of religious freedom in China. Links to these sites and other websites relating to Higher Modern Studies can be found at: LECKIE&LECKIE Learning Lab

For you to do

- Why do the majority of Chinese not follow any religious beliefs?
- Why does the Chinese Government attempt to control religious organisations?

Women's rights

The Chinese constitution gives equal rights to men and women across all aspects of life. However, CPC or Government policy takes precedence over individual rights, so any individual rights which conflict with CPC or Government policy are effectively lost. This is most obvious in the family planning policy.

The one-child policy

The **one-child**, or **planned birth**, policy has been a strict policy of birth control that forbids married couples in urban areas from having more than one child. The policy has its roots in the pragmatic economic reforms launched in the late 1970s, when it was recognised that overpopulation could be a barrier to successful economic development and growth.

The one-child policy is criticised by some human rights groups on the grounds that it breaches rights of reproduction and is discriminatory. It is also opposed by some anti-abortion and evangelical Christian groups. There is some evidence that the policy has been enforced through compulsory abortion, compulsory sterilisation and even the killing of infants (especially girls). In early 2007, the head of China's National and Family Planning Commission announced that the Chinese Government would reduce fines for low-income couples that are found to have violated the policy. Reasons given for this relaxation of the policy include redressing the imbalance between rich families (who could afford to pay the fines) and poor families (who could not) and also an attempt to address the gender imbalance that the one-child policy created.

Ethnic minorities in China

Most of the population of China belong to the Han ethnic group. There are 55 ethnic minority groups recognised by the government, and they should all enjoy the same human rights according to Article 4 of the constitution. However, there are a number of ways in which members of ethnic minorities are discriminated against.

Ethnic minorities are disadvantaged by the *hukou* registration system. Under this system, most citizens must be registered in an official place of residence. In order to move from one place to another, citizens require the **permission of the authorities** of the place they want to leave and the place they want to go to. As part of the Government's urbanisation strategy, the hukou system has recently udergone reform to enable rural migrants to gain access to social services, primarily education for their children.

Other human rights issues

Other issues which give human rights campaigners concern include:

- the use of the **death penalty** – there are 68 crimes which are punishable by death, ranging from murder and drug trafficking to tax fraud and corruption (Amnesty International estimates that at least 1,770 people were executed in 2005)
- **organ harvesting** – where the internal organs of executed prisoners are removed (possibly without their previous consent) and then sold for transplants
- **torture and ill-treatment** of prisoners – prisoners are regularly beaten, denied adequate food, and placed in solitary confinement for extended periods
- **arbitrary detention** – hundreds of thousands of people are detained without trial each year, and are not allowed access to lawyers
- **workers' rights** – workers cannot form or join independent trade unions, but must join official state-recognised unions.

The 2008 **Olympic Games** will be held in Beijing. The award of the Olympics is a great mark of international status, and many human rights campaigners hope that the Beijing games will help promote a greater degree of respect for human rights in China. One of the major issues will be the right to free speech, with thousands of foreign journalists in the country. There are also reports of the demolition of thousands of homes and forced evictions as land is cleared for the games stadiums and the athletes' village.

Internet research

Visit the Amnesty International website and read about China's uses of the death penalty.
Visit the Human Rights Watch website and read more about the group's concerns over the impact of the Olympic Games. Monitor the situation to keep up to date with new developments.
Links to these sites and other websites relating to Higher Modern Studies can be found at:

For you to do

- To what extent does the one-child policy conflict with human rights?
- Critically examine China's record on human rights. Consider issues such as freedom of speech, religious belief, race and sex discrimination, and treatment by the police.

STUDY THEME SUMMARY

China is a one-party state, with a great deal of overlap between the membership of the Government and the Communist Party of China. There is a complicated committee structure linking the Party and the Government, and there are many levels of government from national Government at the top, down to village committees. Democracy is restricted to open elections at village level.

The only political party with any power is the Communist Party. There are a number of small parties which are allowed to participate in discussions, but they have no power or influence, and there are few opportunities for free political activity. Parties that are explicitly pro-democracy, or partisan nationalist or separatist groups, are illegal.

China has undergone major economic reforms since 1980, and it is rapidly becoming one of the biggest economies in the world. Poverty levels have declined rapidly, but the economic reforms have had some damaging effects. Unemployment has increased as a result of the closure of many old, inefficient, state-owned industries. These industries often provided high levels of social, education and health care support which has now been lost. Rapid industrial expansion has been accompanied by environmental problems, with high levels of water and air pollution. Despite the economic growth, there are still major inequalities between different sections of the population (in particular between men and women, and between urban and rural populations).

Many Western governments and organisations have major concerns about China's human rights record. Chinese citizens do not enjoy the same practical levels of human rights, with restrictions on their freedom of speech, freedom of religious belief and freedom of political activity.

Exam-style essay questions

'China's political system has become more democratic in recent years.' Discuss.

To what extent has recent economic and social change in China reduced the pressure for political reform?

Critically examine the claim that economic reforms have made China a more unequal society.

STUDY THEME 3C:
The United States of America

In this study theme you will be expected to have a detailed knowledge and understanding of:

- ## THE USA POLITICAL SYSTEM
  The role and powers of the USA Government at federal, state and local levels.

- ## POLITICAL ISSUES
  Participation and representation; immigration. Political parties and support from different groups. Political trends.

- ## SOCIAL AND ECONOMIC ISSUES
  The nature and extent of social and economic inequalities; demands for change; the effectiveness of Government responses and the consequences for different groups.

BACKGROUND

The United States of America is the world's richest, and arguably, most powerful nation. Its wealth and resources give it enormous influence in the world economy and international politics.

Land makes the USA a powerful country

The USA covers 9.6 million square kilometres. It has a varied climate and extensive natural resources. As a result, the USA has an enormous agricultural output and is one of the world's leading producers of minerals such as metals, coal, gas and oil. With such vast resources the USA dominates world trade. In 2005, the GDP of the USA was about **one-quarter of the world's total output**.

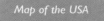

Map of the USA

FACT

- **Location:** North America, bordering both the North Atlantic Ocean and the North Pacific Ocean, between Canada and Mexico
- **Area:** 9,631,420 sq km, about half the size of Russia, slightly larger than China, about two and a half times the size of the European Union
- **Population:** 298,444,215 (July 2006 est.)
- **Ethnic groups:** White 69%, Hispanic 12.5%, Black 12.3%, Asian 3.6%, native Amerindian and Alaskan 1%, native Hawaiian and other Pacific islander 0.2% (2000 Census)
- **Religion:** Protestant 52%, Roman Catholic 24%, Mormon 2%, Jewish 1%, Muslim 1%, other 10%, none 10% (2002 est.)
- **Economy:** the economy is marked by steady growth, low unemployment and inflation, and rapid advances in technology
- **Unemployment:** 5.1% (2005 est.)
- **Population below poverty line:** 12% (2004 est.)
- **Military spending:** $518.1 billion (2005 est.), 4.06% of GDP

Population

The population of the USA is about 300 million. Of this, about 70% is classified as white. Most of the white population is descended from the European settlers who migrated to the USA over the past 400 years. At various times, the USA has been seen as a haven for refugees from political and religious persecution. The **population of the USA is very mixed** and becoming more so. Different groups within the population experience varying levels of social and economic success.

The US population is changing

The black and Hispanic populations are the biggest minority groups in the USA, each comprising about 12% of the total population. The **Hispanics** are the **fastest growing group** and have recently overtaken the blacks to become the largest of the minority populations. Most of the Hispanic population comes from Mexico. At the current rate of growth, **whites will cease to be the majority population by 2050**.

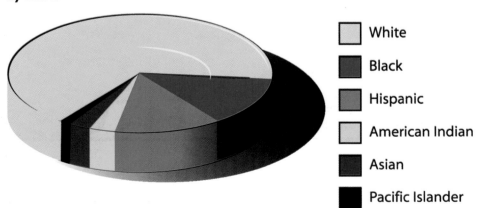

The population of the USA

White
Black
Hispanic
American Indian
Asian
Pacific Islander

Hispanics

Hispanics are the fastest growing group because the average age of Hispanics is younger, the average family size is larger and fertility rate for Hispanic women is higher. Mexican Americans make up two-thirds of all Hispanics. **Most (about 90%) live in the South and South-West** in states such as Texas, Arizona, New Mexico and California. Poor Mexicans are attracted by higher living standards in the USA. They work for low wages as field hands, gardeners and housemaids or in sweatshops in large cities. They are economic migrants and earn far more than in Mexico.

Many are illegal aliens who are smuggled across the border. Their illegal status means they can be exploited by employers in the US. Wages and working conditions are poor. They face dismissal without pay, being beaten or forced to work in illegal and dangerous environments. An estimated 8–11 million Hispanic illegal aliens are in the USA.

The remaining Hispanics are mostly Puerto Ricans and Cubans. Many of the Cubans are refugees who fled to the USA after the 1959 revolution. They regard themselves as exiles. Many have become wealthy in the US.

Blacks

Just over half (55%) of blacks live in the South. They are the descendants of slaves who worked on the cotton and tobacco plantations. In the years after the Second World War, large numbers migrated to the cities of the North and West looking for work and to improve their living standards.

Industrial decline led to poverty for many and they also suffered discrimination and segregation. There is now a reversal with many blacks moving south trying to escape the 'rust belt' cities of the North. Many middle class blacks are choosing to segregate themselves in black-dominated communities.

Of those blacks still living in the cities of the North and West, over two-thirds are trapped in the inner city **ghettoes**. Life in the ghettoes often means poverty, unemployment, poor education and health, the breakdown of traditional family life and high levels of crime. There is a distinct **black underclass** trapped in the ghetto, where their lives may be affected by drugs, violence and AIDS.

WORD BANK

Ghetto: a section of a city occupied by members of a minority group who live there because of social restrictions on their residential choice.

Native Americans

Native Americans include American Indians, Eskimo (Inuit) and Aleut. The Eskimo and the Aleut live in Alaska. American Indians are concentrated in western states, mainly on tribal reservations.

Native Americans have experienced significant discrimination, and until the 1980s the average income on the reservations was 25% of the US average. American Indians suffered from poverty, unemployment, alcoholism and malnutrition. In 1980 the Indian Gaming Act made gaming legal on reservations. Gambling provided jobs on the reservations and the income it generated was spent on improving health, education and welfare facilities.

Asians

Asians are concentrated in the West (particularly California) and in the cities of the North-East and the South. Asians have done well in the US education system and as a result have secured well paid employment, mostly in science and education.

Many first-generation immigrants have opened small businesses in areas such as the ghetto where others would not. Through the 1990s Asians — comprised mainly of Chinese, Japanese, Koreans, Filipinos, Thais, Cambodians and Vietnamese — accounted for 31% of migrants to the USA.

Internet research

Visit the USA pages of the CIA World Factbook website to learn more facts about the USA.
Visit the website of the US Census Bureau and make more detailed notes on the different ethnic groups and their population and distribution.
Links to these sites and other websites relating to Higher Modern Studies can be found at: **www.leckieandleckie.co.uk** by clicking on the Learning Lab button and navigating to the Higher Modern Studies Course Notes page.

Ideology and economy

The USA has a **capitalist market economy**, based on the ideas of private ownership, the profit motive, the market and competition. Most US people also believe that the Government should not interfere with the economy.

- **Private ownership** means that most production and services should be owned and run by private individuals and companies. Some services such as the police and the army have to be provided by the Government.
- **Profit motive** is what encourages people to invest. They hope to be successful and earn a profit from their investment. However, businesses can fail and investors lose money.
- The **market** drives capitalism and encourages competition. As prices of a commodity rise, profits will rise. This encourages investment in businesses to supply what is required. As the supply increases, several businesses will be in competition to attract the available demand. Only the most efficient businesses will survive, those providing best quality for the best price. As a result consumers will get the best deal and enjoy high living standards.

In theory, there should be no Government involvement in a market economy. However, capitalist theory does not always work. Some businesses become so powerful they dominate the market and destroy the competition. For example, Microsoft has been able to manipulate the software market to push out competitors.

There has to be Government involvement to regulate areas of the economy, and laws and regulations are needed to protect the consumers, investors, employers and workers.

Internet research

Visit news sites such as CNN and make more detailed notes on how powerful the US economy is and also some examples of the reality of capitalism.

Links to this site and other websites relating to Higher Modern Studies can be found at:

Capital: money a person has saved or borrowed then invested in a business.

For you to do

- Make notes on the main features of capitalism in the USA:
  —private ownership
  —profit motive
  —market
  —competition.
- For each of the main US ethnic groups – whites, Hispanics, Native Americans, Asians, and blacks – design a table or diagram to show:
  —proportion of the population
  —distribution
  —social and economic position

THE SYSTEM OF GOVERNMENT IN THE USA

The Government of the USA is based on the **US Constitution**, written in 1787 and drawn up following the Declaration of Independence from Great Britain (1776). The USA comprises a federation of 50 states. Each state has its own Government (known as the *State Assembly*) but there is one Federal Government for the whole of the USA. **The Constitution describes what the Federal Government is allowed to do.** Any powers not specified in the Constitution are reserved for the states or the people. Under the terms of the Constitution, the Federal Government has the power to:

- settle disputes between states to prevent them going to war
- take charge of the armed forces
- be responsible for foreign affairs
- issue currency
- run the postal service.

The Constitution also lays out the rights of the individual.

The Constitution can be amended, and over the years, 27 amendments have been added to the Constitution, including amendments to give freedom of religion, to set voting ages, to give voting rights to women, to abolish slavery and to set the lengths of the terms of office of the President.

The system of government is set out in the Constitution which specifies the way the people are represented in **Congress**. There are two chambers in Congress – the **Senate** and the **House of Representatives**. The Senate consists of 100 Senators, with two Senators elected from each state. The House of Representatives has 435 members, with each state represented in proportion to its population. The Head of State is the President.

Internet research

Visit the website of the US Constitution to read the full text of the Constitution and the Bill of Rights.
Visit the website www.bensguide.com.
Make some brief bullet point notes on
- the election of the President and Vice President
- the election of Senators
- the election of Representatives.

Links to this site and other websites relating to Higher Modern Studies can be found at:

The US
Constitution

The powers of the President

The Head of State in the USA is the **President**, who is elected every four years. The powers of the President are laid out in the Constitution. The President has important roles in national security and in the appointment of his Cabinet, judges in the Supreme Court, and in the approval of new legislation. Many of the powers of the President are subject to **checks and balances** applied in Congress.

Commander-in-Chief of the armed forces

The President is **Commander-in-Chief of the Armed Forces** and it is nominally his responsibility to defend the USA from all threats. He can order the use of troops overseas but he cannot declare war without the approval of Congress. He can make treaties with other countries, but they must be approved by the Senate.

Power of appointment

The President appoints US ambassadors, Supreme Court Justices and other officials, but these appointments must have the agreement of the Senate.

Legislative power

Every January the President gives his **State of the Union Address** to Congress. He outlines what his administration has achieved in the past year and what it intends to do in the coming year. This includes the laws it wants to introduce. The President cannot introduce Bills directly. He can propose a Bill, but a member of Congress must submit it for him.

When both Houses of Congress pass a Bill, they send it to the President for his approval. If he agrees with the Bill, he signs it and it becomes a law. However, if the President does not like the Bill, he can use his veto, and return the Bill to Congress unsigned with a list of reasons to explain why he vetoed it. It requires a two-thirds majority in both Houses to overturn a Presidential veto.

The President may use a *pocket veto*. The Constitution says that the President must sign a Bill within 10 days. If he does not sign and Congress is in session, then the Bill becomes law without his signature. However, if Congress is adjourned before the 10 days are up, then Congress is not in session and the Bill fails.

The President can by-pass Congress in certain circumstances by issuing an **Executive Order.** An Executive Order has the power of law but does not need the Congress to pass it, so the Executive Order gives the President the power to make changes to the legal framework of the USA with no check from Congress.

Executive power

The President is responsible for **carrying out the laws passed by Congress**. He appoints Secretaries of State to run departments of Government whose officials do the work of Government.

Changes in Presidential power

The President is often described as the **single most powerful person in the USA**. Since 2001 the President's office has increased its power. Following the 11 September terrorist attacks in New York and Washington, the President issued an Executive Order to create the Department of Homeland Security (DHS) which came into existence in 2003. This increased the powers of the administration to monitor people in the USA and elsewhere in the world. The DHS increased the potential for the Government to use its intelligence and surveillance capacity to monitor the lives of US citizens as part of the war on terrorism.

The new powers include the power to overrule the courts if they order the release of any person the Attorney General deems to be a terrorist or who he says has links with terrorism. Executive Orders giving a President such an extension of power were meant

to be time-limited to the period of an emergency. President Bush intends to retain these powers as long as terrorism is a threat. This could go on indefinitely because terrorism in some form or other is always present.

President George W. Bush addresses Congress

Internet research

Visit the White House website to find out more about Federal Government.
Take a tour of the building.
Listen to the State of the Union Address to find out what the current administration proposes to do.
Visit the BBC News website to find out more about the increases in Presidential power and to find out about President George W Bush's use of the Presidential veto.
Visit the website of the *New York Law Journal* to find out more about how President George W. Bush has increased his power of veto.
Links to these sites and other websites relating to Higher Modern Studies can be found at: LECKIE&LECKIE Learning Lab

The separation of powers

In addition to defining the powers of the Federal Government and setting out the rights of individuals, the Constitution includes a series of measures to prevent too much power being given to any one person or group of people. An essential part of these measures is **the separation of legislative, executive and judicial powers**.

A Government must be able to make laws, carry out laws and apply justice according to these laws. If all three functions are controlled by the same individuals then the Government will become a **dictatorship**. The US Constitution ensures these three functions are under separate control.

- **Legislative function** – The power to make laws for the USA is the responsibility of the **Congress**. For a Bill to become a law it must be passed by a majority in both the House of Senate and the House of Representatives.

- **Executive function** – The power to carry out the laws of the United States is the responsibility of the **President**. The President appoints Secretaries of State to run departments of Government whose officials will do the day-to-day work of governing. There are 25 Secretaries of State including departments such Agriculture, Defense, Education and Homeland Security. These Secretaries of State and the President make up the **Cabinet** which meets regularly to decide what the Government needs to do to run the USA.

- **Judicial function** – The power to judge according to the laws of the USA is the responsibility of the **Supreme Court**. It is made up of nine Supreme Court Justices (judges) who decide what the laws of the United States actually mean and how they should be applied in the courts.

Checks and balances

The Constitution applies a number of **checks and balances** to the powers of all elements of Government, from the President down. The system of checks and balances means that it is not possible for any part of the Government to act in a way which is not deemed to be in the best interests of the country.

The checks and balances can be applied by **elected members of Congress** or by **unelected members of the Supreme Court**.

Checks on the Federal Government

The US Constitution reserves all power for the people or the states. The Federal Government can only do those things the Constitution allows it to do, so the power of the Federal Government is balanced against the rights and powers of the states individually and the people. If the Federal Government wants to increase its power, it must change the Constitution. Changes to the Constitution require:

- the agreement of two-thirds of the House of Senate and House of Representatives
- the agreement of the President
- the agreement of three-quarters of the State Assemblies.

Checks on the President

The President has very considerable powers, but is subject to checks and balances applied by Congress and the Supreme Court. Checks by Congress over the President include:

- the requirement that **Congress must pass changes to laws**, even when it is the President who proposes the changes. In 2005 the Senate refused to extend parts of the Patriot Act and make most of it permanent
- the requirement that **new Bills must be introduced by members of Congress**. The President cannot introduce new Bills into Congress
- the ability of Congress to **over-ride a Presidential veto** by a two-thirds vote
- the requirement that Congress must **approve spending** for any new policies proposed by the President
- the ability to **impeach the President** for any suspected wrongdoing.

Impeach: to charge a Government official with offences committed while in office.

Checks by the Supreme Court over the President include:

- a **judicial review** of any Act of Congress, whether proposed by the President or Congress, to decide whether it is unconstitutional. The nine judges on the Supreme Court review the law in relation to what they think the Constitution intended. If a majority decide the law is not allowed by the letter or the spirit of the Constitution then it is declared unconstitutional and cannot be applied in the courts anywhere in the USA. In 2005 two Federal courts challenged the President's approval for unauthorised spying on US citizens since 11 September 2001.

Checks on Congress

Congress is also subject to a range of checks and balances, to ensure that a powerful Congress, perhaps with large majorities for one party, does not pass legislation which does not have the support of the President or which is unconstitutional. Checks by the President over Congress include:

- the ability to **veto bills** passed by Congress. It is difficult for Congress to ignore this check because two-thirds of both Houses would have to vote to over-ride the veto
- the power to **recommend legislation** to Congress. This happens every year in the State of the Union address.

Checks by the Supreme Court on Congress include the **judicial review** of any Act of Congress.

Checks on the Supreme Court

The Supreme Court is the highest court in the USA and leads the judicial function of the Federal Government. It is a very powerful body, and the opinions of the individual Justices on the Supreme Court are very influential. Checks by the President on the Supreme Court include:

- the power to **nominate judges**
- the power of **pardon**
- the right to openly **support** or **criticise the court** (and in so doing, influence their decisions).

Checks by Congress on the Supreme Court include:

- the **confirmation** or **rejection of appointments** to the court
- the right to **set the number of Justices** on the Court. Congress may pass a law requiring the President to increase the number and so change the balance in the court
- the right to **impeach a Justice**
- the right to initiate constitutional amendments which allow them to **overturn decisions of the Court**. Recent attempts have included decisions on abortion, school prayers and desecration of the American flag. They all failed.

Elections

Another balance written into the Constitution is the system of elections. The President is elected for four years with a two-term maximum. Members of the House of Representatives are elected to serve for two years, and Senators are elected for six years.

One third of the Senate is re-elected every two years.

A strong President can only remain in office for eight years during which time a new House of Representatives is re-elected every two years, as is one-third of the Senate. If the voters in the US do not like what the President is doing, they can elect representatives to check his power within two years. No individual can become the President for life and gather more and more power.

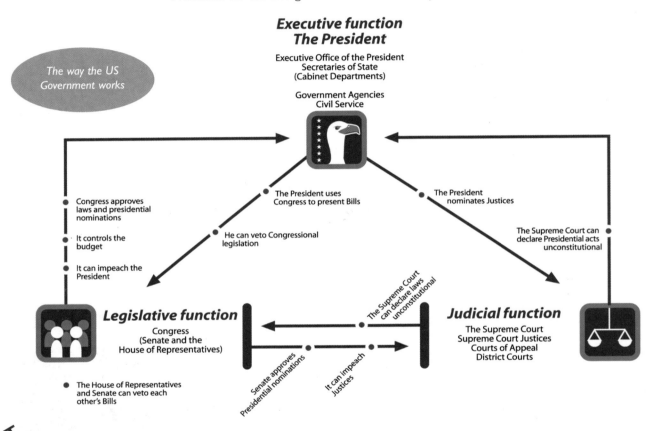

The way the US Government works

Executive function
The President

Executive Office of the President
Secretaries of State
(Cabinet Departments)

Government Agencies
Civil Service

- Congress approves laws and presidential nominations
- It controls the budget
- It can impeach the President

The President uses Congress to present Bills

He can veto Congressional legislation

The President nominates Justices

The Supreme Court can declare Presidential acts unconstitutional

Legislative function

Congress
(Senate and the House of Representatives)

- The House of Representatives and Senate can veto each other's Bills

The Supreme Court can declare laws unconstitutional

Senate approves Presidential nominations

It can impeach Justices

Judicial function

The Supreme Court
Supreme Court Justices
Courts of Appeal
District Courts

FACT

Electoral College

An American President is not chosen directly by the people, but is elected by an Electoral College, which reflects the votes cast in each state. Each state has a number of votes in the Electoral College which equals number of Senators (always two) and its Representatives. The State with the biggest population is California, and has two Senators and 53 Representatives, so it has 55 electoral votes. There are 538 electors in the College. Using a First-Past-the-Post system, the winner in each state gets all the Electoral College votes in that state. To become President, a candidate needs 270 Electoral College votes. The winning candidate does not need to win the national popular vote.

Internet research

Visit the website of the US Constitution to find out more detail on the separation of powers and checks and balances.

Links to this site and other websites relating to Higher Modern Studies can be found at:

LECKIE&LECKIE
Learning Lab

For you to do

- Make notes on the following terms
  — Constitution
  — Federal Government
  — Legislative function
  — Executive function
  — Judicial function
  — Separation of powers.
- Draw up a table to show the checks and balances which limit the powers of each of the following:
  — Federal Government
  — The President
  — Congress.
- To what extent is the President is the most powerful person in the USA?

POLITICAL PARTIES AND THEIR SUPPORT

The two main political parties in the USA are the **Republican Party** and the **Democrat Party**. Their support comes from different geographical areas and different groups of people. There are a number of smaller independent parties, but it is very rare for them to gain any kind of electoral success in the Congressional elections.

Republican Party

Historically, the Republicans are the **right-wing conservative** party in the USA. Most of their support comes from the South (e.g. Texas and Florida) and from the agricultural states in the Midwest and West. Republican support is stronger in rural areas and in suburban or *small town America*.

In 2004, 62% of white male voters and 55% of white females voted Republican, showing solid support in affluent 'middle America'.

Republican influence

The Republicans were the **majority party in Congress** between 1995 and 2006. Americans are increasingly more conservative in their attitudes, for example, supporting Workfare (see page 237) and limits on Government assistance to the poor, which are Republican policies. However, The Republican Party lost conrol of both houses of Congress in 2006 because of US involvement in Iraq.

The Republicans have promoted an image of **traditional family values** which has gained support amongst those concerned about the breakdown of the family and amongst voters in **Bible Belt America**.

The war on terrorism initially benefited the Republicans as many Americans are strongly patriotic and the Republican Party is considered by many to be the party which will do more to stand up for American values. However, some influence is

Republican Party symbol

being lost as significant numbers of voters are questioning the loss of American lives in Iraq and the cost of US involvement in the Middle East. Many ethnic minorities feel the Government response to Hurricane Katrina in 2005 was inadequate and discriminatory.

Democratic Party

Democrats are more **liberal** than the Republicans, and draw their support from the states on the East and West Coasts. Much of the support is concentrated in larger cities.

The Democrats draw particular support from **lower income groups, women and ethnic minorities**. In 2004, 67% of non-white men and 75% of non-white women voted Democrat.

Democrat influence

The Democrats were the majority party in Congress until 1995 but their influence is shrinking as their support shrinks. There is less public support for policies aimed at reducing inequality in society such as welfare and Affirmative Action Programmes, which were traditional Democrat issues.

Significant numbers of ethnic minorities (who would normally be considered core Democrat voters) are increasingly opposed to policies that are traditional liberal-thinking Democrat issues such as pro-abortion or homosexual rights. However the Democrats regained control of both the senate and the House of Representatives in 2006 because of the unpopularity of the Iraq War.

Democratic Party symbol

Election results in 2004

Republican majority ■

Democrat majority ■

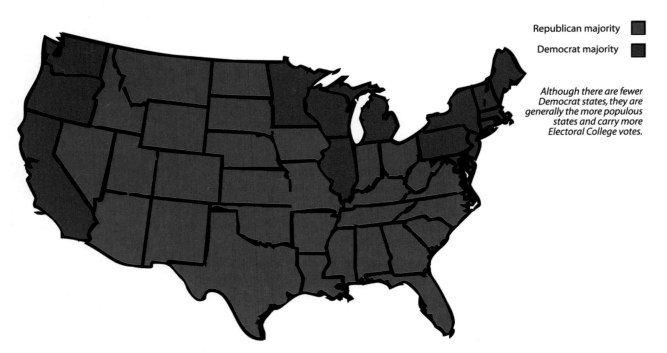

Although there are fewer Democrat states, they are generally the more populous states and carry more Electoral College votes.

THE ETHNIC MINORITY VOTE

With ethnic minorities comprising 30% of the population, both Democrats and Republicans are keen to secure their votes in elections.

Blacks

Black representation is increasing. Following the 2004 elections, there were 43 black members of the House of Representatives, compared with 25 only 10 years before. In the early 1990s, the Democrats introduced **majority–minority districts**, in which boundaries were changed to create voting districts with large majorities of either blacks or Hispanics. Black or Hispanic candidates would be elected in these districts. This single act increased Black representation from 25 to 39 members.

However, influence has not increased in the same proportions. The introduction of majority–minority districts means there are overall fewer Congress members elected as a direct result of black support and there are fewer Democrat Party Representatives.

Why has black influence decreased after the introduction of majority–minority districts?

If an electoral area were to return three representatives and all three depend on gaining black support to win their District, then generally three white Democrats would be elected, since black voters support the Democrats in large numbers. Black Democrat candidates have a low chance of being elected as the Districts are made up of mostly white voters with a few blacks. However, each of these representatives will have to be sympathetic to black needs.

If the boundaries are changed so that all the black voters are in one district (that is, according to majority–minority districts) then it is more likely that a black Democrat representative will be elected in that District. Black representation will have increased. However, the remaining two representatives will be elected by a mostly white electorate who tend to vote Republican. Two white Republicans will be elected and neither of them will need to have any concern for black issues.

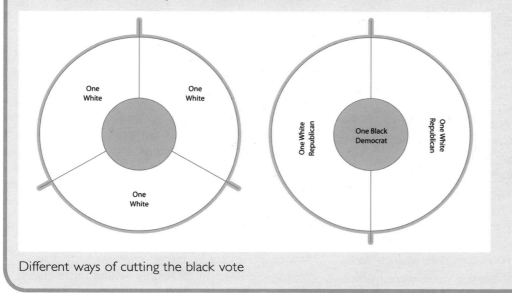

Different ways of cutting the black vote

Blacks are still under-represented at Federal level

In 2005, blacks had 10% of the seats in the House of Representatives. Since blacks comprise 12% of the population, they are slightly under-represented in the House of Representatives. In the Senate, Barack Obama was the only black Senator (out of 100). Blacks are failing to make it into the top level of politics in significant numbers.

Black influence in Congress is effective

The 43 black Representatives are all **Democrats** and together they make up a **Black Caucus**. As a group they agree how they are going to vote on issues in the House. Together they have 20% of the votes needed to pass a Bill.

- The Black Caucus makes up the largest united voting group and so wield considerable influence. Representatives will support them on black issues in return for votes in other areas.
- President Bush has sought the support of the Black Caucus in return for his support on issues important to them. This has crossed party political lines as he is Republican and they are Democrats.

Registration and turnout

Blacks are less likely to register to vote, with 69% of blacks registered to vote compared to 75% for whites. Voter turnout is lower among blacks than among whites. In 2004, 67% of whites voted but only 60% of blacks did. Reasons for this are varied and complex.

- Many blacks still suffer economic and social inequality and voting has not changed that. Many feel that politics and politicians have little to offer them.
- Those with a lower level of education are less likely to vote and blacks are more likely to be poorly educated.
- Blacks tend to be concentrated in areas where the result is a foregone conclusion – a black Democrat will be elected to represent a black area – and so they do not bother to vote.
- Many feel the system discriminates against them. In Florida if a person has been jailed for a crime at any time then they are not allowed to vote. More blacks are jailed than whites and so **felony disenfranchisement** discriminates against blacks.
- In Florida in the 2000 election there were many

reports of further discrimination through electoral malpractice:
- —polling cards were not received
- —there was intimidation at the polls
- —voter registration was falsely claimed to be problematic.

Action to win the black vote

Both major parties have taken specific actions to try to win more votes from black people. In the 1990s, **Motor-Voter laws** were introduced by the **Democrats** to allow voter registration at the same time as people licensed their cars. However, Republican voters took most advantage of this. Republicans tend to be better off and are more likely to be car owners. The outcome was an increase in votes for the Republican Party which was the majority party in the House of Representatives until 2006, and in the Senate until 2007.

Blacks mostly vote Democrat but the Republican Party has tried to win some black votes by targeting young, middle class blacks. By meeting with various black organisations and church groups the Republican Party hopes to win votes for its strong views on family, anti-abortion and anti-gay rights. If they win 5–10% of the black vote they will challenge several Democrat Senators and make it difficult for Democrats to win a presidential election.

The importance of the black vote is reflected in high-level appointments by President Bush of black people to run State Departments, such as Condoleezza Rice as Secretary of State.

Hispanics

Hispanic representation is increasing but they are also under-represented. In 1990, there were only 10 Hispanic members of the House and no Senators. In 2005 there were 26 Hispanic members in the House of Representatives and two Senators. This represents approximately 5% of the House and 2% of the Senate, yet Hispanics make up 13% of the population. Majority–minority districts helped increase the number of Hispanic representatives.

Registration and turnout

Many Hispanics are economic migrants with little interest in politics. In 2004, only 58% of those eligible to vote registered (representing just 35% of the total Hispanic population). However, many Hispanics are not citizens and only 16 million out of 27 million Hispanics in the USA are eligible to vote. Turnout amongst those eligible to vote was 47%, but because of the low levels of voter registration, this turnout represented just 28% of Hispanics of voting age. With such low turnout politicians paid little attention to Hispanic issues.

Action to win the Hispanic vote

Anti-immigration policies in the 1990s meant many Hispanics voted against the Republican Party. However, Hispanics are the fastest growing group in the USA so the Republican Party could not afford to lose their vote to the Democrats.

The Republican Party introduced policies aimed at Hispanic issues such as allowing illegal immigrants to get legal status and eventual citizenship. They also began party political broadcasts in Spanish. In 2000 they won 35% of the Hispanic vote, and they increased this to 45% in 2004.

President Bush has appointed several Hispanics to high level positions, most notably Alberto Gonzales, appointed Attorney General in 2005.

Why the Hispanic vote is important

The Hispanic vote is concentrated in particular geographical locations. In 2004, Hispanics made up 8% of the national vote, but in some states like New Mexico they make up 30% of voters. They are the **swing vote**. California, Florida, Texas and New York are enormously important states in presidential elections, as together they have nearly half the electoral college votes. These states also have the biggest concentration of Hispanics, so their votes could determine the outcome of future elections.

Swing vote: a block of votes which can cause the outcome of an election to swing one way or the other.

Traditionally, **Hispanics have largely voted Democrat**. The Democrats were identified with policies for better welfare provision and health care which appealed to poor Mexican Americans and Puerto Ricans. The Democrats were also identified with the Catholic vote and so attracted the Catholic Hispanic vote. Many second- or third-generation Hispanics are now becoming middle class. They now identify with the Republican Party policies on private enterprise. The Republican positions on anti-abortion and family values also appeal to the strongly family-orientated Hispanics. This is leading to a decline in the Democrat vote amongst Hispanics. In 1996 they had 70% of the Hispanic vote, but in 2000 this fell to 62% and in 2004 to 55%.

Internet research

Go to the website of the White House to find other examples of minorities in the US Cabinet.

Go to the website of the Southwest Voter Registration Education Project and make notes on campaigns aimed at increasing the Hispanic vote, such as:

- 10-4 Campaign
- Campaign for Communities.

Links to these sites and other websites relating to Higher Modern Studies can be found at:

For you to do

- Draw up a table to show the variation in support for the Democrat Party and the Republican Party. Consider:
  — geography
  — socio-economic group
  — gender
  — ethnic group
  — social outlook/attitude.
- Outline the reasons why the Republican Party currently dominates US politics.
- Explain why majority–minority districts were both good and bad for black representation.
- What is the Black Caucus and why is it influential?
- Make up a diagram to summarise the reasons why black voters are still disenfranchised.
- Assess the importance of the ethnic minority vote to the main political parties in the USA.

SOCIAL AND ECONOMIC INEQUALITY

Despite the great economic strength of the USA, there are considerable levels of social and economic inequality. Social and economic factors are closely related and one affects the other. Social factors include access to **decent housing**, **education** and **healthcare**, and **vulnerability to crime** and **fractured family structures**. Economic factors include **income levels** (including welfare benefits) and **employment rates**.

Poverty

Poverty levels in the USA declined between 1990 and 2001 but there is still great inequality. **Blacks are three times more likely to be poor than whites.** Hispanics are only slightly better off than blacks. Asians have similar rates of poverty to whites.

Federal Poverty Level

In the USA, the official measure of poverty is the Federal Poverty Level (FPL). It was introduced in 1964 and was based on the cost of a family food budget multiplied by three (because in those days families spent roughly one-third of their income on food). In 2001, using the same formula, the FPL was set at $18,000 for a household of four persons. However, in 2001 the proportion spent by the average family on food had fallen to one-fifth of total income, so the FPL should really be set at five times the cost of food spending which would be $30,000. The true extent of poverty is hugely underestimated.

The FPL does not take into account the variation in cost of living in different places. Some places are more expensive to live in than others For example, other measures have set the poverty level for a single parent with two children at $52,000 in Washington DC.

Causes of poverty

Blacks and Hispanics are three times more likely to experience poverty than whites. However, there are considerable differences in the reasons for black and Hispanic poverty.

For black people, long-term discrimination has created a distinct black underclass. Blacks in poverty tend to be:

- single parent female-headed households
- welfare dependent
- marginally educated, e.g. high school dropouts
- chronically unemployed
- criminal **recidivists**.

WORD BANK

Recidivist: someone who is repeatedly arrested for criminal behaviour.

Most (70%) of blacks in the cities of the North and West live in ghettoes with poor employment opportunities and few positive role models. Many become stuck in a **cycle of poverty** that continues for generations.

Hispanic poverty is largely the result of poor economic migrants from Central and South America who are willing to take even very low paid jobs in the USA because their prospects are still better there than in their home country.

Hispanics are more upwardly mobile and many start up businesses which helps them move out of poverty. Extended families will use their joint income to invest in better housing. Second- and third-generation Hispanics are less likely to live in poverty than those in the first generations.

Poverty is not equally distributed amongst Hispanics. Cubans are more likely to be middle class compared to Mexican Americans. In 1999 only 17% of Cubans were poor compared to the average figure of 22% for Hispanics.

Income and unemployment

Income levels vary considerably among the different ethnic groups. The chart shows the variation in median incomes in 1999.

In 2001, 26% of blacks lived on incomes below $20,000 compared to only 14% of whites. High levels of black unemployment mean that more are forced to live on welfare. Changes in the welfare system in the past 10 years have badly affected the level of income for groups like blacks who are welfare dependent.

Low income among Hispanics is caused by many having low paid jobs rather than being unemployed and living on welfare.

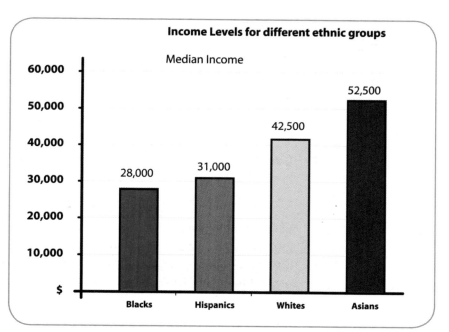

Income Levels for different ethnic groups

Median Income

Group	Median Income
Blacks	28,000
Hispanics	31,000
Whites	42,500
Asians	52,500

The high income among Asian is related to their generally higher level of education, and many are well represented in the top levels of employment in business and education. They tend to experience low levels of unemployment. In 2001, 34% of Asian households had incomes over $75,000 compared to only 26% of whites.

The chart shows how unemployment levels vary considerably across the different ethnic groups.

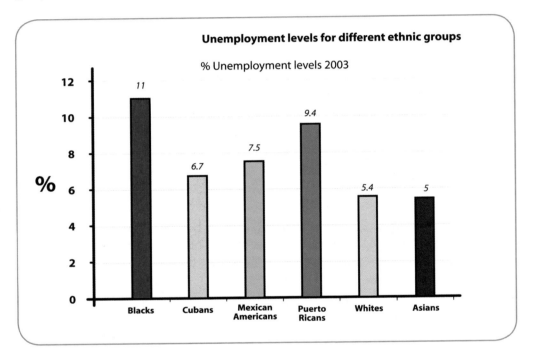

Hispanics are more likely to be in work than blacks. In 2001, 64% of Hispanics were economically active compared to 67% of whites (but only 58% of blacks), but a high proportion are in low paid employment.

Unemployment is more common among Hispanics than among whites but the levels are not evenly distributed. Cuban unemployment is relatively low as the Cubans are a more stable group whereas there are far more immigrants among Mexican Americans and Puerto Ricans. Puerto Ricans are about 40% more likely to be unemployed than Cubans.

This has a great impact on levels of Hispanic poverty.

Causes of unemployment

Unemployment rates vary with changes in the economy and with personal circumstances, such as educational attainment and discrimination.

Changes in the economy

If the economy is strong then more people will be in work while during a recession unemployment increases. The first to lose employment in a recession are lower paid unskilled workers and they are the last to be hired during an upturn. Blacks are more likely to be in low skilled work and are most likely to suffer this 'last in, first out'. More Hispanics are self-employed and therefore fewer become unemployed during a recession.

The effects of the US welfare system

The 1996 Welfare Act introduced Temporary Assistance for Needy Families (TANF). This places the responsibility for running welfare assistance on individual states. Although the state funds are decided at federal level, each state can develop and implement its own programme. Features of the TANF system include:

- a **five-year lifetime limit** for welfare for any individual
- the requirement for claimants to **work in return for welfare** (sometimes called **Workfare**)
- the requirements for claimants to undergo **training in skills** for work
- the right of the state to decide what is **suitable work**
- **child support** for lone parents.

The 1996 Welfare Act did not change the Food Stamp programme. Under this scheme, poor families get coupons to exchange for food at specified food stores.

The number of families claiming welfare has dramatically reduced. Between 1996 and 2000 families claiming TANF fell from 4.4 million to 2.3 million. Black families were the most affected by changes to welfare; 80% of families receiving TANF are Black, 17% are White and only 1.3% are Hispanic.

Families who leave TANF face poverty. More than half (60%) of families leaving TANF after the five-year limit find low paid work earning between $12,000 and $17,000, below the FPL. The remaining 40% receive no income. Blacks are worst affected by this cause of poverty.

Children are badly affected by the changes to welfare programmes. The number of children living in families on incomes below $9,000 has increased, and emergency assistance to families for hunger and homelessness has increased. Hospitals report increases in malnutrition among infants and toddlers.

In 2003, the 1996 Welfare Act was amended to increase the level of compulsion in the system. At the same time, finance for the support programmes such as child care, transport costs and job training was frozen.

Educational attainment

Levels of employment and income are directly related to levels of education. In 2002, the unemployment rate amongst blacks who dropped out of high school was 14%, compared to 9% of those who graduated. In 2003, 20% of blacks dropped out of high school compared with 15% of whites.

Race discrimination

Amongst those who did not complete high school, blacks are almost twice as likely as whites and Hispanics to be unemployed. Among high school graduates 9% of blacks were unemployed compared to only 5% of whites. The same variation applies to unemployment rates across the education attainment spectrum. At all levels, discrimination affects employment prospects and income and as a result contributes to poverty.

Hispanics are the exception. In 2003, 43% of Hispanics dropped out of high school, but their income and employment rates are better than those among blacks. Hispanics tend to drop out of high school to go into work, often in family businesses. They are often self-employed and so do not appear in unemployment statistics.

For you to do

- Summarise the differences in poverty amongst the main ethnic groups, in particular:
  — rates
  — causes.
- Make notes on inequality in income and unemployment for the main ethnic groups. Try to use a table to bring the information together, looking at:
  — welfare dependency
  — unemployment
  — pay levels.
- What are the main causes of unemployment for blacks and Hispanics?

Education and income levels

The higher a person's level of education, the higher their income. The average income of someone with a professional degree such as a doctor or lawyer is much higher than a person with a school diploma. Educational disadvantage will generally result in reduced incomes.

Blacks

Black children face educational disadvantage in schools in inner-city ghettoes, which are poorly equipped and staffed. Many of the teachers are from different race backgrounds from their students and research suggests this can put these students at a disadvantage.

Many black children are negative about education and as a result are often disruptive. Poor blacks cannot afford entry to university and college courses such as maths, science, the law and medicine that lead to well-paid employment.

Blacks who manage to study for degrees still face discrimination in income. The average income of a black person with a bachelor's degree is 25% below that of a white person with the same qualification while at professional degree level the difference is 37%.

Asians

Asians have done well in the US education system. In 2000, 44% of Asians were college graduates compared to only 26% of whites.

In Texas, competition for university places is based on being in the top 10% of a school graduation group. Many white parents are taking their children out of the highest achieving schools because of the competition from Asian children. Educational success is resulting in Asians earning higher incomes and potentially becoming the wealthiest group in the USA. The Asian population is currently concentrated in areas with high-tech industries such as Silicon Valley in California (electronics and science-based industry), Seattle (with jobs in Boeing engineering) and in Houston (with employment around the space centre).

For you to do

- Compare the educational success of the blacks, Hispanics and Asians.

Health

The USA does not have a state-funded health service like the NHS in the UK. People have to **pay for healthcare** and for most this means having private health insurance. Those on welfare may receive Medicaid which provides basic healthcare.

Blacks

Health indicators for blacks show significant inequality compared to other groups:

- in 2000, the life expectancy of blacks (72.2) was five years less than for whites (77.1)
- the infant mortality rate is over twice as high for blacks than whites
- in 2002, the proportion of babies of low birth weight was 13.3% for blacks compared with 6.8% for whites and only 6.5% for Hispanics.

Some of the reasons for this inequality include:

- 25% of blacks do not have health insurance due to low income or low status employment that does not provide insurance, compared with only 10% of whites who have no insurance
- there are twice as many black teenage mothers compared to whites and about two-thirds of all

births are to unmarried mothers; the babies have low birth weight due to their mothers' poor diet, smoking, drinking and drug dependency during pregnancy

- obesity is a particular problem in the black community
- crime also has an impact: the most common cause of death among young black males is being shot
- AIDS is a major health problem; between 1981 and 2000, blacks had 47% of all reported cases of AIDS in the USA.

Hispanics

At 80.5, life expectancy is higher for Hispanics than for whites and infant mortality lower but there are still a number of health inequalities:

- 33% of Hispanics have no health insurance, more than any other group; this is related to the number of Hispanic economic migrants who have no residency rights and therefore no access to Government health insurance such as Medicare or Medicaid
- Hispanics suffer the second highest levels of HIV/AIDS comprising 20% of all diagnoses
- Hispanics have higher rates of obesity, strokes, diabetes and cirrhosis than whites; these are all problems related to lifestyle and income
- the two main causes of death for young Hispanic males are traffic accidents and homicides.

Asians

Asians have the longest life expectancy in the USA. In 1997 life expectancy for an affluent Asian American was 92.

- Asians have the lowest rates of deaths from AIDS and cancer. This is related to Asians' more self-disciplined lifestyle with low levels of drink or drug abuse. Teenage births are also low.
- The main health problems for Asians are stomach cancer (caused by dietary factors), tuberculosis and leprosy.

For you to do

- Note the health inequalities for blacks, Hispanics and Asians compared to whites in the following areas
  — infant mortality rates
  — health insurance
  — AIDS
  — serious illness
  — lifestyle.

Housing

Housing inequality is closely linked to income and contributes to health inequality. Different ethnic groups experience degrees of poor housing.

Blacks

Fewer than 50% of blacks own their own home compared to 66% of whites. Low income makes it difficult to get a mortgage. Racial discrimination also makes it twice as difficult for blacks to get a mortgage compared to whites. **Redlining** means mortgage lenders draw a red line around areas of towns where they do not offer loans. These are predominantly black areas.

Most blacks live in rented inner city housing. Prices elsewhere are too high. Inner city housing developments, known as projects, have high population densities with few social facilities, creating huge social problems.

Blacks still face segregation in housing due to *White flight*. Affluent whites living in the suburbs either prevent blacks from moving into their area or move away to all-white suburbs. The suburbs around many cities are a series of segregated housing areas.

Hispanics

Hispanic home ownership rates have increased over recent years and reached 47% in 2001. This is still less than the figure for whites. The average Hispanic household spends over one-third of its income on housing. This is due to the high cost of housing in relation to a low average income. Hispanics are twice as likely as whites to have problems with the quality of the buildings they live in.

Discrimination

The US Department of Housing and Urban Development has reported that between 1989 and 2000, there was a decrease in the level of discrimination for both blacks and Hispanics buying a home but discrimination is still a problem. The main form of discrimination occurs when black and Hispanic people are told houses are unavailable when they are still available to whites.

Housing agents give Hispanics less help with getting finance and between 1989 and 2000, there was an increase in quoting Hispanics higher rents for properties.

Asians and Pacific Islanders face discrimination, with homebuyers experiencing adverse treatment relative to whites 20% of the time. Systematic discrimination occurs in housing availability, inspections, financing assistance, and agent encouragement.

Internet research

Visit the website of the US Census Bureau to get the most up-to-date information on poverty, income and health for the different ethnic groups in the USA.
Visit the website of the Centre on Budget and Policy Priorities and make some additional notes on the effects of TANF and other welfare programmes.
Links to these sites and other websites relating to Higher Modern Studies can be found at: LECKIE&LECKIE *Learning Lab*

For you to do

- In what ways do discrimination and segregation continue to affect blacks and Hispanics in housing?

Crime and justice

There are considerable differences in crime rates and inequalities in justice in the different ethnic groups. In general, black people experience more crime and are more likely to be in prison than any other group.

Blacks

Blacks are eight times more likely than whites to be in prison and three times more likely than Hispanics. In 2002, 47% of all jail inmates were black despite the fact that only 12% of the population is black.

The main causes of black crime are unemployment, street gangs and drugs. Crime is attractive to young unemployed blacks as it pays more than the low paid jobs that are available in the ghetto and more than the low levels of income provided by welfare. Family life in ghettoes is severely disrupted, and the patterns of behaviour contribute to the high levels of crime.

About two-thirds of children in the black community are born to unmarried mothers and over 80% of black households are lone parent families. Many women have several children while they are still in their teens, often fathered by different men who do not stay to support their children.

This lifestyle has created a culture of **welfare dependency** because there are so few permanent males of working age in households.

Lack of respect for women in the ghetto has created huge social problems. Without a father in the household, children (particularly boys) show little respect for the female head of the household and go on to treat young women in a similar manner. A cycle of fatherless households has developed.

Blacks also face **inequality in justice**. Nearly half (45%) of the prisoners under sentence of death in the USA are black. This is partly due to the high levels of serious crime in the ghetto but a recent Amnesty International report found that a black person found guilty of murdering a white person is 15 times more likely to be executed than a white person found guilty of murdering a black person.

Barrio: a neighbourhood (usually poor) with largely Spanish-speaking residents.

Hispanics

Hispanics are more likely to be the victims of crime than whites but are less so compared with blacks. Hispanics in the **barrio** become involved in crime for the same reasons as blacks in the ghetto. However, the influence of the strong extended family means large numbers of poor Hispanics work hard and avoid crime. Hispanics also have more positive role models.

Internet research

Visit the website of the US Department of Justice to get more detailed and up-to-date statistics on crime for ethnic minorities.

Visit the website of Amnesty International to read their report on racial prejudice in the US justice system.

Links to these sites and other websites relating to Higher Modern Studies can be found at:

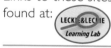

For you to do

- Summarise the statistics that show the black community is disproportionately affected by crime.
- What evidence is there that the disintegration of family life does not affect all the minority groups equally?
- To what extent are ethnic minority groups in the USA socially and economically disadvantaged?

THE IMMIGRATION DEBATE

Immigration is the subject of a major political debate in the USA. Despite the historical fact that the USA is a nation of immigrants, there are concerns that the current levels of immigration are not good for the country and that steps need to be taken to reduce the numbers of people being allowed into the USA.

Arguments in favour of immigration include:

- employers want **cheap labour**
- immigrants are **young and economically active**, and contribute to the economy by as much as $30 billion per year
- **cultural diversity** is enhanced by immigrants
- immigrants bring **new skills and create new jobs**. This is particularly true of Asians.

Arguments against immigration include:

- **wage levels for the poorer paid are kept low**
- immigration is **costing the taxpayer too much** for health, education and welfare payments (an estimated $30 billion)
- **American culture is being overwhelmed**, and English is no longer the main language in many areas
- when the economy is in decline many complain that **jobs and college places are being taken by immigrants**. The 'Angry White Males', blacks and resident Hispanics also complain about the new immigrants – the Asians and 'new' Hispanics.

Government responses

Legislation was introduced in California in 1994 by disgruntled Californian taxpayers who felt the Government was failing to take action to deal with the significant increase in the number of Hispanic and Asian immigrants. The legislation, known as Proposition 187, tried to discourage illegal immigration to California by denying illegal aliens and their children access to education, health and welfare benefits. It was declared unconstitutional by the Supreme Court.

In 1996 the US Government introduced the Immigration Reform Law which doubled the Border Patrol on the US–Mexican border to reduce the number of illegal immigrants. In the same year the Welfare Reform Law tried to deter immigration by stopping welfare for legal immigrants until they had lived in the USA for five years and by preventing access to welfare for illegal immigrants altogether.

One of the results of the terrorist attack on the World Trade Center in 2001 was a tightening of the immigration laws. The USA PATRIOT Act introduced new reasons to stop people entering the USA. It gave the Attorney General the power to **declare an alien as a terrorist without trial** and **detain suspected terrorists for an indefinite time**. The PATRIOT Act also increased the number of the border patrols.

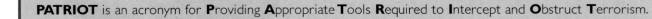

PATRIOT is an acronym for **P**roviding **A**ppropriate **T**ools **R**equired to **I**ntercept and **O**bstruct **T**errorism.

The Border Security Act (2001) increased the budget for the Immigration and Naturalisation Service (INS) and Customs Service. Different agencies had to share information, airlines and shipping companies had to inform the authorities about passengers, and colleges had to keep the authorities informed about foreign students.

Internet research

Visit news websites such as CNN to find out more about criticism of federal plans for immigration. Links to this site and other websites relating to Higher Modern Studies can be found at:

LECKIE&LECKIE
Learning Lab

The USA has strengthened border controls along its border with Mexico

The Department of Homeland Security was formed in 2003. It brought together existing Government agencies such as the INS and formed the US Citizenship and Immigration Services (USCIS). This organisation only grants visas following extensive checks which can take many months. Anyone whose record prompts any suspicion is denied access. These changes have had a big impact in reducing the number of immigrants and asylum seekers to the USA.

For you to do

- Draw up a table to note the main social and economic arguments for and against immigration in the USA.
- Make notes on the recent reaction to immigration
  — at state level
  — at federal level
  — after 2001.
- Critically examine the view that attitudes towards immigration in the USA have hardened in recent years.

AFFIRMATIVE ACTION

In the 1960s, a series of measures known as **Affirmative Action** were introduced in an effort to eradicate discrimination in employment and education for minorities and women. Programmes included actions to create racial balance in schools and to end discrimination in businesses applying for Government contracts.

Education

In order to create racial balance in schools, children were bussed to different areas of cities with different ethnic profiles. **Bussing was hugely unpopular** and created hostility. It led to further segregation as middle class families, both white and black, moved to avoid being involved. It also diverted funds from other areas of education. It was ended in 1995 by the Supreme Court.

Business

Companies that wanted either Federal or State Government contracts had to have Affirmative Action

Programmes (AAPs) in place. These programmes required companies to work towards changing the race profile of their workforce to reflect the population profile in that area.

Legal challenges to Affirmative Action

Affirmative Action has been a controversial issue in the USA, and a number of legal challenges have effectively ended Affirmative Action.

- In 1978 the Supreme Court ruled that setting aside places for minority students was **reverse discrimination**. However, it also stated that universities could consider race as one factor in admissions.
- In 1996 Proposition 209 abolished all public service AAPs in employment, education and contracting in California. The Supreme Court refused to hear a challenge to Proposition 209 and so it effectively ended AAPs in California. Other states such as Texas, Washington, Georgia and Florida followed and abolished AAPs.
- In 2003, the Supreme Court ruled that Michigan University could take race into account when allocating student places, but that its system of awarding extra points to ethnic minorities (20 on a scale of 150) was unconstitutional.

There are arguments both for and against AAPs.

- After 30 years of programmes the **problems of the past should have been eliminated**.
- There have been **vast social and economic improvements for minorities** and now there should be a level playing field.
- Affirmative Action is **reverse discrimination** and therefore wrong.
- Companies are forced to take on **second rate employees** to meet targets
- People do not want to be employed as '**token**' minorities.
- Minorities might have made **greater advances on their own** without the tokenism.

However, despite any flaws in AAPs, minorities still suffer inequalities. AAPs have helped make the USA a more tolerant society. The ending of AAPs in university admissions in various states has reduced the number of minority admissions. Thirty years of gains could be lost.

Internet research

Read the article on the USA Today website on the end of bussing and attitudes to racial integration in education today.

Review some of the stories and views on AAPs in the 1990s found on the website of the Washington Post. Links to these sites and other websites relating to Higher Modern Studies can be found at: **LECKIE&LECKIE** *Learning Lab*

For you to do

- Describe, with examples, how Affirmative Action worked.
- Why can it be argued that Affirmative Action is effectively ended?
- Describe why both whites and ethnic minorities might be against AAPs.
- Summarise the arguments for and against Affirmative Action in a table.
- Critically examine the success of Affirmative Action Programmes in improving the social and economic position of ethnic minorities in the USA.

STUDY THEME SUMMARY

The USA is the wealthiest country in the world and has huge reserves of natural resources. It has a robust capitalist market economy which emphasises the role of the individual over that of Government. The Government is based on the US Constitution and has three linked functions, the legislative, executive and judicial functions, responsible for passing laws, carrying out the laws, and administering law respectively. The Government is headed by an elected President. There is a strong system of checks and balances to prevent any one person or group of people gaining too much power.

There are two main political parties in the USA, the Republicans and the Democrats. Support for these parties varies considerably according to location, gender and ethnicity. Ethnic minorities are under-represented in Congress, and they are less likely to vote in elections than white people. However, as the populations of ethnic minorities grow, their votes will become more important and both parties are developing policies to attract these votes.

The USA has a mixed population, comprising mainly whites, but with sizeable black, Hispanic and Asian populations. These ethnic minority groups are growing in number and in importance. However, there are still significant differences in the lives led by the different groups, particularly in terms of health and wealth. Black people suffer most in terms of ill health, unemployment, poor education, poor housing and discrimination. Hispanic people also experience these problems, but to a lesser extent than blacks. By contrast, Asians have higher than average incomes and enjoy better health. The American system of welfare still has the capacity to leave people in poverty. Various measures have been taken to address the inequalities suffered by ethnic and other minorities, with varying degrees of success. There is a vigorous political debate over immigration levels, with some Americans expressing concern that too much immigration is bad for the USA and its citizens.

Exam-style essay questions

- Critically examine the system of checks and balances on the different institutions of the US Government.
- Ethnic minorities are under-represented in the political system of the USA. Discuss.
- Critically examine the reasons for the social and economic inequalities experienced by ethnic minorities in the USA.
- To what extent has the issue of immigration had an impact on the politics in the USA?

STUDY THEME 3D:
The European Union

In this study theme you will be expected to have a detailed knowledge and understanding of:

- ## AIMS, GROWTH AND ACHIEVEMENT OF THE EUROPEAN UNION (EU)

  The main institutions and their influence within the Union.

- ## CO-OPERATION AND CONFLICT WITH REFERENCE TO POLITICAL, SOCIAL AND ECONOMIC ISSUES

  Constitutional arrangements; enlargement; the single market and single currency; regional and social policy.

- ## CASE STUDY OF THE COMMON AGRICULTURAL POLICY AND THE COMMON FISHERIES POLICY

BACKGROUND

The World Wars of the first half of the 20th century provided the impetus for the establishment of a more cooperative Europe. The wish to avoid further conflict and to rebuild the ruined economies of Europe and the need to deal with the new realities of the Cold War provided the background for the replacement of conflict with cooperation.

The European Union has grown significantly in size and in its aims and purpose since the original cooperative agreements, leading to the establishment of the present day (2007) European Union of 27 member states.

The aims of the European Union include:

- the establishment of a peaceful, united Europe
- the rebuilding of the war-ravaged economies of Europe and the return to production for peaceful purposes
- the development of democracy and human rights
- the establishment of a counterweight to the two superpowers, USA and USSR
- the development of a large market to gain economies from large scale production for business.

HINTS & TIPS

The early growth and original aims of the EU are for background only and will not be asked about specifically in the exam.

EARLY GROWTH OF THE EUROPEAN UNION

The first post-war cooperative activity was the establishment of the European Coal and Steel Community (ECSC) in 1951. The ECSC pooled the resources of France, West Germany, Italy, Belgium, Luxembourg and the Netherlands.

These six countries went on to establish the European Economic Community (EEC, also known informally as the Common Market). The EEC was a customs union which aimed for the free movement of goods and services within the member countries. The six original members signed the Treaty of Rome in 1957, establishing the EEC (which was then implemented on 1 January 1958). The same countries also formed Euratom, an organisation developed to promote nuclear energy, in 1957.

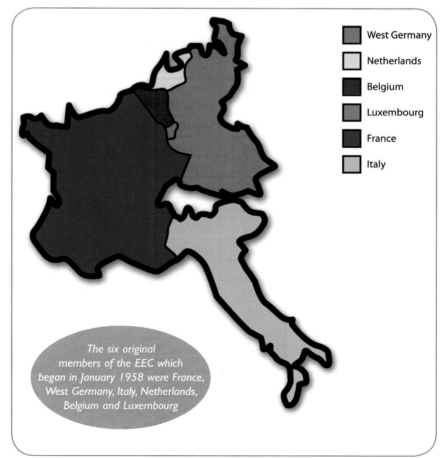

Legend:
- West Germany
- Netherlands
- Belgium
- Luxembourg
- France
- Italy

The six original members of the EEC which began in January 1958 were France, West Germany, Italy, Netherlands, Belgium and Luxembourg

DECISION MAKING IN THE EUROPEAN UNION

The European Union has grown from a group of six countries with limited aims to a much larger organisation of 27 countries, with further expansion likely in the future, and a wide range of policies. The practical difficulties of reaching agreement and making decisions in a union with so many countries of widely varying population size and area, language and cultural differences and economic variation should not be underestimated. The European Union attempts to strike a balance between two approaches to decision making – intergovernmentalism and supranationalism.

Intergovernmentalism is a system of decision making whereby power is retained by the individual member states and decisions are based on the principle of all members reaching unanimous agreement. Representatives of the organisation have advisory powers only or are responsible for implementing policies decided by the representatives of each government. Supporters of this system argue that it is the only way to maintain democratic control over the European Union since it is the individual governments in each member state which have democratic legitimacy in representing the interests of their citizens. They also argue that vital national interests and differences can only be maintained under such an arrangement. More **Eurosceptic** nations, such as the UK, Denmark and Sweden, favour this approach to decision making.

Eurosceptic: a term used to describe a person or group opposed to European integration or 'sceptical' of the EU and its aims; sometimes relating to the wish to protect national sovereignty.

Supranationalism is a system of decision making where power is held by officials of the organisation or by representatives elected by the people of the member states. Individual member states still have powers but they must share them with other bodies of the organisation. Decisions are made by majority rather than unanimity. Supporters of this form of arrangement within the EU argue that this allows a faster pace of integration and quicker decision making. The *Benelux* countries (Belgium, the Netherlands and Luxembourg) and France, Germany and Italy have tended to favour this system.

Attempts to agree a Constitution for the EU have failed because of difficulties in reaching agreement between the member states and the refusal of voters in some countries to ratify the proposed constitution in referenda.

The institutions of the European Union

The EU comprises a number of separate institutions which carry out different functions. The institutions include the European Parliament, with directly elected representatives from all member states, the Council of the European Union, the European Commission and the European Court of Justice.

European Parliament

The European Parliament is **elected every five years using proportional representation**. At the moment it has 785 members (known as MEPs). The number of members from each country depends on the size of its population so Germany elects 99 members while Malta has five members. The UK elects 78 members using the party list system within regions. Scotland is counted as one region and has **seven members who represent the whole of Scotland** rather than specific constituencies. Once elected, members do not sit in national delegations but join party political groupings with those of similar views from other countries. Almost one third of MEPs are women.

Parties in European Parliament

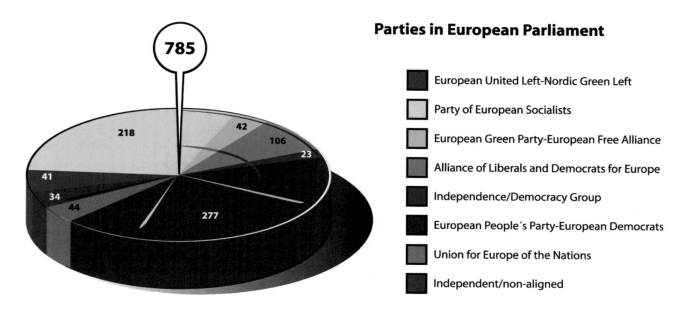

785

218   42
106
41   23
34
44   277

- ■ European United Left-Nordic Green Left
- □ Party of European Socialists
- ■ European Green Party-European Free Alliance
- ■ Alliance of Liberals and Democrats for Europe
- ■ Independence/Democracy Group
- ■ European People's Party-European Democrats
- ■ Union for Europe of the Nations
- ■ Independent/non-aligned

The roles of the European Parliament include:

- **passing European laws:** this responsibility is shared with the Council of the European Union. Depending on the issue involved the Parliament has the right to amend, veto or be consulted on legislation. The Parliament cannot itself propose new laws
- **approving the President** and other members of the European Commission
- **approving the budget** of the European Union (jointly with the Council)
- the power to **dismiss the European Commission**.

As the Parliament has grown, the powers have increased.

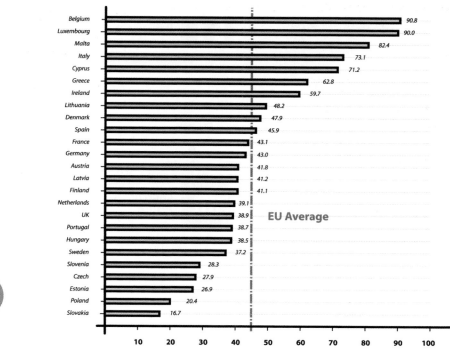

Percentage turnout figures in 2004 elections

Belgium	90.8
Luxembourg	90.0
Malta	82.4
Italy	73.1
Cyprus	71.2
Greece	62.8
Ireland	59.7
Lithuania	48.2
Denmark	47.9
Spain	45.9
France	43.1
Germany	43.0
Austria	41.8
Latvia	41.2
Finland	41.1
Netherlands	39.1
UK	38.9
Portugal	38.7
Hungary	38.5
Sweden	37.2
Slovenia	28.3
Czech	27.9
Estonia	26.9
Poland	20.4
Slovakia	16.7

EU Average

Turnout varies considerably in the election to the European Parliament 2004

The Council of the European Union

The Council of the European Union (formerly known as the Council of Ministers) is made up of a **Government Minister from each member state**. The Minister who attends will depend on the issue being discussed, so, for example, if agriculture is being discussed then the Agriculture Minister from each country will attend. When votes take place each country has a number of votes related to its size (although consideration is given to the smaller countries to make sure they cannot be outvoted by a few large members). Some issues, such as taxation, immigration and foreign policy, are not decided by majority votes due to their importance and national sensitivity. When the heads of governments in each state meet in summits, known as the European Council, broad issues of policy are discussed.

How decisions are made in the EU

The Commission proposes a new law to the Council of the European Union. The Council discuses and votes on the proposal. On most subjects the European Parliament must also agree on the proposal before it can become European law. In most cases a vote is taken and decisions can be reached using a **qualified majority vote** (QMV). On matters that are seen to be very important to individual member states, such as tax, defence and foreign policy, unanimity is required.

Under QMV, each country has a number of votes, related to their population. The big four countries – Germany, France, UK and Italy – each have 29 votes with other countries having fewer. To pass a new law:

- at least 232 votes must be in favour
- more than 50% of member countries must vote in favour
- the votes must represent at least 62% of the population of the EU.

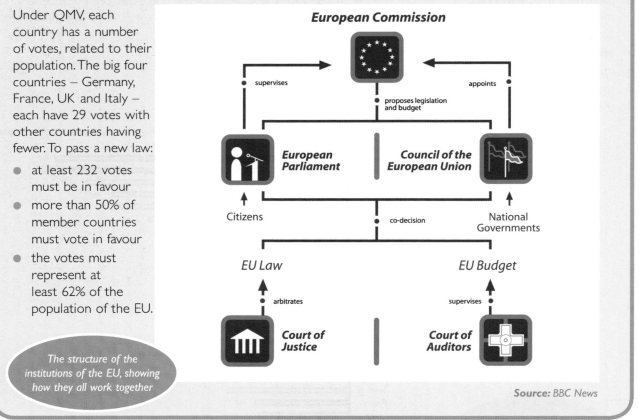

The structure of the institutions of the EU, showing how they all work together

Source: *BBC News*

Although the Council of the European Union shares legislative responsibility with the European Parliament, it is the Council which has greater power within the EU. It has the main responsibility for making policy decisions within the EU.

The European Commission

The role of the European Commission is to represent the interests of Europe as a whole and not the national interests of individual countries. Each country appoints one member of the Commission, with each Commissioner being responsible for specific policy areas. They do not represent the government or country they were appointed from. Commissioners are appointed for five-year terms.

The roles of the European Commission include:

- **making proposals** for new European laws
- **day-to-day running** of EU policies and spending
- checking that countries and organisations abide by **EU treaties and laws**
- **promoting European integration**.

Peter Mandelson

- Born 1953 in London
- Labour Party campaign manager in 1997
- Elected as Labour MP for Hartlepool in 1992
- Held various UK Cabinet positions including Secretary of State for Trade and Industry and for Northern Ireland
- Resigned from Cabinet twice over financial affairs
- Appointed as EU Commissioner by British Government in 2004
- Made EU Commissioner for Trade

Jose Manuel Barroso, President of Commission

- Born 1956 in Lisbon, Portugal
- Former revolutionary, later joined Social Democratic Party in Portugal
- Member of Portuguese Parliament
- Government Minister and Prime Minister 2002–2004
- Chosen as 11th President of European Commission in 2004

The Court of Justice

The Court of Justice ensures that EU laws are applied as intended and interpreted uniformly across all member countries. Decisions of the Court are binding on member states and large fines can be imposed against countries and companies who fail to comply with EU law. Each member country has one judge on the Court.

Relationship of the EU to member states

The members of the European Union have voluntarily transferred a considerable amount of sovereignty (decision-making power) to the European Union. The European Parliament is directly elected, the Commission acts in the interests of the EU as a whole and many decisions are made in the Council by majority votes, so the EU could be seen as a *supranational* body.

However, the EU does not have the power to transfer further powers to itself without the permission of the member states. In many areas of policy such as foreign relations and defence, member states have given up relatively little national sovereignty so the EU retains many features of an intergovernmental body.

The debate over the proposed European Constitution may determine what kind of body the EU becomes or whether it evolves into a body with its own unique structure.

For you to do

- What are the difficulties in reaching agreement between the members of the EU?
- Explain the difference between intergovernmentalism and supranationalism.
- Describe the role of each of the main institutions of the EU.
- Explain the relationship between the main institutions of the EU.
- Examine the decision-making processes of the European Union.
- Where does real power lie in the EU? Explain your answer.
- The EU is fundamentally undemocratic. Discuss.
- To what extent has the EU taken over the powers of its member states?

Internet research

Visit the website of the European Parliament to find out the current composition of the EU in terms of representatives from different countries and different political parties.
Find out about the members of the European Parliament for your area.
Links to this site and other websites relating to Higher Modern Studies can be found at: LECKIE&LECKIE Learning Lab

HINTS & TIPS

Have some idea of how decision making and democratic accountability compares with the UK.

Achievements of the EU

- Growth from six to 27 members
- Countries still applying to join
- No countries have left the EU
- Peaceful relations between member states
- Former dictatorships absorbed into EU as well as former Communist states
- World's largest economy
- Economic growth and prosperity
- Increasing areas of cooperation
- Introduction of single European currency
- Beginning to take on international defence role
- Major force in international negotiations
- Free movement of citizens across Europe

COOPERATION AND CONFLICT IN THE EUROPEAN UNION

As a grouping of 27 countries, the European Union has great scope for conflict over political and economic issues. The political issues include the development of a European Constitution, and the degree of sovereignty to be retained by member states. Economic issues include the single European currency and trade relations. However, issues which might initially appear to be straightforward economic issues often end up as political issues because of the different stances taken by different countries.

Political issues

A Constitution for the European Union

Between 2002 and 2004 a Constitutional Convention under former French President Valéry Giscard d'Estaing produced a draft Constitution for the European Union. The Constitution was thought to be necessary to bring together the various laws and treaties that had been enacted since the formation of the EU. It would also clarify the powers of the institutions and prepare the way for the expansion of the membership of the EU. The process came to halt in 2005 when both the French and Dutch voted against the Constitution.

The Constitution proposed:

- **subsidiarity** – the principle that the EU will only act in areas where the member states have decided to give it the relevant power and where the aims are better achieved at a European rather than national level
- an **increased role** for the EU in some areas of policy, most controversially in asylum and immigration
- an **extension of foreign and defence policy**; however, member states will still retain their veto in this area and be able to maintain their own foreign policy

- an **extension of QMV** to more decisions in order to speed up decision making in an EU of 27+ members. Members would retain a veto in foreign policy, defence and taxation. The European Parliament would have an equal say on issues requiring a QMV
- a **European President**, who would be elected for a period of 2.5 years (renewable once). The President would be elected by the European Council and be confirmed by the European Parliament. The President would become the representative of the EU internationally and be the major figure in driving forward EU policies
- a **Minister of Foreign Affairs**, who would act as Foreign Minister for the EU's foreign and security policy
- a reduction in the number of **Commissioners** so that the Commission would consist of the President of the Commission, the Union Minister of Foreign Affairs and 13 Commissioners appointed by countries on an equal rota
- an enhancement of the role of the **European Parliament** giving it the power of co-decision with the Council of the European Union on those issues that require a decision by QMV. This would enhance the democratic nature of the EU since the Parliament is the only institution in which voters have a direct say
- **consultation with national parliaments** on European legislation. If one-third of them believed a law would be better carried out at the national level then the Commission would need to review the legislation
- the establishment of a **charter of fundamental rights**
- the establishment of the EU as a **legal identity** of its own, able to enter into international agreements. EU laws would take precedence over national laws in agreed areas
- a procedure for **countries leaving the EU**.

The proposed Constitution provoked considerable debate across the EU. Some see it as not going far enough, missing the opportunity to create a deeper union with greater integration of more policy areas, and to build a United States of Europe. Others claim that the constitution is a step along the road to greater integration which they oppose.

In order for it to come into force, the 25 EU member states (at the time) were required to ratify the Constitution by the end of October 2006. By May 2006, 15 countries had ratified the Constitution. However, French and Dutch referendas rejected the proposed Constitution in 2005 and it appears to have foundered.

Various explanations have been put forward for opposition to the Constitution, including:

- **erosion of national sovereignty** and national identity
- **general uneasiness** with the EU
- **amount of legislation** from Brussels and the increasing number of policy areas
- **possible Turkish membership** of the EU
- **economic liberalism** reducing the focus on 'Social Europe'
- concern over the effects of **globalisation**
- **loss of national influence** in Europe
- EU **integration going too fast**
- EU **influence over issues close to citizens**
- **lack of democracy** within the EU
- impact of the **Euro**.

HINTS & TIPS

> The debate over the European Constitution will go on for several years – be aware of the discussions going on and whether or not any progress is being made in the acceptance of the Constitution by all members.

For you to do

- Explain why a new Constitution was thought to be necessary for the European Union.
- What were the main proposals made for the new Constitution?
- Explain the arguments made against the proposed EU Constitution.
- Critically assess the view that the EU will not be able to function effectively unless it can reach agreement on the new Constitution.

Political debates in Europe

In addition to the ongoing discussions regarding the Constitution, there are a number of areas of debate in Europe, such as democracy, stability, integration and foreign policy. These debates are summarised in the following table.

Internet research

Visit the website of the BBC or newspapers to find out the current state of progress of the EU Constitution. Find out opinions in different countries of the EU. Links to these sites and other websites relating to Higher Modern Studies can be found at: LECKIE&LECKIE *Learning Lab*

DEMOCRACY	
Reasons why the EU is thought to be undemocratic	*Reasons why the EU is thought to be democratic*
● The EU is undemocratic with decisions being made by faceless officials in Brussels. ● Decision-making power is being taken away from national parliaments. ● High levels of hostility or indifference to the EU in many member states as shown by declining turnout in EU elections mean that MEPs aren't really democratic representatives.	● European Parliament is elected by voters in all member states using systems of proportional representation. ● The interests of national governments are represented on the Council of the European Union and countries have the right to veto issues of national importance to them. ● Most people within the EU would wish to retain membership.

STABILITY	
Reasons why the EU is not thought to be stable	*Reasons why the EU is thought to be stable*
● EU did not prevent war in former Yugoslavia. ● New countries joining make it more difficult to make decisions in the EU and in the future may fundamentally alter the nature of the EU. ● Countries are joining for economic benefits of membership.	● The EU has maintained peace in Europe for 50 years. ● The EU has preserved democracy and human rights with newly democratic countries seeing membership as a way of preserving their new-found rights. ● More countries wish to join and as yet no countries have left the EU.

INTEGRATION	
Arguments against integration	*Arguments for integration*
● Further integration leads to loss of national identity. ● National sovereignty is lost as more and more decisions are made in Brussels. ● Further integration will lead to more disagreements and put greater strain on the EU.	● Countries are able to maintain their own language and social and cultural traditions within EU ● Principle of subsidiarity ensures only those decisions best taken at EU level are given to EU institutions. ● The EU is a voluntary agreement of countries with important safeguards built in to protect vital national interests.

FOREIGN AND DEFENCE POLICY	
Arguments against a common foreign policy	*Arguments for a common foreign policy*
● A common foreign policy could conflict with the national interests of member states. ● Moves towards a common defence policy could weaken commitment to NATO and alliance with USA. ● The creation of another superpower in international affairs could create more instability in the world.	● A common foreign policy would give Europe a greater voice in international affairs. ● NATO would still be seen as the main focus for European defence and security. ● A united Europe could counter-balance US influence and possible Chinese power in the future.

For you to do

● Overall the EU has provided political benefits to the people of Europe. Discuss.

Economic issues

The primary objectives of the European Community (now the European Union) were to ensure peace in Europe and develop the economies of the member states. Both of these objectives were to be aided by the creation of a single market amongst the member states. The single market would lead to greater trade, larger economies of scale and greater economic efficiency. Also, countries whose economies were interdependent would not go to war with each other.

Single European market

Since its formation the EU has taken steps to create a single European market (SEM) and although this was said to have been completed by 1992 it remains an ongoing project. The SEM has many aspects:

● **free trade** of goods and services within the EU through the removal of internal tariffs and quotas and the removal of most border controls

● the establishment of an **EU competition law** which can be used to regulate anti-competitive practices of companies and also restricts the ability of governments to provide state aid to domestic industries

● **freedom of movement** for citizens to live, work and study within any EU state and be entitled to social protection in their country of residence. This allows workers to go to where there are labour shortages

● the **free movement of investment capital** within the EU

● a **harmonisation of laws** relating to safety and technical standards, trademark regulations and company laws

● **value added tax** (VAT) adopted as a common system of indirect taxation (although countries retain the right to set their own level)

● the creation of the **Eurozone** – the countries who adopted the euro in place of national currency (see pages 259–261 for more detail)

● a **common external customs tariff** imposed on trade with non-EU countries. The EU acts as a single body in international trade negotiations.

Advantages and disadvantages of the SEM are shown opposite.

For you to do

● What are the political and economic purposes of the SEM?
● Describe the main features of the SEM.
● To what extent are the benefits of the SEM outweighed by the disadvantages?

Advantages	Disadvantages
● The EU has grown into the largest trading bloc in the world.	● Economic growth in the EU has been slower than in other parts of the world.
● After enlargement in 2007, firms selling in the SEM have access to over 480 million consumers.	● Countries within the EU still pursue their own national economic interests rather than the greater good of the EU.
● The Commission claims that the SEM has helped create 4.5 million new jobs and generated €800 billion in additional wealth since 1993.	● The Common External Tariff has placed trade barriers against imports from developing countries.
● The EU has a stronger voice in international trade negotiations than individual states would have on their own.	● The USA and increasingly China are the major trading countries in the world today.
● Countries which do not abide by EU competition law can face sanctions (such as the French being forced to allow British lamb imports).	● Some countries apply the EU competition laws more rigorously than others placing their own domestic industries at a disadvantage.
● Workers can move to areas of skill shortage allowing economic growth to be maintained, for example, many Polish tradesmen have come to work in the British building industry in recent years.	● The migration of workers may put the jobs of existing workers at risk and cause a drain of skills from certain countries.
● Investment can move around the EU, creating jobs in poorer parts of the union and allowing companies to earn profits.	● The ability to move capital from one country to another without restriction could put jobs at risk as firms close factories in one country and move to another area where labour costs are lower.
● The introduction of the euro has made trade easier and provided benefits for individual travellers.	● Not all EU member states have adopted the euro.

Single European currency

An important aspect of the SEM has been the establishment of a single European currency, with the **euro** as the unit of currency. Economic and monetary union (EMU) has been an important aim of the EU since its earliest days. The debate about EMU has been one of the most controversial within the UK, with supporters and opponents of British membership of the euro basing their cases on both economic and political arguments.

The current single currency was preceded by a number of attempts by member states to bring their currencies into line with each other. The first attempt to align exchange rates in the early 1970s collapsed after only two years. The exchange rate mechanism (ERM) set up in 1979 created a European currency unit (ECU) but was again unsuccessful and caused huge economic problems for the British Government in the early 1990s.

The **Maastricht Treaty** (1991) laid down firm plans for a single European currency. The euro was launched in 1999 in an electronic form as a commercial means of payment. In 2002, **euro notes and coins** were issued and the euro became legal tender in 12 members of the EU, known as the Eurozone.

Participating countries had to agree to fix the exchange rates between their currencies, with national governments giving control of their monetary policy to the European Central Bank. The Growth and Stability Pact brought broad economic policies into line (for example, limiting the amount of government borrowing by countries).

The Eurozone consists of 13 member states of the EU (the UK, Sweden and Denmark did not join at the outset) with a population of over 316 million people.

Introduction of the euro, 1 January 2002

It was predicted by many that 'E-day' would result in massive disruption with concerns about the huge cost of conversion for businesses, possibility of fraud, and shortages of the new notes and coins. In fact, the preparations, involving printing 14.5 million notes and minting 56 billion new coins, resulted in a smooth transition. The main concern was the belief that in some countries business had taken advantage of the changeover to increase prices unreasonably.

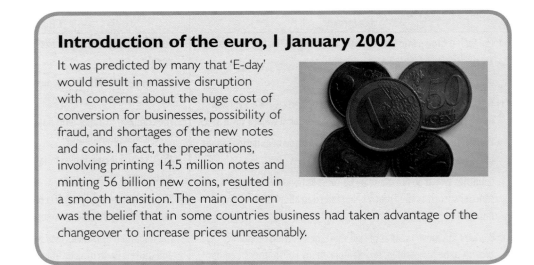

All Eurozone countries have the **same currency** and the **same interest rate**. The interest rate is set by the European Central Bank, based in Germany. The Council of Finance Ministers determine economic policy for the EU.

Most of the recently joined members of the EU are due to join the Eurozone within the next few years. Only Britain and Denmark have agreement from the EU to stay outside the Eurozone. However, the British Government have declared it is their aim to join the euro when five economic tests have been met.

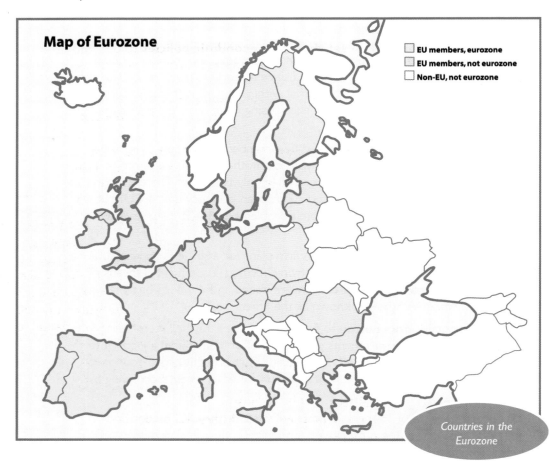

Map of Eurozone

☐ EU members, eurozone
☐ EU members, not eurozone
☐ Non-EU, not eurozone

Countries in the Eurozone

Advantages of the euro

- It is claimed that a single currency will result in **greater stability of exchange rates** giving exporters greater certainty and thereby leading to conditions in which trade will increase.
- **Businesses face fewer charges** in having to take steps to protect themselves against currency fluctuations.
- The discipline of the single currency should result in **lower interest rates** as all currencies would be influenced by traditional German economic prudence.
- Politically, the euro is a **major step forward in European integration**. Individual currencies are a major feature of individual national identity, but by establishing a single currency across all of the EU a big element of nationalism is removed.
- Consumers **do not incur commission charges** when exchanging currency to visit other countries. The use of a single currency avoids confusion and makes price comparisons easier, resulting in greater competition.

Disadvantages of the euro

- Opponents of the euro argue that it is **impossible in the long term to maintain the same exchange rate** across so many countries with different economies. Economic union requires a degree of labour mobility which the EU does not have (not least because of language barriers).

> **'Monetary union is the motor of European integration.'**
>
> Former Belgian PM Jean-Luc Dehaene

- Countries **lose the ability to set their own economic policies** to deal with domestic economic problems (such as borrowing more in order to create more jobs if unemployment is rising).
- Different countries tend to go through **economic cycles at different times**. Decisions made by a single central bank cannot take account of the **different phases of the economic cycle** in different countries.
- The **loss of national sovereignty** is seen as a major problem by opponents who believe that the economic arguments given for the euro are less important than the increased impetus to integration and the growth in the power of trans-European institutions.

Britain and the euro

The British Government is in favour of euro entry. However, Britain will join only after the British public have voted in a referendum and after five economic tests have been met. Those tests are:

- evidence of **sustainable convergence** between Britain and the economies of a single currency
- whether there is **sufficient flexibility** to cope with economic change
- whether the effect on **investment** will be positive
- whether the impact on our **financial services industry** will be positive
- whether it is good for **employment**.

> **'Monetary union is a fundamentally undemocratic project. It has stripped member states of their power to tailor economic policy to local and national circumstances and placed it instead in the hands of an institution which is open to neither scrutiny and democratic audit nor influence.'**
>
> Caroline Lucas MEP

Arguments in favour of and in opposition to the euro are summarised below.

In favour	In opposition
● The Government would embark upon a major publicity exercise explaining the advantages of the euro to voters. For example, more people already have experience of using the euro on holiday.	● Membership of the euro seems to be unpopular in the UK with significant forces such as Rupert Murdoch's *Sun* newspaper very much opposed to membership.
● If Britain doesn't join the euro, it will lose out on investment as companies will prefer to locate in those parts of the EU where their costs are reduced by being able to use the euro.	● The British economy has been doing well outside the Eurozone —employment, inflation and growth have all been performing well and this economic performance would be put at risk by joining the euro.
● Existing members have not lost any of their national identity as a result of being in the Eurozone and giving up their traditional currencies.	● Britain would lose the pound, which has been an important part of the British identity for hundreds of years.
● Britain will lose influence inside the EU and in negotiations with outside bodies if it is not seen to be a full member of the EU by not signing up to the euro.	● Strains have already been shown in the Growth and Stability Pact with both Germany and France being able to flout the rules, particularly on levels of national debt.

For you to do

- Explain how the single European currency helps to achieve the SEM.
- Describe the introduction of the euro in 2002.
- To what extent does the introduction of the euro limit the economic sovereignty of those countries that have adopted it?
- What are the 'five tests' of British membership of the euro?
- Britain would be seriously disadvantaged by not adopting the euro. Discuss.

Internet research

Visit the website of the UK Government and find out the present position regarding joining the euro.
Visit the websites of UK newspapers and try and find out the view of different newspapers regarding joining the euro.
Visit the website of a polling organisation and find out the view of the public regarding membership of the euro.
Links to these sites and other websites relating to Higher Modern Studies can be found at:

HINTS & TIPS

The debate over Britain's membership of the euro will continue over the next few years. Find out the views of the different political parties in the UK. How do newspapers treat the issue? What are the views of different newspapers?

ENLARGEMENT

The European Union has grown from its original six members to the current 27 members, in seven stages. The biggest influx of new members took place in 2004 with 10 countries joining, increasing the area of the EU by a quarter and its population by a fifth. It is not only the size of the expansion that is significant. The nature of the member countries will significantly alter the nature of the EU.

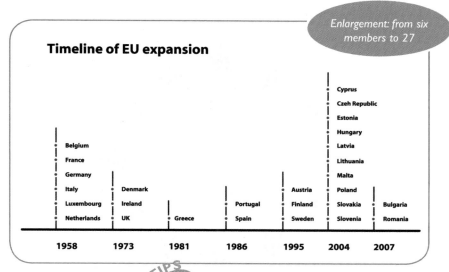

Enlargement: from six members to 27

Overall the new members have significantly less developed economies compared with the existing members. They have lower GDP levels per person and higher proportions of the workforce employed in agriculture.

This phase of expansion shifts the EU towards Eastern Europe with most of the countries joining until recently being part of the former Soviet Union itself (Estonia, Latvia and Lithuania) or part of the Soviet Bloc of countries and part of the Warsaw Pact military alliance. Until the fall of the Iron Curtain and the end of Communist control in Eastern Europe, these countries had a completely different economic and social system as well as being regarded as enemies.

Be aware of how the countries which joined in 2004 are coping with membership and be aware of the state of negotiations with possible future members.

In order to qualify for membership, candidate countries must:

- **guarantee democracy, human rights and the rule of law**
- have a **functioning market economy** able to cope with EU membership
- **incorporate European law** into their own system of laws.

Bringing in so many new members has implications for the running of the EU. Changes have been necessary in the institutions of the EU, increasing the numbers attending the Council of the European Union,

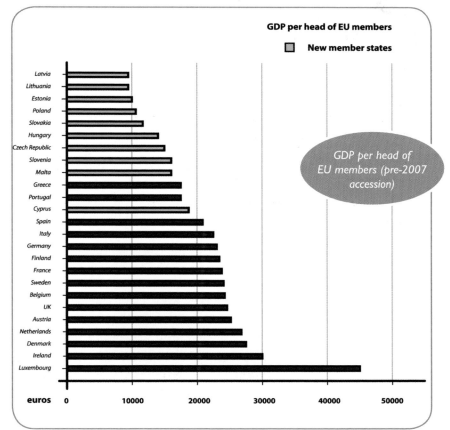

GDP per head of EU members (pre-2007 accession)

the Commission and the European Parliament. Enlargement was a major factor behind the proposal to introduce a European Constitution. With more members, decision making is more difficult and the traditional dominance of France and Germany may be weakened.

There are also concerns about the ability of poorer countries to compete with the more developed members and about the movement of people from poorer areas to richer parts of the EU. As poorer areas in the EU, most of the new members will be entitled to regional assistance, possibly at the expense of areas which have benefited from this assistance in the past.

The expansion of the EU may also provide the impetus to reform institutions of the EU such as the Common Agricultural Policy (see pages 270–273). Expansion of EU membership can be seen as an opportunity to slow down the progress of integration since it will become more difficult to establish common policies across a larger number of more diverse countries.

Expansion comes at a considerable cost to the existing members, although one study has suggested existing members will gain £6 bn while new members will gain £15 bn.

For many, the economic costs and benefits of enlargement are secondary and the real benefits are in greater political influence for a larger and more powerful union as well as greater stability and security in Europe. Lasting peace is achieved with former enemies being so interlinked that there is no possibility of war between them. There is some concern that Russia would oppose the loss of countries that were its former allies.

Future expansion

Two other states are candidates to join. Croatia has already been accepted as a member and should be able to join within a few years. Much more controversial is the future membership of Turkey. The Commission has agreed to continue negotiations with Turkey about its future membership which has been accepted in principle. However, despite some progress, there are still major concerns, for example, about Turkey's human rights record and its attitude towards its Kurdish people.

Some existing members are also concerned about the 'European-ness' of Turkey – it is not generally regarded as a European state, since is it mainly located in Asia. In its culture, traditions and in particular its religious beliefs it is seen to be significantly different from the rest of the EU. Turkey is an overwhelmingly Muslim country while the other countries in the EU come more from a Christian tradition and in some cases the Christian religion is an important part of their national identity. Turkey is also a large country in both area and population. The problems caused by absorbing poorer countries already in the EU would be made worse if a country as poor as Turkey were also to be integrated. These differences will make it harder to incorporate Turkey into the community than other countries that have more of a shared identity with the existing members.

Supporters of Turkey's accession point to the progress that Turkey has made in both modernising its economy and improving its human rights record. They also point out that many existing EU countries have significant Muslim populations and that it would send a very negative image to them if Turkey were to be refused membership on the basis that the majority of its citizens were Muslims.

For you to do

- Explain fully why Britain has consistently had problems with the EU budget.

For you to do

- In what ways does its recent expansion pose challenges for the EU?
- What conditions must candidate members fulfil to become full EU members?
- Give arguments for and against expansion of the EU.
- Explain why the possible membership of Turkey is a problem for the EU.
- The expansion of the EU will lead to benefits for both existing members and new members. Discuss.

Internet research

Visit the website of the EU and find out which countries are applying to join the EU. What are the conditions being applied to these candidate members? What is the likelihood of future expansion?

Links to this site and other websites relating to Higher Modern Studies can be found at:

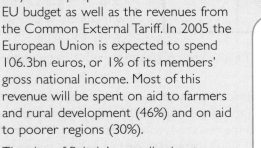

HINTS & TIPS

New members are set to join the EU. Countries will become part of the Eurozone and debates will take place on fundamental issues within the EU. Keep up to date with recent developments that you can include, where relevant, in your essay answers.

The EU Budget

EU income comes largely from the member states, in line with how wealthy they are. A proportion of VAT revenues from each country is paid into the EU budget as well as the revenues from the Common External Tariff. In 2005 the European Union is expected to spend 106.3bn euros, or 1% of its members' gross national income. Most of this revenue will be spent on aid to farmers and rural development (46%) and on aid to poorer regions (30%).

The size of Britain's contribution to the budget has long been a source of grievance for British Governments, with Margaret Thatcher negotiating a rebate in 1984. Tony Blair has agreed to give up much of this special arrangement, given Britain's relatively improved economic position and in light of the expansion of the EU in return for reform of the Common Agricultural Policy (CAP).

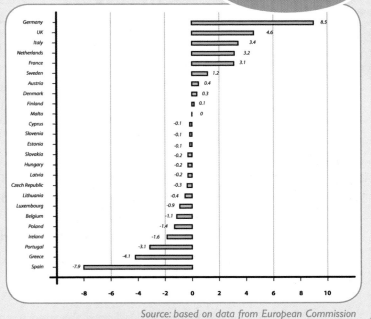

Net givers and takers in the EU, 2004

Country	Value
Germany	8.5
UK	4.6
Italy	3.4
Netherlands	3.2
France	3.1
Sweden	1.2
Austria	0.4
Denmark	0.3
Finland	0.1
Malta	0
Cyprus	-0.1
Slovenia	-0.1
Estonia	-0.1
Slovakia	-0.2
Hungary	-0.2
Latvia	-0.2
Czech Republic	-0.3
Lithuania	-0.4
Luxembourg	-0.9
Belgium	-1.1
Poland	-1.4
Ireland	-1.6
Portugal	-3.1
Greece	-4.1
Spain	-7.9

Source: based on data from European Commission

REGIONAL POLICY

The European Union is one of the richest parts of the world. However, it still contains considerable economic diversity and the addition of the new members has widened the gap between the richest and poorest regions of the EU. Regional policies aim to help economically and socially disadvantaged regions by transferring resources from richer areas to poorer ones. This will improve unity across the union by narrowing the gaps in income and wealth across the regions.

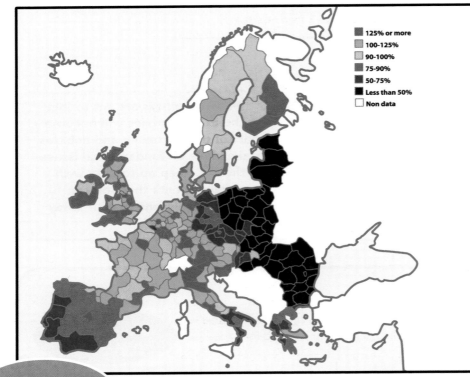

125% or more
100-125%
90-100%
75-90%
50-75%
Less than 50%
Non data

GDP per head as percentage of EU average, 2002

Even before expansion in 2004 there were differences in prosperity within the EU. The 10 richest regions had a level of GDP per person three times higher than the 10 poorest regions. The enlargement in 2004 doubled the level of inequity within the EU, with the population of the EU increasing by 20% while the GDP increased by just 5%. The Baltic States have a GDP per person of 45–60% of the EU average, while the newest members, Bulgaria and Romania, have per capita GDPs of about 30% of the EU average. Almost all regions in the new members qualify for regional assistance.

About one third of the EU budget is devoted to policies designed to remove the differences in wealth across the EU.

Inequalities may be a result of geographical remoteness. It can be seen from the map that most of the poorer areas are on the edges of the EU. Many of the inequalities are longstanding, while others may be the result of more recent social or economic change such as the decline of traditional industries that certain regions depended upon.

The EU policy to reduce regional disparities is built on four structural funds:

● the **European Regional Development Fund**
● the **European Social Fund**
● the section of the **Common Agricultural Policy** devoted to rural development
● financial support for fishing communities as part of the **Common Fisheries Policy**.

These funds will pay out about €213 billion, between 2000 and 2006.

A further €18 billion is allocated to the **Cohesion Fund**, set up in 1993 to finance transport and environment improvements in member states with a GDP less than 90% of the EU average at the time (Greece, Ireland, Spain and Portugal).

Where the money goes

- A total of 70% of funding goes to areas where GDP is less than 75% of the EU average, known as **Objective 1 regions**. About 22% of the EU's population live in the regions benefiting from these funds. The funds are used to improve basic infrastructure and encourage business investment.
- Another 11.5% of regional spending goes to **Objective 2 regions** (areas experiencing economic decline because of structural difficulties such as the decline of industries) to help with economic and social rehabilitation. About 18% of the EU population live in such areas.
- **Objective 3** focuses on job-creation initiatives and programmes in all regions not covered by Objective 1. About 12.3% of funding goes towards the adaptation and modernisation of education and training systems to promote employment.
- Additional funds are available specifically to help new members adjust to membership of the EU and begin to tackle the inequalities which exist between them and the EU average.

Problems with regional policy

- Whether or not regions are designated as areas entitled to support is often the result of **political wrangling** between countries.
- Many believe that **insufficient resources are devoted to regional aid**.
- Areas which have been entitled to aid in the past may **suffer if aid is withdrawn** – transitional funds have been given to make this adjustment easier.
- The growth of the EU to encompass poorer countries will put considerable strain on the EU regional budget. This will result in the **transfer of resources from the richer countries** which may be politically damaging for these governments.
- As a result of the membership of new countries, **existing members may no longer find themselves entitled to receive EU regional support** (because poorer countries lower the overall average).

For you to do

- Why has the EU felt it necessary to give regional assistance to some areas?
- Explain why some areas are poorer than others.
- Describe the help available to poorer areas of the EU.
- Explain why the new members of the EU will place a greater strain on the EU's regional aid budget.

Internet research

Visit the website of the EU and find out what assistance is given to areas in the UK.

Links to this site and other websites relating to Higher Modern Studies can be found at: LECKIE&LECKIE *Learning Lab*

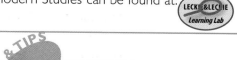

Keep a note of a few local examples of projects that have received EU funding.

HINTS & TIPS

SOCIAL ISSUES

The EU has been sensitive to the criticism that it is primarily concerned with economic issues and the interests of business. It has increasingly pointed to ways in which the EU has a positive impact upon the everyday lives of the people of Europe.

Apart from the benefits deriving from rising living standards and a peaceful Europe, the EU claims that citizens gain these benefits:

- **freedom to travel, live, work and study** anywhere in the EU
- **a ban on discrimination** on the grounds of nationality
- **acquisition of European citizenship** to complement national citizenship
- **protection of fundamental rights** covering non-discrimination on grounds of gender, race, religion, age and sexual orientation
- **guarantees of workers' rights and social security** throughout the EU.

Effects of social policy

The policy of free movement of citizens within the EU has led to a number of concerns, particularly with the growth to 27 members and beyond. The 1985 Schengen Agreement removed most of the internal barriers to movement between the majority of EU states. (The UK and Ireland felt unable to sign up to all aspects of the agreement and have retained many of their controls on entry.)

Concerns over crime

The EU has attempted to deal with worries that greater freedom for citizens would also provide more opportunities for criminals to operate in different countries and make it easier for international terrorists to develop their networks more effectively and evade detection and arrest. There are also concerns about levels of organised crime networks. The nature of some crimes means that they can only be tackled effectively through internationally coordination action.

There are a number of EU measures to tackle concerns over crime.

- There is **police cooperation** through Europol, which gathers intelligence on organised crime and

gives member states an assessment of the dangers from organised crime and suggests ways to tackle it. Europol is involved in cooperation to tackle people trafficking.

- The **European Police Training College** trains police forces in cross-border cooperation.
- **Good practice** is shared between national police forces.
- The **European Arrest Warrant** was established to make extradition between countries easier and quicker.
- **Drug use and trafficking** are being targeted.

Concerns over immigration

The admission of new members to the EU led to widespread fears of a massive wave of immigration from the former Communist countries of Eastern Europe. This fear was stronger in Britain than in most other areas of the EU.

> Britain was warned last night it faces a massive benefits bill to pay for the looming influx of immigrants, including gypsies, from Eastern Europe. Tens of thousands of poor, unskilled workers seeking benefits are preparing to head for the UK by exploiting our lax border controls, ministers were told.
>
> *The Express*, 9 February 2004

To deal with these concerns only Malta and Cyprus were given full rights of entry when the EU was enlarged in 2004. Existing members were able to place restrictions on entry from the other eight countries. In the UK a five-year plan was introduced involving a Workers' Registration Scheme whereby workers may come into the UK but they must register within 30 days of finding a job. Other countries have imposed more stringent restrictions.

Recent European immigration to the UK

A number of concerns have been raised about the level of recent European immigration to the UK.

- Large numbers of workers from Eastern Europe have entered the UK. Many more have arrived than were expected. It was predicted that about 15,000 would enter the UK, but it has been estimated that there have been over **half a million arrivals**.

- It is estimated that about **20% of these arrivals have not registered** and are therefore working illegally and are not paying tax, so there is a loss of revenue to the Government and councils.
- Some argue that **the influx of workers reduces job opportunities** for established residents and that the low wages earned by many of the incomers put a downward pressure on wage rates for other low paid workers.
- The concentration of these workers in the South-East of England is placing strain on services such as **housing and education** in some London boroughs.
- Many will **send their wages back to their dependents in their home countries** reducing the benefits of their earnings on the UK economy.

However, it is also claimed that the UK economy benefits from such immigration.

- These **immigrants come to work**, not claim benefits.
- They are **filling skill shortages** in the UK economy which otherwise would hinder economic growth (such as tradespeople like plumbers and joiners in London).
- They are **filling public service jobs** (such as dentists in Scotland).
- Their **low wages keep inflation down** and they will often do jobs that are not attractive to native-born residents.
- They are helping to address Scotland's **declining population** and **skills shortage**.
- Most **do not intend to stay permanently in Britain** but will return to their own country when they have made some money.
- Most **do not bring dependants** with them.
- They provide a **young workforce** which counteracts Britain's ageing population.

HINTS & TIPS

Immigration is an issue on which people often have strong views. If you have to answer a question on this issue, make sure you are able to give a balanced answer that deals fully with all sides of the debate.

For you to do

- In what ways does membership of the EU provide social benefits for its citizens?
- In what ways has EU membership increased worries about a rise in criminal activity?
- How has the EU tackled crime across the borders of its members?
- Critically assess the view that free movement of labour within the EU has benefited the UK.

Internet research

Visit the websites of the BBC News or the UK Government and find out how much immigration has taken place.

Visit the websites of different newspapers and find out their views on immigration from the EU.

Links to these sites and other websites relating to Higher Modern Studies can be found at:

LECKIE & LECKIE
Learning Lab

THE COMMON AGRICULTURAL POLICY

The system of support for farming in the European Community known as the Common Agricultural Policy (CAP) was one of the earliest common policies in the EU. It has also been the most costly policy and the most controversial. When the CAP was established, Europe was still in an era of food shortages and farming incomes were low and unstable. The original aims of the CAP were:

● to guarantee food supplies
● to support farmers' incomes and maintain the rural way of life.

Britain was not a member of the EU at the time the CAP was established. By the time Britain joined, the CAP was already operating in a way that suited the original members, in particular, France. Having a very different industrial structure and markedly different agricultural sector, Britain was not well placed to benefit from the CAP. UK Governments, both Labour and Conservative, have consistently pushed for reform of the CAP.

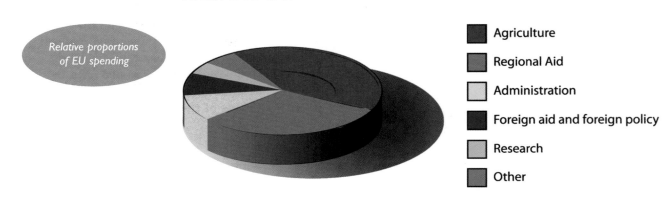

Relative proportions of EU spending

■ Agriculture
■ Regional Aid
□ Administration
■ Foreign aid and foreign policy
□ Research
■ Other

Source: European Commission

How much does the CAP cost?

CAP has always been the largest item in the EU budget although it has now fallen to less than half of total spending. The system operated by guaranteeing farmers a set price for their products. If the price farmers received in the market fell below this set price, then the CAP would intervene and buy any unsold output.

This helped to deal with Europe's food shortage and made sure that farmers received an income. However, the system of intervention encouraged farmers to produce more and more, since they knew they would be paid whether consumers wanted their products or not. The CAP **paid for unsold food** and also paid to store huge amounts of unwanted food in so-called *butter mountains* and *wine lakes*. In addition, the CAP **subsidised the export of surplus food** to markets overseas. **Food imports were also taxed** so that European consumers were unable to take advantage of cheaper food prices from around the world.

The CAP paid out €49 bn in 2005 and it has been estimated that it has imposed additional costs to consumers of €55 bn (in 2003).

Serious reform of the CAP was not attempted until the 1990s, with the aim of reducing the impact on the EU budget. As EU policy has embraced other areas, the share of the budget spent on CAP has fallen steadily. In 2002, EU Ministers agreed to hold CAP spending steady, in spite of the growth in membership, leading to a real reduction in agriculture's share of the EU budget.

CAP funds are not distributed equally.

- Countries with larger agricultural industries receive more.
- France is the largest recipient.
- Ireland and Greece receive levels of subsidy well above the EU average.
- The new member states will begin to receive agricultural subsidies at the rate of 25% of existing members but this is set to rise.
- Most of the money goes to the biggest farmers, large agribusinesses and hereditary landowners.
- Most (80%) of the funds go to 20% of farmers while the smallest 40% of farmers share just 8% of the funds.

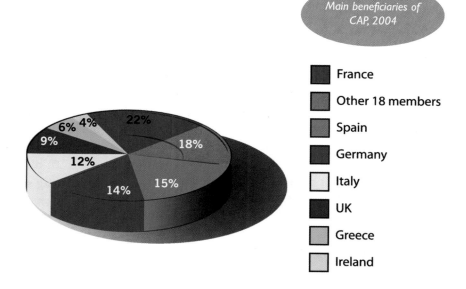

Main beneficiaries of CAP, 2004

- ■ France
- ■ Other 18 members
- ■ Spain
- ■ Germany
- □ Italy
- ■ UK
- ■ Greece
- □ Ireland

Reform of CAP

In 1992, the EU changed the price support system by **reducing guaranteed prices** and breaking the link between subsidies for farmers and production (known as **de-coupling**). Farmers were required to take part of their land out of cultivation in a *set-aside programme*.

Single payments were made to farmers to encourage the **development of rural areas**, **diversification** and **modernisation of farms**. In 2003 and 2004 additional reforms were introduced to link payments to **food safety**, **improved animal welfare** and **environmental improvements**.

In international negotiations, the EU has offered to **reduce import tariffs** on agricultural produce and **cut exports subsidies** if other countries, such as the USA, do the same.

Reform of the CAP was necessary:

- to deal with the **rising costs** of agricultural support
- because of **pressure from members** such as Britain who clashed with France over the question of CAP reform
- under **international pressure from the World Trade Organisation** because of export subsidies
- to avoid **escalating costs** as the EU expanded to include countries with **large and undeveloped agricultural industries**.

Benefits and problems of the CAP

CAP provides these benefits for EU members:

- **European self-sufficiency** in food due to increased agricultural output
- support for farmers to provide **stability in incomes** and support for modernisation of agriculture
- **maintenance of rural communities** which provides important environmental benefits for non-agricultural communities
- **stable prices** for consumers
- cost of agriculture as a percentage of EU budget is declining
- reform of CAP has placed greater emphasis on issues such as environmental protection, animal welfare and food safety
- new member states will have the opportunity to **modernise their farming industries**.

Alongside these benefits, there are problems, however:

- agricultural support is **costly**
- **overproduction** is encouraged

- **environmentally-damaging intensive farming methods** are encouraged
- there have been allegations of **fraud** and **misuse of funds**
- **consumers** pay higher prices compared with world market prices
- there are concerns over the **impact of new member states** with a high proportion of agricultural industry in old-fashioned and inefficient farms
- most of CAP funds go to **large farms and agricultural businesses** rather than to small farms where incomes remain uncertain and low
- funds are **distributed unevenly** to countries
- **exporting subsidised surplus food stocks** in world markets has a detrimental impact on producers in developing countries and other countries that sell into the same markets
- **import tariffs** keep out produce from other (developing) countries
- other industries (such as car manufacturing) complain that agriculture receives **unfair preferential treatment** in state aid.

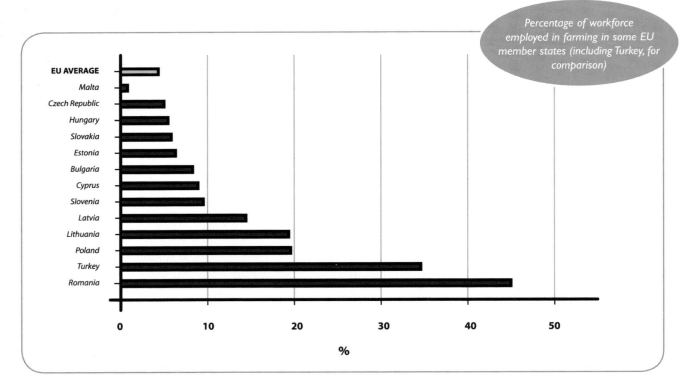

Percentage of workforce employed in farming in some EU member states (including Turkey, for comparison)

%

Source: Eurostat

For you to do

- Why was the creation of a CAP such an important policy in the early days of the EU?
- Describe how the CAP supported farmers' incomes.
- What are the main criticisms of the CAP?
- What reforms have been made to the CAP in recent years?
- Membership of the CAP has been a disaster for Britain. Discuss.

Internet research

Visit the website of the EU and find out how much is being spent on CAP. Find out the current aims and priorities of the CAP.

Visit the UK Government website and find out the present Government's position on CAP.

Links to these sites and other websites relating to Higher Modern Studies can be found at:

THE COMMON FISHERIES POLICY

The fundamental problem for the fishing industry is the fact that no-one effectively owns the seas, so no-one has the responsibility for maintaining fish stocks. Scientific research has highlighted the decline of fish stocks and the impact upon the marine environment of some of the practices of the fishing industry. Changing technology has also seen the greater use of *factory ships*. These have contributed to over-fishing in some areas, and onboard processing has resulted in a loss of jobs on shore.

The Common Fisheries Policy (CFP) was set up in 1983. It aimed to:

- **monitor fish stocks**
- **protect the standard of living** of those involved in fishing
- **protect the interests of the consumer**
- develop a **sustainable approach** to fishing
- monitor the **impact of fishing** on the marine environment.

In order to meet these aims a number of measures have been adopted.

- **Fishing quotas** were introduced which limited the amount of fish that could be caught by each boat. Total Allowable Catches (TACs) are determined and allocated among member states.
- **Restrictions** are placed on the **number of days** and **time of year** in which boats could go out fishing.
- **Controls** are placed on the **size of nets** to reduce the number of immature fish caught.
- Grants are given to fishermen to find alternative employment and thus reduce the size of the fishing fleet.

Many of these measures have been extremely unpopular in fishing communities. Although fishing is not a large employer overall, employment in fishing is largely localised in small communities which rely heavily on the income from the industry. Proposals to impose total bans upon the fishing of some species have been criticised since fishermen believe that the industry in certain areas would die out and not be able to benefit from any subsequent replenishment of the fish stocks. Many fishermen also dispute the advice of scientists about their claims that fish stocks are declining.

The difficulty of policing and enforcing the CFP, and the feeling in some parts of the community that not all countries apply its provisions equally rigorously, have led to opposition to the policy.

Opposition to the CFP has been particularly strong in Scotland. The SNP has called for withdrawal from the policy and has charged the UK Government with abandoning Scotland's interests in fisheries negotiations.

Impact of the CFP in Scotland

The Scottish fishing industry has great significance in purely economic terms. The landings into Scotland by all vessels in 2000 were valued at almost £310 million and Scottish boats landed nearly £70 million worth of fish abroad. Since the fishing industry is mainly located in parts of the country which have limited job opportunities, the impact of EU fisheries policies will be felt disproportionately in those areas.

SNP leader Alex Salmond has been very critical of the CFP, arguing that it does not operate in the interests of fishing communities in Scotland. He has said Britain should pull out of the EU fisheries deal because it is designed 'to rob fishermen of their birthright'. The SNP leader has said that Britain should withdraw from the CFP and control of fisheries should be given to the Scottish Executive.

Salmond agrees with the majority of Scottish fishermen who dispute much of the scientific advice given to the European Union about the state of fish stocks and the conservation measures proposed. They claim the restrictions on catches to allow cod stocks to recover (which also involve restrictions on other species which are not so depleted) will make it impossible for Scottish fishermen to make a living. Furthermore they argue that small and individual boat owners are at a huge disadvantage when competing with massive industrial-scale fishing vessels common in other countries. Any ban on fishing to let stocks recover will mean that that, as Alex Salmond has claimed, 'The sea is teeming with fish but it may soon by empty of our fishermen.'

Be aware of the impact of the CAP and CFP upon Scottish farmers and fishing communities.

For you to do

- Why is there a very strong argument for the fishing industry to be regulated by a common EU policy?
- Why are so many in the fishing industry in Britain opposed to the CFP?

Internet research

Visit the website of the BBC in Scotland or Scottish newspapers and find out the views of those in the fishing industry in Scotland about the CFP.
Links to these sites and other websites relating to Higher Modern Studies can be found at:

STUDY THEME SUMMARY

The European Union has grown considerably in membership and in scope. The growth of the EU has made the process of decision making more complex and time consuming. The need to accommodate the interests of the diverse countries that make up the EU and meet the democratic aspirations of the people of Europe has led to the proposals for a Constitution for the EU. The controversy surrounding the proposal has called into question the future direction and nature of the EU.

The wide range of political, economic and social issues with which the European Union is concerned is having an increasing impact on the day-to-day lives of the citizens of the EU. Integration is increasing in areas such as the introduction of the euro and economic opportunities are opening up for the new members. However, major debates are still going on about how far Europe should continue to adopt common policies and to what extent national governments have control over political, economic and social policy.

While the Common Agricultural Policy no longer consumes the vast bulk of the EU's budget, it is still the largest single item of expenditure and has a major impact on all citizens of Europe as consumers of food as well as the agricultural sector itself. Reform of the system is still a major aim of countries such as the UK and the membership of new members with large and relatively backward agricultural industries will increase the pressure for reform. Although fishing is a smaller industry, its localised nature means that any policies have a major effect on particular parts of some countries.

Exam-style essay questions

- Assess the achievements of the European Union.
- Critically evaluate the benefits of enlargement of the European Union for existing and new members.
- Evaluate the debate regarding a European Union Constitution.
- Evaluate the benefits of either the single European currency or the Common Agricultural and Fisheries Policies.

STUDY THEME 3E:
The politics of development in Africa

In this study theme you will be expected to have a detailed knowledge and understanding of:

- **HEALTH AND HEALTH CARE ISSUES**

  Access to education, food and safe water. The links between health, education, food and development.

- **ECONOMIC, POLITICAL AND SOCIAL FACTORS AFFECTING DEVELOPMENT**

- **THE RESPECTIVE ROLES OF AFRICAN GOVERNMENTS, THE AFRICAN UNION, THE EUROPEAN UNION, NON-GOVERNMENTAL ORGANISATIONS, THE UNITED KINGDOM AND THE UNITED NATIONS IN PROMOTING DEVELOPMENT.**

BACKGROUND TO AFRICA'S LAND AND PEOPLE

Africa is the second biggest continent, and has the second highest population, after Asia. It comprises 53 countries covering over 20% of the land area of the world and has more than 12% of the population. The land varies from desert in the north and parts of the south, with vast tropical rainforests in the equatorial regions.

Africa has huge reserves of natural resources such as diamonds, metal ores, gold, and petroleum. It is also a major agricultural producer, producing cotton, coffee and cocoa beans for export. However, these reserves are not evenly distributed, and there are countries with little or no resources.

Africa is a desperately poor continent. In 2005, almost 70% of the population lived on less than $2 per day. Many African countries suffer from very high levels of debt resulting from aid packages from Western countries. Many countries are heavily reliant on overseas development aid

Agriculture accounts for a large proportion of the gross domestic product (GDP) of many African countries. Over 30% of the population are reliant on agriculture for their livelihood (but in some countries, this figures rises to more than 90%). For a continent where drought has such devastating effects, it might seem surprising that only 1% of agricultural land is irrigated. The countries which are highly reliant on agriculture for their income are very vulnerable to changes in the world market and to the impacts of adverse weather.

Virtually all of Africa was colonised by European countries in the 19th century in the **Race for Africa**. The dominant European colonisers were Great Britain, France, Belgium, Portugal and

HINTS & TIPS

Although Africa is an overwhelmingly poor continent, remember there are over 50 countries in Africa. Avoid making points in your answers which give a too stereotypical picture of Africa.

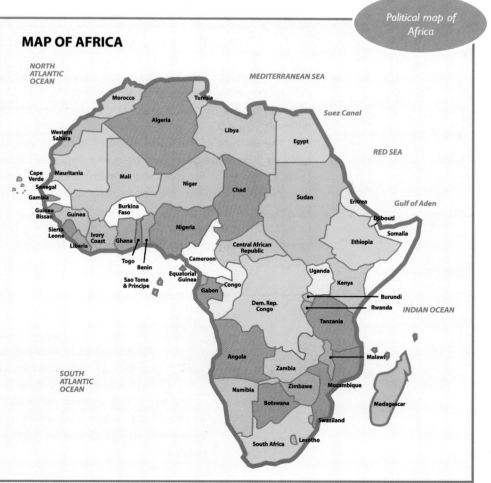

Political map of Africa

Germany. This colonisation resulted in the countries whose borders we now recognise in Africa, but the establishment of African countries was entirely for the convenience of the colonising powers and often bore little or no relation to existing political or tribal regions.

Most African states remained colonies of European states until the 1960s, when the independence movements gained momentum. Unfortunately, the post-colonial years of many African countries have been marked by poverty, corrupt and authoritarian governments, and political and economic instability. Many countries have undergone military coups and dictatorships, and there are few successful democracies in Africa. There continue to be tensions and conflicts between neighbouring tribes, and disputes over European-imposed borders and territory are common.

According to the United Nations Human Development Report (UNHDR) in 2006, 29 of the 30 countries in the 'Low Human Development' category were African (the other being Haiti, in the Caribbean). Only the island states of the Seychelles and Mauritius were in the 'High Human Development' category. The UNHDR uses a range of indices to measure development, such as life expectancy, literacy rates and per capita GDP, and in all these areas, many African countries have fallen a long way behind the rest of the world.

Internet research

Visit the website of the United Nations Development Programme and read about the Human Development Reports. What are the factors which are used to calculate levels of development? Why is it important to be able to compare levels of development in different countries?

Visit the website of the CIA Fact Book. Choose five African countries and make a table to summarise and compare some important statistics, such as life expectancy (overall, as well as for men and women), mortality rates, birth rate, health statistics, literacy levels, land use, environmental issues, GDP, employment rates, debt and aid figures, disputes, etc.

Links to these websites and other websites relating to Higher Modern Studies can be found at: **www.leckieandleckie.co.uk** by clicking on the Learning Lab button and navigating to the Higher Modern Studies Course Notes page.

HINTS & TIPS

Although this study theme is 'The politics of development in Africa' you should not refer to South Africa in your answers. You should use examples from any of the many other countries in Africa with countries in sub-Saharan Africa being the most relevant.

UNITED NATIONS MILLENNIUM DEVELOPMENT GOALS

In 2000, the United Nations set a series of Millennium Development Goals (MDGs), which set out the priorities for aid and development programmes for developing countries. The aim is to achieve these goals by the year 2015.

The goals are kept deliberately simple, but are very ambitious. It is intended that the MDGs will be used to guide all the development programmes carried out by all the various aid and development agencies in a coordinated way, so that there is no conflict of activity and no unnecessary duplication of effort.

There are four key elements to the overall MDG campaign:

- practical assistance to support priorities
- monitoring progress in each country
- monitoring progress across the world
- research to determine the best ways of achieving the MDGs in each country.

Millennium Development Goals

Goal 1 Eradicating extreme poverty and hunger

Goal 2 Achieving universal primary education

Goal 3 Promoting gender equality and empowering women

Goal 4 Reducing child mortality

Goal 5 Improving maternal health

Goal 6 Combating HIV/AIDS, tuberculosis and other diseases

Goal 7 Ensuring environmental sustainability

Goal 8 Developing a global partnership for development

HINTS & TIPS

In order to score high marks in essays it is important to make developed points with relevant examples. Use recent examples from specific African countries, mention particular aid projects and agencies and make reference to recent events to back up your answers.

Internet research

Visit the UN website and read about the Millennium Development Goals. As you work through this unit, make notes on the way each topic fits within each Development Goal.
Links to this site and other websites relating to Higher Modern Studies can be found at:

LECKIE&LECKIE
Learning Lab

For you to do

- Using the expanded MDGs given on the UN website, make notes on the way the eight different MDGs are linked. You may find it useful to draw a diagram or mind map to show the links and overlaps – the interrelationships between different factors. Add to this diagram as you discover further links.

HEALTH AND DEVELOPMENT

Health and health care are essential components of a developed country. Without a healthy workforce, it is not possible for the economy to function properly, since there are not enough healthy people to do the work, there are too many ill people draining the resources, and there are too many people spending time caring for ill people instead of being able to work.

One of the standard indicators for the state of a country's health care systems is the average life expectancy at birth. In the UK, the average life expectancy is 78.5 years, but for many African countries, the life expectancy is under 50, and in the case of Zimbabwe, it is just 36.6 – less than half of the expectancy in the UK.

In 2001, the African Union held a special conference in Abuja (in Nigeria). The aim was to set a series of goals for improvements in health care across the whole continent. One of the most important goals was the agreement from all governments to commit to spending 15% of their national budget to health spending, with particular emphasis on HIV/AIDS.

Many of Africa's health problems are related to poor sanitation and limited availability of fresh water, endemic diseases such as malaria and HIV/AIDS, and poor availability of health care.

Water supplies

The lack of clean water is one of the most pressing issues in many parts of Africa. In many rural areas, the only sources of water are rivers, lakes and waterholes which are seasonally affected and which do not provide clean water throughout the year. In many places, there are no piped water supplies, and people (almost always women and children) have to walk many miles to collect water.

In urban areas, there may be piped water supplied, but there is often little in the way of sanitation, so sewage is untreated and often pollutes water supplies. Over the whole continent, only about half of the population has access to clean water and sanitation. Dirty polluted water is a major carrier of disease, and diarrhoea and water-borne diseases are responsible for the death of hundreds of thousands of children each year. Water shortages contribute to crop failures, resulting in malnutrition and further deaths.

The chart shows the proportions of the Ethiopian population with access to clean water and decent sanitation; 69% have no toilet facilities at all apart from the local fields and forest.

Availability of fresh water (left) and sanitation resources (right) in Ethiopia

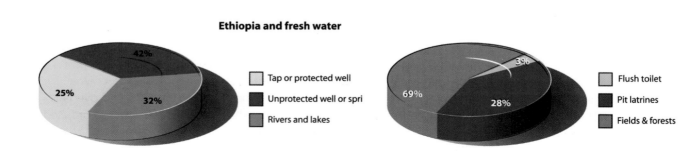

Ethiopia and fresh water

42% — 25% — 32%

- Tap or protected well
- Unprotected well or spri
- Rivers and lakes

3% — 69% — 28%

- Flush toilet
- Pit latrines
- Fields & forests

As well as having an impact on health, the lack of clean water also affects poverty levels. Clean water improves living standards in a number of ways:

- less illness means less time lost from work
- less time wasted in collecting water can be used for productive activities
- less illness saves money that might have been used for medical treatment
- less money spent on treating these illnesses means more money can be spent on addressing other health care issues
- improved agricultural production reduces vulnerability to hunger and can increase income.

Across the continent, there are hundreds of programmes to improve water supply and sanitation. Every African country has a range of projects underway. Many are supported by aid funding from international bodies such as the World Bank, and from non-governmental organisations (NGOs) such as WaterAid. WaterAid is critical of the approach taken by the World Bank, which involves private sector management of water utilities. In some of these projects, there is controversy over the involvement of water companies from Europe and the USA in the provision of water supplies. These companies have been brought in to help manage the water infrastructure – the boreholes, purification plants and pipe networks – but they charge higher prices for clean water and poor families are unable to pay for the water they need.

Poor households are often not connected to mains water supplies, and rely instead on water sellers who may charge five to ten times more per litre of water than wealthy people in the same city have to pay for their mains supply. Rural populations are even more likely to experience difficulty in getting access to clean water at a price they can afford.

According to the UN Human Development Report 2006, it will take until 2040 before sub-Saharan Africa reaches the MDG goal for clean water. Even then, there will still be millions of Africans without access to clean water.

Water shortages are forecast to get worse over coming years as a result of climate change. In parts of Africa like East Africa, the Sahel and Southern Africa, it is predicted that as rainfall declines and temperatures increase, there will be considerable agricultural losses to staple foods, with production of maize down by 33%, sorghum down by 20% and millet down by 18%.

Internet research

Visit WaterAid's website and take notes about the impact of poor water availability on health and related issues. Read the report 'Looking Back' and write a brief summary of some specific achievements and ongoing problems.

Links to this site and other websites relating to Higher Modern Studies can be found at:

For you to do

- Why is access to clean water such a big issue in Africa? List all the ways in which the lack of access to clean water hampers development.
- Add any new factors or issues to your diagram on the MDGs.

Availability of health care

Lack of comprehensive health care is one of the major problems in Africa. In most African countries, there is little or no free health care available to everyone. Access is often reserved for employees of public sector organisations and private sector companies. However, this only accounts for about 10% of the workforce, so the other 90% of the workforce are doubly disadvantaged by having to pay for health care but often being unable to afford it.

The NGO Save the Children estimates that almost 800 children die every day because their parents cannot afford to pay for medical treatment. Many of these deaths are caused by diseases such as measles, pneumonia and malaria, which could all be prevented with adequate treatment. The provision of free health care is a key priority for African development. However, many African governments cannot afford to fund free health care, and many of the free clinics are run by NGOs such as the Africa Foundation and US Doctors for Africa.

Health care delivery is also affected by the numbers of doctors and nurses. Over recent years, the NHS in Britain has been criticised for recruiting doctors and nurses from African countries to work in the UK. African doctors and nurses are also travelling to the USA to work – in 2004, it was estimated there were more doctors from Ghana working in the American states of New Jersey and New York than were working in the whole of Ghana.

Another factor in the difficulties faced by African countries is the need to repay debts which have built up over the years from aid loans. Many countries have very large debts which consume significant proportions of their income. In 2002, Cameroon spent 3.5 times as much on debt repayment as it did on health, and Mali spent 1.6 times as much.

The prevalence of major diseases like HIV/AIDS and malaria has major implications in the fight against poverty in Africa. Many AIDS sufferers are young men, who are often the main income earners in a family. When they die, their family is left without their income. At the same time, many people have to stay at home to look after AIDS/HIV and malaria sufferers, again depriving the family of an income. Education is affected – teachers may be sufferers, and children may be carers, or may be forced into work if their parents are sufferers. Businesses and organisations such as schools and hospitals are hampered by these diseases, as they have to replace ill staff.

Disease in Africa creates a vicious circle. It stops people working, putting a brake on economic growth and requiring more public spending on health. All this slows development, and gets in the way of Africa's ability to deal with the diseases.

For you to do

- How do the actions of developed countries like the USA and UK interfere with African health care?
- Describe the impact of health care issues on development in Africa.

Malaria

Malaria is a common infectious disease in tropical regions, caused by parasites which are transmitted by mosquito bites. It causes fever, chills, muscle aches, anaemia and organ failure. Malaria can be successfully treated using drugs. However, for treatment to be most successful requires patients to be diagnosed and treated within 24 hours of the symptoms appearing, but in many parts of Africa, this is not possible. Health care facilities are not always easily accessible, and families may not be able to afford to travel to clinics.

Malaria

- Responsible for about 900,000 deaths in Africa each year
- Estimated to reduce Africa's GDP by $12 billion per year
- Responsible for 20% of the deaths of children aged under five
- Accounts for 40% of all spending on health care
- Many children who survive suffer in later life from brain damage
- Prevention programmes include provision of mosquito nets and insecticides

HIV/AIDS

Human Immunodeficiency Virus (HIV) is a virus which damages the human immune system. It can lead to the development of Acquired Immune Deficiency Syndrome (AIDS), which is a general term applied to the collection of symptoms, infections and tumours developed by sufferers. HIV is transmitted by direct exchange of bodily fluids containing the virus. Common methods of transmission include unprotected sex, blood transfusion, maternal transmission and dirty hypodermic needles.

Sub-Saharan Africa holds 10% of the world's population, but is home to 60% of people living with AIDS. In 2004 there were 25.4 million people living with AIDS in the region, and 2.3 million had died that year from AIDS-related illnesses. Only 3% of people with AIDS received the treatment they needed. Most sufferers are between the ages of 15 and 49.

AIDS prevention programmes could be considered to be more important than treatment programmes, but they are being overshadowed by treatment programmes. Prevention is the most cost-effective intervention, particularly through the provision of condoms, but it requires considerable education and changes in behaviour.

In countries where prevention programmes have been undertaken, they have proved to be effective. The main prevention activity is aimed at reducing the numbers of people participating in unprotected sex. In Uganda, prevalence of HIV dropped from 15% of the adult population in the early 1990s to 5% in 2001, and similar declines have been seen in Kenya, Zimbabwe and urban areas of Zambia and Burkina Faso.

Mother-to-child transmission is the other common form of transmission, and occurs when pregnant women have HIV and pass it on to their infants, either at birth or through breast milk. This form of transmission can be prevented if women are provided with the right drugs, but this does require that women are aware of their HIV status. This requires a testing programme for all pregnant women. Lack of drugs and lack of testing facilities means that this continues to a major cause of HIV transmission.

AIDS treatment programmes work through the provision of the correct antiretroviral drugs (ARVs). Less than 20% of the population of Africa with AIDS are receiving ARVs. Proper provision of ARVs requires a decent health care system with sufficient doctors and nurses, but few African countries have these resources. Botswana has been the most successful country in delivering ARVs, with about 85% of the affected population receiving the drugs they need in 2002. However, this success has not been matched elsewhere, and while there are signs of improvement, the scale of the problem is proving difficult to deal with. In countries such as Ethiopia, Ghana and Nigeria, fewer than 10% of the affected population are receiving the drugs they need.

In 2005, the G8 Summit at Gleneagles launched the **All by 2010** campaign, which aims to ensure full availability of ARVs by the year 2010. This campaign pledges considerable international support to African countries. The **President's Emergency Plan for AIDS Relief** (PEPFAR) was launched by President Bush in 2003 and committed $15 billion to tackling AIDS in poor countries over a five-year period. Much of this funding is aimed at providing sufficient ARVs to treat 2 million people by the end of 2008. At the end of March 2006, PEPFAR was supporting treatment for around 561,000 people.

Internet research

Visit the Aids in Africa website to see the most up-to-date figures for the numbers of new infections, deaths, victims and life expectancy. How do these figures compare with the figures for 2004 given above? Using the Country Reports in the Statistics section on the Aids in Africa website, pick three countries and chart the changes in the estimated numbers of deaths and the numbers of children orphaned by AIDS since 1999. For your selected countries, are things getting better or worse?

Visit the Roll Back Malaria campaign website, and make notes on key points – numbers affected, death rates, direct and indirect costs of the disease, and progress in fighting the disease.

Links to these sites and other websites relating to Higher Modern Studies can be found at:

For you to do

- Make notes on all the different ways in which ill health affects the African population. In particular, consider the impacts on education, health care, agriculture and business.
- Add to your mind map as appropriate.

EDUCATION AND DEVELOPMENT

For a continent to develop economically, it needs an educated workforce. Unfortunately for Africa, much of the population is lacking many of the basic literacy and numeracy skills needed for a developing economy. Adult literacy rates in the poorest countries are low, and overall, only half of African adults can read, and only 60% of children go to school. Less than 10% of the workforce has completed secondary school, and in 22 African countries, enrolment in secondary schools is less than 20%. Many African children who should be attending secondary school are either at home looking after other family members, or they are working to add to the family income.

In 1990, a UN conference launched the **Education for All** initiative (EFA), with the aim of ensuring that all children in the world would have the opportunity of receiving good quality basic education by the year 2000. That target was missed, and the EFA target date has been moved to 2015. However, it looks as though even this target will be missed by 15 African countries.

Illiteracy rates are highest in the countries with the highest levels of poverty, and even in those countries with lower levels of poverty, it is the poor who have the lowest standards of literacy. In countries such as Rwanda and Senegal, there is a gap of more than 40% in the literacy rates in the poorest and wealthiest households.

There are big differences in literacy levels between men and women. In Sub-Saharan Africa, there are 76 literate women for every 100 literate men. In some countries like Benin, Chad, Mali and Niger, the ratio is even worse, with fewer than 50 literate women for 100 literate men. These are the countries with the lowest overall literacy rates, so women are in a particularly poor position. Women are more likely to be denied access to education, especially when they are expected to act as carers and undertake household burdens such as fetching water.

There are also big differences in literacy levels in urban and rural areas. For example, in Ethiopia, literacy rates are 23% for the rural population compared with 74% of the urban population. Rural populations in Africa are often nomadic, and these groups may be excluded from education programmes.

Very few children have access to any formal nursery education. Only 63% on average enrol at primary schools and about 40 million primary school age children are not enrolled. Over half these children are girls, so the disadvantages of gender start at a very early age.

Enrolments in secondary education are even lower. In 2002, only 28% of the eligible population attended secondary school (compared with 58% in all developing countries). Only 3% of the eligible population go on to any kind of tertiary education (again, more men than women).

School attendance is key to improving literacy levels, and the countries with the lowest levels of school attendance are the countries with the lowest levels of literacy. Literacy is also associated with the quality of teaching, and many children do not receive adequate schooling because of difficulties in teaching. These difficulties include:

- a lack of properly trained teachers (in Malawi and Namibia, fewer than 60% of teachers have undergone proper teacher training)
- overcrowded classrooms (with up to 70 pupils in primary school classes in countries such as Chad and Congo).
- a lack of teaching resources, including textbooks.

Improving educational standards requires greater levels of funding. In the period between 1998 and 2002, education spending in Cameroon and Cape Verde doubled, but in many countries, spending is still less than 4% of national income, compared with a recommended level of 6%. In order to achieve the Education for All goals by 2015, it is estimated that $7 billion per year is needed, but at the moment, only $2.1 billion is being given in education aid.

Internet research

Visit the UNESCO website and read about the six goals of the Education for All initiative. Compare these goals with the Millennium Development Goals. How do the EFA goals contribute to the MDGs?

Visit the Schools and Health website and read the executive summary of the Global Campaign for Education report. Make notes in particular examples, especially the relationship between education and health.

Links to these sites and other websites relating to Higher Modern Studies can be found at:

For you to do

- What are the different circumstances faced by children in urban and rural areas? How will these different circumstances affect the relative levels of poverty in urban and rural areas?
- What are the factors which affect the levels of education that children receive in different parts of Africa? Include the issue of gender in your response.
- How does access to education affect development? How are health care and education related?
- Add to your mind map as appropriate.

FOOD AND DEVELOPMENT

Food shortages and hunger are probably the first things we think about when we hear about aid to Africa. In fact, most children in Africa do have enough to eat, although there are still large numbers who do not. In Sub-Saharan Africa, 28% of children under five are underweight. Of all these children, about 37% are in Nigeria and Ethiopia, and in Ethiopia, 47% of all children are underweight.

Children living in rural areas are more likely to be underweight, with 31% of children under five in rural areas underweight compared with 20% in urban areas. There is virtually no difference between boys and girls.

Reducing extreme hunger is one of the Millennium Development Goals, so it has been a funding priority. However, there has been little improvement in most of Africa, with just a 2% improvement in the numbers of underweight children in the period from 1990 to 2004. This percentage improvement masks an actual increase in the total number of underweight children because of the increasing population of the region.

There are many reasons why African countries face food emergencies. This list shows the reasons for food shortages in 2001.

- Angola: Civil strife, population displacement
- Democratic Republic of Congo: Civil strife, internally displaced persons and refugees
- Eritrea: Internally displaced persons, returnees and drought
- Guinea: Civil strife, population displacement
- Liberia: Past civil strife, shortage of inputs
- Malawi: Floods
- Rwanda: Drought in parts
- Somalia: Drought, civil strife
- Tanzania: Food deficits in several regions
- Burundi: Civil strife and insecurity
- Republic of Congo: Past civil strife
- Ethiopia: Drought, internally displaced persons
- Kenya: Drought
- Madagascar: Drought/cyclones
- Mozambique: Floods
- Sierra Leone: Past civil strife, population displacement
- Sudan: Civil strife in the south, drought
- Uganda: Civil strife in parts, drought

Source: Food and Agriculture Organisation

Few African countries are self-sufficient in food, and are reliant on imports and food aid. Although donor countries are good at providing emergency aid, longer-term development aid aimed at improving agricultural techniques and productivity declined by 43% from 1990 to 2002.

Africa's ability to grow and distribute its own food is affected by:

- the high incidence of diseases which reduce the workforce
- armed conflict, corruption and mismanagement of food supplies
- environmental degradation such as soil erosion
- world trade policies and exchange rates
- poor transport infrastructure.

African food production will also be affected by climate change. One estimate suggests that cereal production will be reduced by about 10% by 2080, increasing the risk of hunger by 20%.

For you to do

- Looking at the list of causes of food shortages, sort the shortages into those caused by human activities such as civil strife and those caused by natural events such as drought. Which is the more serious problem?
- In addition to civil strife, what are the other human activities which affect food production and distribution?
- Add to your mind map as appropriate.
- To what extent is it true to say that drought is the major cause of hunger in Africa?

Internet research

Visit the BBC News website and read the discussion about the causes of hunger in Africa. Make notes and take examples of any new factors not previously covered.
Links to this site and other websites relating to Higher Modern Studies can be found at: LECKIE&LECKIE *Learning Lab*

CONFLICTS IN AFRICA

Africa is more affected by armed conflicts than any other continent. Many of the conflicts are civil wars (or internal conflicts) and are the result of unresolved disputes following independence from European states. Since 1960, there have been more than 20 major civil wars in Africa, and there are currently 13 countries affected by conflict. It has been calculated that there are more than 26 million people forced to leave their homes as a result of fighting.

War has been a major barrier to development in Africa in a number of ways:

- it disrupts food production and availability, and often contributes to famine
- it is much more difficult to deliver successful education and health care programmes in a country at war
- the costs of military activity divert spending away from development programmes. Military spending is expected to reach $9.5 billion in 2007. At the moment, half of all military spending comes from three countries – Algeria, Morocco and South Africa.

Some of the wars and armed conflicts receive coverage in the British media, like the war in Darfur (in Sudan), but there are many others which do not receive much attention. For example, there has been a 19-year civil war in Uganda between government forces and the Lord's Resistance Army (LRA). The LRA has abducted thousands of children. Boys have been forced to fight as soldiers and girls forced to 'marry' LRA soldiers. Thousands of civilians have been killed and nearly 2 million people were forced from their homes into refugee camps, where thay had little access to education and health care, and were unable to earn a living. All these people were reliant on emergency aid to keep them alive.

In 2004, the African Union established its Peace and Security Council (PSC), with the aim of creating a forum to promote peace, security and stability in Africa, and to improve the prospects of development in Africa. This is a sign that African governments recognise the harm that is being done by the continuation of armed conflict in the continent, but the PSC does not appear to have made much impact.

Internet research

Look at the map of world conflicts on the Global Security website. How does Africa compare with the other continents? How might this affect Africa's ability to compete with Asia or South America in the world economy? Choose a couple of areas of conflict and research them, noting how they affect people's access to water, food, education, etc.

Links to this site and other websites relating to Higher Modern Studies can be found at:

War in Darfur

Darfur is a region in the west of Sudan. It has a population of about 4 million people, of whom about 60% are subsistence farmers. Darfur has experienced drought on a regular basis and crop yields and livestock have suffered as a result of the droughts, so it is a very fragile environment to live in. The region experienced long-running conflict in the neighbouring country of Chad over many years in the 1980s and this left much of Darfur in a state of lawlessness.

Fighting in Darfur broke out in 2003 between the Sudanese Liberation Movement (and its allies) and militia groups generally known as the Janjaweed, directed by the government of Sudan. There is a complicated range of ethnic divisions in the regions, and the Janjaweed are accused of acting on behalf of the Government to force certain ethnic and tribal groups out of Darfur.

Over 2 million people have been forced from their homes, and most of these people are living in refugee camps in Darfur and in Chad. Even here they are not safe, with many camps and aid workers being attacked. The African Union and United Nations have provided 7,000 troops to try to monitor a ceasefire, but they are spread very thinly on the ground and are outnumbered by the Janjaweed. The attacks on aid workers resulted in most humanitarian organisations withdrawing their staff from the region, leaving the refugees in an even more desperate situation.

Internet research

Visit the BBC website and read the latest articles about the Darfur region of Sudan. Do the African Union and United Nations have the situation under control?

Links to this site and other websites relating to Higher Modern Studies can be found at:

For you to do

- What is the impact of conflict on development in Africa?
- Add to your mind map as appropriate.

THE IMPACT OF DEBT ON DEVELOPMENT

Africa – the poorest continent in the world – owes massive amounts of money to rich countries. Africa has received billions of dollars in aid from governments, banks and charities, mostly in Europe and America. This money should have been spent on development programmes, but much of that money has been lost due to corruption and poor administration.

Some aid money is given as loans, which need to be paid back over time. Interest is charged on the loans, so the amount that has to be paid back over the loan period may be very much greater than the original loan. Trying to repay these loans is a major problem for many African countries, and loan repayments often divert money away from useful projects such as health and education development programmes.

In 2005, the leaders of the world's leading economies met at the G8 summit in Gleneagles and agreed to cancel the debt of the 14 poorest countries in Africa. However, even after that debt cancellation, it was estimated in 2006 that Africa still owes $200 billion, requiring annual payments of $14 billion. Africa still repays more in debt than it receives in aid.

Internet research

Read the article on the *Guardian* website about the conditions imposed by the IMF on some of the countries which were supposed to have had their debts cancelled. Why does the IMF think it is important to attach these conditions to debt relief? Read the other article on the *Guardian* website reviewing achievements one year after the G8 agreement in 2005. Summarise the achievements as well as the problems preventing full delivery of the promises. Links to these sites and other websites relating to Higher Modern Studies can be found at:

LECKIE&LECKIE
Learning Lab

Check the websites of the Debt Relief campaigns or the Department for International Development to see what progress is being made in cancelling African countries debt.

AFRICAN AGRICULTURE AND THE WORLD ECONOMY

Cash crops

Farmers can grow crops for themselves (subsistence farming) or for sale. Crops grown for sale are called **cash crops**. Many African countries try to produce cash crops as a way of raising money. The most important cash crops are coffee, cocoa, bananas, cotton and oranges. These are all products which are sold in an international market, and prices set are based on total world supply and demand, which can mean that African growers do not always get the best possible price for their goods. For example, if South American coffee growers have a bumper harvest, supply is greater than demand and prices go down. The African growers have to accept the same prices, regardless of how much it actually costs them to produce their coffee.

Agricultural products such as coffee and cocoa need expensive processing before they can be sold to the public. However, import tariffs in America, Europe and Japan imposed on processed goods mean that Africa can only export low-value unprocessed goods instead of high-value processed goods. This means it is not economically viable to build processing plants in Africa and it is unable to develop its agriculture sector to compete with developed countries. Without sufficient income, it is also difficult to invest in agricultural technology which would help increase crop yields.

WORD BANK

Tariff: a tax or charge imposed on imported produce. The practical effect is to increase the final price in the country importing the produce.

A further barrier to the African agricultural industry is the practice of dumping cheap subsidised produce in Africa. For example, in Senegal and Ghana, unwanted chicken thighs and wings from Europe are sold at half the price charged by local chicken farmers. These imported thighs and wings now account for 89% of the market, so many local farmers have been forced out of business.

Many of the difficulties faced by African farmers are a result of the Common Agricultural Policy (CAP) of the European Union. The CAP provides subsidies to European farmers and sets guaranteed prices for some products. European farmers who grow sugar beet are guaranteed a price three times the world market price and restrictions on imports into Europe, along with very high import tariffs, make it impossible for African growers to sell in Europe. At the same time, European export subsidies allow European sugar to be dumped at low prices in Africa. It has been calculated that this imbalance costs Mozambique more than £70 million a year. European sugar subsidies were ruled illegal by the World Trade Organisation in 2005, but there has been no agreement on how to reform the industry in Europe.

African farmers are also at the mercy of changes in exchange rates. International commodities such as coffee and cocoa are priced in US dollars, so farmers often have no control over increases in the international price of their products.

Agriculture is very closely linked to the overall development of Africa. Low life expectancy and high levels of disease and illness have reduced the capabilities of the farming population. This affects productivity and investment potential. Poor productivity affects the availability of food and leads to malnutrition, debt and dependency on aid, and increased poverty. This is another of the vicious circles that Africa is struggling to escape from.

For you to do

- List the things that developed countries do which make it hard for African countries to repay their debt.
- How have developed countries helped the poorest African countries escape from their debts?
- What impact does debt have on development? Add to your mind map as appropriate.

LAND OWNERSHIP AND LAND TENURE

Africa is hugely reliant on the land and its natural resources for its income. These natural resources may be agricultural, such as coffee and cocoa, or they may be mineral resources like gold and diamonds. Over 70% of the population earn their livelihood from the land, so the relationship between the land and the people is vitally important.

'Land tenure' is the phrase used to describe the rights that a person or organisation holds in a piece of land. The organisation may be a family or a village, or a business or a government. Often, different organisations will claim tenure rights over the same piece of land, and often, there are no formal records to show who holds the rights to certain areas.

The status of tenure rights is complicated. Many rights were assigned to white European farmers, plantation owners and miners when Africa was colonised. Since independence, some governments have tried to reassign rights along traditional lines, but at the same tried to keep some control of resources (particularly valuable mineral resources). In some countries, white farmers have been forcibly evicted from their farms, which have been handed over to favoured members of the local population. In Zimbabwe, this has contributed to a catastrophic collapse in the economy. In other cases, pre-colonial land tenure was ignored and land was handed back in ways that have created new ethnic divisions. This has contributed to the unrest and conflict found across the continent.

Getting land tenure right is important because it affects what is done with the land. Unfair distribution of land is often associated with poor use of the land. Farmers do not use their crops and livestock in the most productive ways, affecting food supplies and contributing to shortages. Conflict over land can also result in over-use or competition for different uses, such as arable or pastoral agriculture.

By contrast, where land rights are clearly assigned, there is an incentive to invest in the land:

- farmers are more likely to adopt more efficient and productive agricultural practices
- longer-term planning is feasible, perhaps with other local farmers in agricultural associations and cooperatives
- these associations can help to raise money to invest in new equipment for production and processing.

For you to do

- What is meant by land tenure?
- What can happen if there is conflict over land rights? How does this affect development?

Women and land ownership

Women are responsible for 60–80% of agricultural production, so their access to land suitable for farming is very important. However, women are often excluded from land ownership for cultural reasons, and land is only held by men and passed down through the father's side of the family. In the event of the death of the man in a family, the woman may have no hereditary rights to the land.

Some African countries do have equality legislation, but this often excludes agricultural land from inheritance schemes, and women continue to be discriminated against in land law reforms. In some places, traditional systems which have protected women's rights have been eroded under the pressures of over-population. This is particularly the case when men migrate from rural to urban areas in search of work, leaving behind women without the appropriate authority to manage their land.

A series of law reforms in Eritrea in the 1990s aimed to provide greater equality between men and women with respect to ownership of land. The Government retains the right to assign land tenure rights, and every Eritrean citizen whose main source of income comes from land use has a lifetime right to use land and make a profit from it, even when the land formally belongs to someone else (or to the Government). All land rights granted in this way are recorded with the Government. Land rights granted this way cannot be transferred to anyone else, and are not inherited on death. The Government can grant land rights to any Eritreans when they reach the age of 18, regardless of gender.

These laws are often in conflict with traditional tribal laws, and in many cases, there is a gap between what the law says and what actually happens, so women are still not being given access to land in the ways the law intended.

Internet research

Read about women and land tenure on the FAO website. Why is it important to address issues of land tenure and women?

Links to this site and other websites relating to Higher Modern Studies can be found at:

For you to do

- Why do women experience discrimination in relation to land tenure?
- Write a short paragraph describing how and why African women experience more deprivation than men. Refer to issues such as health, education, poverty and agriculture and describe the links between them.

DOMESTIC POLICIES OF AFRICAN GOVERNMENTS

In the 50 years from 1954 to 2004, there were 186 military coups in Africa. In the same period, 15 African presidents were assassinated. There aren't many stable governments in Africa. But stability of government isn't necessarily good for a country – Zimbabwe has had the same President since 1980, but the country is experiencing major problems, with falling life expectancy and a serious health care problem in AIDS, very high levels of inflation and a failing economy.

African governments are proving to be poor at creating and implementing policies for the development of their countries. Many governments are spending more money on their armed forces than on health and education and/or have been subject to extensive corruption. The African Union reported in 2002 that corruption was costing Africa $148 billion a year, with money being siphoned off from government accounts into the personal accounts of politicians and civil servants. It is estimated that 50% of tax revenues are 'lost' to corruption.

In many places, corruption is a way of life, and it is necessary to bribe civil servants to get things done. This can affect simple things like access to health care, but also affects international companies who have to pay bribes in order to do business. This can represent a major cost of doing business in Africa. In Nigeria, the oil company Shell has admitted to paying money to the military, and in 2003 dismissed 29 members of staff for corruption. In Ghana about two-thirds of households pay about 10% of their income in bribes to civil servants, and 44% of businesses make similar payments.

International aid is also subject to corruption. In many cases, money is transferred directly out of aid accounts. In 1996, it was estimated that up to $30 billion was lost from aid loans and transferred to accounts outside Africa. This figure is about double the total GDP of Ghana, Kenya and Uganda put together.

One of the main criticisms made about African governments is their poor **governance** – in other words, their inability to govern effectively. This inability relates to the way they develop and implement policies, and the way the state is accountable to the people. It is now generally recognised that poor governance has been one of the major causes of Africa's problems over recent years, and that this must be addressed if all the international aid and development programmes are to succeed.

One of the difficulties for national governments is that they have major commitments to public spending (such as the health care and education spending discussed earlier), but they also have to undertake economic policies which will encourage faster economic growth. Getting the balance right is difficult even in developed countries with strong governments and relatively efficient civil services, but in many developing countries, governments are not sufficiently stable and the civil servants do not have the necessary skills.

Governance: the method and system of government.

In Uganda, the Government has set out a Poverty Eradication Action Plan (PEAP) with the specific aim of creating development policies to reduce poverty in the country. The main policies are:

- increased private investment
- the modernisation and commercialisation of agriculture
- the expansion and diversification of exports
- modernisation of civil service to reduce corruption.

A second set of policies also include:

- increasing electric power generation
- improving regional transport networks and reducing trading obstacles
- improving banking services
- improving government services to businesses.

For you to do

- What are the reasons for poor governance in Africa?
- What effect does poor governance have on development?

The PEAP is part of an ongoing series of reforms in Uganda, and has helped Uganda achieve growth rates of about 6% for the last few years. This is very good compared with European growth rates (typically between 2% and 3%), but it is estimated that growth needs to increase to at least 7% to achieve the Millennium Development Goals related to poverty. However, despite this high level of growth, many Ugandans feel they are getting poorer and that corruption is getting worse. Some critics are concerned that some of the privatisation programmes, where businesses owned by the state are sold to private investors, end up with friends of the President being given preferential treatment in buying shares in the businesses.

THE ROLES OF GOVERNMENTAL AND NON-GOVERNMENTAL ORGANISATIONS IN PROMOTING DEVELOPMENT

There are many different organisations involved in promoting and working towards development in Africa. These can be divided into governmental organisations and non-governmental organisations (NGOs). Government organisations include individual governments and government departments (such as the Department for International Development in the UK), and groups of governments such as the African Union, the United Nations and the European Union. NGOs can be charity organisations such as Oxfam, Save the Children, and Forest Action Network. Some NGOs concentrate on emergency aid and support, like Médecins sans Frontières, who provide emergency medical aid in disaster areas. Other NGOs will concentrate on long-term development projects.

African Union

The African Union (AU) is an international organisation which works for the good of all African countries. It was founded in 2002, replacing the Organisation of African Unity (OAU). Morocco is the only African state which is not a member of the AU.

The AU has a number of main objectives, with the overall aims of:

- promoting peace and security across Africa
- promoting and representing the African interests to international organisations
- accelerating economic growth and development
- working with international partners to tackle health care problems, particularly with respect to preventable diseases.

The African Union is responsible for the New Partnership for Africa's Development (NEPAD), which outlines a framework for the development needs of Africa. The main objectives of NEPAD are to:

- eradicate poverty
- ensure that African growth and development is sustainable and stable
- ensure that Africa plays a full part in the global economy
- accelerate the empowerment of women.

The AU has only existed for a few years, so it is hard to assess its effectiveness across a range of situations. The way the AU was set up and will be run is a reflection of the growing strength of democracy in Africa. Under previous national leaderships of unelected military governments, the previous all-African body, the OAU, had little interest in promoting democracy. One of the aims of the AU is to promote democratic principles and institutions, popular participation and good governance, and it can launch reviews of countries which fail to meet certain standards. It will also intervene in countries where genocide and war crimes are reported.

The AU has tried to play a role in bringing peace to Darfur, with limited success. It has a military force of about 7,000 troops in the area (more than six times bigger than Scotland). With so few troops, it's virtually impossible for them to act as a peace-keeping force. Despite this, they have managed to help people, by monitoring the situation and their presence has reduced the numbers of children being abducted into armed

forces. They have helped refugees return to their homes and protected aid workers in refugee camps. The evidence suggests that the AU presence helps reduce the levels of conflict. Unfortunately, there are not enough AU troops to bring about peace.

Internet research

Visit the BBC website and read about the African Union. Make notes about the aims and objectives of the AU. What difficulties will the AU have in achieving its aims? Links to this site and other websites relating to Higher Modern Studies can be found at: **LECKIE&LECKIE** *Learning Lab*

For you to do

- Draw up a table with the headings Organisation; Aims; Achievements; Problems/Failures; Effectiveness. Complete the table as you read and research the different organisations involved in development in Africa. Begin with the AU.

The European Union

The European Union (EU) is the biggest donor to Africa, and is its most important trade partner. Through its colonial past, many people also feel that Europe has a special responsibility towards Africa. The EU divides its work between short-term emergency aid (through ECHO, the humanitarian aid department of the European Commission), and long-term development aid across a wide range of sectors including trade, education, health care, infrastructure development, and governance and administration.

The EU collaborates with the AU to deliver development programmes. The objectives and priorities are set out in the AU's New Partnership for Africa's Development, and were spelt out in the EU Strategy for Africa, announced in December 2005. This sets out the long-term framework for actions to be taken by individual European countries and the EU as a whole to help Africa in achieving the Millennium Development Goals. The EU has agreed to increase the development funding it gives to Africa, and aims to give $24 billion per year by the year 2010.

In 2005, ECHO gave €236 million to African states to help in emergency aid relief. The biggest recipient was Sudan, where ECHO provided €45 million to assist in the Darfur region. This aid has helped provide the victims of the war with food, access to clean water and sanitation, health care and protection from attacks.

The EU has adopted a number of tactics in its work in Darfur. At a high level, it works with the UN and other international organisations to raise awareness of the conflict. This is important to get the necessary diplomatic initiatives to work, and to get sufficient humanitarian aid from other donors. At a lower level, ECHO works with other aid agencies to provide humanitarian help such as:

- food aid, including the purchase, transport and distribution of cereals (using local resources wherever possible)
- shelter, such as the provision of plastic sheeting or local building materials
- provision of seeds and tools to farmers able to grow their crops and care for livestock
- non-food items, such as clothing, blankets, soap, cooking utensils and fuel, water containers, sleeping mats and mosquito nets;

- water and sanitation, through the repair of existing water sources and provision of sanitation in refugee camps
- health care, including nutrition programmes, disease prevention programmes and emergency care for victims of the violence.

For you to do

- Why is the EU involved in development in Africa?
- What are the different ways in which the EU helps countries in Africa?
- Add to your table as appropriate.

Non-governmental organisations

Non-governmental organisations (NGOs) can be relatively small single-issue campaign groups or they can be major international bodies with a range of development activities. NGOs do not have to operate in the country they are trying to help – some of the most effective work undertaken by NGOs in recent years has been the Drop the Debt campaign, which sought to have the debts of the poorest countries written off. All the work for this campaign was undertaken in the world's richest countries, and it used public pressure to persuade politicians to help Africa in this way.

However, most NGOs do their work in Africa, and will provide a vast range of development aid, such as:

- FARM-Africa helps farmers manage their resources
- Centre for Democracy and Development promotes democracy and human rights
- Conserve Africa Foundation promotes and implements sustainable development
- WaterAid helps provide access to clean water and sanitation
- African Educational Opportunities Foundation provides scholarships to poor students to allow them to carry on their studies.

Sustainable development: development that meets the needs and aspirations of the current generation without compromising the ability to meet those of future generations.

There are international NGOs, which may be based in Europe or North America, and there many African NGOs. In 2004, there were over 3,500 African NGOs, such as:

- the Evergreen Club of Ghana promotes environmental awareness and supports the national forestry plans
- the Mazingira Institute in Kenya has helped promote political reforms
- Harvest Help provides practical support through sustainable farming and increased self-reliance to communities in rural Africa
- PDH Togo is a small humanitarian project which helps AIDS/HIV sufferers, orphans, children in need and victims of abuse or family problems
- the TunaHAKI Foundation helps orphans and street children in Tanzania.

NGOs have a vital role to play in African development. They often have specialist skills and can act with more independence than government and international development agencies. NGOs can act as intermediaries between local populations and government agencies, and can help influence policy and raise awareness of issues.

NGOs in Africa have a difficult balancing act to achieve. Many of the governments are very sensitive to criticism, so NGOs have to be careful about the ways they set about their work without making adverse comments about the government. Governments tend to favour NGOs which provide basic services such as education, welfare and health care, which the government itself might usually be expected to provide. By contrast, NGOs which do criticise governments (such as human rights organisations and NGOs which work on governance and corruption) may find it hard to carry out their work without interference.

International NGOs often work with African NGOs and government agencies. In Niger, Oxfam has worked with ADD, *Action pour un Développement Durable* (Action for Sustainable Development) to build 15 new schools and employ teachers, to provide education for the local children. These new schools have provided education for 630 children, who otherwise would not have learned to read and write. Oxfam have also helped pay for a community education facilitator, who makes sure that all the local children (and in particular young girls) are able to go to school. As well as teaching the usual lessons, the school also helps the whole village by offering advice on hygiene and sanitation. Local villagers are able to participate in the running of the school, so the programme helps promote concepts of local democracy.

However, NGOs do not have all the answers, and there can be problems with the way they act. Some critics suggest that there are NGOs which are very good at attracting development money from funding agencies but do not deliver the promised projects. There are occasions when NGOs will do things their way, rather than coordinating efforts with other agencies or with regional and national governments. For example, in Kenya, an NGO worked with coffee growers to improve the yields that the growers achieved from their plants. This part of the project was a success, but nothing was planned to help the farmers get their products to the market or to help them sell their produce – NGOs sometimes do not look at the bigger picture. Other concerns about the effectiveness of NGOs include:

- lack of understanding of problems in the rural context, because NGOs are often urban-based
- NGOs aren't always able to operate independently of their funding sources
- projects are issue-based and time-limited, often ignoring the historical background
- sometimes NGOs unrealistically regard the societies they deal with as a harmonious whole, disregarding ethnic and tribal differences.

There are also concerns that NGOs may help create a dependency culture – when local populations become so dependent on NGOs to provide aid and relief that they are unable (or unwilling) to take responsibility themselves.

Internet research

Visit the FarmAfrica website and read about its goals. Choose a country where it runs programmes and summarise its achievements and any problems it faces. Links to this site and other websites relating to Higher Modern Studies can be found at: **LECKIE &LECKIE** *Learning Lab*

For you to do

- What are the advantages and disadvantages of having NGOs involved in development programmes?
- Why might some governments not want NGOs working in their country?

UK government

The UK is one of the biggest aid donors in the world. In 2004, it provided £357 million in aid to Africa. All this aid is managed by the Department for International Development (DFID). This is a Government department headed by a Cabinet minister.

In common with most organisations involved in aid and development, DFID uses the Millennium Development Goals as outlines for the structure of its work. It works in collaboration with governments, NGOs, private sector organisations, and international institutions like the World Bank, UN agencies and the European Commission. It currently works in 31 countries in Africa, either with direct funding or through other agencies.

As well as working in Africa directly in development projects, DFID works internationally to negotiate policies and programmes which will help countries meet the MDGs. These negotiations include trade talks to ensure that Africa can compete in world markets without suffering unfair tariffs or subsidies.

DFID is sometimes criticised for some of the work is does. These criticisms are often similar to those levelled at NGOs. One particular criticism which used to be made was that UK development projects were 'tied' to British companies, so for example, if DFID gave money for a new bridge to be built, the bridge-building contract had to be given to a British company. Since 2001, all British aid has been 'untied'.

> **The Secretary of State for International Development is a political figure and in recent years has been in the Cabinet. Clare Short held the position until she resigned from government and was replaced by Hilary Benn. Check the British Government website to see who currently holds the position.**

DFID in Mozambique

In recent years Mozambique has made impressive progress towards meeting the MDGs. With poverty rates falling to 54% in 2003 there are nearly 3 million fewer Mozambicans living in absolute poverty than would have been the case had poverty remained at 1997 levels. There were 1 million more children enrolled in primary schools in 2004 than there were five years earlier. Under-five mortality fell by 19% between 1997 and 2003 (from 219 deaths per 1,000 live births in 1997 to 178 in 2003) meaning on average one less child in every 25 is dying before their fifth birthday and maternal mortality rates have fallen by over 50% since 1995.

DFID is one of the largest donors in Mozambique. Its aid framework for 2005/06 is £55 million and remains at this level for 2006/07. Of the £55 million, £35 million (64%) is provided directly to the Government's budget, through a partnership agreement between the Government of Mozambique and 18 donors (called the Programme Aid Partners). This approach helps the Government to finance and achieve the service delivery objectives in its own programme. In addition, DFID has large programmes in health, education, infrastructure and HIV and AIDS. It also supports key processes of government, including public financial management and tax collection.

Source: DFID

Internet research

Visit the DFID website. Using the AiDA Database link, do a search for development projects in an African country. (In the Start date field, choose the year 10 years ago from now.) Make notes on the different types of projects that DFID has been involved in, using the Sector Group column of the table. What are the biggest and smallest projects? Select some of the projects and make notes on the other organisations involved in the projects (using the 'Org involved' field).

On the DFID website read the pages about Mozambique. What were the special circumstances in the 1980s and early 1990s which affected life in Mozambique? Make notes on what has happened since then and how the lives of poor people have been improved. How successful has DFID been in Mozambique? Has DFID been successful on its own, or has it helped other organisations make a difference?

Links to this site and other websites relating to Higher Modern Studies can be found at:

United Nations Specialised Agencies

The United Nations has a number of specialised agencies involved in international development. Each agency works in a specific field such as education, health care and agriculture. Their work often overlaps with that of other agencies, so it is important that they work together, and that they work in partnership with countries with development programmes. Sometimes they will work on regional programmes, covering a number of neighbouring countries.

The priorities of eight agencies are directly related to the MDGs. Two of these agencies are the World Bank and the International Monetary Fund. These are financial institutions which are involved in lending money and ensuring financial stability. The other six agencies are directly involved in social and economic development. They are:

- Food and Agriculture Organisation (FAO)
- International Fund for Agricultural Development (IFAD)
- International Labour Organisation (ILO)
- United Nations Educational, Scientific and Cultural Organisation (UNESCO)
- United Nations Industrial Development Organisation (UNIDO)
- World Health Organisation (WHO).

Food and Agriculture Organisation

The main aim of the FAO is help poor countries develop sustainable food and agriculture systems which will help eliminate hunger. Special attention is given to rural areas, since 70% of hungry people live in these areas and are generally responsible for growing crops and livestock.

Internet research

Visit the website of the Food and Agriculture Organisation. Make notes about the TeleFood project, noting in particular the types of projects it helps with and the countries in which it operates.
Links to this site and other websites relating to Higher Modern Studies can be found at:

International Fund for Agricultural Development

IFAD has a similar role to the FAO in addressing world hunger. It works by providing finance for agricultural development projects. It also promotes social development, gender equality, income generation, improved nutritional status, environmental sustainability and good governance. It helps give the poorest people a voice in development programmes and improve their ability to participate in society.

International Labour Organisation

The ILO works to promote basic standards for employees, such as the abolition of forced labour, equality of opportunity and treatment at work and the right to organise in trade unions. It also helps with training for small businesses, setting up cooperatives in rural areas and working with governments to revise labour laws. In Africa, it is particularly active in work to reduce the numbers of children being forced to work. In Kenya, 1.9 million children between the ages of five and 17 are in work, but only 3.2% of these children have had a secondary school education, and 12.7% have no formal education at all.

United Nations Educational, Scientific and Cultural Organisation

UNESCO encourages the use of education and science to promote peace and sustainable development. It helps develop projects which enable people to make full use of their talents and available resources. In Africa, it is active in developing education programmes to allow all children to get a good education, and it puts particular emphasis on literacy, HIV/AIDS prevention education and teacher training.

United Nations Industrial Development Organisation

The role of UNIDO is to help develop industrial capacity and to promote clean and sustainable industrial development. By helping poor countries to develop an industrial infrastructure, UNIDO helps them to participate in the world economy as something other than just a provider of raw materials. In Africa, its main emphasis is on agricultural industries and small- and medium-sized businesses.

World Health Organisation

The aim of the WHO is quite simply to promote the general health of all the people in the world. Major roles include the development and delivery of projects to combat disease and to promote health education programmes. It is involved in the development and distribution of vaccines and drug treatments for diseases like malaria, HIV/AIDS and polio.

In 2006, the WHO coordinated a massive vaccination programme in Somalia, Ethiopia and Kenya. Nearly 3 million children under the age of five were given vaccinations against polio by teams of health care workers travelling about the region by cars, trucks, horses, camels and donkeys. The aim is to eradicate polio completely from the region.

Internet research

Visit the websites of some of the UN Specialised Agencies, and make notes about some of their programmes.
Links to these sites and other websites relating to Higher Modern Studies can be found at:

For you to do

- How do the UN agencies decide their priorities?
- Add to your table as appropriate.
- Assess the effectiveness of government and non-governmental organisations in helping African countries with development.

HINTS & TIPS

**In exam questions you will be asked to 'discuss' an issue or asked to decide 'to what extent' something is the case.
Your answer must contain analysis and balance and consider the topic or issue from different viewpoints before reaching a conclusion.**

STUDY THEME SUMMARY

Africa has a wide range of problems which are preventing it from developing at the same rate as most countries in the rest of the world. Some of the problems are the result of the colonial past, when European countries ruled African countries as colonies. In the aftermath of independence from Europe, many countries have undergone years of civil war and armed conflict. Poor government, often accompanied by widespread corruption, has meant that few African countries have had stable systems in which their economies can grow.

Most African countries have poor levels of health. HIV/AIDS and malaria are particularly devastating diseases, and across the continent, millions of people die each year from these and other preventable diseases. Life expectancy in most countries is low. Standards of health are affected by limited access to clean water and sanitation, and by poor nutrition, often as a result of food shortages. Ill health, malnutrition, poor access to water and good sanitation, and low education rates cause vicious cycles from which it is difficult to escape. Women are more likely to be affected than men.

Restrictive international trade rules make it hard for African countries to participate in global markets for anything other than raw materials (either agricultural goods or minerals). In order for African economies to grow enough to lift the population out of poverty, many of these rules have to be changed.

The Millennium Development Goals direct the aid and development programmes undertaken by a wide range of organisations, ranging from international and governmental agencies like the UN and DFID to NGOs like Oxfam and local groups. The programmes range from major regional projects across a number of countries right down to small-scale projects with very specific local aims.

Exam-style essay questions

Critically examine the factors which limit the production of food and its distribution.

What is the biggest obstacle to the achievement of the Millennium Development Goals in Africa?

To what extent is it true to say that debt to donor countries prevents Africa from becoming responsible for its own development?

Critically examine the claim that provision of fresh water will be the most urgent problem in Africa by 2015.

STUDY THEME 3F:
Global security

In this study theme you will be expected to have a detailed knowledge and understanding of:

- ## THE ORGANISATION AND ROLE OF THE UNITED NATIONS (UN)

  Aims, membership, institutions, decision making procedures, reforms/changes.

- ## THE ROLE OF THE NORTH ATLANTIC TREATY ORGANISATION (NATO)

  International role, reforms/changes.

- ## ORIGINS AND CONSEQUENCES OF RECENT THREATS TO PEACE AND SECURITY

  Including international terrorism, demanding an international response.

- ## INTERNATIONAL RESPONSES

  The EU, NATO and the UN responses to recent threats to peace and security including international terrorism.

ORIGINS OF THE UN AND NATO

The UN and NATO are probably the most important security institutions in the world. They both have their roots in the aftermath of the Second World War, and have major roles in shaping international politics and diplomacy. Although they have quite different roles, they both have to face new challenges as the nature of world politics changes.

The United Nations

The two World Wars of the first half of the 20th century led to the setting up of the United Nations. After the Second World War, the victorious Allies convened a conference to establish the UN. Fifty countries signed the original charter in June 1945, committing them to the maintenance of world peace through international cooperation. The United Nations came into being on 24 October 1945.

The membership of the UN has grown to 192 members in 2006. Virtually every nation in the world is represented with a seat in the General Assembly. The main UN headquarters are in New York but other parts of the UN are to be found in Geneva, The Hague, Vienna, Montreal, Copenhagen and Bonn.

Article 1 of the Charter states that the purposes of the United Nations are:

- To maintain international peace and security, and provide peaceful means to resolve disputes
- To develop friendly relations among nations based on the principle of equal rights and self-determination
- To achieve international co-operation in solving economic and social problems, and in advancing human rights
- To be a centre for nations working together.

The aims of the UN are listed in the Charter of the United Nations.

Charter of the United Nations

WE THE PEOPLES OF THE UNITED NATIONS DETERMINED

- to save succeeding generations from the scourge of war, which twice in our lifetime has brought untold sorrow to mankind, and
- to reaffirm faith in fundamental human rights, in the dignity and worth of the human person, in the equal rights of men and women and of nations large and small, and
- to establish conditions under which justice and respect for the obligations arising from treaties and other sources of international law can be maintained, and
- to promote social progress and better standards of life in larger freedom,

AND FOR THESE ENDS

- to practise tolerance and live together in peace with one another as good neighbours, and
- to unite our strength to maintain international peace and security, and
- to ensure, by the acceptance of principles and the institution of methods, that armed force shall not be used, save in the common interest, and
- to employ international machinery for the promotion of the economic and social advancement of all peoples,

HAVE RESOLVED TO COMBINE OUR EFFORTS TO ACCOMPLISH THESE AIMS

For you to do

● What provided the impetus for the formation of the United Nations?
● Explain how the aims of the UN help to make the world more secure.

Internet research

Visit the website of the United Nations and research the formation of the UN. Summarise the key points.

Links to this site and other websites relating to Higher Modern Studies can be found at: **www.leckieandleckie.co.uk** by clicking on the Learning Lab button and navigating to the Higher Modern Studies Course Notes page.

The North Atlantic Treaty Organisation

After the Second World War, the world was divided between the two competing ideologies of capitalism and communism. The USA emerged as the leader of the capitalist countries. The Soviet Union (also known as the USSR) was a communist country. Each believed its own system to be superior to the other. The USA and its allies were concerned that the USSR was imposing communism on to the Eastern Europe states it had occupied after the war.

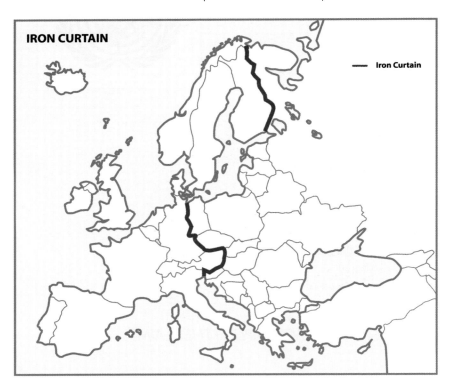

IRON CURTAIN

— Iron Curtain

They also feared that the USSR would try to extend its influence into pro-American, capitalist countries. The Soviet Union constructed what it claimed was a defensive barrier across Europe. Europe was divided politically by the building of what became known as the 'Iron Curtain'.

In 1949, 12 countries signed the North Atlantic Treaty, setting up NATO. The alliance brought countries in Western Europe together with the USA and Canada. The military power of the USA was seen as a safeguard against the ambitions of the USSR.

The aims of NATO are set out in the North Atlantic Treaty.

Article 1: undertakes to settle any international dispute by peaceful means.

Article 2: commits the members to the development of peaceful and friendly international relations by strengthening their free institutions, and by promoting conditions of stability and well-being.

Article 3: members agree to maintain and develop their individual and collective capacity to resist armed attack.

Article 4: consult together whenever the territory, independence or security of any members is threatened.

Article 5 states:

> The Parties agree that an armed attack against one or more of them in Europe or North America shall be considered an attack against them all. Consequently they agree that, if such an armed attack occurs, each of them, in exercise of the right of individual or collective self-defence recognized by Article 51 of the Charter of the United Nations, will assist the Party or Parties so attacked by taking forthwith, individually and in concert with the other Parties, such action as it deems necessary, including the use of armed force, to restore and maintain the security of the North Atlantic area.

Article 5 is the key aim of NATO. It provides for mutual and collective self-defence in which an attack on one member is seen as an attack on all. The treaty was invoked for the first and only time following the attack on the Twin Towers in New York on 11 September 2001.

Membership of NATO

NATO currently has 26 members, grown from the original 12 members.

TIMELINE OF MEMBERSHIP	
1949	Belgium, Canada, Denmark, France, Britain, Iceland, Italy, Luxembourg, the Netherlands, Norway, Portugal and the United States of America
1952	Greece and Turkey
1955	West Germany
1982	Spain
1999	Czech Republic, Hungary and Poland
2004	Bulgaria, Estonia, Latvia, Lithuania, Romania, Slovakia and Slovenia
2008?	Albania, Croatia, Macedonia

For you to do

- Why was NATO established?
- Explain how Article 5 of the NATO Treaty attempts to maintain peace.
- Describe the changes in NATO membership since its foundation. Mention the changes in both size and composition in your answer.

Internet research

Visit the website of NATO and find out its present membership.
Links to this site and other websites relating to Higher Modern Studies can be found at:

ORGANISATION OF THE UNITED NATIONS

From the initial group of 50 countries who signed the UN Charter in 1945, the UN has grown and now has representatives of virtually every country in the world. Growth has happened as African and Asian countries have joined and also as new countries have come into being, particularly in Eastern and Central Europe.

NUMBER OF UN MEMBER STATES	
1945	50
1960	100
1970	127
1980	154
1994	184
2006	192

The United Nations is sometimes referred to as a family of organisations. The main bodies are the General Assembly, the Security Council, the Economic and Social Council, the International Court of Justice and the Secretariat.

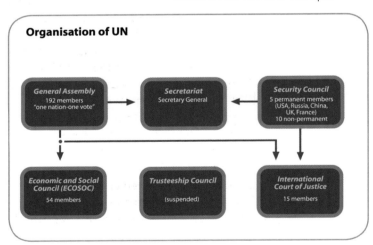

Organisation of UN

The General Assembly

All countries in the UN are represented in the General Assembly. This is often referred to as a 'parliament of nations' with each member state, irrespective of its size, having one vote. Decisions are reached by a simple majority, although important decisions on key areas such as peace and security, admission of new members, and the UN budget are decided by a two-thirds majority. Decisions are often now reached by consensus without a vote being taken. Decisions are not binding upon members but have a moral and political authority.

For you to do

- Describe the growth of UN membership.
- What changes has the growing membership meant for the nature of the UN organisation?
- Describe the composition and function of the General Assembly.
- Why is the General Assembly described as a 'talking shop'? Is this a bad thing?

The Security Council

The Security Council is the most powerful part of the United Nations. It has the responsibility for maintaining peace and international security. The Council can be called together at very short notice at any time, whenever peace is threatened.

There are 15 Council members. Five of these are permanent members – the UK, China, France, Russia and the United States. The other 10 are elected by the General Assembly for two-year terms. The aim is to achieve a regional balance of members with three African states, two Asian, two South American, two West European and other states, and one East European.

Draft resolutions are drawn up by one or more members and circulated among the other members. Drafts can be negotiated or changed and then formally proposed to the Council. Each member has one vote and decisions made by the Council require nine **yes** votes out of 15. A decision cannot pass if there is a **no** vote or a **veto** from one of the five permanent members, but a resolution can be passed if a permanent member abstains.

During the Cold War the use of the veto severely hampered the ability of the UN to intervene in international disputes. The different ideological positions of the USA and the Soviet Union meant that almost inevitably one would refuse to support the other. Since the early 1990s and the end of the Cold War, the major powers have been much more willing to cooperate and the number of actions in which the UN has been involved has increased.

When the Council considers a threat to international peace, it can take a number of actions:

- it may suggest a settlement through discussion and negotiation and provide a means for the various parties to a dispute to come together
- it can try to mediate between the countries involved, acting as a go-between when two sides refuse to talk to each other
- if fighting has begun, the Council will try to secure a ceasefire
- it may also send a peace-keeping mission to help maintain a truce and to keep opposing forces apart. For example, UN forces have been maintaining the ceasefire in Cyprus since 1964, and more recently UNIFIL has been carrying out this role in Southern Lebanon

- it can impose economic sanctions such as a trading ban. UN sanctions were imposed against Iraq in the years before the beginning of military action in 2003
- it may order a ban on arms sales to countries
- the Council has authorised member states to use 'all necessary means,' including military action, to see that decisions are carried out. This would be the last resort and only authorised after all other means have failed.

Criticisms of the Security Council and proposals for change

Although the Security Council is the most important forum in the UN, there are a number of problems with it:

- The structure of the permanent members reflects the victorious Allies at the end of the Second World War, so the membership has remained the same since 1946 (with Russia taking the seat of the Soviet Union after the break-up of the USSR). The changed nature of the world has led to other countries pressing for permanent member status. These other countries have included Germany, India, Japan, Brazil and the African Union. Increasing the size of the Security Council would allow wider representation, but would also make it a more unwieldy body.
- The permanent members' veto is seen as discriminatory and has meant that at times (particularly during the Cold War) the Security Council has been powerless.
- Many Arab countries have been critical of the Council. They believe it has been very lenient with alleged Israeli breaches of resolutions while a much harder line was taken against Iraq.
- The lack of agreement in the Security Council on action against Iraq prior to the 2003 invasion led the USA, the UK and other countries to take action without the approval of the UN Security Council.
- The UN has also been criticised for taking action too late and being ineffective as disasters occurred such as the Rwandan genocide in 1994 and the Srebrenica massacre in 1995.
- The Security Council does not have a standing military force at its disposal. If a UN force is required to address a crisis, it can take some time to assemble the necessary military force. This may result in a force which is ill equipped, poorly prepared and difficult to command effectively.

For you to do

- Describe the role and composition of the Security Council.
- Why has the veto held by the some members of the Security Council been criticised?
- What actions can the Security Council take to deal with conflicts?
- The Security Council is in need of reform. Give reasons to support this view.

The Secretariat

The Secretariat is responsible for providing the support work necessary to carry out the decisions made by the General Assembly or the Security Council. At its head is the Secretary-General, who is the main figurehead of the UN. The Secretariat consists of departments and offices with a total of 14,000 staff, drawn from over 170 countries. The Secretary-General is elected by the General Assembly on the recommendation of the Security Council, for a period of five years (which may be renewed). The job of Secretary-General has been acknowledged to be one of the most difficult in the world.

The Charter describes the Secretary-General as 'chief administrative officer' of the organisation, who shall act in that capacity and perform 'such other functions as are entrusted' to him or her by the Security Council, General Assembly, Economic and Social Council and other UN organs. The Charter also empowers the Secretary-General to 'bring to the attention of the Security Council any matter which in his opinion may threaten the maintenance of international peace and security'.

These guidelines clearly define the Secretary-General's role but also provide a great deal of scope for the holder of the office to act independently. The Secretary-General must act on behalf of the members of the UN and uphold the ideals and principles of the organisation. This means that he may sometimes challenge or disagree with member states.

One of the most vital roles played by the Secretary-General is the use of his 'good offices' – steps taken publicly and in private, drawing upon his independence, impartiality and integrity, to prevent international disputes from arising, escalating or spreading. During his term of office as Secretary-General, Kofi Annan made use of his good offices in a range of situations, including Cyprus, East Timor, Iraq, Libya, Nigeria and Western Sahara. In the period before the military intervention in Iraq Kofi Annan made great diplomatic efforts to avoid the war, although without success.

Current Secretary-General Ban Ki-moon

In October 2006, Ban Ki-moon of the Republic of Korea was appointed as the eighth Secretary-General, to succeed Kofi Annan. Minister Ban took up his new post on 1 January 2007.

> **HINTS & TIPS**
>
> **Ban Ki-moon recently became Secretary-General of the United Nations. Try to find statements he has made or actions he has taken to include in your answers.**

Internet research

Visit the website of the United Nations and make a list of the various parts of the UN. Summarise the role of each of the main bodies that make up the United Nations. Links to this site and other websites relating to Higher Modern Studies can be found at:

UN peace-keeping forces

When the Security Council authorises a peace-keeping force it must rely on troops contributed by UN member nations. These troops are often known as 'blue berets' or 'blue helmets' because of their distinctive headgear. Before they take part in a peace-keeping mission the rules for deployment have to be agreed by all parties to the dispute. The UN force is required to be unbiased and may only use force of weapons for self defence.

In May 2006, the UN was involved in 18 peace-keeping operations across the world, comprising about 89,000 troops, police and civilian personnel. This is more than a five-fold increase in forces since 2000. After the USA, the UN has the largest number of military forces deployed in the world.

The size of the UN's peace-keeping operations and the increasing complexities of their missions have put enormous strain on the UN's ability to respond to conflict around the world. In addition, major powers such as the USA and the UK are already heavily committed to military interventions in Afghanistan and Iraq, putting more pressure on other countries, often poorer developing nations with limited military capabilities, to provide the forces for UN missions.

Following a range of criticisms, the UN has taken steps toward reforming its operations. The Brahimi Report was the first of many steps to improve the working of peace-keeping missions. The report pointed out the need for improved management and financial control of the growing numbers of UN missions. It encouraged member states to increase the support they gave to peace-keeping missions by providing political support, materials, personnel and finance. It recommended an increase in the UN's ability to deploy forces rapidly but did not recommend the establishment of a UN standing force.

For you to do

- Summarise the main recommendations of the Brahimi Report.
- What is the role of the Secretariat of the UN?
- What is the role of the Secretary-General?
- Describe the role of the UN Secretary-General and the Security Council in maintaining global security.

Internet research

Visit the website of the United Nations and find where UN peace-keeping forces are operating today. Make notes on two of the current missions.

Links to this site and other websites relating to Higher Modern Studies can be found at:

Finance of the UN

The UN is financed by its members.

- Members pay compulsory subscriptions largely on the basis of their ability to pay. For example, the USA, the biggest source of UN funding, contributes about 22% of the UN budget.
- Countries with lower than average rates of GDP per person or large amounts of debt are given rebates on their subscriptions.
- All countries must pay a minimum contribution set at 0.01% of GDP.
- Permanent members of the Security Council pay a higher share of the budget, reflecting their special position with regard to peace-keeping.
- Member states also make voluntary contributions to special UN programmes.

The United Nations and all its agencies and funds spend about $20 billion each year, or about $3 for each of the world's inhabitants. The size of the budget and bureaucracy has been criticised, but the budget is not disproportionately large, considering what the UN has to do. The cost of UN peace-keeping in 2005–06 was $3.55 billion – well under half of one per cent of world military spending.

The effectiveness of the UN's ability to carry out its functions has been limited because some members have not paid their full subscriptions. As of May 2006, members' arrears topped $1,206 million, of which the United States alone owed $675 million. The failure of the USA to pay its full contribution is a source of discontent amongst some other members.

Some critics claim that the USA is withholding payments as a bargaining tool, to encourage the UN to do things the way the USA wants. Although the USA pays most, its critics argue that it also gains financially because the UN headquarters are located in New York and diplomats and world leaders bring income to New York when they meet there.

Some suggestions to tackle the UN funding crisis include a global tax on currency transactions, while others propose environmental taxes and taxes on the arms trade. However, member states responsible for the highest contributions are reluctant to reform the system, fearing they would lose influence.

Oil for Food scandal

The UN and Kofi Annan were criticised for corruption that took place in the administration of a scheme that was set up in 1995 to allow Iraq to sell a quantity of oil so that the proceeds could be used for humanitarian purposes. Kofi Annan's son, Kojo, was also implicated in the scandal. Some have claimed that the affair was exaggerated in the USA by those who wished to criticise the UN.

For you to do

- How is the UN financed?
- Why does the UN face financial problems?

Internet research

Visit the website of the United Nations and find out the names and countries of origin of the past and present Secretary-Generals of the United Nations.

Find out which countries are paying the most into the UN and which countries owe contributions to the UN. Links to this site and other websites relating to Higher Modern Studies can be found at:

Influence of the USA on the UN

Political change in countries such as the USA and UK can affect these countries' policies towards the UN and NATO.

The picture of the UN as a family of organisations with the General Assembly at its centre, where each member has the same rights to speak and each has one vote, is misleading. The reality is that the Security Council is the most powerful part of the UN institutions. Within the General Assembly, the permanent members clearly have the additional power of veto, putting them above the other 10 members without this power, whose membership only lasts for two years at a time.

Within the General Assembly, the USA has the most power. The United States played a major role in the establishment of the UN and since then many have viewed the UN as a tool of US foreign policy. Since the end of the Cold War, the USA emerged as the main political, social, economic and military power in the world. The USA has used this power to gain influence amongst other member states, and smaller and less powerful countries often appear to be pressured to back US policies.

As the major financial contributor to the UN, the USA has used its economic power to increase its influence. For a period the USA refused to meet its full financial obligations because of disagreements with UN policies. This dispute has now been settled with the USA gaining a number of concessions (although the accumulated debt has still to be paid).

In the early 1990s, the USA persuaded the membership of the UN and Security Council members to support the first war against Iraq, following that country's invasion of Kuwait. In 2003, the USA failed to gain UN Security Council backing for its invasion of Iraq. Members of the Security Council, including France and Russia, indicated that they would veto any UN military force, thereby stifling US proposals. The USA and its allies took military action without the approval of the UN.

The USA has frequently found itself in disagreement with the UN over criticism of Israel. The USA has used its veto to stop resolutions it views as being too critical of Israel while Arab countries and supporters of the Palestinians believe that the USA has used the UN to favour Israel and weaken attempts to find a lasting solution to the Palestinian problem.

Some within the USA are critical of the policies of the UN and even the very existence of the organisation. This disagreement within the USA means that policy towards the UN and the level of influence of the USA can vary. President George W. Bush has been relatively unenthusiastic about the effectiveness of the UN.

Some believe that the UN needs to be fundamentally reformed to address the composition of membership today and the needs and priorities of developing countries rather than relying on a 60-year-old structure which gives greater influence to those who were the main powers at the end of the Second World War.

For you to do

- To what extent is it true to say that the UN is merely an instrument of US foreign policy?
- Evaluate the arguments for reform of the UN.

END OF THE COLD WAR AND NEW THREATS TO PEACE AND SECURITY

The era of *glasnost* in the Soviet Union led to the eventual end of the Cold War. The Iron Curtain was dismantled, the Soviet Union was broken up and many Eastern European countries and former republics of the USSR were transformed into democracies.

Initially, the lessening of tension brought about by the end of the Cold War was seen as the beginning of a new era. The UN was able to take steps to deal with conflicts around the world, as the Security Council was able to make decisions without the use of the veto. The role of NATO was reviewed as the reason for its establishment was now gone. Countries hoped they could divert military spending towards peaceful projects.

However, the relative stability of the Cold War appears to have been replaced by an era of uncertainty and instability. Regional conflicts have become more serious. Conflict between India and Pakistan has the potential to develop into a major war (possibly involving nuclear weapons). The break-up of the former Yugoslavia and the Soviet Union created new states and old rivalries and conflicts surfaced. Countries such as Iran and North Korea have ignored international opinion to try to develop their own nuclear weapons capacity.

Ethnic and religious conflict has resulted in instability in various parts of the world. International terrorism has raised the level of tension around the globe with terrorist attacks against many targets including Indonesia, New York, London and Madrid. There are concerns about an era in which the only superpower is the USA, which feels it has the right to exert its power throughout the world. As China, with its massive population, moves closer towards achieving economic superpower status, it may seek further political influence. The European Union has a combined population and economic power to match the USA, but does not always speak with a single voice on international political and security matters.

The post-Cold War era has thrown up a new set of security issues requiring a new set of answers.

- The patterns of conflict have changed, with more than 90% of conflicts taking place within, rather than between, states.

- There is instability in the former Soviet empire, shown most graphically in the former Yugoslavia, resulting in years of ethnic and nationalist violence.
- Conflict, often within a country, can take place for ethnic or religious reasons.
- Conflict between countries may be caused by claims for land or natural resources such as water, oil or diamonds.
- There is concern over the proliferation of weapons of mass destruction and the spread of weapons to unstable regimes such as North Korea, Iran and Iraq.
- International terrorism has become a major force. Many countries have been affected, with the attack on the World Trade Center in New York and the Pentagon on 11 September 2001 being the most violent single incident.

For you to do

- How have the main issues of global security changed since the end of the Cold War?
- To what extent is it true to say that the world is a more dangerous place now than during the Cold War?

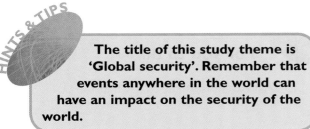

HINTS & TIPS

The title of this study theme is 'Global security'. Remember that events anywhere in the world can have an impact on the security of the world.

CHANGES IN THE MEMBERSHIP OF NATO

NATO was set up following the Second World War in the face of Soviet expansion. The original membership linked Western Europe with North America. The military strength of the USA was thought necessary to counter the perceived threat from the USSR. When West Germany joined NATO in 1955, the USSR responded by setting up its own military alliance – the Warsaw Pact – dominated by the USSR but made up of the Eastern European states that had fallen under Soviet domination after the war.

The **Cold War** was characterised by the rivalries of the competing superpowers, the USA and the USSR, and their respective allies. The geographical division of Europe was the practical manifestation of this ideological split and the setting up of NATO and the Warsaw Pact was the military representation of the Cold War conflict. Each side saw the other as the enemy and felt that any military attack would come from the other side of the Iron Curtain. NATO's over-riding purpose was to provide a means of collective security against an expected attack from the USSR and its allies. Its military resources were deployed to deter and respond if necessary to such an attack. Its military strategy was based on the assumption that any attack would come from the East.

WORD BANK

Cold War: a period of political and military rivalry between the United States and the Soviet Union (1945 to 1991) that fell short of actual war. The Cold War existed because of the competing ideologies – communism and democratic capitalism – of the Soviet Union, the USA, and their allies.

The Warsaw Pact

The Warsaw Pact was established in 1955 to counter the alleged threat from the NATO alliance. It was made up of the Soviet Union, East Germany, Czechoslovakia, Bulgaria, Hungary, Poland, Romania and Albania.

The Pact lasted throughout the Cold War until members began withdrawing in 1991, following the collapse of the Eastern bloc and political changes in the Soviet Union.

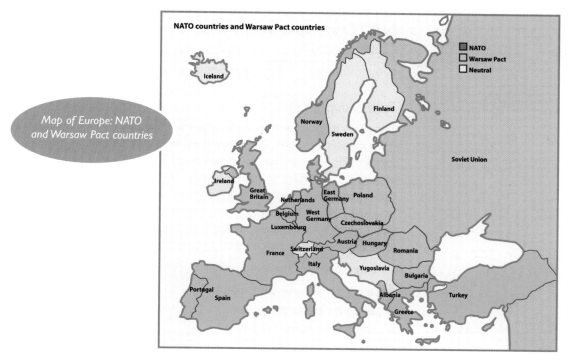

Map of Europe: NATO and Warsaw Pact countries

In the late 1980s, the situation in Europe began to change fundamentally:

- countries in Eastern Europe began to demand greater freedoms from the Soviet Union
- Mikhail Gorbachev (Soviet leader in the late 1980s and early 1990s) signalled that the USSR would no longer be prepared to intervene in the internal affairs of the countries of Eastern Europe
- the Berlin Wall came down in 1989 and East and West Germany were reunited in 1990
- the USSR began to break into separate parts as former Soviet Republics demanded their own independence
- the Warsaw Pact was dissolved in 1991 and the Cold War came to an end.

The basis on which NATO was established no longer existed: Europe was no longer divided, the USSR was no longer a threat, and Russia was economically weakened.

These changes in Europe also led to major changes in the membership of NATO. Former members of the Warsaw Pact and former republics of the USSR applied for and were granted membership of NATO. NATO membership grew to its present 26 member states. The new members are drawn from former communist states in Eastern Europe such as Poland and Hungary, former Soviet republics such as Latvia and Lithuania, and states formed after the break-up of the former Yugoslavia.

In order to join, applicant states must agree to accept the values of NATO with regard to freedom, democracy and respect for human rights. They are also required to reform their political and economic systems where necessary, to bring them into line with other members, as well as being prepared and able to contribute to the military aspects of the alliance.

The fall of the Berlin Wall allowed East and West Germany to be reunited

NATO cooperation with other countries

Since the end of the Cold War, NATO has taken a series of steps to improve cooperation with other countries, most of which had once been seen as enemies.

Partnership for Peace

The main form of cooperation was the establishment of the Partnership for Peace (PfP) project in 1994. There are presently 20 countries in the PfP project, with 10 former PfP partners having joined NATO in the two most recent phases of NATO expansion in 1999 and 2004. The aim of the PfP project is to improve security and opportunities for peaceful cooperation, as well as preparing the ground for those countries which may wish to become full members of NATO. The Partnership for Peace programme allows participating countries to share information and take part in joint exercises and peace-keeping operations.

Partner countries make a number of commitments as part of their PfP agreement:

- apply democratic principles
- abide by international law
- commit to human rights
- accept disarmament and arms control agreements

- do not use threats or force against other states
- respect other states' borders
- settle disputes peacefully.
- openness in national defence planning
- democratic political control over armed forces
- take to steps to work with NATO in peace-keeping and humanitarian operations.

HINTS & TIPS

> When writing answers to global security questions make sure to explain any points you make and back up your answers with recent examples.

NATO consults with any PfP partners who feel threatened, giving greater security without full membership of the alliance. There is no single agreement that all PfP partners commit to, and each country makes a partnership agreement based on its particular circumstances and needs. Cooperation focuses mainly on defence and military matters but can also deal with all aspects of NATO interests including training, communications, crisis management, and emergency planning.

Relations between NATO and Russia

The relationship of NATO with Russia has been a very sensitive issue. Russia has seen its former allies and former Soviet Republics cooperating with NATO and taking NATO membership. Soviet suspicion increased as NATO's borders touched Russia's own territory.

Links and cooperation between Russia and NATO have been developed. The first step was the creation of the North Atlantic Cooperation Council in 1991 (later renamed the Euro-Atlantic Partnership Council). This was established to allow for consultation and to encourage a new cooperative relationship with the countries of Central and Eastern Europe. A further link was made in 1994 when Russia joined the PfP programme.

The NATO–Russia Permanent Joint Council was established in 1997 to give Russia a consultative role in discussions of matters of shared interest. Although Russia was given a voice, it often felt that its views were ignored. When former Warsaw Pact members the Czech Republic, Hungary and Poland joined NATO in 1999, its concerns increased.

The attacks on the USA on 11 September 2001 led to a change in the relations between NATO and Russia. Russia's support for the USA after the attacks resulted in an improvement in relations with NATO.

The NATO–Russia Council (NRC) was established in 2002. This gives Russia an equal role with the NATO countries in decision making on policy to counter terrorism and other security threats. Although NATO and Russia will not always agree on everything and differences remain on some issues, there is a new spirit of cooperation based upon the common threats to world peace and security faced by Russia and NATO members.

NATO in the 21st century

To some, NATO has been a great success. It was set up to resist the threat of military expansion from the Soviet Union, through mutual self-defence. Not only did it achieve this throughout the years of the Cold War but it also eventually saw the defeat of the system of Communism, as the ruling ideology, in the USSR and its Eastern European allies.

It could also be argued that the very success of the alliance and its now much closer links with Russia, indicate that there is no longer any need for such an alliance. Some argue that NATO has done its job and should now end.

Others strongly disagree. While accepting that its original aims have now been overtaken, they would argue that NATO still has a major role to play in the 21st century:

- The principles of mutual self-defence are still valid.
- The more members the NATO alliance has the less risk there is of conflict breaking out between them.
- Many of the new members believe that membership of NATO protects them against any external threat from Russia. Although Russia does not currently appear to be a threat, some neighbouring countries fear that this could change in the future depending upon who holds power within Russia.
- NATO membership requires member states to adopt democratic political systems and protect human rights. These obligations act as a safeguard against those within the countries who may wish to return to less democratic systems.
- NATO membership provides an economical way for new member states (which are generally economically weaker and militarily less developed) to safeguard security and provide for defence while allowing the military forces to modernise.
- The world is an uncertain place and there are still threats and challenges to international peace and security. NATO was successful in meeting the challenges of the Cold War era. It can change its methods of operation and emphasis to respond to new threats such as nationalist struggles, international terrorism and nation building.

There are criticisms of the expansion of NATO and the extension of its activities into new areas.

- Widening of NATO membership may make it less effective. Too many members with different military structures and resources could weaken the power of NATO forces. Many of the new members bring little to the military power of NATO and may be a drain on NATO's resources and capability.
- As in any alliance of nation states there will always be differences and disputes. In NATO, France has often been critical of US domination. The increase in membership increases the potential for disagreements and makes consensus more difficult.

- NATO activities have extended into new areas, outside the original remit of NATO and also beyond the North-Atlantic area. Interventions, such as military action in Bosnia and Kosovo and later in Afghanistan, have led to disagreements over the nature and extent of the action being taken. Military intervention led by the USA into Iraq caused a major split between NATO members with the USA, Britain and others supporting the action while France, Germany and others indicated that they were opposed to military intervention.
- Russia is uneasy that its former allies and even former Soviet republics have joined NATO. Although Russia now has its own links with NATO (via the NATO–Russia Council), some within Russia see the extent of NATO forces on their borders as a potential threat.
- Although still the most powerful part of the NATO Alliance, the USA has chosen to act independently against the Taliban in Afghanistan and against Saddam Hussein in Iraq. Apparently ignoring the views of their fellow members of NATO has been seen as a lack of commitment to the Alliance.

For you to do

- Why was the Warsaw Pact established?
- Describe the changes that took place in Europe in the late 1980s and early 1990s.
- In what ways has NATO's relationship with Russia and the former members of the Warsaw Pact changed?
- Explain the conditions for membership of the Partnership for Peace programme.
- Describe the ways in which NATO's membership and its role have changed.
- NATO is no longer needed. Discuss.

Internet research

Visit the website of NATO and find out the present membership of the PfP programme. Links to this site and other websites relating to Higher Modern Studies can be found at:

Changing role of NATO

Despite the political changes that came with the ending of the Cold War, NATO is changing the way it operates in order to respond to new threats to peace and security.

Since 1991 NATO has engaged in a number of actions, all of which are far removed from its original purpose.

> *Clearly, a large-scale invasion of our territory is no longer our dominant concern. Today, the survival of our countries can be put at risk by developments that happen entirely within the borders of another country. This is as true for the kind of terrorism that was allowed to breed in Afghanistan as it is for the proliferation of weapons of mass destruction.*
>
> *In light of such challenges, a passive, reactive approach will not do. These threats need to be confronted when and where they emerge.*
>
> *Simply put, we have moved away from the narrow, geographical approach to security that characterised NATO for almost five decades. We demonstrate this with our operation in Afghanistan, and with our training mission in Iraq. And we may demonstrate it again soon by offering logistic support to the African Union's peace-keeping mission in Darfur.*
>
> Adapted from a speech by NATO Secretary-General, Jaap de Hoop Scheffer (May, 2005)

TIMELINE OF NATO ACTIVITIES	
1992	NATO provides assistance to UN peace-keeping operations in the former Yugoslavia.
1995	NATO embarks on its first military campaign by launching air strikes against Bosnian Serb positions and shooting down four Serb aircraft, which were violating the UN-mandated 'no-fly' zone. These actions help to bring pressure for a negotiated peace settlement. A NATO peace-keeping implementation force (Ifor) is put in place to monitor and implement the ceasefire in Bosnia and Herzogovina.
1996	The Russian Parliament votes to send Russian forces to Bosnia to join Ifor.
1999	NATO launches its first large-scale military operation. An 11-week air campaign is launched against Serbian positions to force an end to the conflict in Kosovo. It is NATO's first campaign without UN backing. NATO helps establish the KFOR whose peacekeepers are installed in Kosovo, bringing it under NATO's protection. Responsibility for peace-keeping in Bosnia is handed over to a European Union led force (Eufor) in 2004.
2001	NATO begins disarmament operations in the former Yugoslav republic of Macedonia. After the 11 September attacks on New York and Washington NATO invokes the mutual defence clause for the first time in its history. The USA chooses not to involve NATO in the subsequent USA-led war in Afghanistan.
2003	NATO takes command of the International Security Assistance Force (ISAF) in Afghanistan, the first time NATO takes charge of a mission outside the North Atlantic area.
2004	NATO commits itself to training Iraqi security forces.
2005	NATO provides air transport for African Union (AU) peace-keepers in the Darfur region of Sudan. NATO also provides training to AU officers.
2006	A NATO-led force takes over military operations in the south of Afghanistan from USA forces (see map on page 318 for details).

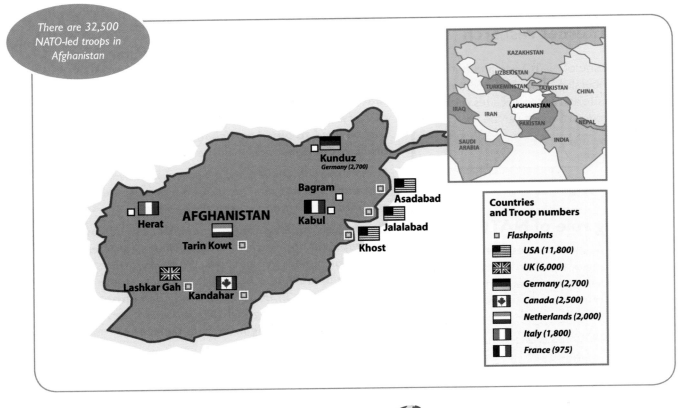

There are 32,500 NATO-led troops in Afghanistan

Countries and Troop numbers

- ▢ *Flashpoints*
- *USA (11,800)*
- *UK (6,000)*
- *Germany (2,700)*
- *Canada (2,500)*
- *Netherlands (2,000)*
- *Italy (1,800)*
- *France (975)*

Although the actions listed in the timeline on the opposite page are far removed from NATO's original purpose it could be argued that all are still aimed at securing a safer and more peaceful global situation. It can be claimed that the threat to the security of NATO members comes from a range of conflicts of varying kinds, taking place in different parts of the world. In tackling these sources of conflict and instability, wherever they occur, NATO is being true to its original intention – to maintain the security of its members.

Yesterday's NATO guarded our borders against military aggression. Tomorrow's alliance must continue to safeguard our shared security while contending with new threats that recognise no borders – the spread of weapons of mass destruction, ethnic violence, and regional conflict.'

Former US President, Bill Clinton

For you to do

- Give examples from the timeline above which support the view put forward by NATO Secretary-General, Jaap de Hoop Scheffer.

Internet research

Visit the website of NATO and find out in which areas of the world it is presently operating.
Links to this site and other websites relating to Higher Modern Studies can be found at: LECKIE&LECKIE *Learning Lab*

CHANGING MILITARY FORCES

Since its formation NATO has changed its approach to defence. The initial strategy of 'massive retaliation' was replaced in the 1960s by the notion of 'flexible response', designed to create uncertainty in the mind of any potential aggressor, who would not know how NATO might respond to an attack on a member state. The strategy of 'flexible response' was designed to ensure that aggression of any kind would be seen to involve unacceptable risks to the aggressor.

Arms race

The arms race is the name given to the competition between the former Soviet Union and the USA in the area of military weapons systems, especially nuclear weapons. Each side continually built up larger stocks of more powerful and sophisticated weapons systems in order to gain superiority over the other.

Weapon type	USA	Russia
Intercontinental ballistic missile	2,151	3,444
Submarine-launched ballistic missile	3,616	2,024
Bomber	1,528	626
Total	7,295	6,094

Source: BBC, Jan. 2001

Even during the Cold War there were negotiations to reduce the risks inherent in the arms race and various arms control negotiations took place between the superpowers and their allies.

With the end of the Cold War, NATO began to work towards improved security for Europe as a whole. In 1999, the alliance confirmed its essential purpose was to:

'... safeguard the freedom and security of its members by political and military means. It affirms the values of democracy, human rights, and the rule of law and expresses the commitment of the Allies not only to common defence but to the peace and stability of the wider Euro-Atlantic area.'

NATO Handbook

This reaffirmed the idea of collective defence but also identified new activities in crisis management and partnership to enhance the security and stability of the Euro-Atlantic area. As early as 1991 NATO concluded that 'the threat of general war in Europe has virtually disappeared' but anticipated more significant risks in the future. These risks included ethnic conflict, the abuse of human rights, political instability, economic fragility and the spread of nuclear, biological and chemical weapons. At this time, the threat of international terrorism was not evident.

HINTS & TIPS

> **Essays may require you to discuss or to assess the extent to which something is the case. Make sure your answers contain balance and you come to conclusions.**

NATO's military capabilities were shifted from deterrence to response to crisis operations. NATO also encouraged cooperation and a greater role for a specifically European aspect to defence with an increasing role for the European Union. NATO's crisis response operations in the Balkan states of Bosnia and Kosovo were examples of the new approach to security.

NATO forces had to adapt to the new circumstances. To engage with opposing forces, they needed to be able to deploy forces quickly and with a high degree of mobility. Their forces had to be able to maintain operations in hostile environments for a sustained period of time. NATO actions would also involve forces from different countries working together. By the late 1990s NATO forces would be a mixture of nuclear and conventional forces.

The NATO operations in Bosnia and Kosovo demonstrated how far NATO's military strategy had moved away from the initial concept of massive retaliation. It was involved in a wide range of peace-keeping and peace-enforcing operations as well as humanitarian actions.

Nuclear weapons

KEEP NUCLEAR WEAPONS	ABOLISH NUCLEAR WEAPONS
The destructive power of nuclear weapons is so great that if they were used in retaliation against an aggressor, they would inflict so much damage and destruction that there would be no military advantage to the aggressor. This is known as the concept of **deterrence**.	Nuclear weapons are so dangerous, not only in their immediate power but also in the secondary effects of radiation and the longer term environmental impact that any use of nuclear weapons is inconceivable. This means they are morally reprehensible and ineffective as a deterrent since they can never be used.
The existence of the nuclear deterrence maintained peace between the superpowers during the Cold War era.	**Proliferation** – the spread of nuclear weapons – to more countries increases the risk of their use.
NATO's more flexible approach to its deployment and possible use of nuclear weapons creates a situation of uncertainty for potential aggressors, which protects its members against attack.	Since 11 September 2001, there has been concern that terrorists could acquire nuclear weapons and are prepared to use them against targets since they would have less fear of retaliation.

Since their development and use at the end of the Second World War, nuclear weapons have been controversial with arguments being put forward both in their support and for their abolition.

NATO argues that the retention of its nuclear forces is more political than military since they are believed to be necessary to demonstrate their commitment to preserving peace. The retention of US nuclear forces on European soil demonstrates the USA's commitment to maintaining the Atlantic alliance. However, the reliance on nuclear forces has been reduced.

NATO's nuclear powers (USA, France and the UK) have reduced the size of their nuclear forces. These unilateral actions were in addition to the bi-lateral and multi-lateral arms control agreements made under the Strategic Arms Reduction Treaties and the Strategic Arms Reduction Talks.

Nuclear states

Officially there are five nuclear weapon states in the world: the USA, Russia, the UK, France and China. Three more states – Israel, India and Pakistan – have developed nuclear weapons. South Africa developed nuclear weapons but scrapped them in 1991. Ukraine, Belarus and Kazakhstan acquired nuclear weapons after the break-up of the USSR but have now either scrapped them or sent them back to Russia.

North Korea demonstrated its nuclear weapons capability in 2006 and Iran has a nuclear power programme which some states believe to be a means of developing a nuclear weapons capability.

Nuclear proliferation – 2006

Throughout 2006, international tension increased as Iran and North Korea were accused of seeking to develop a nuclear weapons capacity. The UN Security Council discussed the imposition of sanctions against Iran, as they were not convinced that Iran's programme of uranium enrichment was for peaceful purposes (for nuclear power stations).

The Iranian President, Mahmoud Ahmadinejad, described the USA as 'tyrannical' and stated that Iran would not yield to international pressure to suspend its programme. It claimed that the West was applying double standards against Iran since the same pressure was not being placed upon other countries with a proven nuclear capacity or who were developing civilian nuclear programmes, but were US allies.

Western countries are fearful that Iran is using its nuclear power programme as a cover for its intention to develop nuclear weapons. President Bush stated that the USA will not permit Iran to develop nuclear weapons and while he has declared that he wishes to find a diplomatic means to resolve this problem, he has not ruled out other means. Israel, which bombed an Iraqi nuclear reactor in 1981, is also believed to have plans to intervene should Iran develop its own nuclear weapons.

In October 2006, North Korea tested a nuclear weapon. This was a gesture of defiance against the UN, which had imposed sanctions against the country. Although North Korea's nuclear capability is limited, there are fears that countries in the eastern Asia area will be under pressure to develop their own nuclear forces. Tension has been high since President Bush labelled North Korea as part of the 'axis of evil' in 2002.

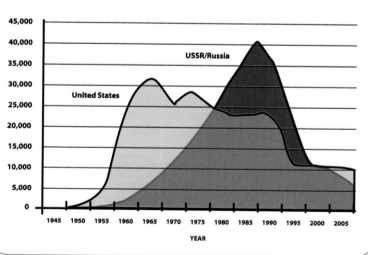

Growth and reduction of US and Soviet Union/Russia nuclear stockpiles

The events of 2006 around Iran and North Korea demonstrated the altered security situation after the end of the Cold War with the danger of nuclear proliferation. The extension of nuclear weapons capability to what are regarded as 'rogue states' is seen as a danger to global security. It increases the number of states with weapons they can use and it increases the risk that these weapons will fall into the hands of other states and terrorist groups.

NATO Response Force

NATO established a NATO Response Force (NRF) in 2002, in order to be able to react quickly to crisis situations around the world. NATO must be able to 'field forces that can move quickly to wherever they are needed'.

The NRF can consist of up of 25,000 highly equipped air, ground and sea troops, who can be deployed quickly to trouble spots around the world. It can undertake missions such as evacuations, disaster management, counter terrorism, and, if necessary, be able to clear the way for larger forces to follow at a later time. The NRF was not declared fully operational until November 2006.

For you to do

- Explain how the end of the Cold War resulted in a changed military strategy for NATO.
- Explain the meaning of nuclear proliferation.
- Which countries are nuclear powers?
- How have the numbers of nuclear weapons changed in recent years?
- Describe the role of the NATO Response Force (NRF).
- Nuclear weapons continue to have a role to play in preserving world peace and should be kept. Discuss.
- Describe NATO's role in maintaining global security.

Internet research

Find out which countries have a nuclear capability. Try visiting the website of the International Atomic Energy Agency (IAEA), news websites such as the BBC, and general reference sites such as Wikipedia.

Links to these sites and other websites relating to Higher Modern Studies can be found at:

INTERNATIONAL RESPONSES: CASE STUDIES

Libya

Libya is an example of a country that was long seen as a major threat to global security but has now come into the mainstream. After taking power in 1969, Colonel Gaddafi was one of the West's strongest critics and supported a broad range of militant groups, including the Irish Republican Army and the Palestine Liberation Organisation. Libya's alleged involvement in attacks in Europe in the 1980s triggered USA military strikes in 1986.

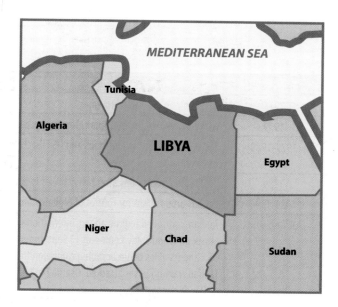

Libya was blamed for terrorist attacks on aircraft including the Lockerbie plane bombing in 1988. Following international pressure, Libya formally took responsibility for the incident in 2003 and agreed to pay $3 billion compensation to the families of the 270 victims, leading to the lifting of UN sanctions. Months later, Libya renounced weapons of mass destruction, leading the way for further improvement in relations with the West.

Libya continued to make policy changes in order to improve its relations with the West and since 2003 the country has developed normal links with the European Union and the USA. It is an example that shows what can be achieved through negotiation rather than force when there is goodwill on both sides.

The example of Libya is seen as a positive one. It is hoped that it may provide a model for diplomatic solutions to problems with countries such as Iran and North Korea, which presently are seen in the same way Libya once was.

For you to do

- In what way can the case of Libya be seen as a positive one for global security?

Internet research

Visit the website of the Foreign and Commonwealth Office and find out the present state of relations between the UK and Libya.
Links to this site and other websites relating to Higher Modern Studies can be found at:

Afghanistan

Afghanistan is an extremely poor country, which for centuries has been fought over by foreign armies. It is strategically placed between the Middle East, central Asia and the Indian subcontinent. Ethnic, religious and regional differences make it an extremely difficult country to govern. Since the overthrow of the King in 1973, it has been the subject of constant conflict.

TIMELINE OF EVENTS IN AFGHANISTAN	
1973	King Zahir Shah is overthrown.
1979	Soviet troops invade to support Moscow-backed regime.
1979-1989	Civil war between Soviet troops and USA-backed 'mujahideen', including Osama Bin Laden. Afghanistan becomes Cold War battleground.
1989	USSR withdraws troops after heavy losses in defeat.
1989-1994	Various groups fight for control of Afghanistan. By 1994 the 'hard-line' Islamic Taliban emerge as most powerful force.
2001 onwards	Taliban-controlled regime angers international community by providing shelter for Osama Bin Laden and al-Qaeda after attack on World Trade Center on 11 September 2001. USA and its allies begin bombing campaign to oust Taliban and capture Osama Bin Laden. Taliban forced from power and Taliban training bases attacked. Osama Bin Laden not captured. Thousands of US troops in Afghanistan hunting Taliban and al-Qaeda supporters.
2004	New constitution signed, elections held, won by Hamid Karzai.
2005	New parliament inaugurated.
2006	Worsening security situation as Taliban continue campaign against US and NATO forces. Growing casualties amongst civilians, Taliban fighters and foreign troops.

The government of President Karzai faces many problems. Afghanistan remains extremely poor in spite of aid from the international community. There are many different regional militias making central control of the country very difficult. Many of the regional chiefs are responsible for drug production and trafficking. Afghanistan produces about one third of the world's opium.

International involvement

Following the attacks on the World Trade Center and Pentagon in the USA on 11 September 2001, NATO responded. NATO members invoked Article 5 of the NATO Charter and confirmed that an attack on one member is an attack on all – if one member is attacked, then all members are obliged to come to their defence. All NATO members were now required to cooperate in military and intelligence activities to assist the USA in fighting whoever was responsible for the 11 September attacks.

The USA and its NATO allies launched a bombing campaign against Afghanistan in October 2001 with the aims of removing the Taliban regime from power, destroying al-Qaeda training camps and capturing or killing al-Qaeda leaders, in particular Osama Bin Laden. US forces have not yet been successful in destroying all Taliban forces nor in capturing Osama Bin Laden and US troops remain in Afghanistan. Part of this lack of success can be attributed to the difficult circumstances the military forces have to operate in, including mountainous conditions and very hot dry summers and harsh winters.

President Hamid Karzai

Under UN authority NATO has, since 2003, been taking over responsibility for security in Afghanistan. Through the International Security Assistance Force (ISAF), NATO is helping to establish the conditions in which Afghanistan can develop democratic government and peace and security.

NATO took over full command of ISAF in August 2003. This is the first mission outside the Euro-Atlantic area in NATO's history. Initially restricted to providing security in and around Kabul, NATO–ISAF has now extended to cover approximately 75% of the country's territory. There are about 18,500 troops from 37 NATO and non-NATO countries.

ISAF's role is to help the Government of Afghanistan and the international community in maintaining security within the force's area of operations. ISAF is supporting the Afghan Government to expand its authority across the country, and is attempting to provide a secure environment in which democratic government can develop and reconstruction work be undertaken. The role NATO is undertaking in Afghanistan is quite different from the role envisaged for the alliance when it was first set up as a defensive alliance against a possible attack from the Soviet Union. The tasks of ISAF are:

> **The military campaign in Afghanistan is ongoing. Keep an eye on media reports of casualties, successes and setbacks.**

- to provide security in and around the capital, Kabul
- to extend and maintain security over the whole of Afghanistan's territory
- to provide support in setting up participative governmental institutions
- to operate Kabul's international airport
- in coordination with USA-led forces fighting under Operation Enduring Freedom to eliminate Taliban and al-Qaeda forces
- to train Afghan security and police forces
- to eliminate drug production and trafficking.

ISAF is not a UN force, but is a force deployed under the authority of the UN Security Council made up of willing NATO members, commanded by NATO and financed by the nations who have contributed troops. It is an example of a peace-building force in the early part of the 21st century where the security interests of western countries are seen to be served by the development and strengthening of democratic institutions and the establishment of rights and the rule of law.

In addition to the military action in Afghanistan, the UN is involved in trying to tackle the deep poverty in Afghanistan and help to develop the country after decades of war.

For you to do

- Although Afghanistan is a very poor country, the situation there has been a threat to global security. Why?
- Why was Afghanistan attacked by the USA and its allies in 2001?
- Describe the role of NATO and the ISAF in Afghanistan.

Internet research

Visit the website of the Foreign and Commonwealth Office, NATO and the Ministry of Defence and find out the present involvement of NATO and the UK in Afghanistan.

Links to this site and other websites relating to Higher Modern Studies can be found at:

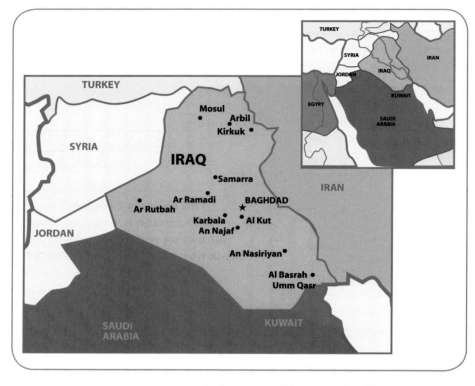

Iraq

The invasion of Iraq in 2003 and the subsequent conflict has been the biggest issue threatening global security in recent years. The Iraqi regime, led by Saddam Hussein, was accused of developing weapons of mass destruction (WMD). A number of UN resolutions demanded that weapons inspectors be allowed to monitor and assess its activities. In the 1980s, Saddam Hussein's regime had been supported by the USA, particularly when it was in conflict with the USA's main enemy at the time, Iran. Saddam's invasion of Kuwait led to the first Gulf War in 1991 and the removal of Iraqi forces led by UN-sanctioned forces, mostly from the USA and under US control. Saddam was not removed from power at this stage.

Following the 11 September attacks in 2001, the USA became increasingly impatient with the UN's failure to force Saddam to comply with its resolutions, although there was no evidence to connect Iraq to the 11 September attacks. In spite of economic sanctions, Saddam did not cooperate fully with UN weapons inspectors.

Supporters of the war in Iraq say...	Opponents of the war in Iraq say...
It was appropriate to remove Saddam Hussein from power since he was an evil dictator who abused the human rights of Iraqis and had invaded Kuwait in 1990.	The West previously supported Saddam when he fought against Iran. Also, the USA has not gone to war against other dictators.
Saddam was a risk to other countries in the region as he was believed to be developing WMDs.	No WMDs were found in Iraq. The invasion was based on false information.
Saddam supported international terrorism and could have provided weapons to al-Qaeda.	No links between Iraq and al-Qaeda have been found. The war has increased international terrorism.
Saddam ignored UN resolutions relating to Iraq's alleged WMDs over several years despite sanctions being imposed against his regime. It would damage the credibility of the UN if Iraq were seen to be flouting UN resolutions.	Other countries have flouted UN resolutions without receiving such severe punishment. The invading countries ignored the will of the UN which wished to find a diplomatic solution. Many believe the invasion to be an illegal act.
An Iraq without Saddam would create the conditions for democracy. A more stable and peaceful situation in the Middle East would be created. Elections have already been held to choose a democratic government.	Iraq has descended into civil war, provoking greater instability in the whole of the Middle East. Iran is threatening to develop a nuclear capability, and there is increased conflict between Israel and Southern Lebanon.

The eventual decision to launch an invasion of Iraq, taken by the USA and supported by the UK and other partners in the coalition, was very divisive. France and Germany (fellow members of NATO), Russia and China all indicated that they were opposed to the invasion. The USA argued that the action was necessary to maintain the credibility of the UN, while their opponents argued the opposite, claiming it showed an arrogant disregard for international opinion and made any negotiated settlement through the UN impossible to achieve.

Three years after the invasion, US and other troops are still bogged down in a conflict which has been described by some media sources as a 'civil war' between the different ethnic and religious groups in the country. Thousands of people have died in the Iraq conflict since the US-led coalition invaded. Estimates of civilian deaths vary widely, ranging from 50,000 to over half a million. Over 3,000 soldiers from the coalition had been killed by the end of 2006.

MILITARY DEATHS IN IRAQ UP TO NOVEMBER 2006	
USA	2,968
UK	126
Italy	33
Ukraine	18
Poland	18
Bulgaria	13
Other (from 12 countries)	39

The impact of the invasion and conflict since 2003 has had a major influence upon global security.

- The invasion by the US-led coalition led to massive protests by people around the world and the expression of hostility towards US foreign policy.
- It has demonstrated splits between western countries which are usually allies, as well as other countries, many of which opposed the invasion.
- There has been an increase in hostility towards the USA, in particular, from Muslim countries who believe the invasion was an attack on Islam.
- Terrorist attacks have increased, including bombings in Madrid in 2004 and London in 2005, with some believing that the invasion resulted in more recruits for extremist groups.
- Although no evidence of an al-Qaeda presence in Iraq before the invasion was found, al-Qaeda has now established itself there and is believed to be heavily involved in the **insurgency**.
- The credibility of the USA and the UK have been damaged as many people believe that the war was undertaken on the basis of false information.
- The credibility and authority of the UN have been damaged as the USA was prepared to act independently of the UN when it could not persuade the members of the Security Council to back the invasion.

It has been argued however that:

- the war has shown the determination of the USA and some of its allies to take decisive action to rid the world of evil dictators and regimes which are a threat to world peace and security. Saddam Hussein was tried and executed in December 2006.
- this decisive action was a factor in Libya's decision to abandon its own programme of weapons development and to establish normal relations with the rest of the world. Such resolute actions may persuade other 'rogue' states such as Iran and North Korea to respond to diplomatic pressure.
- although it will take a long time to achieve and will come at a considerable cost in both money and lives, democracy is being built in Iraq. Other countries, especially those in the Middle East, may come to see this as a system of government they may wish to emulate in the future.

For you to do

- Explain how the invasion of Iraq has had both a positive and a negative impact upon global security. Overall has the impact been positive or negative?

Internet research

Use the BBC website to research the current position in Iraq.
Links to this site and other websites relating to Higher Modern Studies can be found at:

Insurgency: armed rebellion by an irregular armed force against a recognised authority, government or administration.

STUDY THEME SUMMARY

The United Nations and NATO are among the most important political, military and diplomatic bodies in the world. They were both set up in the aftermath of the Second World War with the aim of promoting peace and security, and preventing such wars breaking out again. In the United Nations, considerable power is held by the five permanent members of the Security Council – the USA, the UK, Russia, China and France. In NATO, the USA is the dominant partner. The strength and influence of the USA in these international bodies is a concern to some people.

Both organisations are adjusting to a new set of challenges which have developed since the end of the Cold War. Ethnic and religious conflicts and international terrorism are now bigger threats to world peace and security than 'traditional' conflicts between neighbouring states.

Military intervention in Iraq and Afghanistan has not proved to be the success that had been anticipated. Although the military action has succeeded in removing the regimes that were in place and which were hostile to Western interests, the new governments have not succeeded in achieving a peaceful settlement. It remains to be seen whether other Middle Eastern states will see democracy as a system of government they wish to adopt.

Exam-style essay questions

Examine the changing role of the United Nations in peace-keeping. Refer to at least one conflict outside Europe.

To what extent is it true to say that the United Nations must reform in order to ensure future success in peace-keeping?

Critically evaluate the recent success of NATO in peace-keeping operations.